FIRESIDE

THE CELEBRITY SEX REGISTER

101 LUMINARIES LISTED

*Cross-indexed, Annotated, and Compiled
from Biographies (Authorized or Otherwise),
Autobiographies and Tell-all Memoirs*

BY

SHIRLEY SEALY

with An Introduction by
BRUCE WILLIAMSON

A FIRESIDE BOOK
Published by Simon and Schuster
New York

DEDICATION

To Britt, Eddie, Hedy, Linda, Jackie, Shelley,
Stewart, the Joans and Elizabeths—and
Howard Hughes. Also to Rosa and Ira who
stayed married for fifty years while all this
was going on.

Copyright ©1982 by Shirley Sealy and Bruce Williamson
All rights reserved
including the right of reproduction
in whole or in part in any form
A Fireside Book
Published by Simon and Schuster
A Division of Gulf & Western Corporation
Simon & Schuster Building
Rockefeller Center
1230 Avenue of the Americas
New York, New York 10020
FIRESIDE and colophon are trademarks of Simon & Schuster.
Designed by Elaine Golt Gongora
Manufactured in the United States of America
Printed and bound by Fairfield Graphics
10 9 8 7 6 5 4 3 2 1
Library of Congress Cataloging in Publication Data
Sealy, Shirley.
The celebrity sex register.

"A Fireside book."
Includes bibliographical references and index.
1. Actors—Biography. 2. Actors—Sexual behavior.
3. Entertainers—Biography. 4. Entertainers—Sexual
behavior. 5. Biography—20th century. I. Title.
PN2205.S45 1982   792'.028'0922 [B] 82-5941
ISBN 0-671-44296-1

CONTENTS

ACKNOWLEDGMENTS

Bruce Williamson's brainstorm started this project, his gentle browbeating helped finish it. Also, many passages of *The Celebrity Sex Register* were set aglow by his brightly polished puns, his illuminating bons mots. Thanks. And thanks as well to those friends and researchers—they know who they are—whose assistance, suggestions and appreciative chuckles encouraged me to get on with it.

AUTHOR'S NOTE

The *Celebrity Sex Register* is not meant to be a complete and thorough documentation of the sex lives of those celebrities listed herein. Our information is based entirely on facts and allegations that have appeared in book form, primarily autobiographies and biographies. A few anthologies have been consulted to fill in certain gaps, and a very few items that are considered common knowledge (Ryan and Farrah, Woody and Mia) have been included where appropriate.

Some editorial discretion was exercised in selecting the subjects to be listed in *The Celebrity Sex Register,* but obviously our initial choice was limited to those people whose romantic escapades are interesting enough to have been recounted in published form by themselves or others. It happens that most of these people are film stars, and most of the books by or about them have appeared in very recent years. This material therefore is contemporary—whether the subject discussed is living or dead—reflecting contemporary attitudes toward freedom of information in a new, more permissive social climate.

Under each subject, the alphabetized main listing is followed, in most cases, by a section headed *"Miscellany."* The main listing includes all liaisons that are known to be *serious,* and/or amusing, if not explicitly sexual. Whereas *"Miscellany"* includes case histories of relationships that were purely platonic—or *probably* so—but nevertheless hold some fascination.

It will be noted that many of our main subjects are cross-referenced *under* listings for others. Thus SHELLEY WINTERS, for example, will be found under main listings for, among others, MARLON BRANDO, ERROL FLYNN and HOWARD HUGHES, with a notation to consult the main listing for WINTERS. Also, some people rate a listing of their own despite the fact that there has been no book about them, simply because their names crop up so frequently in the basic source material. This is the case with Warren Beatty, for example, or Aly Khan.

Although the source of every direct quote from a book is not indicated except where it seems of particular importance to cite the source, every quote can be traced to one of the books listed at the beginning of each chapter.

Finally, our apologies are extended in advance for any omissions which may be the cause of hurt feelings.

INTRODUCTION

Though I am professionally acquainted with many actresses, I have learned—unfortunately, the easy way, manuscript open before me as an armchair sexual athlete—that to make love to a movie star is either arrogance, pure folly, or a heroic adventure at least as perilous as hang-gliding. The crash comes, of course, a decade or perhaps several decades later, when she brings out her book and tells all the world about you. No, not your perfect musical pitch or incredible perception, not your total recall of Rudyard Kipling's *If* or Shakespeare's sonnets or selections from Robert Frost. Who cares, after all? What the lady will remember is your staying power. How good you were, and how often. And expect no mercy for any of your shortcomings. Neither thinning hair, insufficient funds, temporary impotence, nor premature ejaculation can stay these tattletales from the ruthless completion of their memoirs.

Is anything sacred today? Very little, it seems. Everyone kisses and tells. Some tell and sue for palimony as well. So many naughty secrets have already been spilled that comedienne Joan Rivers, as a guest reviewer of John Huston's autobiography in the *Hollywood Reporter,* began her appraisal by noting: "Hooray! John Huston never slept with Shelley Winters!" Along with Shelley, whose professional accomplishments are substantial, of course, came Susan Strasberg, Elizabeth Ashley, Evelyn Keyes, and a bevy of other bruised but relatively insignificant mini-stars whose careers held far less interest than their bouts with drugs, booze, bad marriages, and the men they had taken to bed. The assumption seems to be that a celebrity "into OD Sex" (Ashley's phrase) is automatically newsworthy, or at least worth wading through. Well, maybe. The problem for Hollywood folk may be that a good biographer is hard to find, while an autobiography (with or without a ghost writer) frequently deteriorates into a sexual performance roster, naming names and rating prowess in the sack, with major film credits and critics' quotes tucked between the sheets, so to speak.

Which brings us straight back to the book you are holding, an attempt to create some order out of the sexual chaos found between the hard and soft covers of innumerable memoirs, confessions, indictments, unauthorized exposés, and loosely edited collages of hanky-panky among the high and mighty. Call it a wry critique masquerading as a compendium. This cheerfully mischievous tome may have found a way to satisfy a reader's prurient interest without excessive foreplay. Sure, it's fascinating to learn how *The Wizard of Oz* was made, but for every film-school zealot there must be a dozen gossip-hungry fans out there who simply want to know who did what and to whom, and whether they did it on a casting couch or in the back of a Rolls or in Flagrante Delicto (I am told that's an Italian resort frequented by showfolk and other Beautiful People).

A reminder. In the catalogue of indiscretions that follows, there's obviously material included beyond mere pillow talk by ladies who cannot keep a secret. Bitchy bios as well as autobios. There are famous persons mentioned who have little to do with films, though they usually have some gilt by association with one or two—or four, or ten, count 'em—glamorous figures on the contemporary scene. Movie gods and goddesses tend to hog the limelight in every era. If their lives are the kinds that entice tycoons or politicos or titled gentry or madcap heiresses to fly near the flame, or if their amours have been dazzling enough to inspire a scandalous biography, they are apt to show up, oversexed and extensively cross-indexed. Testifying against themselves, willingly or otherwise, they are damned if they do what most of them indubitably did.

Some people are conspicuously absent. You won't find Liv Ullmann because her perceptive best-seller, *Changes*, was not a book about bed partners despite her acknowledged long relationship in Sweden with Ingmar Bergman, by whom she had a child. Nonetheless, Sophia Loren and Ingrid Bergman and Lauren Bacall earn their places in the registry—granted that their respective autobiographies are several cuts above the tell-all variety—because their private lives have become virtual soap operas, known to millions, with all-star international casts (Loren's *Living and Loving*, in fact, was televised with Sophia playing the lead opposite John Gavin, now U.S. Ambassador to Mexico, as Gary Grant). Countless other current names are omitted, however frequently they appear in *TV Guide* or in the gossipy context of *People* and the *Star* and the *National Enquirer*. "Victoria Principal meets Andy Gibb" may fascinate the viewers of television talk shows, but the purview of *The Celebrity Sex Register* excludes the stars of *Dallas* and *General Hospital* as well as teenybopper idols whose biographers are as yet unborn, and whose autobiographies should not hit the stands, God willing, until most of us are happily extinct. Janis Joplin, yes. Jean Harlow, yes. The Fonz and Erik Estrada, no. With notable exceptions, the emphasis is on an older, golden generation of superstars whose personal lives may have been as trashy as they were flashy, but were seldom irredeemably dull.

It would be pleasant to pretend, as Bing Crosby's earnest biographers do, that the film colony and its denizens are just simple folk, Ma and Pa Kettle in Bel Air. They write: "Contrary to popular belief, most people in the entertainment industry live more decent lives than people in almost any other profession. But owing to the industry's high profile, it only takes one Errol Flynn to give the entire industry a reputation it can't live down." That's cute, though utterly unconvincing, particularly when Hollywood no longer has its militant house mothers, Hedda and Louella, to tidy up or sweep under the rug most of the sleazier local scandals. Mel Gussow, in his Darryl Zanuck biography, came closer to the truth: "The movies, an industry founded on commercialism, nurtured by egotism, and aimed at exhibitionism, *were* sexier than the rest of America." Of course. And perhaps that is one of the reasons we love them. If we accept Hollywood Babylon as a hardworking factory town, the town would be Peyton Place with Lana Turner in residence and all the shades up. Who could ask for anything more?

It's curious but true that many more women than men seem ready to shuck off their inhibitions in print, and there lies a subject worth study by Kinsey, Hite, or Masters and Johnson. The facile explanation would be women's lib, a lot of wronged females finally getting their own back in a world where men make the rules. Possible. But this tradition got up steam as far back as 1936, when Mary Astor's scandalous diary broke into headlines from coast to coast, and gave all her former lovers heartburn. Mary, Mae West, Hedy Lamarr, and Linda Christian wrote the first explosive autobiographies from 1959 to 1966. Only recently are men beginning to demand equal time. A strange phenomenon. If you were brought up, as I was, to believe that a real gentleman doesn't talk to his pals in the pool hall or behind the barn about any girl whose favors he has enjoyed (I'm sounding old-fashioned for a reason), there is some cultural shock in realizing that the chicks probably had a great giggle together about such misplaced gallantry. Witness the case of Warren Beatty, a most intelligent actor-producer and a passing acquaintance of mine for the past fifteen years. It's scarcely a professional secret that Beatty has a reputation as one of the great Hollywood womanizers of our time, and his name will appear with some frequency hereafter—as a partner in dalliance with a number of ladies. Yet I know of no book devoted to listing Beatty's conquests, he is unlikely to write one himself, and I have never heard him boast about women he seduced or vice versa. Even so, a good half-dozen actresses have confided in me, on surprisingly short acquaintance, that their nights with Warren were memorable in one way or another. Do women simply talk too much? Gloryosky, Daddy, is it as simple as that?

Even when they do take up their pens, the menfolk tend to be markedly more reticent. Stewart Granger, Eddie Fisher, and Jackie Cooper were far franker than most in their 1981 autobiographies, while John Huston's *An Open Book* maintained a closed-door policy on a good many pungent details, even to the point of omitting the name of his least favorite wife. In his chatty bestselling memoirs—two volumes so far, and a third to come—David Niven showed typically good form, everything cricket. Or nearly. While he reveals very little about his own errant youth as a young man about Hollywood, except in general terms, Niven is not averse to naming names in juicy anecdotes about other people. And he has known them all.

Quite a few have known Niven, too, and that's another striking aspect of the social chemistry accomplished when a hundred or more celebrity bios become one. Niven himself shows up here and there where you least expect him. Amazing combinations occur— Jackie Cooper with Joan Crawford, Tyrone Power with Errol Flynn, Howard Hughes with practically everyone *but* Jackie Cooper. And long before an actor became President, what a flow of sexual electricty hummed between Hollywood and Washington, D.C. The mind boggles. Each book appears, at times, to have been written partly for the purpose of correcting or contradicting all the others. The truth, if there is any, goes through so many permutations—filtered through so many eccentric sensibilities—that the cumulative effect becomes like a parlor game. A kind of erotic *Rashomon*, with famous players as the pieces on the board. Happily, nearly everyone scores.

Should you fail to meet all the people you hope to meet in the following pages, despair not. Spicy new books are in progress or imminent from June Allyson, James Stewart, Rita Gam, John Mills, Ann Todd, Lana Turner, Bette Davis (second volume of her autobiography), and Shelley Winters (ditto). They had better be spicy, or else. Marlene Dietrich attempted an autobiography, they say, and had her act so cleaned up that her publisher thought she had accidentally written the life of Dame May Whitty—at last report, Dietrich's memoirs were still shelved. Elizabeth Taylor's own reminiscences are said to be so hot they have been locked in a Swiss vault to marinate, at least for the duration of her tenure as a Senator's wife. The end of that liaison is in sight, they say, which may give Taylor a green light, though Liz will have to go some to outdo Kitty Kelley's "unofficial" bio of her.

If you are a celebrity yourself, given to impulsive liaisons within your peer group, you'd better line up a literary agent and beat your next partner to the punch. Keep in mind that she, or he, may be given a six-figure advance to recall your pathetic, fumbling advances at a patio party in Malibu. Incorrigible bastards who don't want to find their names in future editions of this book may choose several courses of action: (1) Don't sleep with anyone who owns a notebook or tape recorder. (2) Don't sleep with anyone. (3) Ask your conquests to sign a waiver. Otherwise, just pull the covers over your head and devil take the fine line between true love and *True Britt*.

Bruce Williamson
Film Critic and Contributing Editor/
Films, Playboy *magazine*

—

ASHLEY, ELIZABETH
(b. 1939)

Frenetic, outspoken southern-born actress once called "a dirty Audrey Hepburn," who has achieved her greatest successes on stage, in *Barefoot in the Park* and a revival of *Cat on a Hot Tin Roof*, for example. Her movie appearances, from *Ship of Fools* in 1965 to a virtual cameo role in *Paternity* (1981) with Burt Reynolds, seldom bring out the best she can do. A couple of serious emotional breakdowns, combined with a quick temper, a sharp tongue, her acknowledged fondness for getting stoned, and other forms of self-indulgence, have considerably slowed the momentum of Ashley's career. In her breathy, energetic autobiography, she admits: "My sexuality has always been very erratic. There are times when I couldn't be less interested in it and other times when I'm hardly interested in anything else."

PRIMARY SOURCE: *Actress: Postcards from the Road*, by Elizabeth Ashley with Ross Firestone (Fawcett/Crest, 1978).

★*FARENTINO, JAMES* New York actor and Ashley's first husband. She became pregnant by him just before her first big break on Broadway in *Take Her, She's Mine*. A risky abortion. Later, "We decided to get married when his Catholic background leapt up and grabbed him by the throat." One night they were out drinking with Shelley Winters when Farentino impulsively told Ashley, "Listen, you can't have me for my body alone." Elizabeth cracked up, surprised to hear a man mouthing that line. "Honey, *every* girl ought to be married to an Italian *once*," offered Shelley. "She didn't have to encourage me. Any woman who wouldn't have opted for Farentino's body would have had something the matter with her brain." Of course, once is not forever.

★*FINNEY, ALBERT* British actor. He was on Broadway playing *Luther*, Ashley was a big hit in *Barefoot in the Park*. Her fiancé, George Peppard, had to go back to Hollywood; "Well,

keep an eye on my girl, will you?" he told friend Albert. And Finney did. At first Ashley was simply in awe, then in love. "For the first time in my life I was in love with two men at the same time. George was offering to take care of me . . . Finney was offering me nothing at all except some of his time and body." Being pulled in both directions at once, says Ashley, had something to do with her ending up in a psychiatric clinic. When she came out, Finney was on the road.

★*McGUANE, TOM* Novelist and screenwriter who wrote the script for an Ashley "western," *Rancho Deluxe* (1975). Their long affair, which began on the Montana movie location, apparently had the blessing of McGuane's wife Becky (who later married Peter Fonda). Elizabeth describes her behavior with McGuane as "flagrant, scandalous, slatternly, offensive, high and wonderful and low, mean and dirty." Item: On very short acquaintance McGuane said, "Let's fuck." Despite her protests that she *couldn't* with a married man, they spent the next night in his camper in the parking lot behind her motel. Item: Tom followed her to Connecticut while she rehearsed a new play, and they went to the movies one afternoon. Sure that they were alone (they weren't), he pulled out a joint and started making moves. Ashley rasped loudly, "We *cannot* get laid in the movie theater in Milford, Connecticut, in the middle of the afternoon while watching *The Sting*." But they did, and it was more fun than anything she'd done in her life. Ashley muses that to her, the best of all possible worlds, sexually, is "two *takers* in bed with each other. Which is exactly how it was with McGuane. The one-on-one combat was precisely the thing he liked best about it. And for the first time in my life, I met my match . . . a worthy opponent." Ended in a draw.

★*NARDINI, TOM* Young actor who had a role with Ashley in a TV movie, *Harpy*. She recalls they had a wonderful time "getting stoned, riding horses and running around in the fields barefoot in our jeans." Ashley was still married to George Peppard, who, on returning home from London, decided to fly to

Ashley's location in the middle of the night. She was shacked up with Nardini, but an alert hairdresser spotted Peppard and called Nardini's room to warn Mrs. Peppard. She arrived in her own room just seconds before George knocked. He walked in, put down his briefcase, looked at the unused bed and said, "All right, who have you been fucking?" She wanted to kill him; instead they just had a knock-down-drag-out fight and were reconciled within the hour.

★*PEPPARD, GEORGE* TV and film star, Ashley's second husband. She was already a big fan of Peppard's when she won the lead opposite him in *The Carpetbaggers* (1964). George still had a wife, but that didn't keep the co-stars from lighting up their own little hideaway in Benedict Canyon. The love affair was terrific, although Elizabeth had qualms early on about their perpetual disagreements. "I didn't change my principles, I just stopped talking about them around him. Of course, that's where the first drop of poison in the well goes down, but who knew?" So she gave up her own acting career, they married in 1965, and for six years Ashley played the dutiful Hollywood wife. They had a son, Christian (whose mere existence proved to his mother that she was part of the human race). But George's lofty ambitions for his career and gentleman-rancher lifestyle just did not materialize, and he became a bitter man, says Ashley. "You can only live with a man who is enraged and despairing and desperately unhappy for so long. . . . I started to hate him." She also started to get restless about her own forsaken career. But it took a few more drunken, physically violent scenes to make her resolve to sue for divorce.

MISCELLANY

Ashley implies there were many other lovers before and after (and sometimes during) her marriages. There was one period in New York, for example, when "I smoked a lot of dope, I made it with a lot of guys. I tried every way I could think of to act just as bad and outrageously as I could."

ASTOR, MARY
(b. 1906)

Her father decided she should become an actress, "and my father had never been wrong." Father also explained the facts of life in such a crude way she became, in her words, "as cold as ice." She arrived in Hollywood in 1923, just short of her 17th birthday; the fabled John Barrymore was her first co-star and her first love. She would have four marriages, make eighty films, fall victim to alcoholism and poverty—and become the first major Hollywood star to write a "tell-all" memoir. Mary kept a diary all her life, and it was introduced as evidence in her second divorce. The real diary was tame, she claims, compared to the forgery that appeared which "named every bigwig in Hollywood with pornographic detail." The real diary was impounded by the court, kept in a vault until 1952, then burned, unread. At the age of 53, while writing her autobiography, Mary found God. With the help of a friendly Catholic priest, she "removed the detonator to my self destruction—which was ignorance. I could look back on my life and see it as bizarre, fantastically foolish and unnecessarily miserable."

PRIMARY SOURCES: *Mary Astor: My Story,* by Mary Astor (Doubleday, 1959; Dell, 1960); *Hollywood Babylon,* by Kenneth Anger (Associated Professional Services, 1965).

★*BARRYMORE, JOHN* He was 40, she was a virginal 17 when he asked her to be his leading lady in *Beau Brummel* (1923). Both were "startled," said Mary, when they fell in love. Barrymore convinced Mary's protective parents that he must give her dramatic coaching. Alone. While he was performing his historic *Hamlet,* they set up an "almost domestic" arrangement in his New York hotel room, even though he still had a wife somewhere. The romance lasted almost two years, until Barrymore became the paramour of his *Don Juan* leading lady Dolores Costello.

When wounded Mary confronted him, he tenderly said, "Dear Goopher, I'm just a son of a bitch."

★*BRADBURY, RUSSELL* Studio executive. At first she resisted his pursuit, even though her marriage (to Hawkes) left a lot to be desired. When she finally succumbed, "the affair was conducted in the upper brackets of sophistication." Until she became pregnant, "and an abortion is an abortion whether it is accompanied by the music of Sibelius or by the caterwauling of tomcats in an alley."

★*DE CAMPO, MANUEL ("Mike")* Mexican dandy, educated at Cambridge, a gentleman "until the family fortunes ran out." Over Christmas in 1936, Mary and Mike eloped to Arizona; he was husband no. 3. She was 30, he 24. His Catholic family protested, "and I began seriously drinking." They had a son in 1939; Mike went away to war in the early '40s. When he came home on leave the couple "amicably discussed divorce" and got one.

★*GLASS, BILL* "A nobody." But on the rebound from Barrymore, he was "fun to be with." They talked marriage but she lost interest while in Texas filming *The Rough Riders.* (See SAUNDERS, below.)

★*HALL, FERRIS* Actor. Mary returned to the stage in her 40s, met Ferris, who "wasn't much of an actor, but I was in desperate need of a man to lean on." Their strongest bond was booze. While on tour she began to seriously consider his marriage proposal, and rushed back to Hollywood to tell him so. He met her plane, and Mary, happily babbling on, asked what he'd been doing that made him look so good. "I got married—three weeks ago," he said.

★*HAWKES, KENNETH* Producer and brother of director Howard Hawkes. Very Ivy League. Astor's first husband. Their courtship had very little sex, lots of "small-town evenings," as he called them. Mary would make fudge and they'd sit on the porch swing. But then, every night on their honeymoon he simply kissed her and went to sleep. She began the affair with Bradbury about the same time Ken lost a lot of money in the stockmarket

and "became annoyingly ill." Ken Hawkes was killed in 1930, taking part in an aerial stunt scene for a film. After two years of marriage, Mary was a widow at 24.

★*KAUFMAN, GEORGE S.* The playwright. Mary met him on a trip east. He introduced her to literature, music, and Edna Ferber, Moss Hart, Alex Woollcott, Oscar Levant, George Gershwin, etc. She found him extremely attractive "for all his ungainly frame and saturnine mien." In Hollywood, their affair and Astor's career flowered (she made *Red Dust* with Gable and Harlow) while her marriage fizzled. During the divorce action with Dr. Thorpe (see below) Mary's so-called "Blue Diary" jottings about Kaufman were published in Los Angeles. One heady sample: "Sat around all day—lunch in the pool with Moss and George and the Rogers—dinner at The Dunes—a drink in the moonlight *without* Moss and Rogers. Ah, desert night—with George's body plunging into mine, naked under the stars. . . ." Cornered in New York for comment, Kaufman offered only: "You may say *I* did not keep a diary."

★*SAUNDERS, JOHN MONK* Screenwriter, author of *Wings,* the first Oscar-winning film, shooting on location in Texas as Mary was filming *Rough Riders.* They had all the romantic trappings of a Hollywood romance: "A Texas summer, a harvest moon, dancing the last dance at the outdoor pavilion at the country club." The magic dissolved. Fourteen years later he hanged himself.

★*THORPE, FRANKLYN, M.D.* Second husband. He nursed her through tuberculosis, then his visits became more personal than professional, and "he was a trapped man." Once wed, he seemed to prefer his boat to his wife; she began having a series of public affairs. They had a daughter in 1932, and he used the famous Astor diary in court to win custody of the child. Afterward, writes Mary, "Sexually, I was out of control, I was drinking too much. I found myself late in the evening thinking someone terribly attractive, and wondering the next morning, 'why, why?' "

★*VERY PROMINENT ACTOR* "We had

candlelit dinners, listened to Gilbert and Sullivan." He said he'd get a divorce if Mary would marry him. She said sorry.

★*WHEELOCK, TOMMY, SGT.* Serviceman she met at a wartime pool party. He was a Boston blueblood, and struck Mary as "the dullest man I've ever met." Yet in 1945, Wheelock became husband no. 4. She thought he had money, he thought she did. After five years of marriage they were over $30,000 in debt. Mary hit bottom, then discovered Catholicism, converted, realized she was "living in sin." At her urging, Wheelock signed a paper agreeing they would not have sexual relations. Soon after, they "began to bicker," and she demanded a divorce.

★*WINSLOW, BILL* Studio publicity man. She developed "a blind, all-consuming infatuation." He taught her to fly, he made her laugh. "I realized Bill did not love me . . . but just being with him made the difference between living and not living." The studio transferred him to New York.

MISCELLANY

★*ASH, JIMMY* Actor who got a role with Mary in stage production of *Time of the Cuckoo*, because he'd quite simply been in love with her all his life. She was then drinking heavily, and credits Jimmy with helping her get through the engagement.

★*REALTOR* Well known and successful in Hollywood. He tried and failed to blackmail Mary into an affair by producing evidence of her relationship with Bradbury. It didn't work.

BACALL, LAUREN
(b. 1924)

New York actress-model, spotted on a *Harper's Bazaar* cover in 1943 by the wife of director Howard Hawkes, promptly cast opposite Humphrey Bogart in Hawkes's *To Have and Have Not*. The rest is history. She made her best movies with Bogart (*The Big Sleep*, 1946; *Key Largo*, 1948), but

seemed to lose her zest for Hollywood after he died. Bacall regained prestige as a major star—in fact, she topped herself—by appearing on Broadway in *Cactus Flower* (1965) and *Applause* (1970), the musical version of *All About Eve*. *Time* magazine once called her "the kind of sex symbol a fella could swap wisecracks with and then bring home to mother." Her bestselling autobiography certified Bacall's standing as a leathery, glamorous showbiz veteran recently enjoying her third Broadway triumph in *Woman of the Year*, a recycled Hepburn-Tracy movie.

PRIMARY SOURCE: *Lauren Bacall by Myself,* by Lauren Bacall (Knopf, 1978; Ballantine, 1980).

★*BOGART, HUMPHREY* First co-star, first film, first husband, father of son Stephen and daughter Leslie. They met making the Hemingway film with Howard Hawkes, and Bacall stole the show when she purred, "Just whistle . . . You know how to whistle, don't you? Just put your lips together—and blow." Thrice-married Bogart was still tied to Mayo Methot, but that couldn't stop what was happening on the movie set between Bogie and Baby. "Anyone with half an eye could see there was more between us than the scenes we played," writes Bacall. Hawkes noticed, and sternly warned the fledgling actress to stop "fooling around with Bogart . . . when the picture's over, that's the last you'll ever see of him." Little did he know that B & B were a match made in heaven. "At the age of twenty I had grabbed at the sky and had touched some stars," concludes the lady who would be the first to agree there was no star brighter than Bogart. (See also BOGART listing.)

★*CARIOU, LEN* Broadway leading man, her co-star in *Applause*, considerably younger than Bacall, and single—but involved emotionally with another actress. "I held him at arm's length for a while. But only for a while." When he left the show, Bacall was shocked ("Another ending—I felt the bottom of my world dropping out") but soon recovered.

★*DOUGLAS, KIRK* Her first big crush when both were New York drama students in the early '40s. Bacall trembled when they met. She had never had a love affair. "Nice Jewish girls stayed virgins until they were married . . . necking in dark corners was about my speed." Douglas joined the navy, apparently just in the nick of time, but has remained a close friend.

★*ENGLISHMAN, MARRIED* After Broadway and Cariou, her London triumph in *Applause* was enhanced by "six completely happy months" with an unnamed Briton. "The relationship was brought to a devastating end through circumstance—bad timing—bad luck." Never a quitter, Bacall vowed to find another good relationship before her time was up. "Having tasted the fruit, I flatly refuse never to taste it again."

★*GUARDINO, HARRY* Movie-TV tough guy and current co-star on Broadway, with the Tracy role in musicalized *Woman of the Year.* Though too late to make Bacall's bio, Guardino is widely rumored to be her man of the hour offstage and on.

★*ROBARDS, JASON* Leading Broadway actor and film star, foremost interpreter of Eugene O'Neill characters. Second husband, father of Bacall's third child, a son named Sam, born December 1961. Bacall was already pregnant when she and Robards decided to marry. It all started on New Year's Eve: "He was feeling no pain, and we hit it off instantly." Jason's drinking, however, became a problem, and "a romantic letter" from another woman ultimately helped Lauren to see that "there's nothing deader than a terminal marriage." Some people thought Robards a Bogart look-alike, but Bacall found scant resemblance.

★*SINATRA, FRANK* Singing superstar, a Bogart crony and Bacall's great new love a year or so after Bogie's death. "I hated feeling that my life was over at thirty-two." Frank turned out to be moody and unpredictable, but asked her to marry him, then abruptly dropped her when a mutual friend leaked their plans to the press. "Frank did me a great favor—he saved me from the disaster our marriage would have been." Yet to this day she resents Sinatra's rude, unfeeling treatment of her. (See also SINATRA listing.)

★*STEVENSON, ADLAI* Politician, Presidential candidate, and great good friend of innumerable ladies. Sitting in a Washington room with several of them after Stevenson's death, Bacall mused mournfully about the "richness" of knowing him, and thought, "He had an uncanny knack for keeping all of us, and more, dangling—happy for anything he threw our way. I thought to myself: *I know things they don't know—I've been places with him they haven't been, shared times they haven't. I'm more special than they know.* And they were clearly thinking those same thoughts. Women are a joke! (To say nothing of men!)"

BANKHEAD, TALLULAH
(1903–1968)

International theatrical star intermittently active in films and radio, she was the daughter of Alabama Congressman William Brockman Bankhead, once Speaker of the House, and rose to fame on the stage in London during the '20s. An outrageous character throughout her career, considered a first-rate actress at her best, Tallulah became the husky-voiced high queen of camp in later years after many flamboyant escapades with heterosexuals, homosexuals, lesbians, finally men half her age whom she dryly described as "caddies." Bankhead's most famous bit of self-mockery was her succinct admission to being "pure as the driven slush," and she once summed up her attitude toward carnal knowledge by telling an interviewer: "I don't know *what* I am, dahling. I've tried several varieties of sex. The conventional position makes me claustrophobic, and all the others give me either stiff neck or lockjaw."

PRIMARY SOURCES: *Miss Tallulah Bankhead,* by Lee Israel (Putnam, 1972; Dell, 1973); *Tallulah Darling: A Biography of Tallulah Bankhead,* by Denis Bryan (Pyramid, 1972).

★*ALINGTON, NAPIER GEORGE HENRY STUART* The third Baron Alington, or "Naps." Her first London conquest and possibly the greatest love of her life. He was "blond, tubercular, well-cultivated, bisexual, with sensuous, meaty lips, antic charm, a history of mysterious disappearances, and a streak of cruelty." Tallulah promptly fell in love, and lost her "technical" virginity to him. At a Beautiful Young Thing costume ball they dressed as twin brothers from the court of Louis XIV, wearing skin-tight blue breeches. Once, after an unexplained absence of a year, he appeared in "a smart lounge suit with a Pekingese puppy under his arm. For you, Lulas," he said. She melted. They called the dog Napoleon. Her dreams of being Mrs. Naps were destroyed when he wed someone else, a lady of noble birth. Alington was killed in the Battle of Britain, at 44.

★*BARRYMORE, JOHN* Legendary actor, one of the Algonquin crowd when starstruck, teenaged Tallulah lived at the famed hotel. She was "so terribly in love with him," yet repelled his advances when he came at her "making fervent little animal noises." She let him kiss her, then ran scared.

★*COOK, DONALD* Respected actor, romantic-comedy matinee idol. They toured in a revival of *Private Lives;* both were known for their romantic entanglements with co-stars, and theirs was a torrid affair. It all ended when Tallulah forbade him to drink and both realized that an emotional involvement with Tallulah was "incompatible with extended sobriety." They were friends forever, however.

★*COOPER, GARY* She once claimed that she went to the theater with Cooper and he didn't say a word all evening. As a friend observed, "he might have said 'yup'—I know he didn't say 'no.' " (See also COOPER listing.)

★*DE BOSDARI, COUNT ANTHONY* Colorful Italian with commanding presence, "his dark hair waved in front like shallow water at low tide." He bought her a diamond necklace; they became roommates and set the date. The ceremony was postponed, and finally canceled when the legality of his divorce came into question *and* it was learned he hadn't paid for that necklace.

★*EMERY, JOHN* Actor who strongly resembled John Barrymore. After admiring his work in a play, Tallulah went backstage to congratulate him and took him home with her that night. He moved in the next day and before the week was out they announced they would be married. They were, on August 31, 1937, in her father's house in Jasper, Alabama. She said she married for love. After a couple of years the union fell apart and Emery began making disparaging public remarks about Tallulah as a lover. Domestic problems were exacerbated by her growing success on stage and in films, while his career went into eclipse. Tallulah got the divorce in Reno, making Emery promise to wait a year before he married his new sweetheart, ballet dancer Tamara Geva. John was Tallulah's only husband.

★*FAIRBANKS, DOUGLAS, JR.* Tallulah met Doug and his new bride, Joan Crawford, on a train west. Said she to Joan: "Darling, you're divine. I've had an affair with your husband . . . you're next."

★*LANGFORD, WILLIAM* Young actor who was an understudy in the touring company of *Private Lives* until Tallulah took him as a lover. She fired another actor to give Langford a role. Tallulah was 46, he was 25. He died ten years later while living with Signe Hasso. Tallulah said he was the last man she ever loved.

★*MADEVILLE, LORD* Son of the then Duke of Westminster. He proposed to Talu six times.

★*MEREDITH, BURGESS* He had just become a Broadway star, Tallulah already was one. She invited him up to see her sometime and he went—with "great expectations." She greeted him with a passionate kiss, immediately told him they were destined to mate, and in no time, "she was wandering around stark naked."

★*SOCIETY GIRL/ACTRESS* Tallulah, at 20, was smitten to the point of "obsession" and referred to her as "the only woman I ever loved." Actually, she loved others, some much older than she. "My father warned me about men and booze, but he never mentioned a *word* about women."

★*WELL-KNOWN MOVIE ACTOR* He gave Tallulah the clap; gonorrhea, to be exact. The infection spread, causing severe pain, fever, and weight loss, necessitating a total hysterectomy. She was 31.

★*WHITNEY, JOHN HAY "JOCK"* Handsome, dashing, and very rich sportsman. The idea of marrying him "appealed enormously" to Tallulah. But he had a wife. What the heck. They remained friends.

★*WILSON, TONY* Hot-eyed Englishman from a very distinguished family. Tallulah once again was in love; along came sister Eugenia, who took a shine to Tony and vice versa. Tony followed Eugenia to Paris; Tallulah didn't speak to her sister for many years.

MISCELLANY

★*AMORY, CLEVELAND* Mutual friend Katharine Hepburn sent him to Tallulah "to complete the young man's education." He became a groupie at Windows, Tallulah's country house, but never a captive.

★*BEATON, CECIL* Her friend, and the one who noted that "Tallulah burns her candle at *every* end."

★*BRANDO, MARLON* He said they had "bad chemistry," she said she didn't like his nose-picking. Both agreed Tallulah lusted after him when he appeared with her, very briefly, on Broadway, in *The Eagle Has Two Heads.* (See also BRANDO listing.)

★*BUSINESSMAN* Her favorite escort in 1962. He was awed by her and she, in turn, awed his children when she greeted them wearing "a red maribou smoking jacket and dragging on a cigarette holder that resembled a pole vault."

★*CARTEN, KENNETH* He was 11 when they met and he fell in love. To him she was either a mother or a playmate, depending.

★*CAVENDISH, DOLA* Wealthy Canadian girl who *adored* Tallulah and became her faithful companion, living at Windows. Talu

said, "I know what people think—but I've never even seen Dola in a slip."

★*CHURCHILL, WINSTON* So taken by Tallulah he sat through Noel Coward's *Fallen Angel* five times. And he reportedly paid her a secret visit in the U.S. When Tallulah acquired her pet lion she named it Winston.

★*COLE, STEPHAN* Tallulah's first full-time in-residence "caddy," as she called them; one of the lads who moved in to take care of her. He joined the army in 1942.

★*DA COSTA, MORTON* Actor-director and "caddy" at the country house. She introduced him to her friends thusly: "This is Morton Da Costa. He's a poir-fect gentleman. This morning, we were lying on the veranda, I broke wind, and he never raised an eyebrow."

★*DIETZ, HOWARD* Famed lyricist. Immortalized in Talu's crowd by uttering the line "A day away from Tallulah is like a month in the country."

★*DU MAURIER, SIR GERALD* Great actor-director in England. "Most of his stars fell in love with him, and Tallulah was no exception." It was while appearing in Sir Gerald's *The Dancers* that Tallulah began to notice her "fanatical, burgeoning following of Cockney girls."

★*GARROWAY, DAVE* Radio-TV personality. They had a "marvelous relationship but were thought of as a very odd couple. He'd end his radio show with 'Goodnight, Tallulah.' "

★*"GEORGE"* Anonymous wealthy publisher. One lover remembers that in the middle of the sex act, Tallulah screamed: "Please stop now, *stop* now! *I'm engaged to George!*"

★*GRIFFIN, MERV* He was a young, handsome, blue-eyed singer when he shared the bill with Tallulah in Las Vegas. He found her shocking—asking what he thought of her recently lifted breasts, greeting him in her dressing room while sitting on the john. But they got along, and spent one very drunken night in the casinos "winning thousands."

★*HALL, PHILLIP* Her secretary-companion for five years. On occasion, exhausted, they'd fall into bed together. In the morning

Tallulah would ask, "Did we byze last night?" "Byze" was her euphemism for making love—derived from "going to beddy-byes."

★*HERLIHY, JAMES LEO* Novelist who convinced Tallulah to star in his play *Crazy October*. To him, she was the most interesting person ever. She also did what he told her to do.

★*HOOK, TED* Young dancer who first met TB in Las Vegas. She was later in Hollywood and he called her on a whim. She just as whimsically asked if he wanted the job of taking care of her. That was 1958. He remained with her through some of the rough years, trying to regulate the drinking and the pill-taking. She finally told him to go and get a better job, because "there's less fun and more nursemaid in your job everyday." Today, Ted Hook's *Backstage* is a popular after-theater spot in New York.

★*KEITH-JOHNSTON, COLIN* Lanky, blond English actor Tallulah saw a great deal of while still married to John Emery.

★*KIRKWOOD, JIMMY* Co-starred in Tallulah's summer-stock production of *Welcome, Darlings*. At his "audition" she talked nonstop for an hour, then told him he was absolutely perfect. A frequent guest at Windows.

★*LAKING, SIR GUY* The first of Talu's "freaks," a fat, lisping eunuch who resembled a cretinous Charles Laughton. He served as court jester to Tallulah; she adored his silly gossip.

★*LEVY, JESSE* Self-proclaimed retired playboy who, at 45, met Tallulah and began managing her life. Was with her until she died in December 1968.

★*MURROW, EDWARD R.* Her last romance, or so she said. She fell in love when he interviewed her at Windows for his *Person to Person* TV show. By all accounts it was unrequited, "but it made her happy as a girl over her first romance."

★*RANDALL, TONY* Buddies and campaigners together for Stevenson and Kennedy. "She was a little girl show-off, being bad all the time to get attention, being naughty and being darling."

★*TILDEN, BILL* Wimbledon tennis champ. She went with him to Paris for the Davis Cup matches.

★*WEISSMULLER, JOHNNY* The new Tarzan who took Tallulah's mind off Gary Cooper, not as attentive to her as she wished when they made a film together. Between takes, she said, "Cooper sat cross-legged whittling on such lumber as was available." She, for one, seemed to find Tarzan more of a swinger.

★*WILLIAMS, ROBERT* One of her "boys," who went back with her temporarily in the early '60s.

BARDOT, BRIGITTE
(b. 1934)

French love goddess whose entire life evolved into a montage of international incidents after her beautiful bare body embellished *And God Created Woman*, a 1956 film directed by her husband Roger Vadim. For the sexpot soon known throughout the world as BB, a harvest of lovers, husbands, movies, and headlines followed in tumbling profusion—the movies themselves often flops, seemingly of less interest to the public than the golden mademoiselle herself, who today lives in semiretirement as undefeated champion in the battle of the sexes. She was the sexual revolution's *avant-garde*, a new breed of feminist commando. French writer Marguerite Duras observed: "When a man attracts her, Bardot goes straight to him. Nothing stops her. It does not matter if he is in a café, at home or staying with friends. She goes off with him on the spot without a glance at the man she is leaving. . . ." BB freely acknowledges having many lovers, though she adds: "But now they are successive. Never do I have more than one at a time."

PRIMARY SOURCES: *Bardot: Eternal Sex Goddess*, by Peter Evans (Leslie Frewin Ltd., London, 1972); *Bébé: The Films of Brigitte Bardot*, by Tony Cralley (Citadel, 1977).

★*ALBOU, PAUL* Well-to-do Parisian dentist with fashionable clientele. Removed one of BB's wisdom teeth in 1965, then danced with her in a disco, and the duo disappeared for a week. Presumably, BB showed up smiling.

★*BROZECK, MIROSLAV* Blond actor, later successful sculptor. Man of the moment with whom BB was rumored to be pondering marriage and adopting a child in 1977 as *Bébé* went to press. But the Brozeck boom faded.

★*CHARRIER, JACQUES* Bardot's second husband, married in 1959 after co-starring in *Babette Goes to War*. Charrier found their wedding, in a French village overrun by photographers, "nauseating, primeval." BB had a baby, her only child, Nicholas Jacques, born Jan. 11, 1960. Charrier went into the army, had a nervous breakdown, and was discharged after three months. Following his second suicide attempt and a fistfight with Sami Frey (Bardot's co-star in *La Vérité*), Brigitte slashed *her* wrists and swallowed a bottle of sleeping pills. That was in September, 1960. Their stormy marriage ended in 1962.

★*CONNERY, SEAN* Co-star in the English-language western *Shalako*, filmed in Spain. "Bloody marvelous," said Sean when informed who his leading lady would be. Their first summit meeting was reportedly a *succès fou:* "They looked at each other and you knew what she was thinking, and you knew what he was thinking. You could have cut it with a knife." Onscreen, alas, the magnetic combo appeared to have been sliced a bit thin.

★*DISTEL, SACHA* French singer-guitarist whose six-month liaison with BB considerably shortened his climb to the top of the charts: "I met Brigitte—and one week later I was *the* man in the world." No other performer on her preferred list ever reaped comparable fringe benefits. Said Bardot: "He brought music into my life."

★*ENGELS, MICHAEL* Art publisher in Paris.

★*FREY, SAMI* Bardot's co-star in Clouzot film, *La Vérité*, winner of a screen test that had every virile male in French cinema breathing through a love scene abed with BB. "The only man who can make me vibrate fully as a woman," said Brigitte. The vibes didn't last, but the movie was Bardot's biggest hit in France.

★*GAINSBOURG, SERGE* French songwriter married to actress Jane Birkin.

★*GILLES, PATRICK* First of Bardot's younger lovers (he was 23 to her 35) who was not an actor to be rewarded with a role in one of her films, *Les Femmes*, 1969.

★*KALT, CHRISTIAN* Another handsome young companion, former bartender at a chic après-ski club, close to BB during the early '70s. Kalt later wrote a series of newspaper articles about how wonderful it had been chez Brigitte.

★*MALLE, LOUIS* French director of three Bardot films, including the quasi-autobiographical *Vie Privée* (about a suicidal sex symbol, made in 1961, the year after Bardot's own widely publicized effort to end it all), and *Viva Maria* (1965) with Jeanne Moreau. Presently married to Candice Bergen.

★*RIZZI, LUIGI* Italian nightclub owner, photographed at La Madrague, Bardot's villa in St. Tropez, sunbathing in the nude with BB, who was still married to Gunther Sachs. Said Gunther: "I think the end is in sight."

★*ROJO, GUSTAVO* Spanish actor who notified the press about a weekend rendezvous with Bardot, and said he planned to marry her. This annoyed her then-*amant* Trintignant, whom BB wanted to marry. Jean-Lou's wife (Stephane Audran, later Mme. Claude Chabrol) wouldn't grant him a divorce. Said BB succinctly, "It's a mess."

★*SACHS, GUNTHER* German tycoon Count Gunther Sachs von Opel, Bardot's third husband. They eloped to Las Vegas on Bastille Day, 1966. "Marriage must be like a stroke of madness," said BB. A couple of months later, she found Sachs's world of business getting dull. "He took me by storm. I was on a flying carpet—serenaded in Venice, baccarat in Nice, marriage in Las Vegas. But when the carpet landed—bang! He was dry, artificial, obsessed with making an impression, to exhibit me to the Shah of Iran."

★*SARNE, MICHAEL* Former pop singer, actor, and, eventually, director (of *Myra Breckenridge)*. Appeared with Bardot in the Anglo-French *À Coeur Jolie*, made in England. Going underground for a few days with BB rendered Sarne rapturous, having had a legend in his own bed: ". . . more fun and more excitement in a short time than with any woman I have ever known."

★*TERZIEFF, LAURENT* French stage actor and BB's top leading man, at her insistence, in *À Coeur Jolie*. His screen presence somehow just missed, and Terzieff was by now personally running a lackluster fourth after Sarne, Zaguri, and Sachs.

★*TRINTIGNANT, JEAN-LOUIS* Major French film star, BB's quarry in *And God Created Woman* and partner in some steamy love scenes occasionally continued after Vadim cried *"Cut!"* Thus the director launched his sex goddess, but lost his wife. BB adored Jean-Lou's jealousy, though amour went AWOL when the army called him up. She hated uniforms.

★*VADIM, ROGER* First husband and lifelong friend and star-maker also instrumental in shaping the careers of Jane Fonda (whom he also wed), Catherine Deneuve, and Annette Strogberg (wife no. 2). The discovery and development and wooing of BB, begun when she was a virginal 15-year old ballet student, also established Vadim's reputation. "You," he told her, "are going to be the respectable married man's unattainable dream."

★*VALLONE, RAF* Italian actor who taught her to appreciate Beethoven and Brahms, and briefly managed to escape banishment by Bardot's rigid RFC rating—Ready for Chrysanthemums—usually applied to any man over 40.

★*VERGEZ, LAURENT* Still another *beau jeune homme*, whose nude photographs of Bardot at 40 adorned *Playboy* and other magazines.

★*ZAGURI, BOB* South American businessman she met at Cannes Festival in 1963. When her "heart turned over," she dropped Sami Frey. Dropped Zaguri, who was still at her St. Tropez villa, when she impulsively married Sachs. Said Robert: "I thought she was shopping in Paris."

MISCELLANY

Male model, muscle man, bit player, mechanic, waiter, athlete. Usually dark, medium height, strikingly handsome, nearly always young. When her longtime agent, Olga Horst-Primuz, once questioned her choice of companions, Bardot sulked: "I have always adored beautiful young men. Just because I grow older, my taste doesn't change. So if I can still have them, why not?"

BAUTZER, GREG
(b. 1918)

Slick, handsome showbiz attorney and one of Hollywood's foremost men-about-town. Bautzer worked for Howard Hughes at one time, and ran his former boss a close second as frequent escort to a galaxy of scrumptious superstars. The partial list here includes, for the most part, only those who have been linked with Bautzer in biographies. Not even the Bar Association knows all the ladies with whom this high-flying legal eagle has scored.

PRIMARY SOURCES: *Joan Crawford: A Biography*, by Bob Thomas (Simon and Schuster, 1978); *Zsa Zsa Gabor: My Story*, "written for me by Gerold Frank" (World, 1960); *Jayne Mansfield and the American Fifties*, by Martha Saxton (Houghton Mifflin, 1975); *Lana: The Public and Private Lives of Miss Turner*, by Joe Morella and Edward Z. Epstein (Citadel, 1971).

★*BARRIE, WENDY* British B actress, later TV personality, onetime girlfriend of notorious Bugsy Siegel. Bautzer began to date Wendy while he was still seeing Lana.

★*COBB, BUFF* Beautiful socialite-model—an instant celebrity of her time. She finally hooked Bautzer in marriage—but only briefly—in the mid-1940s.

★*CRAWFORD, JOAN* The perpetually tanned, patient Bautzer made the perfect escort for Joan. Per her instructions, he would follow two paces behind on entering any public place, he carried her poodle and knitting bag, even placed her "serviette" in her lap at mealtime, and didn't seem to mind when his friends mocked him as "Greg the Greek." The obsequiousness was for public display; privately, he managed to exert some control over Crawford, always at the risk of violent backlash. "When provoked, Joan was capable of throwing whatever was handy at the moment, from a highball to—on one memorable occasion—a leg of lamb." After one fight, when Joan had locked him out, Greg climbed the rose trellis and broke into her bedroom. She thought he was *wonderful.* The Bautzer-Crawford relationship lasted four years, which was par for her marriages too. The ending came rather suddenly: On the way home late one night she asked him to get out and check a tire. "As he was gazing down at the tire, Crawford gunned the motor and sped off on Sunset with a screech of rubber . . . the romance was over." (See also CRAWFORD listing.)

★*GABOR, ZSA ZSA* She was one of the many, *many* famous filmland beauties who spent beaucoup time in Bautzer's company. In fact, she was with him the night she met husband-to-be Conrad Hilton. However, Gabor's autobiography says less about Greg than about the gown she was wearing at the time. (See also GABOR listing.)

★*MANSFIELD, JAYNE* He was "Mr. Standby" to Jayne—"always there to take a girl out to the most elegant parties." And "even though he dates the most famous women in the world, he makes a girl feel like she is the only one. He is extremely attentive. Greg will dash across the room to light a girl's cigarette." The secret of his success, no doubt. Bautzer on Mansfield is something else: "I found her simpatico. She was so vulnerable and insecure." But, for all her voluptuousness, Bautzer didn't find Jayne sexy. (See also MANSFIELD listing.)

★*TURNER, LANA* Greg was Lana's first *publicized* Hollywood affair, and everyone approved—MGM and her Mom most of all. The studio liked Bautzer's maturity and steadying influence on 19-year-old Lana; Mom liked him because he was rich and good-looking. Their engagement was taken for granted. Later, Lana would say, "I *was* engaged to Greg Bautzer. That is, if anyone can claim actually to be engaged to this astute escape artist." Anyway, their relationship went poof when Lana eloped with Artie Shaw. (See also TURNER listing.)

★*WYNTER, DANA* Second lady to bring Bautzer to the altar; the marriage endured from 1956 until 1968, producing a son, Mark.

MISCELLANY

Jot down the names of every acknowledged glamour girl of the past three decades, and divide by two. Sooner or later, at least half are likely to have had a cozy tête-à-tête with Greg.

BEATTY, WARREN
(b. 1937)

He had everything it takes to become just another heartthrob, yet Shirley MacLaine's handsome kid brother, with his tidy good looks and facile boyish charm, did much more with what he had than anyone might reasonably expect. Thanks to shrewd, discriminating choices (as producer-star of *Bonnie and Clyde* in 1967, producer-star and co-author of *Shampoo* eight years later, as producer, director, star and co-author of *Reds,* 1982), Beatty has become an inner-directed impresario whose stardom seems almost an afterthought. His ego drives in the private sector of his life are something else. Despite several important long-term relationships, his reputation as one of Hollywood's great hit-and-run swingers has few parallels since Errol Flynn first went out to play. Unmarried at 45, Beatty shows no sign of slowing down in any department.

PRIMARY SOURCES: *Joan Collins: Past Imperfect,* by Joan Collins (W. H. Allen, 1978); *True Britt,* by Britt Ekland (Prentice-Hall, 1980); *The Diane Keaton Scrapbook,* by Suzanne Munshower (Tempo Star Book/Ace Books/

Grosset & Dunlap, 1979); *Vivien Leigh,* by Anne Edwards (Simon and Schuster, 1977; Pocket Books, 1978); *Jack Nicholson: The Search for a Superstar,* by Norman Dickens (New American Library/Signet, 1975); *Bittersweet,* by Susan Strasberg (Putnam, 1980); *The Greatest Star: The Barbra Streisand Story,* by Rene Jordan (Putnam, 1975); *P.S. I Love You,* by Michael Sellers (Collins, London, 1981).

★*CARON, LESLIE* She had played *Lili* and *Gigi* and married director Peter Hall, of the prestigious Royal Shakespeare company, in 1956. They had two children before Hall sued for divorce in '64, naming Beatty as corespondent. Two years later, in London, Leslie and Warren made a comedy together called *Promise Her Anything.* Whatever promises were made, none were kept. After four more years, Leslie married producer Michael Laughlin instead.

★*CHRISTIE, JULIE* From *McCabe and Mrs. Miller* (1971) through *Shampoo* (1975) and *Heaven Can Wait* (1978), Beatty and Christie were the golden couple of the '70s—offscreen more so than on. To many fans and critics they seemed to be the perfect mating—the sensuous, beautiful, and intelligent British star with one of the sexiest, handsomest, and smartest leading men in American films. But by the late '70s there seemed to be a gulf as wide as the Atlantic Ocean between them.

★*COLLINS, JOAN* She knew and became engaged to Beatty when he was a "shyly myopic, pimply-faced, skinny boy" of 23. In those days, she recalls, he was "sexually insatiable." "Three, four, five times a day *every* day was not unusual for him, and he was also able to accept phone calls at the same time. . . . I had never seen anything like it, and although it was exciting for the first few months, after a while, I found myself feeling somewhat like a sex object." Actually, the result of such unbridled passion was a bit grim: pregnancy and an abortion. Shortly after, Joan visited her friendly astrologer to learn that lover Warren would soon be out of her life, and that in *his* future, "He will need a constant inflation of his ego—one woman will not suffice." (See also COLLINS listing.)

★*EKLAND, BRITT* She quite simply calls Warren "the most divine lover of all. His libido was as lethal as high octane gas. I had never known such pleasure and passion in my life." Britt had met Beatty years before, but nothing clicked until their tryst in London ("Julie Christie, his new love, was foolishly absent, and loyalty wasn't one of his strong points"), which was resumed at his penthouse pad in Beverly Hills. (See also EKLAND listing.)

★*HUSTON, ANJELICA* When the former model first arrived in Hollywood, "she alternated her affections between Warren Beatty and Jack Nicholson before finally settling down with Nicholson"—where she's been, more or less, ever since.

★*KEATON, DIANE* Diane bumped into Warren at about the same time she was breaking up with Woody Allen—and picking up an Oscar for Allen's *Annie Hall.* They spent the first flush of their romance in New York, going out to dinner in out-of-the-way places and reportedly enjoying quiet evenings at home. Diane theoretically learned a lot from Warren; for instance that "great looking guys have the same goals and problems as everyone else." ("Everyone else" meaning mousy mensches like Woody?) (See also KEATON listing.)

★*MITCHELL, JONI* Singer who's known to have been one of Beatty's frequent dates.

★*PHILLIPS, MICHELLE* It was, and still is, a rare thing indeed for Warren Beatty to set up housekeeping with *anybody,* but he and Michelle (and her daughter Chyna from first husband John Phillips) did share a big house on Mulholland Drive for a few years. Still, he retained his bachelor quarters at the Beverly Wilshire Hotel. Just to entertain out-of-town guests, don't you know. (See also PHILLIPS listing.)

★*STRASBERG, SUSAN* She says they met in Rome, as he was completing location shooting of *The Roman Spring of Mrs. Stone,* and he moved in with her "for the remainder of his vacation." He kept her very busy. Even at parties in other people's houses. (See also STRASBERG listing.)

★*STREISAND, BARBRA* They were "an item" circa 1971.

★*WOOD, NATALIE* They were "an item," sometime before that, after Natalie had divorced Robert Wagner on their first marriage-go-round. At the same time, coincidentally, Wagner was in London seeing Joan Collins, Beatty's former live-in girl. "Warren," sniffed Joan, "had not found it disadvantageous to his burgeoning career to be seen dating Natalie, a major star." Between marriages, in 1964, Natalie starred in *Sex and the Single Girl.*

MISCELLANY

★*LEIGH, VIVIEN* Beatty's distinguished co-star in *The Roman Spring* of *Mrs. Stone.* He was half her age, and stories of an intrigue between the London theater's first lady and the rising young stud are balanced by conflicting reports that they were not at all friendly. Ah, well, it's a nice idea.

★*MARGARET, PRINCESS* In a new biography of comic Peter Sellers, known to be a close friend of the Princess's, it is alleged that Her Highness once asked Sellers to fix her up with Beatty. Next time Warren came to London town, Peter rang up and hinted that "someone special" wanted to meet him. Later, climbing into the car and recognizing his blind date, Beatty reportedly gasped, "Jeezers, Pete, ain't that something?" What then? *Qui sait?* Probably not much.

★*MENGERS, SUE* Big Hollywood agent who confided to client Joan Collins one day, "God, I must be the only woman in L.A. or New York that Warren hasn't tried to *shtup.*"

BERGMAN, INGRID
(b. 1915)

After Garbo, Sweden gave Bergman to American movies, and her scrubbed, healthy wholesomeness set a standard for beauty that soon made many of the lacquered film goddesses who came before her look obsolete. As a romantic heroine, of course, *Casablanca* (1943) was her high point, though she won her first Oscar for *Gaslight* a year later, from which she graduated to several Hitchcock classics, *Spellbound, Notorious,* and *Under Capricorn.* Being a woman in jeopardy always seemed to bring out the best in Bergman. Her off-screen travail began in earnest when she went to Italy to make a movie with Italy's prodigious Roberto Rossellini, plunging headlong into a love affair which brought an end to her career in the U.S. Yesterday's scandals are pretty tame by today's standards, but Bergman has sorted out her past effectively—in book form, as well as in *Autumn Sonata,* Ingmar Bergman's 1978 film with Ingrid brilliantly playing an aging performer with career and family conflicts very much like her own.

PRIMARY SOURCE: *Ingrid Bergman: My Story,* by Ingrid Bergman and Alan Burgess (Delacorte, 1980; Dell, 1981).

★*CAPA, ROBERT* *Life* magazine photographer who took some of the most memorable World War II photos in Europe. The romance began in that heady time just after VE Day in Paris, in a chance meeting as Ingrid was enroute to greet the victorious Allied troops. He was 31, "an arresting and original human being . . . an international man, worldly and wise, and yet . . . still vulnerable." Ingrid, at 30, was a suddenly famous movie star and an increasingly unhappy wife. Capa followed her to Hollywood and they were faced with a dilemma, having fallen in love. "That part was not easy," Ingrid writes, "because I was so moral, so prudish you might say." If Capa had asked her to come away and be his wife, she might have. But he didn't. He couldn't live in her shadow, she couldn't follow him on his journalistic junkets. When they agreed to part, Ingrid noted she was "tearing a very dear piece away from my life." Their love affair evolved over the years into a deep, abiding friendship. In 1954, when the French had just begun to do battle there, Capa became the first war correspondent to be killed in Vietnam.

★*COOPER, GARY* They were teamed in *For Whom the Bell Tolls* (1943), but the sparks between them apparently didn't ignite until they made *Saratoga Trunk* (1945). Bergman's book ignores the fact, but their relationship gave off sufficient heat to worry Paramount's publicity department. Bergman played a "wickedly comic" role as a courtesan, and Cooper's biography asserts that "where she'd been protected by Cooper in the Hemingway picture, she was now toying with him in real life." The plot was sexy enough. Flacks feared that an American public still wrapped up in war would react negatively to all the extramarital fun Ingrid and Gary seemed to be having off the set. The movie's release was held up a couple of months while the gossip cooled. A few decades later, they might have built an ad campaign around it. *O tempora! O mores!* (See also COOPER listing.)

★*FLEMING, VICTOR* Director (*Gone with the Wind*, among others) who began working with Ingrid on plans to film her hit New York play *Joan of Lorraine*. Fleming was many years married and 60 years old, twice Ingrid's age, when he declared his love. "She did not for one moment protest . . . it was all part of the flood of creation. What she did not accurately perceive was that Victor was not merely *half* in love, he had toppled over the edge, and his fall . . . was far closer to agony than to ecstasy." They both knew it could not be, and he said of himself, "There's no fool like an old fool." When finally working on the film (retitled *Joan of Arc*), "the intensity of their work gave them no time for anything else."

★*LINDSTROM, PETTER* Ingrid was 21, a most promising young actress, when, in July 1937, she married Petter, a 30-year-old Stockholm doctor. She writes, "Petter and I went about our careers as if we were going to live happily ever after." However, first came their daughter Pia, then World War II, forcing the family to leave Europe. With her success in Hollywood, the marriage began to split at the seams. "He told me what to do and what to say," said Ingrid, and he became convinced she was having affairs with all her leading men. Domestic harmony was not enhanced by the Capa affair—which was reignited briefly in

1947 while the Lindstroms vacationed in Europe—and it totally fell apart in 1948 after Bergman was emotionally swept away by Roberto Rossellini's *Open City*. At that historic moment, "Ingrid Bergman's life changed, Roberto Rossellini's life changed, Dr. Petter Lindstrom's life changed. And children were given life."

★*ROSSELLINI, ROBERTO* Ingrid wrote him this letter: "Dear Mr. Rossellini, I saw your films *Open City* and *Paisan,* and enjoyed them very much. If you need a Swedish actress who speaks English very well, who has not forgotten her German, who is not very understandable in French, and who in Italian knows only 'ti amo,' I am ready to come and make a film with you." He cabled an immediate yes to her proposal and followed up with a long letter outlining his plans for the movie he had in mind with Bergman: *Stromboli.* "Ingrid had known in her heart for a long time that if the right man came along and said the right words, she was ready and willing to go." And so she did. Still married to Lindstrom, Bergman entered into a passionate affair with Rossellini, became pregnant, and bore his son, Robertino—an event that drew such remarkable news coverage that she was hounded by paparazzi even in her hospital room. Her actions were reviled by the world press and condemned on the floor of the U.S. Senate, and for several years she did not get a role in a Hollywood movie. Her eventual marriage to Rossellini produced two more children, twins Isabella and Ingrid. In 1956 Ingrid met and was very attracted to Lars Schmidt, but did not dare think of leaving Roberto. But then *he* found someone else, an Indian actress named Sonali. "I knew now things had changed forever. . . . He had fallen in love again . . . he had left *me.* . . . Now we had *solved it.*"

★*SCHMIDT, LARS* Swedish theatrical producer who had offices in New York, London, and Paris. Ingrid and Lars had much in common: Both were Swedes who had spent their lives as foreigners. They decided to marry—on condition that she like his island, Danhommen, off the coast of Sweden. "That first visit we sat on the big round rocks near the house and I said, 'I love your island.' And Lars said, 'Right, let's get married.' It all sounded very simple, but it wasn't as simple as all that." They were wed just before Christmas 1958, at Caxton Hall in London. In 1970, Lars announced that he had found someone else. She did nothing to end the marriage, until 1975 when by mutual consent the couple obtained a very secret divorce.

MISCELLANY

★*GRANT, CARY* Since co-starring in *Notorious*, Grant and Bergman have been truly good friends. He was on hand in Hollywood to collect Ingrid's second Oscar, for *Anastasia*. Said Cary: "I think the Academy ought to set aside a special award for Bergman every year, whether she makes a picture or not." (See also GRANT listing.)

★*HUGHES, HOWARD* Ingrid was introduced to Howard through their mutual friend Cary Grant; they went dancing, and he told her how lonely he was. "I thought, what a silly thing for a man to say. Here's this very rich and famous man—and he's lonely?" Ingrid adds that Howard's aides called her repeatedly, and had others plead his case, but "I was simply not at ease with him. I knew what he was after." Ingrid remained unimpressed even when Hughes told her he had bought RKO Studios—just for her. But a few years later, Hughes and his studio backed the making of Rossellini's *Stromboli*, and he was the first to be told, *in strict confidence*, that Ingrid was pregnant by the Italian director. He kept the news to himself for approximately five minutes, then phoned Louella. He simply figured that the scandalous headlines would be good publicity for the picture. (See also HUGHES listing.)

BEY, TURHAN
(b. 1920)

While Gable, Stewart, Niven and all the established matinee idols were away fighting World War II, someone had to stoke the home fires. Part of the job fell to Bey (originally Turhan Selahattin Sahultavy Bey), whose exotic sensuality decorated a couple dozen movies including *Ali Baba and the Forty Thieves* (1943) and *The Climax* (1944). Valentino he wasn't, and then came V-J Day. When last heard from, Turhan was making his living as a still photographer in Europe.

PRIMARY SOURCES: *Linda: My Own Story*, by Linda Christian (Crown, 1962); *Ava: A Life Story* (Delacorte, 1974); *Lana: The Public and Private Lives of Miss Turner*, by Joe Morella and Edward Z. Epstein.

★*CHRISTIAN, LINDA* She responded at once to "those curious slanting eyes, the rounded face" and the abundance of charm that was native to his birthplace, Vienna. Theirs was not a "tempestuous love," but they spent a lot of time at the beach and at his place "having long chats about life or listening to records of the Vienna Philharmonic." Turhan seemed to drift in and out of Linda's life, whenever she needed "a touch of romance." (See also CHRISTIAN listing.)

★*GARDNER, AVA* They were a frequent pairing in Hollywood in the early 1940s. Ava had a soft spot for exotic men. (See also GARDNER listing.)

★*TURNER, LANA* She saw him in *Dragon Seed*, and made up her mind to meet him. (Artie Shaw said of Lana that she often discovered her new boyfriends by seeing them first in the movies.) After they did meet, it was only a few months before Lana announced her engagement to Bey. Jealous ex-husband Steve Crane picked a fight with the turgid Turhan one night at a swank dinner party, suggesting the two men go out to the garden to "settle matters." In disgust at such macho antics, "Lana tossed away a diamond ring . . . and walked out with Bey." Seems the ring was one that Crane had given Lana, and he spent the rest of the evening on his hands and knees in the garden looking for it. Within weeks, fickle Lana had tossed Turhan aside for someone new. (See also TURNER listing.)

BOGART, HUMPHREY
(1899–1957)

Ugly-handsome inspiration for the Bogie cult, which actually came into existence a decade after his death—a new generation's tribute to one of moviedom's most unlikely romantic heroes. The loner, the honest tough guy, a hard-boiled sonofabitch with a heart of gold—these were the characters Bogart gave substance to in *The Maltese Falcon* (1941) and *The African Queen* (1951), to name but a pair of his classics. Part of the Bogart legend turned out to be his lively marriage to Lauren "Baby" Bacall, who probably knew better than anyone that his treat-'em-rough manner was mostly a front. His true attitude about women was quite old-fashioned. Example: He attended a stag party one night at which the evening's entertainment was provided by eight young and lovely "models." Bogey seemed moody and downcast all evening, never making a move. After the sweet young things were driven home, he looked up at his buddies, and with the most profound emotion said, "Anybody who would stick a cock in one of those girls would throw a rock through a Rembrandt."

PRIMARY SOURCE: *Bogie*, by Joe Hyams (New American Library/Signet, 1966).

★*BACALL, LAUREN* The great love of his life, as he was hers. She was 19, Bogart was 45 at the time of their historic first meeting—with a hit movie to make *(To Have and Have Not)* and nothing between them but Bogart's firebreathing wife, Mayo Methot. The first line Lauren delivered, shaking all over, was: "Anybody got a match?" Weeks later, Bogie sug-

gested she jot down her phone number on the back of a match cover, and the *real* love story began. Bogart was attracted by her youth, her naturalness, her don't-give-a-damn attitude. They loved each other's company, kidding around, swapping corny jokes ("What did the ceiling say to the wall?" "Hold me up, I'm plastered" is one of Bacall's perfect examples). Divorced from Mayo in 1945, Bogart was free to make Betty—as her intimates call Bacall—his fourth wife. They had a rowdy, exhilarating, idyllic kind of togetherness until his death in 1957. The union produced two children, Steve and Leslie. (See also BACALL listing.)

★*MENKEN, HELEN* Wife no. 1. A temperamental redhead, and a successful actress when they met while he was an unglamorous, poorly paid stage manager. Their first encounter was a fight about the sets; he booted her and she belted him. After their marriage in 1926 it got worse; they'd quarrel over whether "it would be right to feed the dog caviar when people were starving." Years later, Helen took the blame for their eventual breakup.

★*METHOT, MAYO* Wife no. 3. They became known as the "battling Bogarts." She was a beauty, an actress, a drinker, and the daughter of a sea captain—so she shared Bogie's love of the sea and sailing. The marriage was unconventional from the very start, Mischa Auer did a Cossack dance, stark naked, at the reception. She picked most of the fights, and Bogart gallantly fought back—admiring her toughness and her ability to drink most men under the table. He called her Sluggy, nicknamed their home Sluggy Hollow. Sometimes she went too far, trying to stab him with a butcher knife. The fighting invigorated their lovemaking. They split when Bogie met Bacall.

★*PHILIPS, MARY* Wife no. 2, and another actress. He was bawling her out for stealing a scene from him when he suddenly became aware that "here was a girl with whom I could very easily fall in love." Her Irish temperament was a perfect balance for Bogie, and the marriage might have lasted longer had it not been for their long separations, he working in Hollywood, she in New York. She fell in love with Roland Young and he with Mayo Methot.

★*PICKLES* His first romance, during a long Long Island summer.

★*RANKIN, RUTH* They dated during the Roaring Twenties, "slumming in Greenwich Village" and having lots of crazy times.

BOW, CLARA
(1905–1965)

Brooklyn-born tease whose first step toward stardom was winning a movie magazine's Fame and Fortune contest. Labeled the "It" Girl, she scrumptiously embodied the restless flapper spirit of the Jazz Age in movies appropriately titled *Mantrap*, *It*, *Rough House Rosie*, *Red Hair*, *Hula*, etc. Even giddier and more ebullient offscreen than on, Bow's life was a Charleston along that floodlit primrose path where Harlow, Monroe, and other tragically flawed sex symbols would follow. Booze, sex, and scandal eroded public affection for her, particularly after the 1931 trial for larceny of a companion-secretary, Daisy DeVoe, who meanwhile sold her revelations about Clara's uninhibited sexcapades to Bernard MacFadden's *Evening Graphic*, a pioneer yellow journal.

PRIMARY SOURCE: *The "It" Girl: The Incredible Story of Clara Bow*, by Joe Morella and Edward Z. Epstein (Delacorte, 1976).

★*BAER, ABEL* New York songwriter who slept with Clara while writing the score for a film, but said "no repeat performances." Once was enough for Baer, who found her sexual appetite athletic, her personal hygiene below par.

★*BELL, REX* Handsome actor, Clara's only husband, with whom she ultimately retired to a sprawling Nevada ranch to raise two handsome sons. Though she said Rex was the only man she ever trusted, they separated some years later. Bell ultimately entered politics and was campaigning to be governor of Nevada when he died of a heart attack on July 4, 1962.

★*CANTOR, EDDIE* Pop-eyed top comedian of stage and screen; his fling with Clara annoyed Al Jolson, who couldn't imagine why she had said no to him, yes to virtually every other male in Hollywood.

★*COOPER, GARY* At the time, a rising cowboy star and ambitious superstud whose flamboyant affair with Clara earned him her personal endorsement as "a great lay." When they met at a party and discussed making a movie together, Cooper remarked that so far his only leading lady had been Flash the Wonder Horse. "Are you and Flash *goin'* together?" quipped Clara. Nope. They were an instant click, Gary and Clara. She took him home with her that night and was delighted to find a partner with sexual stamina equal to her own. Later, Clara confided to a chum that Coop "could keep pumping away all night and into the morning." Fan magazines began to call him the "It" Boy, but Coop's jealousy of the other men in her life—and she rarely said no to any of them—finally made Clara cool toward him.

★*FLEMING, VICTOR* Virile, womanizing director (famed for *Gone with the Wind* in 1939) who was 40 when he directed *Mantrap* with Clara, and found her insatiable. He'd become violent over her frequent infidelities, but joined Clara's stable of "regulars" after Cooper appeared.

★*GILBERT, JOHN* Hollywood's top screen lover of the silent era, he was romantically linked with Garbo but succumbed briefly to Clara, though his friends found her "trashy." Indifferent to the elegance of Gilbert's lifestyle, Clara eyed the opulent silver service at breakfast one morning and cracked, "You really like all this crap?" Presumably, Cupid cringed.

★*KEITH, DONALD* Romantic leading man. A brief fling.

★*LUGOSI, BELA* Hungarian-born actor trapped in his screen role as *Dracula*. Part of the parade through Bow's boudoir, but left no telltale puncture marks.

★MANNERS, HY Former U. of Pittsburgh football star and bit actor in *True to the Navy* (1930), as was Rex Bell, who shared Clara's favors with Hy for the first few weeks, and ultimately outscored him.

★MARCH, FREDRIC Stage star and co-star of Clara's first talkie (*The Wild Party*, 1929), subsequently known as "the best-looking young lech" at Paramount. Casual intimacies followed by slow fade.

★PEARSON, WILLIAM EARL Irresistible interne discovered after an emergency appendectomy. "Really in love," she continued seeing Pearson, who was married, even after his wife sued her for alienation of affection. More embarrassing headlines.

★RICHMAN, HARRY "Mr. Broadway," a hard-drinking, high-living performer whose sexual staying power was also a legend among showfolk. Though their first date was arranged for publicity purposes, they became fun-loving, ardent lovers, and Clara gave Richman a photo inscribed "To My Gorgeous Lover, Harry, I'll trade all my It for your That." Their off-again-on-again engagement suffered a major setback when Richman found her in bed with a Mexican croupier.

★ROLAND, GILBERT Smolderingly handsome Latin lover. He caught her eye in the supporting cast of *The Plastic Age* (1925), and was so eager to marry her that Clara was scared off despite his ardor and her own admission, "He's the first man I ever cared about."

★ROSENBLOOM, SLAPSIE MAXIE Tough young boxer, then in his prime, later had a so-so movie career as a monosyllabic thug.

★SAVAGE, ROBERT Yale football player, scion of steel manufacturing family, whose suicide attempt after Clara jilted him led to a sanity hearing. Savage told the court his lips "bled and ached for days" when Clara kissed him. The publicity didn't hurt her image as a femme fatale, though Clara responded simply: "Men don't slash their wrists. They use a gun."

★SUTHERLAND, EDDIE Director, who got her to bed while making *The Saturday Night Kid* (1929), later bragged about his conquest.

★THE THUNDERING HERD Name given by press to USC's 1927 football team, who collectively revived her interest in outdoor sports. All-American tackle Jesse Hibbs and team captain Morley Drury were generally thought to be her favorite partners for sexual scrimmaging, after Clara visited the clubhouse and invited the boys home, though some wags insisted she had taken on the entire pigskin squad, man by man. Finally, USC's coach issued an edict: "Clara Bow is off limits to all members of this football team."

★YOUNG PILOT One among many who landed in Bow's bed while on location in San Antonio, Texas, during the making of *Wings*, a 1927 smash hit directed by William Wellman. Typically, this weary flier was reported to say: "When you're with her she makes you feel you're the greatest guy in the world and she couldn't live without you. Then you find out she's laying all of your buddies and they feel the same way. . . ."

MISCELLANY

★"COMPANY" Euphemism for companions she'd pick up on sleepless nights while cruising, incognito if possible, in her roadster. Disillusioned with her love life at this point, circa 1927, Clara said: "The more I see of men, the more I like dogs."

BRANDO, MARLON
(b. 1924)

Nebraska's gift to the acting profession, and a priceless one at his best in such films as *On the Waterfront* and *The Godfather*, both of which brought him Oscars. From *A Streetcar Named Desire* to *Last Tango in Paris*, the rest of the list may seem more remarkable to film buffs than to Brando himself, who has always stubbornly sloughed off the mantle of great artistry. He was originally identified as a mumbling

Method actor, a genius in spite of himself. Exotic women—Latin or Eurasian—seem to intrigue him, judged by his track record as a Lothario. He also devotes himself to minority causes, such as aid to American Indians. In recent years, unless lured away by a good role, he spends as much time as he can on his own Tahitian island—a mutineer enjoying the bounty of the multimillion-dollar paychecks he now commands.

PRIMARY SOURCES: *Brando: The Unauthorized Biography,* by Joe Morella and Edward Z. Epstein (Crown, 1973); *Marlon, Portrait of the Rebel as an Artist,* by Bob Thomas (Random House, 1966); *Brando for Breakfast,* by Anna Kashfi Brando and E.P. Stein (Crown, 1979; Berkley, 1980).

★*ADLER, ELLEN* Daughter of drama coach Stella Adler. She waited patiently, and in vain, for Brando to straighten out.

★*BERENGER, JOSANNE MARIANA* Nineteen-year-old French girl from Toulon. While working as a governess in New York she met Brando at a party. On their second date he brought another friend along, "a girl everyone knew he was balling." Josanne quietly followed him to Hollywood (while he made *Désirée)* and he quietly followed her to France, where they announced their engagement. But marriage plans quietly faded away. When Kashfi asked Brando about Berenger, he replied: "She had bad breath."

★*CUI, MARIE* Philippine dancer who charged that Brando was the father of her daughter, Maya Gabriela Cui Brando, born in February 1963. Blood tests failed to substantiate the claim. But Kashfi *had* walked in on Cui and Marlon in bed, resulting in a three-way skirmish that brought the police.

★*EDDY AND ERIKO* One's Polynesian, the other Japanese; they live on Brando's Tahitian island, presumably tending to his every need.

★*FERMEZ, GISELLE* Dusky Haitian girl, a practitioner of voodoo. After being dropped by Brando she indulged in a few vengeful pranks such as directing a mortician to Brando's house to "pick up the body." She enlisted Kashfi's aid in delivering a curse to the man both despised—a shoebox filled with a dead beetle, a dead mouse, rose thorns, a candle, etc., which was thrown over his garden wall to the accompaniment of an "unintelligible incantation."

★*FORD, ANNE* A 24-year-old blouse designer who dated Brando while he was filming *On the Waterfront* in New York. An interview she gave to *Glamour,* says Kashfi, made Brando sound like "a noodle-brained simpleton."

★*JAGGER, BIANCA* According to Morella and Epstein, the former wife of Mick Jagger "remembers Brando with even less kind remarks than Kashfi." Wot'd she say? Anybody's guess.

★*KASHFI, ANNA* First wife. She claims to have been born in Calcutta in 1934 of unmarried Indian parents. Then, says Anna, when she was two, her mother married a Welshman. Other sources say that Anna's not Indian at all. One part of her biography not in dispute is that she began her film career in *The Mountain,* with Spencer Tracy. Kashfi says she didn't know who Brando was when they met in Hollywood. When she found out, she agreed to date him. "Physically," she writes, "Marlon is not well appointed. He screens that deficiency by undue devotion to his sex organ. 'My noble tool,' he characterizes it with some puffery." Much of their courtship took place in the hospital, while she recuperated from TB. Anna felt he proposed out of pity. They were wed in October 1957, but Marlon had failed to make plans for a honeymoon. "What would you like to do now?" he said. "I don't know, Marlon, what did you have in mind?" Kashfi retorted. After driving around LA for an hour he called his agent and asked if they could spend the night. Son Christian Devi, born exactly seven months later, was the subject of a bitter custody suit that lasted until he reached manhood. The marriage ended one day short of their first anniversary. Then the real fisticuffs began.

★*MONROE, MARILYN* Their brief fling is reported glancingly in Norman Mailer's sumptuous MM bio, where it's suggested the event was not an unqualified success. (See also MONROE listing.)

★*MORENO, RITA*   Latin musical star and, recently, a serious actress. Their twelve-year on-and-off relationship was deep but stormy. She hung in there while Brando married others; she flew across continents and oceans to see him. But he didn't do much for her. Moreno was at Brando's house, alone, when she took an overdose of sleeping pills—but his secretary, Alice Marchak, found her and rushed her to the hospital. That was in 1961. Marlon and Rita subsequently worked together, and today are reportedly fast friends.

★*MOVITA*   Mexican actress. Brando's second wife, and either six or sixteen years older than he. They first met on the set of *Viva Zapata;* Brando married Kashfi and had other liaisons before returning to Movita eight years later. They were wed in 1960; had the marriage annulled in 1968. She is believed to be the mother of Brando's son Miko, but Kashfi has other ideas about that. (See NUYEN, below.) Divorced.

★*NIEL, KRISTA*   Italian starlet who, in 1973, announced that Brando had made her a mother. "I'm proud to be having Marlon's baby," she said, "and I want absolutely nothing from him." And that's just what she got.

★*NUYEN, FRANCE*   Eurasian beauty who starred on Broadway in *The World of Suzy Wong*, but never made the big time thereafter. The affair began during his marriage to Kashfi, who *couldn't stand* young Nuyen, "the epitome of glamour and sensuality." Brando once brought Nuyen home, where she "tut-tutted" Anna's curry and filched her "last mango" from the refrigerator. Anna also recalls that during their divorce proceedings, Marlon called from Guadalajara about 2:00 A.M., to tell her that France had given birth to his child, a son, Miko. He asked Anna, "Would you like to adopt him?" Miko was raised by Brando's second wife, Movita, who's still generally considered the young man's mother.

★*PELLICER, PINA*   Another Mexican actress, "discovered" by Brando (she was then 20) to star in the first film he directed, the misbegotten *One-Eyed Jacks.* Pina never made another American movie and committed suicide in 1964.

★*RENAY, LIZ*   Bosomy blond showgirl and model turned writer, who recalls Brando fondly in her racy autobiography, *My Face for the World to See.*

★*TERIIPAIA, TARITA*   Brando's supposedly still-faithful Tahitian mistress, who has borne him at least two children, son Tehotu, daughter Tarita. She was a waitress when he tapped her to star as Fletcher Christian's woman in the 1962 remake of *Mutiny on the Bounty.* She has lived lo these many years on or near Brando's private Tahitian island.

★*WINTERS, SHELLEY*   Kashfi's view is that Shelley used to love to mother Brando back in the early days in New York, darning his socks and all. Shelley tells it differently. Their association continued when both came to Hollywood. (See also WINTERS listing.)

MISCELLANY

★*BANKHEAD, TALLULAH*   Brando was Talu's leading man in *The Eagle Has Two Heads.* But the chemistry fizzled at the show's out-of-town opening. During one of her major soliloquies, he pulled such tricks as picking his nose, unzipping his fly. Before that, Bankhead had made certain sexual overtures to him; afterward they never spoke. Marlon once saw her in an elegant restaurant, however, and boomed across the room, "Tallulah, how the fuck are you?" (See also BANKHEAD listing.)

★*COX, WALLY*   Brando and the late TV actor may have been more than just New York "roommates." The relationship was "deep, multifarious and enduring." Kashfi recalls that only once did Brando discuss his homosexuality in public; he told a French reporter that he'd had experiences with men, and was "not ashamed."

★*MARQUAND, CHRISTIAN*   The French writer. Brando met him in Paris in 1972, during shooting of *Last Tango in Paris.* Marquand was then romantically involved with Dominique Sanda, who was supposed to have the lead in *Tango* until she got pregnant.

Kashfi writes that Brando has intimated his relationship with Marquand was "of a particularly close nature," and that there might have been *sexe à trois* between Brando, Marquand, and Sanda. *Qui sait?*

★*OTHER WOMEN* Those with whom Brando has been associated (at least those who've had their names in print) include *PIER ANGELI, ESTHER ANDERSON, SUSAN CABOT, JOAN COLLINS, KATY JURADO, JANICE MARS, DIANA ROSS, FRANCESCA SCAFFA . . .*

BURTON, RICHARD
(b. 1925)

He was never quite so important a star in cinema as he was on the stage, and he has yet to win an Oscar, but the Welsh-born classic actor tries to straddle both worlds. His sporadic returns to the theater seem to remind the public that Richard Burton was once considered the natural successor to Olivier, though so far he has not matched Sir Laurence's greatest performances in any medium, nor has he managed to duplicate Olivier's trick of taking the money and running from terrible movies or an occasional TV commercial without the sellout's being noticed. Burton's every move has been noticed since the day he met Elizabeth Taylor, wooed her, won her, married her, divorced her, remarried her, and redivorced her, meanwhile making a series of films that appeared to be about the battling Burtons as much as anything else (worst of the lot was *The Sandpiper*, then the redeeming *Who's Afraid of Virginia Woolf?*). Long before Liz, Burton was a celebrated rake who knew sex would be important to him the first time he stepped on a stage to experience "the strangest sensation in my penis." After that, "throbbing fervors when something important is about to happen. . . . I suppose it's a barometer." And nearly always fair weather.

PRIMARY SOURCES: *Richard and Elizabeth*, by Lester David and Jhan Robbins (Funk & Wagnalls, 1977); *Eliz-abeth Taylor: The Last Star*, by Kitty Kelley (Simon and Schuster, 1981); *Richard Burton, His Intimate Story*, by Ruth Waterbury (Pyramid Books, 1965).

★*BASILE, CARMELA* Twenty-year-old Italian schoolgirl who came to watch the filming of *The Journey* near her village, Noto. Burton asked her to lunch; later he sent his Mercedes around to fetch her after school.

★*BELL, JEANIE* Actress and first black woman to be featured in a *Playboy* centerfold. She and Burton were seen "romping around Nice," and Jeanie kept him company during a "drying-out" period in Switzerland. Burton began recourting Elizabeth Taylor, from whom he was then estranged, and Jeanie quietly left the scene.

★*BLOOM, CLAIRE* She was once "the great love of Burton's life," co-starring with him in *Alexander the Great* and *Look Back in Anger*. But when she appeared with Richard in *The Spy Who Came In from the Cold*, the imposing presence of Elizabeth Taylor—by now his wife—chilled any likelihood of auld lang syne. "In all the months of shooting in Ireland, I was never asked to dinner by the Burtons," said Claire.

★*BUJOLD, GENEVIEVE* Co-star in *Anne of a Thousand Days*, and her youthful beauty captivated Burton. He nicknamed her Gin, which worried Liz. She knew he gave nicknames to all his loves.

★*DELON, NATHALIE* Blond French actress, once wife of Alain Delon. During Liz's absence while he filmed *Bluebeard*, writes Kitty Kelley, "Richard, who was supposed to be shooting late on the streets of Budapest, arrived on the set drunk, took Nathalie Delon by the arm, shoved her into his Rolls, and drove off."

★*ELIZABETH, PRINCESS OF YUGOSLAVIA* In 1974, after his first divorce from Elizabeth Taylor, Burton announced his engagement to Princess Elizabeth, 38, still legally wed to Neil Balfour, British banker. The end came because she couldn't face his drinking and blatant pursuit of other women. The Princess was quoted thusly: "It takes more than a woman to make a man sober."

★*GRIMES, TAMMY* Broadway actress. He nicknamed her Shining. She was "madly in love with him for at least four days."

★*HAYNES, ROBERTA* Actress who replaced Diane McBaine as leading lady in the movie *Ice Palace*. She told intimates that she and Richard were "very good friends."

★*HUNT, SUZY* Golden-girl wife of the golden boy of British racing, James "The Shunt" Hunt. Burton first saw her on the ski slopes at Gstaad, where he and Liz (on their second marriage-go-round) spent Christmas 1975. Almost before she could unbuckle her bindings, Richard asked Suzy to come to New York with him, while he took over the lead in Broadway's *Equus*. Taylor angrily told the young woman, "You'll only last six months with Richard." And Suzy replied, "Perhaps, but those six months will be very worthwhile." Burton credits Suzy with literally saving his life, getting him off the bottle, and rejuvenating him "with her enthusiasm." Their affair made headlines throughout early 1976, and after the second Burton-Taylor divorce, they were wed in August of that year. *However*, Suzy walked out on Richard in August, 1981—a fact not publicly known until many months later, when Burton was a surprise guest at the 50th-birthday bash of la Liz, his twice former wife. Which set the rumor cauldrons bubbling once again.

★*LIL* An usherette at the theater where Burton first performed as an actor. His pal Stanley Baker urged him to take her home; "Go on, boyo, it's wonderful." However, Burton remembers his first time with a woman as a painful experience: "I didn't learn anything about sex from Lil."

★*LOREN, SOPHIA* Liz had just walked out on Burton—for the first time. In Italy to make *The Voyage* with Sophia, Burton moved in with the Italian star and Carlo Ponti, her producer husband. Lonely Richard and sympathetic Sophia spent weekends together on the Ponti yacht, and many evenings playing Scrabble together in the Ponti villa. For public consumption, Burton wrote that he *adored* Sophia, platonically, of course. In private, he

hinted the relationship may not have been limited to searching for seven-letter words. Later, there was a distinct iciness between Taylor and Loren. (See also LOREN listing.)

★*OXFORD GIRL* She provided Burton's first meaningful education in sex. "She was older than I was . . . she showed me what to do. I have never had any problems since." Sure, Richard.

★*PATTERSON, LESLEY* Seventeen-year-old actress, one of Richard's dates after his first divorce from Elizabeth.

★*SIMMONS, JEAN* On Burton's arrival in Hollywood, he and first wife Sybil were long-term houseguests with fellow Britons Stewart Granger and his wife Jean Simmons. Away from the house, Jean and Richard were co-starring in *The Robe*, and that wicked Welsh charm began to work once again. The situation remained stable until a New Year's Eve party—where Richard bussed Jean instead of Sybil as the clock struck twelve. Which prompted mild-mannered Sybil to strike Richard. The Burtons found their own living quarters soon after.

★*"STAR"* She was very big at 20th Century–Fox, her husband an important executive. The story goes, "she simply turned up at Burton's dressing room one day, wearing nothing but a coat which she dropped off. . . . She pouted as she said, 'Nobody would introduce us because they're all afraid of my husband.' "

★*STRASBERG, SUSAN* She was only 20, appearing in her second Broadway play—with Burton. As usual, Richard made no effort to hide his indiscretions; he even threw a back-stage 20th birthday party for Susan and invited all Broadway, plus photographers. His nicknames for Susan ranged from "my beautiful Hebrew princess" to Baby Angel. And, as usual, Burton went back to Sybil. (See also STRASBERG listing.)

★*TAYLOR, ELIZABETH* It was at the Stewart Granger manse that Burton, 25, first met Elizabeth, 19. She seemed to him then "the most astonishing, self-contained, pulchritudinous, remote, removed, inaccessible woman

I had *ever* seen." He thought her face divine, but her breasts "apocalyptic, they would topple empires." Ten years later, Burton himself toppled, while playing Antony to Taylor's Cleopatra on film, a now-classic fiasco. Their affair drew "more headlines than the Cuban missile crisis," and resulted in two divorces (Liz from Eddie Fisher, Richard from Sybil) and their eventual marriage in March 1964. On that fateful day, observing that Richard was dead drunk by 8:00 A.M., Liz confided to her hairdresser, "I don't know why he's so nervous. We've been sleeping together for two years." At the wedding Liz wore Richard's gift, a $150,000 emerald clip—the first of many such baubles, which he was better able to afford because his price shot up astronomically after he trumped in with Taylor. "The marriage was surreal, a drama so loaded with absurdity, love, tears, rage of jealous mates and near-tragedy that no movie audience would ever swallow it." Richard and Elizabeth starred in six films together, spent millions, married twice and divorced twice, the last time in 1976—when he found Suzy Hunt, and she encountered the future Senator John Warner. (See also TAYLOR listing.)

★*TUNDER, PAT* Copacabana showgirl with whom Burton "carried on" in New York while appearing in *Camelot*. She also showed up in Rome during *Cleopatra*. Didn't stay long, Burton was so busy.

★*WILLIAMS, SYBIL* Burton's first wife. She was 18, new to the theater, and, like Richard, from a mining village in Wales. They married in 1951. Later, when they played together at Stratford, "some of her reviews were markedly superior to his." That was when Richard told her to "pack it in." She gave up her career, had two daughters, Kate and Jessica, and stood by Burton through his interminable boozing and flamboyant womanizing. Until Elizabeth Taylor. They were divorced in 1964. Sybil later married Jordan Christopher.

MISCELLANY

★*ANDREWS, JULIE* When she heard about Burton's claim that the *only* leading lady he had *not* taken to bed was his *Camelot* co-star Julie Andrews, she retorted in mock outrage, "How dare he say such an awful thing about me!"

CHAMBERS, MARILYN
(b. 1952)

Major performer in porno films since the early 1970s, though her career is based almost entirely on three skin flicks, *Behind the Green Door*, *The Resurrection of Eve*, and *Insatiable*. Born in Connecticut with a solid middle-class WASP upbringing, a former model, Marilyn was the blond, blue-eyed All-American girl next door in blue movies. That image was fortified—and fully exploited by the media—when her debut as a porn star coincided with her appearance as the Ivory Snow girl, babe in arms, on thousands of soap boxes issued by staid Procter & Gamble. P&G promptly found a new girl. Recently appearing in magazines, books, and her nightclub act as a combination sexual guru and liberated livewire, Marilyn writes of herself with giddy candor, yet leaves the impression she's not much given to fooling around unless there's film in the camera. Says she: "I feel I *am* the way I look, clean and wholesome. I hate the expression *fuck films* . . . and I'd be embarrassed to go to an orgy."

PRIMARY SOURCE: *Marilyn Chambers: My Story*, by Marilyn Chambers (Warner, 1975).

★*ARMAND, MATTHEW* Nom de film for Marilyn's leading man in *Resurrection of Eve*. He was also appearing in *Hamlet* while shooting that one, and was frankly more interested in Shakespeare than hardcore cinema. But Marilyn tried to help him overcome his hangups. "He was very respectful of my suggestions. I put him at ease and made his cock stay hard. That's the way I like it best." But Armand went back to the Bard.

★CHAMBERS, DOUG   Former husband, a mechanic and bagpipe player. He didn't seem to mind Marilyn's line of work, and even agreed it was "good practice." She says they thought of themselves as a typical San Francisco couple, only *she* was the one who went out to work. Then she'd rush home to tell Doug about the day's filming. He'd say, "Well, show me what you did." "I'd just pull down his jeans as he flopped on the bed and start recreating exactly what I'd done at work." Though Marilyn thought their liberated marriage magical, the magic wafted away.

★GREEN DOOR LESBIANS   Six women who undress, kiss, and caress Marilyn intimately to prepare her for Johnny Keyes and company. "As far as lesbian scenes go, I'm really not into it." Though she adds that "every woman has a fantasy of wanting to be raped and done in by six chicks. It's been a pretty prevalent one with me."

★GREEN DOOR STUDS   Four, in all. At least two on trapezes join Keyes for orgiastic climax with Marilyn in a legendary sextette still considered by aficionados to be the ultimate pornographic fantasy on film.

★"HELEN"   Actress appearing in TV commercials, a 35-year-old beauty who introduced Marilyn to grass and lesbian lovemaking. In that order. "We can thank Clairol for the start of that," notes Marilyn, since she met Helen while filming a commercial for *Kindness*, a hair conditioner. "Making love to someone who is exactly like you is a trip like no other," Marilyn enthuses, even though her first trip was somewhat marred by the fact that Helen invited her boyfriend to come along and watch.

★HOLMES, JOHN C.   Top male porno star, aka Johnny Wadd, and Marilyn's partner in the marathon finale of *Insatiable*, a collision of giants. Known largely for his awesome genital endowment (12 or 13 inches, presumably), Holmes claims to have had sex with 14,000 women, a claim set forth in a 1981 semidocumentary film called *Exhausted*. Well, yeah.

★KEYES, JOHNNY   Black former prizefighter and dancer, co-star in *Green Door* as fantasy figure who makes love to Marilyn in front of a nightclub audience, wearing crotchless leotard. Keyes reappeared in *Resurrection of Eve* in an active role, though. Marilyn insists all their sex was strictly professional.

★McDONALD, GEORGE   Busy West Coast porn performer, another co-star in *Green Door*. As narrator, the fantasy is his.

★TONY   Star quarterback of the high school eleven, who claimed Marilyn's virginity when she was 17. The first try in Tony's car was a travesty (she got her foot caught in the horn). By trial and error, they finally managed. "This time we took it slowly and easily and Tony made sure the shift knob was in the Park position . . . it felt better than I'd dreamed it would." It was *coitus interruptus*, however; his brother drove up behind them.

★TRAYNOR, CHUCK   Current mate and manager, to whom Marilyn dedicates her book: "—my Traynor and constant companion. Thanks for making my life so beautiful." As a former airplane pilot, entrepreneur, and first husband of sex queen Linda *(Deep Throat)* Lovelace, Traynor had a more menacing role in her autobiographical *Ordeal*. (See LOVELACE listing.) Linda had already walked out on Chuck when Marilyn moved in. "So I just pushed her dresses aside, and hung up my jeans and tee-shirts. Three weeks earlier, Linda Lovelace had been fucking with Chuck in that bed, and now Marilyn Chambers was going to be sleeping in it!"

MISCELLANY

Nameless but numerous, one would think. For Marilyn, peculiarly discreet in her own way, sex in a porno film doesn't count. Otherwise, "I'm a masturbation freak. I think it's one of the best things in the world. Some people need sex more than others and I happen to be one of them. I love it."

CHAPLIN, CHARLES
(1889–1977)

The gentleman tramp and undisputed king of screen comedy, whose claim to fame was staked forever in silent movies. During the last fifty years of his life he made only nine feature films, ending with *A Countess from Hong Kong* in 1967. Charged with Communist sympathies during the McCarthy era of the 1950s, Chaplin left the U.S. for two decades of somewhat bitter exile in Switzerland. He married 18-year-old Oona O'Neill, fought a messy paternity suit, and began to alienate a public which had previously been laughing too hard to dwell on his failed marriages, scandals, and sundry romantic entanglements. "During work, women never interested me," Chaplin wrote; "it was only between pictures, when I had nothing to do, that I was vulnerable." Never an American citizen, he was barred from reentry to the U.S. during a trip abroad on grounds of "moral turpitude," finally returned in triumph in 1972, to be widely honored and wept over—a fittingly sentimental sendoff to an extraordinary career.

PRIMARY SOURCES: *My Autobiography*, by Charles Chaplin (Simon and Schuster, 1964; Pocket Books, 1966); *Hollywood Babylon*, by Kenneth Anger (Associated Press Professional Services, 1965).

★*BARRY, JOAN* Former girlfriend of Paul Getty, her brief dalliance with Chaplin escalated into damaging publicity, even after his marriage to Oona O'Neill. Their first evening together, Charlie wrote, in his customary florid style, he saw Joan as "a big handsome woman of twenty-two, well-built, with upper regional domes immensely expansive and made alluring by an extremely low décolleté summer dress, which . . . evoked my libidinous curiosity." Barry became a bit of a nuisance, however, harassed Chaplin, once broke into and vandalized his house, finally charged him with being the father of her unborn child. By the time the case came to trial, in the mid-'40s, the child was old enough to have a blood test, which proved Chaplin could not possibly be the father of Joan's daughter. After a second paternity trial, despite overwhelming evidence in his favor, he was forced to pay child support.

★*GODDARD, PAULETTE* Vivacious, acquisitive film actress, an ex-Goldwyn girl who was married to Chaplin—his third wife—from 1933 to 1942. He found her "gay and amusing" and explained that "the bond between Paulette and me was loneliness." One day while they were strolling in San Pedro harbor, she saw a 55-foot yacht and remarked, "Now if you had something like that, we could have a lot of fun on Sundays." They began cruising to Catalina on Charlie's boat, finally married, and Paulette's career boomed while the marriage worsened. *Modern Times* and *The Great Dictator* were the only two films she made with her husband. They were still man and wife, as Charlie tells it, the day she appeared in his dressing room with "a slick, well-tailored young man who looked poured into his clothes." Said Paulette, "This is my agent." He wanted to discuss her billing and a salary hike. Chaplin realized the honeymoon was over.

★*GREY, LITA* The second Mrs. Chaplin, an episode so bitter that Charlie never mentions her name in his autobiography, though she bore him two sons—Sydney and Charles Jr.—from 1924 to 1926. The daughter of a waitress, her real name was Lolita MacMurray, a 16-year-old who was cast in *The Gold Rush* but had to be dropped because she was pregnant. A shotgun wedding to Chaplin was Lita's compensation. They eloped to Mexico, reporters in hot pursuit. Lita threw up. Her dragon-lady mama moved into the house, and two years later Lita's published divorce complaint became an underground bestseller at $10 a copy. No details about the Chaplins' sex life were spared. The "perverted, degenerate and indecent act of fellatio" cropped up a lot. It was even said that he asked her to read *Lady Chatterley's Lover*, and despite her two kiddies, Lita continued: "The Respondent never had marital relations with the Plaintiff in the manner that is usual between man and wife." The case cost him a cool million. Charlie's last word on the subject: "What I've been through has aged me ten years."

★*HARRIS, MILDRED* The first Mrs. Chaplin. They met at Sam Goldwyn's beach house, Charlie recalls: "She was a very silly young girl . . . the only possible interest she had for me was sex." The feeling was mutual. "There were dinners, dances, moonlit nights and ocean drives, and the inevitable happened. Mildred began to worry." Though Mildred's pregnancy ultimately turned out to be a false alarm, Chaplin had already married her. "She was no mental heavyweight," he confided to chums, and soon found his sex kitten to be "exasperatingly feline." She signed a contract with Louis B. Mayer, and the marriage ended amid rumors that Millie's outside interests included an affair with another girl.

★*JOYCE, PEGGY HOPKINS* Described by Chaplin as "the celebrated matrimonial beauty," she was an ex-Ziegfeld girl with a $3,000,000 bankroll collected from five husbands. "I'm a *simple* woman. All I want is to marry and have babies," she told Charlie, rattling an armful of diamond and emerald bracelets. Over dinner, it is alleged, she also asked about his sexual prowess, then accompanied Chaplin on a sail to Catalina for nude bathing and related sports. Meanwhile, Peggy told him of her adventures abroad, and their "bizarre, though brief, relationship" inspired Charles to write his successful *A Woman of Paris* (1923) for Edna Purviance.

★*KELLY, HETTY* His first real love, on the bill with a dancing troupe known as the Yankee Doodle Girls. Young Charlie's ardor frightened her. "You expect too much," she told him when he proposed marriage. "After all, I am only fifteen and you are four years older." He never forgot her, though it didn't work out.

★*O'NEILL, OONA* Daughter of the great American playwright Eugene O'Neill; her father was not at all pleased about the relationship between Chaplin and Oona, who was scarcely seventeen when he interviewed her for a film which was never made. Charlie at 54 was "constantly surprised" by her sense of

humor and tolerance. His fourth and dearest spouse, they married during the black days of the Joan Barry paternity scandal. Oona was already four months pregnant (with Geraldine, born 1944) by the time it ended. When she told Chaplin she no longer wanted a stage or screen career, he rejoiced, "At last I had a wife and not a career girl." He later described his beloved Oona as "a continual revelation," and they had seven more children together by the time the Tramp strolled into his twilight years in Switzerland.

★*PURVIANCE, EDNA* Fun-loving beauty and major silent-film star. Chaplin signed her for *A Night Out* in 1915; they soon became lovers and "inseparable." The affair was important for both of them, but Edna had a jealous streak and tended to fall in a faint if other women paid too much attention to him. Although the romance petered out, Purviance stayed on with Chaplin's film company—and on his payroll until her death in 1958.

★*RIVIERA FRIEND* Charming girl "who had all the requisites to alleviate that blue hour of boredom" when Charlie found himself footloose on the Côte d'Azure. He gave her a weekly allowance, they "dined and tangoed and did all the usual frou-frou." Then she slipped away from him for a rendezvous with her former lover, a young Egyptian. A bit more frou-frou, but the frill was gone despite brief reunions in Paris and London.

★*STRANGERS IN THE NIGHT* Though he knew brothels and bimbos and had his share of carnal folly ("sometimes I was potent, other times disappointing"), Chaplin retreats from any "blow-by-blow description of a sex bout. . . . The circumstances that lead up to sex I find more interesting." His case in point was an interlude with an anonymous young lady he met beyond the connecting door of his hotel room in L.A., way back when. He was humming a popular tune of the day. In the next room, she picked up and hummed the next phrase. They wound up humming together, and she opened the door, "a ravishing young blonde . . . all silk negligee and the effect was dreamy." Turned out to be a humdinger. "The third night I was getting rather weary." Work to do, Charlie locked the door, finally had to check out to escape her insistent knocking.

CHRISTIAN, LINDA
(b. 1923)

Extraordinarily attractive starlet and globe-trotter, probably best known as the wife of Tyrone Power. They were the definitive Beautiful People. Born in Mexico of Dutch-German-French-Spanish parentage, Linda's roots—her name was then Blanca Rosa Welter—may have presaged her taste in men from the four corners of the world. A generally undistinguished film career *(Holiday in Mexico, Athena, The VIPs)* could never compete with her private life, which attracted enormous press coverage, as a jet-set butterfly involved with glamorous men. In her book, written in effusive, lushly filigreed prose, Linda proved to be a true romantic still having girlish tremors at the wonder of it all. When last heard about, she had married into "European nobility."

PRIMARY SOURCE: *Linda: My Own Story,* by Linda Christian (Crown, 1962).

★*BEY, TURHAN* He won Linda with "those curious slanting eyes, the rounded face, his charm." Turhan began with a "touch of romance," which blossomed over the years into "the closest of friendships." (See also BEY listing.)

★*FLYNN, ERROL* She first laid eyes on "this beautiful man" in the lobby of Mexico City's Ritz Hotel; within days he had whisked the 17-year old (still known as Blanca Rosa) off to Acapulco. One night, swooping onto her balcony, *he made her his.* "Don't be frightened," he whispered. And so, "gently, the wonder of the girl was guided toward the passion of the woman . . . tears welled up within me." Errol seemed "astonished" to learn that he had, in fact, *deflowered* Blanca Rosa! That

was just the beginning. Flynn convinced Linda to come to Hollywood, where he had acquired for her an apartment and a screen test. The former was a room upstairs at his place, the latter was a sham. Once lodged on Mulholland Drive, Flynn never let her out and Linda soon learned why: He was then on trial for statutory rape, and Linda herself was still "jailbait." When she moved out, Flynn found her, pounded on the door begging her to come back. "I knelt by the bed and started my prayers." (See also FLYNN listing.)

★*PIGNATARI, COUNT FRANCESCO ("Baby")* Perhaps the last of the great madcap millionaire playboys. When they met in Rome, Linda was already a notorious divorcée. The paparazzi went wild. Baby railed that fighting his love for Linda was making him physically sick. One moment he wanted her gone, the next he'd *die* without her. And so it went throughout their months-long round-the-world trip, an odyssey which ended in Pignatari's native Brazil. Linda suspects that Baby grew jealous of the way his countrymen warmed to her; he threatened to do something rash. The next day, there was a commotion outside Linda's hotel: "A parade of cars moving slowly . . . huge signs strung across their sides and tops, and the message written on every one of them was the same: LINDA GO HOME." Her comment to the press: "how curious, how original." She lingered in Rio to have a ball without Baby. Months later they staged a public reconciliation at El Morocco in New York. But, of course, it was never the same again. . . .

★*PORTAGO, FON* The seventeenth Marquis de Portago of Spain, and a daredevil auto racer. He pursued her in Paris, and once together, they crisscrossed the continent to follow the racing circuit. Her instincts told her not to say yes to Portago's proposal; those same inner voices prompted her to tell him not to race in that spring's Mille Miglia. But he did. At his check point in Rome, Linda scrawled a note, "Te quiero mucho," and pressed it into his hand as they kissed before he hurriedly drove away. Fifteen miles from the finish line

Portago's car skidded off the road, killing himself, his co-driver, and ten bystanders. She would never become his wife.

★*POWER, TYRONE* Beautiful leading man and Linda's first husband. Her romantic prose describes that first fateful encounter in Rome: "There was a pause—as if the room were vibrating and we were each waiting until it ceased before we could go on . . . I felt the incredible chemical reaction of love at first sight." The feeling was mutual, for within days Ty was telling Linda that they would marry—ignoring the fact he had not yet divorced Annabella, *and* that Lana Turner still expected to be the next Mrs. Tyrone Power. But, like a happening in a fairy tale, a year or so later, in Rome, Ty and Linda were wed in a church ceremony that turned into a Circus Maximus, with crowds of thousands chanting "Ty-ro-ne!" The lavish wedding was followed by a private audience with Pope Pius XII, who told the couple: "The eyes of the world are upon you . . . you must show everyone the meaning of a Catholic marriage." Settled in Europe for a while, the Powers had a daughter, Romina Francesca, and Linda's world "seemed complete." Cracks appeared when Ty returned to the stage, staying on tour months at a time. There were rumors of other women. When Linda told Ty she was pregnant once again, he said, "What a shame . . . I want my freedom." They stayed together through the birth of a second daughter, Taryn; then Linda found sympathy for a while in the arms of Edmund Purdom. When Ty packed up and left, he said, "Take care of yourself, Puss." It was over. (See also POWER listing.)

★*PURDOM, EDMUND* British actor who emigrated to Hollywood in the late '50s, got lost as the leading man in a swarm of costume epics. Purdom and his wife Tita were having their own problems when they became "friendly" with the Powers. Edmund and Linda were the friendliest. "No one knew of our affair, for we never appeared in public. Our only meetings were during his lunch hour." But after the divorce from Ty, Linda returned to Europe and other amours before literally bumping into Purdom again on the streets of—where else?—Rome. They had a cup of tea, she was on her way to Naples, he offered to drive her down. "Along the winding Italian coast as night began to fall, we realized this encounter was going to mean much more to us." A year later, Linda Christian took her second husband, Edmund Purdom. "I had learned that whatever is meant to be, eventually comes to pass."

MISCELLANY

★*EPSTEIN, JACOB* English sculptor who asked Linda to pose. The topless statue caused a furor on exhibit in London; Ty had it shipped to their California home, "planted solidly between two camellia bushes."

★*GRANGER, STEWART, and WILDING, MICHAEL* When Linda and her sister visited London early in her film career, they "did the town" with the two handsome English actors.

★*KHAN, PRINCE ALY* A friend, famously fond of beautiful women, gave Linda sole use of his Chateau l'Horizon in Cannes.

★*RIVERA, DIEGO* One of Mexico's greatest artists; Linda posed for him—also in the nude. But to satisfy Linda's mother, he added "a tiny little bikini" to the full-figure painting.

★*SCHLESINGER, ROBERT* Man-about-town. Linda thought him "a sweet boy" and very attentive. For no reason at all (she says they never spent a moment alone together), he started giving her jewels—*lavish* jewels, all of which she returned. A friend advised her to "just take the stuff and make the boy happy," so Linda put the matching diamond ring, necklace, bracelet, and earclips (value $122,000 *then*) into a vault. She was forced to return all but the earrings when it was learned Robert had bounced a check to buy them.

★*TODD, MIKE* They met on a transcontinental flight and he pursued her on the ground, offering "fame, jewels," even all the paintings in his house, if she'd stick with him, kid. He was "going to put her kisser on the screen," he said. When Linda turned it all down, he thought he must be talking to the wrong girl. "Who invents your publicity? I'll kill 'em." (See also TODD listing.)

CLIFT, MONTGOMERY
(1920–1966)

Stage-trained, hypersensitive dramatic actor who made female hearts flutter as a romantic weakling in *The Heiress* (1949) and *A Place In the Sun* (1951), or as a rough rider with the soul of a poet, notably in *Red River* (1948) and *From Here to Eternity* (1953). Off the screen, though few fans of that era knew his problems, Clift was insecure, alcoholic, bisexual, and subject to abysmal guilt. After a nearly fatal automobile crash in 1957, while he was making *Raintree County*, Clift never fully regained that boyish handsomeness which made him irresistible to men and women alike. His instability deepened, and the last sorry decade of his life was divided between work and binges of drink, debauchery, and self-destruction.

PRIMARY SOURCES: *Monty: A Biography of Montgomery Clift,* by Robert LaGuardia (Arbor House, 1977; Avon); *Montgomery Clift,* by Patricia Bosworth (Harcourt Brace Jovanovich, 1978).

★*BALABAN, JUDY* Daughter of Paramount Pictures executive. She was a teenager, Monty well into his 30s when they launched what she calls a "tender and beautiful" affair. Although there was a young actor living with Clift at the time, Judy assumed they were "just friends."

★*CARNEGIE, DONNA* Ambitious young actress who worked her way into Monty's life as secretary and "keeper." She said she loved him; he felt "used."

★*CUNNINGHAM, ARLINE* Beautiful effervescent 19-year-old from Pennsylvania who saw *Red River*, boarded a bus for New York "with the express purpose of meeting Montgomery Clift." She wound up working for him, a loyal companion for five years.

★*DENTIST'S WIFE* Monty had her during early days in Hollywood. She was lovely, "and drove a snazzy convertible."

★*DINO* Italian airline pilot, employed as a waiter when Monty met him in Rome while filming *Indiscretion of an American Wife.* Truman Capote called Dino "an absolute moron. It was a mystery to me what Monty saw in him."

★*ENGEL, LEHMAN* Broadway musical conductor. He was ten years older than 20-year-old Monty. Yet Monty's protective mother approved of the relationship, asked Engel to accompany him on a Mexican holiday. The trip was a disaster; Monty caught the amoebic dysentery which would plague him all his life.

★*HOLMAN, LIBBY* Singer, actress, tragic heiress, probably the love of Monty's life. In 1932, Libby was accused but acquitted of murdering her 20-year-old husband, a Reynolds Tobacco heir. Six months later she gave birth to their son, and also inherited millions. Along with Tallulah Bankhead, Libby in the '20s experimented with cocaine and other exotic highs; she entertained lavishly at her country estate, Treetops. Fourteen years older than Monty, she met him in 1942, and they remained friends, if not lovers, for the rest of his life. One guest at Treetops assumed that Libby and Monty were into "kinky sex" because of the bedroom decor: "Everything seemed faintly decadent, the low lights, the slippery white satin sheets, the overpowering fragrance of Jungle Gardenia perfume, the huge bottle of Seconal."

★*"JOSH"* An aspiring actor, Monty's lover for about two years. They never spoke of homosexuality, both young, both believing that it was a shameful mental illness. "Alone we could be emotional and passionate, but outside we had to hide our feelings."

★*LARSON, JACK* Actor. He describes a Monty Clift who, if he liked you, "couldn't keep his hands off you—he was very physical, very affectionate." And if Monty liked you, says Jack, male or female, ultimately you went to bed with him.

★*LINCOLN, ANN* His leading lady on Broadway in 1945. A beautiful, sweet, and vulnerable girl. Ann told friends that she was engaged to Monty; the elopement didn't come off as planned.

★*LOY, MYRNA* They worked together for the first and only time in the film *Lonelyhearts*, in 1959. Again, she was older, "Monty was impressed by her wit, her compassion, her commitment to liberal causes." She ultimately became "entangled in his romantic life," and many mutual friends felt sure Myrna wanted to marry him.

★*ROSTOVA, MIRA* Russian-born actress, Monty's self-appointed drama coach. Throughout much of his life, and his work on stage and film, Mira was at Monty's side—to the frequent annoyance of directors and his fellow performers. When they finally acted together, in Mira's adaptation of Chekov's *The Seagull* (which was to be Monty's last play), her own acting proved embarrassing. The relationship deteriorated.

★*SCHELL, MARIA* German-born actress. Appeared with Monty in a TV special of Hemingway's *For Whom the Bell Tolls*. They were devoted to each other and inseparable until she returned to Europe.

★*TAYLOR, ELIZABETH* The most beautiful 18-year-old in the world, mouthing obscenities, she bowled him over from the very beginning when they played the doomed lovers in *A Place in the Sun*. Monty was 29. Their screen chemistry sizzled, Liz by all accounts—including her own—was deeply in love with him, and hoped for a while they'd marry. He called her Bessie Mae, and adored her, though opinion is divided as to whether they actually made love. They were certainly intimates in a real sense. When Clift had his near-fatal auto accident, which permanently damaged his looks, it was Elizabeth who shielded him from photographers, crawled into the wreck and pulled out the loose teeth choking him. (He later had them strung on a gold chain for her.) Years later, when fragile health and his many addictions made Clift a poor risk, Liz put up her own hefty salary as insurance to have him cast in *Reflections in a Golden Eye*. Monty didn't live to make it, and Brando got the part. (See also TAYLOR listing.)

MISCELLANY

★*BAGLEY, BEN* Entrepreneur and record producer. He says Monty used to be embarrassed by his small penis, "and talked about it all the time. . . . I think it was the secret tragedy of his life." Bagley knew a lot about the tragedies of Monty's life, as he was one of the friends who stayed around toward the end.

★*DABNEY, AUGUSTA* Actress and wife of actor Kevin McCarthy. Monty and the McCarthys were at one time inseparable. Some thought it was because of Clift's love for "Gussie"; others figured his attentions to her masked an attraction to Kevin. Dabney and Clift obviously shared something special, which she described as "an innocent kind of sexuality." Adds Augusta: "I've never seen anyone who relished the sensual the way Monty did. . . . The way he'd suck meat from a lobster's claw . . ."

★*DEAN, JAMES* The late actor. Clift was his idol, and he would call him repeatedly, "mainly to listen to the sound of my voice," Monty complained.

★*FRAZIER, BRENDA* Glamorous debutante. Monty fell in love from afar, but at her coming-out party was too shy even to ask her to dance.

★*GARBO, GRETA* Monty had "a violent crush on Greta," gave dinner parties for her, took her out several times. After one date he managed to kiss her goodnight and confided to a friend, "Her lips were chapped."

★*GASSLER, IMRGAARD* "Ischy," aka the Baroness. Claimed she roamed the world for ten years hoping to meet Monty and marry him. She carried his pictures everywhere, filled journals with reveries of him. When finally cornered, Monty was awed; "I never knew anyone could love me that much." A friend summed up the Baroness: "About as loony a dame as I've ever met."

★*GREEN, JEANNE* She and husband Fred became "Monty's surrogate family on the West Coast." But, like her good friend Augusta Dabney, Jeanne was "half in love with Monty in a romantic and sentimental way."

★GUNN, BILL   Actor, playwright. Monty befriended Gunn when he was just a "20-year old black kid from Philadelphia." No sex, Gunn recalled; "Monty never let it happen."

★JAMES, LORENZO   Actor, singer, and professional companion. He took care of Monty in his last years.

★JONES, JAMES   The writer. He once asked a mutual friend if Monty was a homosexual. Then he confided, "I would have had an affair with him, but he never asked me."

★JONES, JENNIFER   While filming *Indiscretion of an American Wife* in Rome, on-the-scene commentator Truman Capote saw that Jennifer "got some kind of crush on Monty. And believe it or not, she didn't realize that he really liked fellows." When she found out, she got so upset she went into her "portable dressing room and stuffed a mink jacket down the portable toilet."

★LANGE, HOPE   She feels people didn't understand how Monty transfigured his leading ladies into love objects. "There was romance, but only in Monty's adolescent sense of the word."

★McCARTHY, KEVIN   Durable character actor, and along with his wife (see Dabney, above) maintained a lifelong friendship and professional relationship with Clift. Although some opine that Kevin was "the love of Monty's life," Kevin was flabbergasted when a Hollywood director told him to stop shacking up with Clift or his career would surely suffer. "Monty and I had a man-to-man relationship," Kevin insists. "I never had a clue he was gay all those years."

★MONROE, MARILYN   When they made *The Misfits*, and her marriage to Arthur Miller was breaking up, Marilyn and Monty would go out drinking and talking. But, despite the gossips, there was no romance. She said that Monty was the only one she knew in worse shape than she was. (See also MONROE listing.)

★SILVERBERG, DR. WILLIAM   Monty's psychiatrist and "one of the most controversial people in his life." A "known homosexual," Sil-

verberg soon had Monty hero-worshiping him. Under his care Monty's drinking and drug-taking increased; friends who pointed this out to Silverberg were curtly told they must be mistaken.

★SINATRA, FRANK   It was Monty's coaching, some observers feel, that helped Frankie turn in his Oscar-winning performance in *From Here to Eternity*. They remained close until one night at a party Sinatra saw Clift "come on sexually with a man . . . he had his bodyguards throw Monty out."

★THAXTER, PHYLLIS   Actress. Met when both were very young and starting out on Broadway, and fell in love. They talked of marriage, but Monty just couldn't. Phyllis didn't ask questions, but she sensed, even in her "innocence," that "Monty liked both men and women."

★VON LINDE, MANFRED   A plastic surgeon, unsavory character; was rumored to occasionally supply cadavers to a "homosexual funeral parlor," presumably for gay necrophiles. Monty was unaware of his past when they met and became "good buddies." But they had a falling-out after the doctor botched the surgery to remove the bags under Monty's eyes.

★WALKER, NANCY   Character actress on stage/film/TV. "A tiny, flatfooted brunette with a perpetually disgusted expression." She would sustain Monty during the last years of his life, cheering him up with such flippancies as: "If you hadn't been in that car crash, you'd be just another aging pretty face."

★WALLER, BLAINE   Close friend. Monty asked Blaine to become his roommate. "The message was explicit. . . . but I finally made it clear I didn't swing, and he just smiled and shrugged . . . I wasn't AC/DC; Monty was. No crime in that."

★WILDER, THORNTON   Playwright. Wilder, considerably older than Monty, became his "intellectual mentor . . . the affectionate teacher and surrogate father." One who knew them both observed that Wilder sometimes looked as if he had "an actual crush on

Monty. He would literally feast his eyes on him."

★WILLIAMS, TENNESSEE Playwright. Although Monty appeared in a Williams play (You Touched Me), Williams says he didn't know him well "because I wasn't sexually attracted to him . . . Monty disliked me because I was so open about being gay and he wasn't."

COLLINS, JOAN
(b. 1933)

Sultry sexpot. Britain's "bad girl" imported to Hollywood in the mid-1950s to appear in a series of costume epics, occasionally to disappear in instantly forgettable movies of all sorts. A survivor, Joan kept her career alive through thick and thin by sheer endurance, plus her perennially youthful slow-burning energy source. She has recently starred in two steamy sexploitation films, The Stud and The Bitch, both based on books by her sister Jackie, the novelist. (Joan's own book has so far been published only in England.) Currently Collins is captivating American audiences as the tart-tongued Alexis Carrington on TV's Dynasty.

PRIMARY SOURCE: Joan Collins: Past Imperfect, by Joan Collins (W.H. Allen, England, 1978).

★BEATTY, WARREN He was staring at her in a Beverly Hills restaurant. She blushed. He had pimples, but "all in all, he looked rather appealing and vulnerable." The next night they had dinner together. Driving home, Warren simply announced he was coming up for coffee. And so, says Joan, "the die was cast." They became inseparable; Warren was "insatiable." She was then 23, Warren 21; he called her Butterfly, she called him Bee. They decided to celebrate their eternal love by getting married. "Only Warren would think of putting an engagement ring in a carton of chopped liver," writes Joan. But, alas, after nearly two years of lots of loving and lots of scrapping. Collins decided to end it with War-

ren. "What happened to the glorious romantic fun we used to have?" she asked herself. (See also BEATTY listing.)

★CHAPLIN, SYDNEY Son of Charles, sometime actor, co-star in Joan's first big American film, Land of the Pharaohs. They become fun-loving lovers, longtime friends. Visiting the senior Chaplin in Switzerland once, Sydney informed Joan he'd feel funny about indulging in any hanky-panky under his father's roof. Joan volleyed: "Do you think they're imagining we play gin rummy all night?"

★"THE GENERAL" Joan's autobiography devotes nearly an entire chapter to this "Very Married Man," whom she chooses to leave unnamed, but describes as a "devastatingly good-looking" entertainment industry executive whose wife became one of the biggest TV stars of the 70s, and whose best friend was Marlon Brando. (Other sources indicate The General sounds like George Englund, former husband of Cloris Leachman and former partner with Brando in his Pennebaker Productions.) Collins was convinced that her General was everything she had wanted in a man, except that he was married and had little money. Also, his treatment of her was appalling. Like the time they flew to a tropic isle to celebrate his decision to separate from his wife and family. Throughout the brief holiday he was edgy, upset, and remote. Finally, she could stand it no longer. Throwing herself onto the powdery sand in her teeny white bikini, she started to sob. "I wondered how he could possibly—viewing my lithe suntanned twenty-two-year-old body, my face recently described as the world's most beautiful, not to mention all the clever things he'd taught me in bed—how could he possibly think of wife and kiddies now?" According to Joan, General/George never did leave his "Mabel." (However, Cloris Leachman and George Englund were divorced in 1979.)

★HILTON, NICKY Son of Conrad, the hotelier, and, according to Joan, a "sexual athlete." Seems Nicky used to tell girlfriends that between himself, his brother, and his father, they had a "yard of cock." She adds that that vital statistic was not strictly true. Among the odd things about Nicky were the way he kept track of his lovemaking on a scoreboard, and the paraphernalia he kept on his nightstand—a rosary (the Hiltons were devout Catholics), a gun, pornographic books, and "an amazing array of pill bottles." Joan notes that in a few years Nicky was dead of a drug overdose.

★*KASS, RON* Collins's third and current husband, an American record-company executive once based in England. His birthday, March 30, is the same as that of Warren Beatty and Sydney Chaplin, which Collins interprets as a good sign. When they met, her heart did more than flip-flops, it took "a definite lurch." However, they didn't immediately enter into a "flaming affair." Joan paused to think: "Here was the man I had been searching for all my life, and I didn't want to injure our blossoming friendship and love by jumping instantly into bed." It worked. After a few travails in which they faced the prospect of losing one another, they decided to do it. Marriage came three months before their daughter Katyana was born in June 1972.

★*"KING OF CALYPSO"* Gorgeous and sensual black performer, not named directly in Collins's memoir, yet clearly identified as her co-star in *Island In the Sun.* (That could *only* be Harry Belafonte, but if the lady wants to remain coy . . . ?) Nothing much happened while they were on location, but later, at a Hollywood party, he asked for her address and got it. She raced home wondering if she should slip into something looser than her beige chiffon cocktail dress. "God! It had a thousand hooks and eyes and a waist cincher underneath." Throwing on a simple caftan, calming her nerves with a brandy, Joan answered the doorbell to find her King of Calypso standing there, "the familiar costume of open shirt, tight pants and wide leather belt molded to his body." Joan talks of their subsequent rather brief time together as "a delicious interlude."

★*LOEW, ARTHUR JR.* Scion of one of the "royal families" of the motion picture industry. Collins claims to be "a strong advocate of mo-

nogamy—sequentially, that is." So it was out with Syd Chaplin, in with Arthur Loew. Their life together in his pad in the Hollywood Hills was *divine*—until they considered getting engaged before Joan had to leave for a twelve-week location shooting. Arthur confessed he might not be able to remain faithful that long. Joan bridled, challenging him, "You mean you want to fuck around." To which Loew replied, "Spoken like the queen of England." When they finally parted, it was amicable. (See also LOEW listing.)

★*NEWLEY, ANTHONY* Multi-talented English performer-director-writer. Joan's second husband; wed in 1963, divorced in 1970, meanwhile producing two children, Tara and Sacha. It all began in swinging London, where she saw Tony in *Stop the World, I Want to Get Off* and was deeply moved. Joan says Tony was not the greatest lover she had experienced, but she was "obsessed with the bloody man. . . . I thought he was a genius." A genius with a few quirks. Joan agreed to "try to be understanding about his attraction to adolescent girls," but told Tony he couldn't have *her* unless he married her. He did. In six weeks, Joan was pregnant. "The good years had begun," she writes. Then the decline. Tony was not the most faithful of husbands, but there were compensations, and—with Ryan O'Neal, for one—Joan found she rather "enjoyed being an adulteress." Then she agreed to play a wifely character obviously based on herself in Newley's weird, wanton, autobiographical *Can Hieronymus Merkin Ever Forget Mercy Humpe and Find True Happiness?*—in which Newley appears as a man obsessed by a nubile teenager named Humpe. When she saw the movie, Joan suddenly knew there was no more hope for her marriage.

★*O'NEAL, RYAN* Her hubby Tony Newley didn't care for discos, so Joan took to going out at night alone, to The Daisy. Where she met Ryan. She found him funny and endearing, boyish and droll. He was also the first man she'd been attracted to for a long, *long* time. Collins at first decided O'Neal was forbidden fruit. He happened to phone on Joan's birthday and Tony happened to be out of town. Ryan. however. was available. "A girl should get the best she deserves on her birthday. And he was."

★*REED. MAXWELL*   British character actor who had some film success in the late 1950s. He was Collins's "childhood fantasy hero" and. unfortunately. her first husband. On one of their earlier dates he violently took her virginity by first drugging her into an unconscious stupor. She awoke feeling quite ill: "I threw up endlessly . . . and lay back drained on the zebra skin." It then hit her that she'd finally done it—while out cold. Still. she married the guy. and they went to the Riviera for their honeymoon. which turned out to be a nightmare. When a couple of photographers wanted to take photos of her on the beach. Max slapped her hard and screamed that she belonged to him now. "so don't be looking at other men. *ever*—unless they're the ones *I* choose." Later. for example. Max found an Arab sheik who offered ten thousand pounds for one night with Joan. Flabbergasted. she asked her husband. "Are you *seriously* suggesting I go to bed with that old fart for money? . . . I looked at Abdul. his pendulous jowls wobbling. I looked at my handsome. *loathsome* husband and burst into tears. 'Never.' I screamed!" She decided she had to save herself. which meant leaving Max. Their 1953 marriage lasted seven months. Then Joan took off for Hollywood.

★*STAMP, TERENCE*   English actor. They shared a sweet "interlude" in New York.

★*TRUJILLO. RAFAEL*   It was Zsa Zsa Gabor who arranged a blind date for Joan with her friend Rafael. son of the Dominican dictator. Zsa Zsa mentioned that he was in Palm Beach. Florida. "*Palm Beach!*" Joan gasped. "I'm not going 4,000 miles for a blind date!" But she did; Trujillo was good-looking. had impeccable manners. and he wanted her to stay the night on his yacht. She consented. more out of exhaustion than desire. But Joan couldn't help thinking about The General. "So this finally would be how our affair would end. On a beautiful boat. on a perfect Florida night. with the son of the President of the Domin-

ican Republic." Trujillo later sent her a swell diamond bauble as a thank-you.

MISCELLANY

★*WAGNER. ROBERT*   It was in London. R.J. had just broken up his *first* marriage to Natalie Wood. Joan had just split from Warren Beatty. She thought R.J. was gentle and sweet and far too nice for her to become involved with. "We were—hello cliché—*just good friends.*" However. the British tabloids were quick to point out that their respective ex's. Natalie and Warren. seemed to be hitting it off just fine. "These reports were fairly irksome." sniffs Joan. Virtue is not always its own reward.

COOPER, GARY
(1901–1961)

Born in Montana, educated in England, Cooper became the archetypical shy, strong, silent hero in American films, his image apotheosized in the classic western *High Noon.* Hemingway found him Hemingway-esque, and Carl Sandburg called him one of the nation's "most beloved illiterates." He was a diffident *Good Sam* as well as *The Pride of the Yankees,* yet there was more—or less—to Cooper than the camera ever revealed. In his dressing room, he was a nudist, a totally uninhibited exhibitionist, and famously well endowed. At the start of his career, his proficiency as a boudoir swordsman inspired both envy and mild contempt even in jaded Hollywood. His detractors considered Cooper an opportunistic stud who promoted himself, his biographer notes, "by dallying with influential women who could do him the most professional good. He'd bed-hopped from perfumed percales to satin sheets." Long before he died of cancer in 1961, his flaming youth was long forgotten by a public for whom Coop seemed to be, always, Mr. Right.

PRIMARY SOURCE: *Gary Cooper: An Intimate Biography,* by Hector Arce (Morrow, 1979; Bantam, 1980).

★*BALFE, VERONICA ("ROCKY")* New York socialite and Cooper's *only* wife, who had a brief career as an actress with the nom de film Sandra Shaw. They were wed in 1933, and despite his many affairs (including a separation during his long and serious relationship with Patricia Neal), "Rocky" stayed with Cooper until his death in 1961. They had one child, a daughter, Maria, born 1937.

★*BANKHEAD, TALLULAH* Outspoken stage and screen actress who was more fascinated with Cooper than vice versa. On accepting her first film offer, she quipped: "Darling, they offered me *all* that money, and I thought I'd go to Hollywood to fuck that *divine* Gary Cooper." And so she did. (See also BANKHEAD listing.)

★*BERGMAN, INGRID* Internationally acclaimed actress who co-starred with Cooper in *For Whom the Bell Tolls* and *Saratoga Trunk*. During filming of latter, they had a lot of fun offscreen, though Cooper reported, "Ingrid loved me more than any woman in my life loved me. The day after the picture ended, I couldn't get her on the phone." (See also BERGMAN listing.)

★*BOW, CLARA* "It" Girl of the 1920s. Supposedly described Coop, with typical brashness, as "hung like a horse, and he could go all night." Their torrid affair was common gossip in Hollywood, where cocktail parties hummed about the scratches and bruises she inflicted on him in bed. Cooper's ego suffered, however, knowing he was just one of the chessmen being juggled by Clara, whose freewheeling promiscuity outdid his own. (See also BOW listing.)

★*BRENT, EVELYN* Neurotic starlet who got into movies at age 14, suffered a breakdown before she was 20. Co-starred with Cooper in *Beau Sabreur* (1927), she had a brief affair with him during filming, while he was on the rebound from Clara Bow.

★*DIETRICH, MARLENE* Legendary German actress, met while making *Morocco*, then Coop's co-star in *Desire*. She landed in Cooper's arms on rebound from John Gilbert. (See also DIETRICH listing.)

★*DI FRASSO, DOROTHY, COUNTESS* American-born socialite with Italian title who helped Cooper recover from a "nervous breakdown" in the mid-1930s. The Countess is credited with giving him European polish, a sense of style. She joined him in Hollywood and was his most serious romance before Cooper's one and only marriage to "Rocky." Once Coop was absent from some social function, and Tallulah drawled bitchily, "He must be worn to a Frasso."

★*LOMBARD, CAROLE* Blond comedienne and Coop's steady date until he was lured away by Bow. Lombard, later to marry Gable, didn't mind much—and her biographer notes: "Carole regarded him as a dilettante, markedly effeminate in his mannerisms, and not at all the stalwart he impersonated so effectively on film." She seemed to be the only woman in Hollywood blessed with natural immunity.

★*NEAL, PATRICIA* Intense actress who met Cooper on the set of *The Fountainhead*. "They fell immediately in love," and developed a "big, terrific and important" relationship. The affair almost cost him his marriage, and almost cost Neal, 25 years younger than Coop, a blossoming Hollywood career. It ended on Christmas Eve 1951, and Neal said, years later: "I was very much in love with him. But I got myself into a sticky mess. I lived this secret life for several years, and I was so ashamed. . . . I'm sorry for the damage that was done." When Cooper heard that Pat had married writer Roald Dahl, he reportedly turned pale and muttered, "I hope he's a helluva guy. She deserves nothing but the best."

★*PAYTON, BARBARA* Blond playgirl-actress with whom he had a fling when she played a minor role in *Dallas* (1950), though he was already involved with Patricia Neal. At this reckless point in his life, Cooper seemed to go through some middle-age panic about his sex drive. Said one socialite chum, "He was associating with a different class of women . . . the broads."

★*SCANDINAVIAN ACTRESS* Quick fling he met socially while filming *Friendly Persua-*

sion (1956), in which he played a peaceable Quaker father. They disappeared for the night, followed by an observer from a sleazy exposé magazine, which subsequently published a blow-by-blow account, from the couple's first hello to the crucial moment when the lights went out. "They must have followed me with a stopwatch," cracked Coop.

★TOBACCO HEIR Wealthy young man about Hollywood, with industry influence, cited in Clara Bow bio as further evidence of Cooper's anything-goes ambition. "He had no second thoughts about accepting the attentions of a wealthy young tobacco heir." When Clara heard he'd gone that-a-way, the story concludes, she laced into Gary with "You son of a bitch, and you have the nerve to be jealous of me?" Coop kept mum.

★VELEZ. LUPE Fiery Mexican actress who lived for a while with Cooper and two "free-flying eagles." In Wolf Song, the movie that brought them together, Cooper had a nude swimming scene, during which a male chum studies his physique and tells him someday a woman's going to get hold of him and never let go. Lupe was not the woman. He moved into her Laurel Canyon hideaway, his biographer notes, and launched "the year's noisiest romance, with Lupe supplying most of the din." Their long affair was marked by public scenes. and she once took a shot at him in a railroad station. Missed.

★WEST. MAE They had several trysts in her dressing room. so says a new biography of Mae. (See also WEST listing.)

MISCELLANY

★COLLINS. NAN Studio casting director who changed Coop's name from Frank to Gary, jes' like her Indiana home. Her interest in him was motherly, so she said.

★HAYNES, ROBERTA Budding actress who had a small role in High Noon, at which time Coop was still involved with Neal and "getting strong sexual emanations" from his coolly beautiful co-star, Grace Kelly. The following year, Haynes appeared opposite him in Return to Paradise, and was taken aback when he told her, "Don't be upset if I don't make a pass at you," sheepishly explaining that he was taking medicine that made him impotent. Their relationship was "largely platonic."

★KINGSLEY. GRACE Film-society columnist. Through her, during his early days in Hollywood, Cooper met "the great and near-great," and, presumably, lots of ladies who lust.

★MARION. FRANCES Important screenwriter in the mid-'20s, and responsible for putting Coop in his first screen role. "That's our man," she said.

COOPER, JACKIE
(b.1922)

Played Skippy on film at age 8 and became a famous child star as well as a masterful tearjerker in such movies as The Champ with Wallace Beery, whom he "really disliked." In fact, crying on screen never came easy for him, until a director threatened one day to shoot Jackie's dog and feigned going through with it, with a bang, thus the title of his autobiography (see below). An active television producer-director in adulthood, Cooper's book burgeons with evidence that the onset of puberty—though it was an undeniable setback to his acting career—proved him to be a precocious youth in more ways than one.

PRIMARY SOURCE: Please Don't Shoot My Dog: The Autobiography of Jackie Cooper. by Jackie Cooper with Dick Kleiner (Morrow. 1981).

★CRAWFORD. JOAN She was a friend of his mother's: 17-year-old Jackie would often visit the Crawford manse to play badminton. One day Joan caught him giving her the once-over. She said provocatively. "You're growing up. aren't you?" and then told him he'd better go. "Instead. I made a move toward her. . . . She stood up. looked at me appraisingly. then closed all the drapes. And I made love to Joan

Crawford, or, rather, she made love to me." The performance was repeated at least eight or nine times over the next six months, says Jackie, who called Joan "an erudite professor of love." At times Jackie thought Joan quite a "crazy" lady, but in lovemaking, "she was all business . . . When I left, she would put me on her calendar for the next visit." Finally she told him their affair had to end; he must put it out of his mind—"It never happened." Cooper recalled that he held back the urge to blab. When his friends talked about their conquests with some "pimply-faced teenager," he'd nod and think to himself: "But I have been with one of the Love Goddesses of the Screen." (See also CRAWFORD listing.)

★GARLAND, JUDY Because adolescent Judy and Jackie looked good together, MGM and their respective mothers decided they'd make a fun "item." Their arranged dates would include a movie and a soda with two straws. Once Judy asked if she could kiss him. "And so I was in love." But Judy put an end to the relationship when she fell for an "older man" of 16 (Jackie was 14). Then one night, long years after their early MGM days, Judy asked Jackie to take her home from a party. "We had a rowdy old time. . . . She was a big girl, and I was a big boy, and it was a great night." But that was it. Jackie never tried to call her again. (See also GARLAND listing.)

★GRANVILLE, BONITA Child actress, later TV-movie producer. Fourteen-year-old Bonita got no more than "a friendly hello" when she and 15-year-old Jackie first met. A few years later, though, pow! Their romance was interrupted when Jackie took off on a USO tour, went sour when he came back to discover she was getting attention from a lot of other men.

★HORNE, JUNE Actress, daughter of director James Horne. First wife. At 25, she was about five years older than Jackie, more sophisticated, with a tendency to drink too much. He went into the navy, married June in December 1944, and soon a son, John Anthony, was born. Hollywood did not welcome Jackie with open arms after the war, so he decided to seek his fortune in New York, "although I

knew it would mean almost a certain end to my marriage—as June was a California girl." He was right.

★KRAUS, BARBARA New York girl who was "like letting a breath of fresh spring air float into the musty closet of my head." Third and current wife. They giggled all the way through their wedding (in April 1954). "We were the only ones in on the joke . . . we could see that the judge's fly was open." Offspring are Russell, Julie, and Christina. In the 1970s, when Cooper went through a "change of life" crisis, he left Barbara and moved in with another woman (unnamed actress), then "came to his senses," returned to handsome, blond Barbara. And Jackie, at 60, looks forward to the rest of his life with "quiet, peaceful expectation."

★MRS. MARTIN Cooper was a teenager when Mrs. Martin came to visit his mother; when he drove her home she asked him into her parlor, then into her bedroom. "Mrs. Martin became a regular visitor at our house. And equally regularly, I would drive her home, jump on her, then speed back home, murmuring something about 'heavy traffic' . . ."

★NEIGHBOR LADY She was a winsome wench of 20, he barely 13. He took walks early in the morning when she was alone in the house and just getting up. She started inviting Jackie to join her in her still-warm bed. This was Cooper's introduction to sex, and "pretty hot stuff for a kid my age." Their matinal cuddling continued until his mother figured things out.

★PAIGE, JANIS Bouncy screen comedienne. Co-stars on the Broadway stage in Remains to Be Seen, they soon became roommates. Much later they were thankful they hadn't married. "We were just not that important to each other."

★PARKS, HILDY Broadway ingenue. At the time, Jackie was totally in love with the concept of New York, and Hildy "was everything I thought I wanted in a woman—she was so thoroughly New York." They performed together in one Broadway play, married while he was appearing as Ensign Pulver in Boston. He was tapped to play the role again in London, with Tyrone Power as *Mister Roberts*, and Hildy also had a part in the show. Her fierce independence didn't go over well in postwar London, "and I had problems adjusting to Hildy's strong will myself." When the play closed in March 1951, they toured Europe for a month in his Jaguar—which she hated. It was the beginning of the end. Hildy later remarried—to Broadway producer Alexander Cohen, a union which has lasted over twenty-five years.

★*PROSTITUTE* A bunch of the boys—Cooper, Phil Silvers, Sid Miller, Billy Tracy, and Mickey Rooney—decided to hire a hooker, and drew straws "for position." "The first four made it quick, so to speak, but Mickey was in the bedroom with the girl for about twenty minutes." Rooney came out gloating, "and we were believers." When the prostitute came out to pick up her money, after Mickey had gone home, Silvers demanded the truth: "Was that kid in the saddle for twenty minutes?" The girl said, "Are you kidding? Sixteen minutes of imitations and four minutes of fucking."

★*SHOWGIRL* Jackie, at 13, was on a vaudeville tour when he was "caught naked in bed with this broad," according to an older friend who walked in on the pair. "I slapped him on the ass and told him to get out of there."

MISCELLANY

★*BANKHEAD, TALLULAH* Jackie was just a wee tyke when Joan Crawford arranged for him to be Tallulah's blind date, Joan having assured Bankhead she'd be with young, blond, handsome "Mr. Cooper" (Tallu had not yet encountered Gary). Jackie remembers that Tallulah took the joke well; she was "charming and witty, and called me darling." Much much later, when a magazine wired Bankhead in New York PLEASE CONFIRM ENGAGEMENT TO GARY COOPER, Tallulah wired back IT'S JACKIE COOPER I'M ENGAGED TO.

★*DURBIN, DEANNA* Jackie was the first to kiss Deanna onscreen ("Or was it Robert Stack?") and they stole some offscreen kisses too, "ducking behind the backdrops to find a few precious, although musty, moments of togetherness."

★*GODDARD, PAULETTE* Jackie and chums on the studio lot discovered what they called "the Paulette Goddard scenic view," a vantage point with unobstructed sight lines into the star's dressing room. Miss Goddard, it seems, liked to "loll around topless." Cooper recalls that "until Paulette Goddard's time, I really had seen only one body—my own. There were no centerfolds in magazines for kids to moon over. The bikini hadn't been invented yet."

★*MINICK, FARREL* They were both 12. "After the bottle spun in her direction," Farrel gave Jackie his first real kiss. "She was the first big girl who paid any attention to me, the kind of attention a boy realizes comes because he is liked, not because he has a worm in his pocket."

★*O'DAY, ANITA* Jazz singer (and author of her own bio, *High Times, Hard Times*). Through his association with some of the big bands, he met singer O'Day, who was the first to turn him on to smoking pot. She invited him up to her room, they shared a couple of joints, drank some wine, "and I passed out. That was all. Anita was very nice, she covered me up and let me sleep it off."

CRAWFORD, JOAN
(1906–1977)

Long before her posthumous reputation as *Mommie Dearest*, she made it to the big time with *Our Dancing Daughters* in 1928 and became the definitive flapper—Flaming Youth personified. Joan Crawford had always wanted to be a dancer, back when she was a waitress and shopgirl, and by the time she was 19 she had made it from Broadway to a contract at MGM. She reigned as a movie queen for well over thirty years, then lapsed into cheapie horror films (after *What Ever Happened to Baby Jane?* in 1962, her last good movie) and became more and more a ludicrous parody of the hard-edged glamour girl of yesteryear. Crawford's marriages and men friends, her competitive egomania and passion for self-improvement were once common fodder for fan magazines. While she was never too popular with fellow workers, especially if she viewed them as a threat to her own status, it was one of her own four adopted children, Christina, who told the world that the monster impersonating a movie star all those years was actually Godzilla, heavily retouched.

PRIMARY SOURCE: *Joan Crawford: A Biography,* by Bob Thomas (Simon and Schuster, 1978; Bantam, 1979).

★*BAUTZER, GREG* Handsome, perpetually tanned lawyer and escort to some of Hollywood's most beautiful women in the '40s and '50s. Bautzer learned to satisfy Crawford's unique requirements for a man who was "both bull and butler." The rules were to "follow two paces behind when she made her entrance at a party . . . place her 'serviette' in her lap . . . carry her knitting bag and poodle." On the other hand, after one of their "terrific fights" (Joan's quote), Greg was capable of climbing a trellis, breaking the glass door to her bedroom and . . . *"God, it was beautiful!"* So said Joan. After four years of battles and reconciliations, while driving home one night Joan asked Bautzer to stop, get out, and check a tire. She drove off, left him there on Sunset Boulevard at 1:30 in the morning. The end. (See also BAUTZER listing.)

★*COOPER, JACKIE* He was a precocious 17, she in her ripened 30s. He made the initial pass, she took it from there. Jackie recalls that Joan was extremely businesslike about their affair, scheduling his visits in her datebook. But for him, it was fantasy time, making love to one of the Love Goddesses of the Screen. (See also COOPER listing.)

★*CUDAHY, MIKE* Crawford's first big affair in Hollywood. Good-looking, he was the wealthy heir to the Cudahy meat-packing family. As Joan's dancing partner they were "enough to knock your eye out." Mike was 19, carried a hip flask, and on most nights took too many swigs. Though Mother Cudahy didn't consider party-girl Joan a good influence on her son, the romance lasted a year.

★*DOZIER, WILLIAM* Movie producer. He was between marriages (to Joan Fontaine followed by Ann Rutherford) while dating Crawford in the late 1940s. At one party, Dozier danced with his old friend Barbara Stanwyck; Joan seethed, went home alone, and told Dozier when he called, "I thought you, of all people, would be different." Next day, she sent him a roomful of flowers with a card saying, "Please forgive a poor, frightened little girl." (See also DOZIER listing.)

★*FAIRBANKS, DOUGLAS JR.* He came from Hollywood's first family (Doug Sr. had married Mary Pickford); he was young, handsome, dashing, and marrying him was, for Joan, "like a fairy tale." Totally wrapped up in each other, she called him Dodo, he called her Billie; she bought him a huge electric train, he added to her collection of dolls. In public, they gazed into each other's eyes and murmured endearments in pig latin. Then career conflicts arose; Doug was not as "energetic" as Joan in pursuing parts. Tempers flared. After an attempt at a second honeymoon in Europe they called it quits. Married in June 1929, Doug and Joan were divorced in May 1933. The first marriage for both.

★*GABLE, CLARK* Paired for the first time in *Dance, Fools, Dance* (1931), Gable and Crawford were an instant take—with moviegoers as well as with each other. She said Clark was her greatest love, and in the heat of their initial passion she proposed they get divorces (she from Fairbanks, he from Ria Langham), to marry each other. "Sounds good to me, baby," said Gable. She got a divorce, he didn't. Part of the problem was their boss, L. B. Mayer, who ordered them to "cut out all this foolishness." They remained close friends, however, and even resumed lovemaking in later years between marriages. (See GABLE listing.)

★*MARTIN, CHARLES* Writer-director. Joan had a "lengthy" romance with him.

★*RACKMIL, MILTON* President of Universal Pictures during the time when Joan was on the Universal lot demanding the biggest dressing room, the best leading man, etc., etc.—and getting everything she asked for.

★*STEELE, ALFRED* President of Pepsi-Cola and recently divorced when Joan met him; he decided she was "a woman with a woman's needs" and needed a husband. Their wedding took place in Las Vegas in May 1955; her fourth and last. Telling reporters, "This is the happiest moment of my life," Joan boarded the S.S. *United States* for a European honeymoon with Al. Sounds of both physical and verbal battles emanated from their stateroom. In Paris, Joan encountered Steele's daughter Sally, who suggested her new stepmom might find it fun to ride the Metro. Chewing gum, Joan eyed the girl and muttered, "Listen, kid, you live your life and I'll live mine." Such was not her attitude to hubby Alfred; she wanted him to live like a movie star. Their New York townhouse was refurbished accordingly. They were playing gin rummy there the night in 1959 that he had a heart attack and died. Widow Joan, who became company spokeswoman and joined the board of directors of Pepsi-Cola, said she went to work because she was broke.

★*TERRY, PHILLIP* When Joan married him, six weeks after they met, everyone in Hollywood wondered, "*Who* is Phillip Terry?" An actor and former Stanford University football player, that's who. Although the couple appeared blissful ("At dinner parties, the butler sometimes carried notes of endearment between Joan and Phil at the end of each course"), friends found their marriage "disturbingly mechanical." Joan, for example, even scheduled their "siestas" for sex in the daily schedule issued to her household staff. The Terrys adopted a son, Phillip, Jr. (later changed to Christopher), but didn't have a lot to say to each other. Phillip's career languished while Joan's surged ahead with an Oscar for *Mildred Pierce*. This union, Joan's third, lasted from 1942 to 1946—her customary four years.

★*TONE, FRANCHOT* Debonair, classy stage and screen actor who entered her life after the divorce from Fairbanks and the bust-up with Gable. Joan's second husband. She agreed to become his wife after they spent "a glowing evening" with Alfred Lunt and Lynn Fontanne, and "Joan envisioned a similar life for herself and Franchot." They were wed in October 1935, and Joan's demands soon began to rankle. Said Tone: "Every night Joan comes down the stairs all dressed up for dinner, and she expects me to compliment her on how she looks. Every night! My God, if Venus de Milo walked down the stairs every night, I couldn't continue raving about her." Franchot started drinking and running around; Joan caught him *in flagrante delicto* with a starlet in his dressing room. She asked if this happened every day. Franchot flippantly said, "*Yes*, I have to prove to myself that I am still a man—before I go home to you." Divorced in 1939. During her marriage to Tone, Crawford had several miscarriages, and finally she adopted a daughter, Christina.

★*TRACY, SPENCER* They co-starred in *Mannequin*, and "the combination was electric, before the camera and otherwise." Joan learned a lot about low-keyed acting from old pro Tracy, and off the set he taught her how to play polo. But soon Tracy seemed bored with Crawford; she realized she had been "merely a diversion" for him.

MISCELLANY

★*ASHER, JERRY* A young man Joan took a shine to and helped get a job in the MGM mailroom. He soon advanced to the publicity department and later became a magazine writer—producing dozens of articles about Joan.

★*BERN, PAUL* Irving Thalberg's right-hand man at MGM, a great help to Joan's early career. He later married Jean Harlow and killed himself, allegedly because he was impotent. (See also HARLOW listing.)

★*CHRYSLER, JERRY* One of Joan's favorite dancing partners, they won prizes at the Coconut Grove. He died young.

★*DAVIS, BETTE* According to rumors recently come to light, Ms. Crawford ardently pursued Ms. Davis. But she was rebuffed. (See also DAVIS listing.)

★*GARBO, GRETA* Upon meeting Joan, she gazed upon her and said, "You have a marvelous face." Joan remarked later, "If ever there was a time in my life when I might have become a lesbian, that was it." (See also DAVIS, above.)

★*MINES, HARRY* A Los Angeles reporter who developed a passion for Crawford, became a regular visitor at her Bristol Avenue home.

★*OFFIELD, LEWIS* Chorus boy in *Innocent Eyes*, Joan's first stage musical; they both had a driving ambition to succeed in show business. Next time they met, his name was Jack Oakie, popular movie comic of the '30s.

★*STERLING, RAY* They danced at a prom in Kansas City; he was the first man to "believe" in her. "He believed I had a beautiful soul as well as a dancing body."

★*WALTERS, CHARLES* Director. Joan called him at home one night wanting to come over and show him the jewels she'd selected to wear in *Torch Song*. She arrived with a velvet jewel box, wearing an elegant lounging robe, which, at one point, she stepped out of, displaying her naked body. "I thought you should see what you have to work with," said Joan. The flustered director managed to say, "That's very nice," and remembers that Joan seemed pleased.

Among Joan Crawford's other dates or dancing partners in Hollywood: directors *NICHOLAS RAY, ROBERT ALDRICH, RANALD MACDOUGALL,* and *VINCENT SHERMAN;* actors *BRIAN DONLEVY, GLENN FORD, CESAR ROMERO, ROCK HUDSON, GEORGE NADER, DON "RED" BARRY,* and others.

CROSBY, BING
(1903–1977)

The granddaddy of crooners and top American entertainer for nearly half a century, known in his lifetime as the amiable, easygoing, no-bull sort of guy who made seven musical-comedy *Road* pictures with Bob Hope. Crosby in private life was anything but the pipe-smoking domestic animal his millions of fans imagined. Though he had seven children by two wives, family life was not his bag; he preferred male cronies, golf, and the many business enterprises which made him a very rich man. His casual liaisons with women, in and out of marriage, were mostly ignored by a press convinced that the public did not want to hear tawdry gossip about the man who sang "White Christmas." Now it's being told that Der Bingle was not only a dedicated womanizer but had much more serious character flaws. One of Crosby's publicists had a rule of thumb to discover who'd been banged by Bing, according to biographers Shepherd and Slatzer. Any leading ladies who show up in two successive Crosby films "were likely to have been on the receiving end of Bing's attention," according to this reckless claim, which would invite avid but probably unreliable research since only the ladies themselves know whether the attentions were welcomed.

PRIMARY SOURCE: *Bing Crosby: The Hollow Man,* by Donald Shepherd and Robert F. Slatzer (St. Martin's, 1981).

★*BERNIER, PEGGY* Brunette musical-comedy actress, and maybe the first true love of his life, whom Bing met on the road while she was starring in *Good News*. Her understudy at the time was Dixie Carrol, later Dixie Lee, the first Mrs. Crosby (the second Mrs. Crosby was said to be a ringer for Peggy). In the end, Peggy chose to make beautiful music with another singer.

★*DE BAYSSON, GHISLAIN* Stylish aristocratic Frenchwoman with whom Bing associated whenever he found himself in Paris. He took her dancing at Maxim's sans toupee. Like pal Gary Cooper, who consorted with a countess, Crosby enjoyed rich, important, classy people with inherited titles or wealth.

★*FREEMAN, MONA* Intelligent, fun-loving young movie actress who became steady companion soon after Crosby was widowed, considered by many old friends to be the ideal choice for Bing. Mona had been divorced, however, and Bing was Catholic, which put her beyond the pale as wife no. 2, despite Bing's obviously strong attraction.

★*GRANT, KATHRYN* The second Mrs. Crosby, a plucky Texas-born beauty queen and starlet who was 19 when she began dating Bing in 1954 (some fifteen months after Dixie's death). He proposed that fall, canceled the wedding date four times, finally tied the knot in October 1957. In the next four years Kathryn acted in summer stock, earned a nursing degree, occasionally joined her husband on fishing trips, and bore three children—Harry Lillis, Jr., Mary Frances (who grew up to shoot J.R. on TV's *Dallas)*, and Nathaniel. Obstinately opposed to Crosby's belief that a woman should stay home to mind *her* kids, Kathryn clearly had the key to getting along with Bing. As she wrote in a candid memoir, *Bing and Other Things*, he "only wanted a buddy, not a sweetheart."

★*LEE, DIXIE* Shy, warm, nearsighted singing starlet who met Bing in the spring of 1930, wed him in September, and soon began to see that she ranked low on Crosby's list of priorities. The first of many separations came in March 1931, when Dixie told the press that "we have already found out that we are not suited for each other. . . . Bing is a fine boy as a friend, but married, he and I just cannot be happy." Happy or not, Dixie stayed to beget four sons (Gary, named for Bing's buddy Gary Cooper, twins Philip and Dennis, and Lindsay), and found a friend in the bottle during Bing's frequent absences. Said Dixie, years later: "If you're married to a Crosby, you've *got* to drink."

★*RANKIN, JANE* Akron socialite, million-aire's daughter given to close harmony with music men. She is sometimes assigned the role in Crosby's past more likely played by Peggy Bernier. Jane supposedly wanted Bing to settle down in Ohio with her father's firm.

★*TAYLOR, RUTH* Actress dated by Crosby early in his Hollywood career, the original blonde in the original version of *Gentlemen Prefer Blondes*.

★*TILLER GIRL* Unidentified member of all-English musical group billed as the Tiller Girls. Toured with Bing and his partner-pianist Al Rinker for thirteen weeks in 1925–26 in a traveling revue called *The Syncopation Idea*. Was it a serious romance? Rinker describes all Crosby's relations with women as "casual, very casual."

MISCELLANY

★*FLEMING, RHONDA* Appeared with Bing in *A Connecticut Yankee in King Arthur's Court* (1948), but Rhonda was interested in someone else, later, when the widowed Bing made his intentions known. By the time Rhonda was free, Crosby had Kathryn Grant. Rhonda had regrets.

★*KELLY, GRACE* Actress who became Princess of Monaco, won an Oscar working with Crosby in *The Country Girl* (1954). Bing fell hard for Grace, got an Academy Award nomination at the same time, but lost the Oscar to Brando *and* the girl. He did, however, sing "True Love" to her in *High Society* in 1956—the same year she married the prince.

DAVIS, BETTE
(b. 1908)

Hollywood's dowager queen of tragedy and one of the truly legendary ladies, winner of two Oscars, with a list of film classics covering half a century, from *Dark Victory* and *Now, Voyager* to *All About Eve*, etc. Controversial and tempestuous offscreen as she is on, sprung from tough New England stock, Davis obviously lives to work—but has often fought like a trapped tigress in doing so, whether battling with studio moguls about the quality of the movies she made or battling, in turn, with any of her four husbands (all deceased or decamped by now), who might well suffer an identity crisis in that magnetic presence. Most people—fans, fellow workers, and plain civilians—either love her or hate her. Bette's own passionate loves and hates were spelled out with few specifics in her autobiography, published nearly twenty years ago. More recently, her well-guarded secrets have been dragged into the light like everyone else's.

PRIMARY SOURCES: *The Lonely Life*, by Bette Davis (Putnam, 1962); *Bette*, by Charles Higham (Macmillan, 1981).

★*BRENT, GEORGE*   Handsome, stolid leading man in several Davis pictures, most notably *Dark Victory* in 1939, as the dying heroine's sympathetic doctor-husband. "It was inevitable from our first meeting through the seven films we had made together, that we would one day have a romance," wrote Bette. There couldn't have been a better time, with Davis facing a divorce from her first husband, still reeling from the end of her romance with director William Wyler—according to Higham. She and Brent kept theirs going for the next year.

★*FARNSWORTH, ARTHUR*   Second husband, a New Englander and an aircraft engineer, the slightly beefy, broad-shouldered All-American type male she seemed to like best. They married on New Year's Eve 1940. It was a reasonably stable, unexciting match. In August 1943, "Farny" inexplicably dropped dead on Hollywood Boulevard, carrying a briefcase full of liquor. There were rumors of foul play because he had been involved in secret wartime projects. Most likely cause of the injury that made him collapse, Higham reveals, was a blow on the head two weeks earlier—struck by a lamp in a motel where he'd been caught shacked up with a fellow worker's wife.

★*HUGHES, HOWARD*   High-flying millionaire recluse, a paradox with a pot o' gold in-

vested in RKO, TWA, etc. No recluse when Bette encountered him at a Beverly Hills benefit for her pet charity, the Tailwaggers Club, an organization of dog lovers. Wrote Bette (without naming Hughes): "I became involved in a catastrophic relationship. . . . he was extremely attractive and one of the wealthiest men in the West—or East, for that matter." Biographer Higham spells out the catastrophe juicily: Bette, linked with Hughes after his courtship of Hepburn, told friends she'd helped overcome his impotence. Her estranged, exasperated first husband, Ham Nelson, had their bedroom bugged, taped Bette abed with Hughes, then burst in on them. Bad scene. Bette was hysterical, imagining her career ruined by lurid publicity. Hughes paid Nelson $70,000 to hush the story. Bette repaid Hughes, who accepted the money, but "sent her a single flower every year for the rest of his life on the anniversary of the repayment." The romance withered, though, and years later Davis and Hughes feuded bitterly over a film about divorce, *Payment on Demand* (1951). (See also HUGHES listing.)

★*LITVAK, ANATOLE*   Elegant Russianborn director of *The Sisters* (1938), married at the time to Bette's jealous co-star and archrival Miriam Hopkins. Miriam wrongly suspected them of having an affair. Bette was intrigued, but unready: "It was not until some months later that her fascination with Litvak developed into a brief, ill-fated, much gossiped about romance." Which she came to regret next time they worked together (*All This and Heaven, Too*, 1940).

★*MERRILL, GARY*   Movie actor, fourth husband, a few years younger than Davis and not unlike the character he played opposite her in *All About Eve* (1950). Though the film was a triumph, the marriage did less well than expected. The Merrills adopted two children: Margot, who was retarded and placed in a special school, and Michael, who became the subject of bitter custody battles (today a successful lawyer in Boston). Career problems, personal tragedy, Merrill's drinking, and alleged physical violence hastened their 1960 divorce, though in many respects Gary seemed better able than his predecessors to face the challenge of being Mr. Bette Davis.

★*NELSON, HARMON* First husband, familiarly known as Ham or Oscar, Bette's schooldays sweetheart when both attended Cushing Academy in Ashburnham, Massachusetts. Weakish, charming, and handsome, Ham became a semisuccessful bandleader. Bette was 26 and a virgin when they married, in 1932, egged on by her ever-present mother Ruthie. "Before I became Hester Prynne . . . I couldn't have expected Mother to suggest that we have an affair. Would that she had been that wise." Soon to pay the price for connubial joys, Bette was the breadwinner, he the sullen stay-at-home, and Davis's disillusion deepened when Ham and Ruthie persuaded her to have an abortion for the sake of her career. She named the Oscar after him when she picked up her first Academy Award (for *Dangerous*, 1935), noting that Ham's bare backside looked just like the gold statuette's. The bitter divorce came in December 1938, in the wake of Hughes and Wyler.

★*PUBLISHER* Wealthy man with whom Bette enjoyed what Higham calls "a pleasant, undemanding romance" in her late 50s.

★*SHERRY, WILLIAM GRANT* Dark, handsome "Sunday painter" and former boxer, Davis's second husband and father of daughter B.D., her one consolation. They married in late '45 but seemed to have little in common except a fiery temperament. Bette recalls, "We drove to Mexico on our honeymoon. En route my husband threw me out of the car. . . . this was only the beginning." It ended, after many ups and downs, in 1950; an embittered Bette agreed to pay alimony in return for custody of B.D. Sherry soon afterward married B.D.'s nurse. "There are words for men like this. . . . I am afraid my initial charm to Sherry was tied up in part with my earning capacities."

★*WYLER, WILLIAM* The late great director (died 1981) was the mysterious love of her life, director of three of Davis's best films: *Jezebel* (1938, her second Oscar), *The Letter* (1940), and *The Little Foxes* (1941). Though

Wyler begged her to marry him during their volatile affair, Bette was evidently "terrified of an ego even larger than her own." She wasn't sure she could cope with a man so rich, domineering, difficult, and totally secure—but may have regretted her decision. When he married someone else on short notice, she was reportedly so distraught she wanted to quit *Dark Victory*. However, Davis and the Wylers maintained a touch-and-go professional friendship for the rest of his life.

MISCELLANY

★*CRAWFORD, JOAN* No dice despite her "secret desire for Bette." But there was persistent wooing—all on Joan's part, according to Higham, who reports that Crawford bombarded Bette with flowers, perfume, letters, and urgent invitations to dine: "No lovesick male tried harder to seduce a beautiful woman than Crawford did in her pursuit of Davis." On Bette's side, a blank. She sent everything back. Some eighteen years later, when they made *Whatever Happened to Baby Jane?* (1962) together, Joan's ardor was markedly cooler, especially when co-star Bette aced her out of an Oscar nomination.

DAY, DORIS
(b. 1924)

When the former Doris Kappelhoff of Cincinnati gave up singing her heart out to become the gee-whiz girl of romantic comedy, she seemed destined to ask, again and again, "What happened last night?" From *Romance on the High Seas* (1948) and *Tea for Two* (1950) to *Pillow Talk* (1959) and beyond, Doris became the perennial virgin on the verge. No matter how the script identified her, everyone knew she was really the blond, energetic girl next door, the prom queen, who never came through and *did* anything but always acted as if she wanted to. "Maybe Next Time" should have been Doris's song, not Liza's. As a onetime band singer who grew up to be America's sweetheart in the '50s, Day dug a little deeper when she played the life of torchy song-stress Ruth Etting in *Love Me or Leave Me* (1955) opposite Cagney. Doris had more or less retired from the screen when she took pen in hand to tell the world what went on between stanzas of "Que Sera Sera."

PRIMARY SOURCE: *Doris Day: Her Own Story,* by A.E. Hotchner (Morrow, 1976).

★*ANONYMOUS ACTOR* A New Yorker who, years before, had played a support-ing role in one of Doris's movies. Suddenly back in Hollywood to do a movie-of-the-week, he asked Doris to dinner. Before the main course, "the earth was trembling under my chair." It was not an earthquake, but l-o-v-e, *love.* "It totally consumes me. I want to be with that person every minute of the day, I want to sleep with him and eat with him and talk with him and breathe the air he breathes. . . . I am engulfed in physical desire for him." That's what love does to Doris. Fortunately, the ob-ject of her affection stayed around for over a year this time—his TV movie became a se-ries—then went back to wife and family in the East. As for Doris, the earth finally stood still. "I realized after he left that I did not love him in an enduring way."

★*CARSON, JACK* Comic actor who co-starred with Day in her first film, *Romance on the High Seas.* When they started dating, she thought he was "very sweet, considerate"; they may have made love but she was not *in* love.

★*JORDEN, AL* Trombonist with the Jimmy Dorsey band; Doris's first husband. She was only 17 and an aspiring singer when they were wed. The trouble started right away: He beat her up for giving some members of the band the opportunity to look up her skirt as she climbed a flight of backstage stairs to retrieve a wedding present. Upon learning she was pregnant, Al bought pills to induce an abor-tion, later aimed a gun at her distended belly, threatening to shoot. Despite such prenatal terror tactics, son Terry was born in February 1942. Doris finally concluded: "Al's love was destructive, a fire of uncontrollable jealousy

that eventually burned out of me feelings for him."

★*MELCHER, MARTY* Her agent and third husband. When they met, however, he was still married to Patty Andrews of the Andrews Sis-ters. (It was rumored that Patty appeared at Doris's door one night wielding a baseball bat.) Few who knew Melcher had a kind word for him. Said bandleader Les Brown: "An awful man, pushy, grating on the nerves, crass, money hungry. . . . We used to call him Farty Belcher." Doris took the big step with Melcher on April 3, 1951, her 27th birthday, and stayed married to him until he died seventeen years later. In the interim, he'd have rages in which he'd repeatedly smash his fist against the wall (or sometimes hit his adopted son Terry), their sex life deteriorated, and there were "other things." As a widow, Doris found that Melcher and his lawyer had gone through about $20 million of *her* earnings, and had left her nearly $500,000 in debt. Doris contem-plates her spunky image vs. the bitter truth: "Yes, sir, America's la-di-da happy virgin!"

★*WEIDLER, GEORGE* Sax player with the Les Brown band. When Doris split from Jor-den, she rejoined Brown's group as a vocalist. And, for the first time, she and George "no-ticed" each other. "It is a curious phenome-non, isn't it, the way someone we have been around a lot will suddenly capture our fancy, a daffodil bursting into bloom? . . . In no time at all, I fell in love with George and we saw each other every day and slept together every night." However, she had misgivings about be-coming Mrs. Weidler, "even as I drove to the wedding. . . . There was no joy, no eager-ness. . . . Sex is not enough to sustain a mar-riage." Doris left George, her second hus-band, in 1949, when the call came from Hollywood.

MISCELLANY

★*LEVY, AL* A "dear friend and agent." One day he was lurking in the lobby and followed Doris into her hotel room. "He closed the door, turned off the lights, and pulled me onto the bed. He desperately thrust himself on top of me as though he were some unknown rapist and I were an anonymous victim." She fought him off, ignoring his protestations of love—and changed agents. To Marty Melcher.

★*REAGAN, RONALD* They "dated" in the early '50s. He liked to dance and *talk;* Doris remembers telling him he ought to make speeches. "One night we went up to his apartment and it was the first time I had seen the view from high up there in the Hollywood Hills. . . . I thought it was lovely, and I decided that that was the area where I wanted to live, high above the city lights with that celestial view." What happened *then?* Sorry, that's all she wrote.

★*RUMORED ROMANCES* "According to the press," notes Doris, "I was Lady Bountiful of the Sheets. Some of the best fiction in the Sixties was written about my amorous adventures with an assortment of lovers who could only have been chosen by berserk random sampler." Some examples: Maury Wills, the Dodger shortstop ("My most consistently reported affair. The only times I had seen Maury were at the games"); Elgin Baylor ("baseball seemed to be getting slower. . . . the columnists transferred my affair to the Lakers' star forward"); then Sly of Sly and the Family Stone, whom she had met once through her son Terry. Adds Doris: "But my media affairs were by no means limited to black men. I was reported to be sexing around with Jerry West, Pancho Gonzales, Glen Campbell, Frank Sinatra, and would you believe it?—Jimmy Hoffa! Variety was certainly the spice of my life. I wouldn't know Hoffa if I fell over him."

DEAN, JAMES
(1931–1955)

Though he appeared in only three pictures of any importance during a two-year period, *Rebel Without a Cause* (1955) followed by *East of Eden* (1955) and *Giant* (1956) were enough to burn Dean's image into the consciousness of '50s youth. He be-

came a cult figure almost the day he died for a whole disaffected generation caught between the dawn of the atomic age and the coming Age of Aquarius. Less was known at the time than would be the case today about his bizarre, chaotic private world. Born in Indiana, confused and sickly, he had been abandoned by his father, deeply disturbed by his mother's death. He looked psychologically *hurt,* or as director Elia Kazan expressed it: "The main thing the girls felt, the boys felt about him, the faggots felt about him, was that you'd want to put your arms around him and protect him and look after him—don't worry, kid, I'm on your side."

PRIMARY SOURCE: *James Dean: A Short Life,* by Venable Herndon (Doubleday, 1974; Signet, 1975).

★*ANDRESS, URSULA* Dean's last serious affair before his death. The young Scandinavian beauty felt like an outsider in Hollywood, till she met Dean and got into an argument about American music. "Only then did I feel American," she said. Their first date was a breakneck ride on Jimmy's motorcycle, a daredevil initiation rite he often pulled on new acquaintances. His moodiness and their frequent arguments finally left Ursula unable to cope; she abandoned Jimmy Dean for John Derek. Unable to accept rejection, Dean followed the couple everywhere, sometimes confronting them in restaurants. His tactics didn't work. Ursula stayed with John. Until John moved on to Linda (Evans) and Bo.

★*ANGELI, PIER* Actress, and, intimates say, the only woman Dean ever really loved. Jimmy was 23, Pier 21. During the filming of *East of Eden,* he wore "a locket containing a lock of her hair and a piece of fabric from the dress she wore the day they met." Dean's friends felt that loving Pier made him ultrasensitive to everything, though he didn't show it when *Modern Screen* asked if they had marriage plans: "You mean me and Miss Pizza? Who knows? Right now I'm too neurotic." Pier's domineering Italian mother was unhappy about their affair, and pressured her to marry Italian singer Vic Damone instead. She did, and during their wedding ceremony Dean sat on his motorcycle outside the church, "torturing himself" by waiting for a glimpse of the bride and groom. After Dean's death, Pier said that "he was the love of my youth—perhaps my greatest love." She committed suicide at 40.

★*BRACKETT, ROGERS* Dean was parking cars in Hollywood when discovered by Brackett, a TV director who helped Jimmy get jobs, bit parts on radio and in movies. Within a short time, Dean moved into Brackett's home, just off Sunset Boulevard Drive. Dean assured his agent that Brackett "said we could have twin beds." No hard evidence exists that Dean and Brackett had a homosexual affair, but it was rumored at the time that Jimmy was hanging out in gay bars, allegedly "an instant hit with the fist-fuck set" because he would do things others would not dare. Dean also lived with Brackett—who nicknamed him "Hamlet"—for a while in New York, eventually moving out after he got involved with dancer Dizzy Sheridan.

★*LEWIS, JEANETTA* A classmate of Jimmy's when both studied theater arts at UCLA. She had a terrible fight with Dean when she learned he was seeing someone else (see Wills, below). But after angrily knocking her around, he wept and apologized.

★*MILLE, JEANETTE* She started seeing Jimmy after his breakup with Ursula Andress. One day, in September 1955, he appeared at her door and gave her his beloved Siamese kitten, Marcus—a gift from his *Giant* co-star, Elizabeth Taylor—then left without a word. The next day Jimmy's speeding Porsche Spyder went out of control on the highway and he was dead.

★*MYSTERY WOMAN* Young actress under contract to Universal International. Dean described her as a voluptuous "pinup lady." He was not particularly proud of the affair he had with her in 1955—during the filming of *Giant*.

★*SHERIDAN, DIZZY* A New York dancer to whom Jimmy—then living with Rogers Brackett—confided his confusion about homosexuality. She was sympathetic, and apparently persuasive; Jimmy left Brackett's place and moved into Dizzy's.

★*WILLS, BEVERLY* Teenage actress (and daughter of comedienne Joan Davis) who had been going steady with Dean's roommate Bill Bast. She switched to Jimmy, but left him when she learned he couldn't dance. She just loved to dance. Shortly after, Dean made friends with Rogers Brackett.

MISCELLANY

★*HARRIS, JULIE* Co-star in *East of Eden*, and a fast friend. She thought Jimmy Dean "a beautiful boy," and said, "I was never in the habit of falling in love with younger men. But if I'd had the misfortune to fall in love with Jimmy, I would have been in trouble."

★*NURMI, MAILA* Actress who hung out with Dean and another actor, Jack Simmons. They were a threesome at Googie's hamburger joint and Schwab's. Maila had a strong psychic link to Jimmy. On the train en route to see Jimmy's aunt and uncle after his funeral, Maila inexplicably stole the dining car's sugar bowl. She learned from Jimmy's aunt that he had done exactly the same thing when he was 9, on a train returning from his mother's funeral.

DE HAVILLAND, OLIVIA
(b. 1916)

Oscar-winning actress (for *To Each His Own*, 1946, and *The Heiress*, 1949) and perennial sibling rival of sister Joan Fontaine. She is perhaps best remembered as Melanie in *Gone with the Wind*; she also co-starred with Errol Flynn in seven costume epics before she fought and won her freedom from Warner Brothers in a famous test case, after which de Havilland's career blossomed. Considered one of Hollywood's blue-ribbon bachelor girls in her prime, Olivia subsequently wrote an autobiographical tome (see below) about her years as a proper married lady in Paris—a book of the old school, full of precious franglais humor, household hints, and Elsie Dinsmore prose, e.g.: "We live in Paris in a little white house which is as tall and narrow as a chimney; behind it we have a little garden with our own chestnut tree and a small fountain for the pigeons and sparrows. . . ." What "every Frenchman has," she giggles, is a *liver!*

PRIMARY SOURCES: *Every Frenchman Has One,* by Olivia de Havilland (Random House, 1961). Also see *The Lonely Life,* by Bette Davis (Putnam, 1962); *Bette,* by Charles Higham (Macmillan, 1981); *An Open Book: An Autobiography,* by John Huston (Knopf, 1980); *John Huston: A Biography,* by Axel Madsen (Doubleday, 1978); *No Bed of Roses: An Autobigoraphy,* by Joan Fontaine (Morrow, 1978; Berkley, 1979).

★*GALANTE, PIERRE PAUL* Editor of *Paris-Match* magazine, second husband, father of her daughter Giselle. En route to Cannes while waiting for her divorce from no. 1 to be final, Olivia felt ripe for romance: "Louella was unhappy, Hedda was unhappy . . . and the publicity department at Fox was unhappy. They wanted me to fall in love." Among her welcoming throng at the airport in Paris was lucky Pierre, "the very first Frenchman I met in France. Handsome but hangdog. Clean-shaven and solemn. Didn't speak English . . . and did not kiss my hand." Curiously, she likens their courtship to a French military campaign. Pierre followed her home ("the adversary pursued"), and by August "the tricolor rose triumphantly in the California sunshine over the Shoreham Apartments." Which means they announced their engagement. Olivia "planted her standard on the Left Bank" in October, though their actual marriage was delayed a year or so by snags in French law. It was a lasting, but not eternal, peace. They divorced in 1979.

★*GOODRICH, MARCUS* Writer and first husband, whom she married in 1946, divorced in 1952. Olivia doesn't mention him by name in her own book, but says a lot about their son, Benjamin Briggs Goodrich, born 1949.

At the time of the marriage, Goodrich had written a novel called *Delilah* but was not widely known, and Livvy's sister Joan quipped for publication, "All I know about him is that he's had four wives and written one book. Too bad it's not the other way around." The remark did not boost her stock in the Goodrich ménage.

★*HUGHES, HOWARD* Leave it to Joan to blab about her reticent sis and the billionaire tycoon. Hughes impulsively proposed marriage to Fontaine at a party one afternoon. Quoth Joan, "I was shocked. Olivia had been seeing him steadily. I knew her feelings for him were intense." Despite their domestic differences, she wasn't about to two-time her own sister, though Joan continues, "I'd heard rumors that Howard saw girls in shifts (no pun intended). Olivia was on the early shift. . . ." Actresses the like of Ginger Rogers and Katharine Hepburn were alleged to be on the late swing. After mulling all this over, Joan went home to show Olivia the paper on which Hughes had scrawled his private phone number, "and gently tried to explain that she had given her heart to a heel." All hell broke loose, and the de Havilland–Fontaine sister act grew several degrees cooler. So did the thing with Hughes. (See also HUGHES and FONTAINE listings.)

★*HUSTON, JOHN* Director who had his hands full directing both Olivia and Bette Davis in *In This Our Life* (1942). As Huston's biographer tells it, "John fell in love with Olivia. She responded, and the romance soon had Bette seething." Huston seemed to be giving Olivia all the best close-ups. When Jack Warner showed Bette some footage, "she came close to tearing out every seat in the projection room." The girls became fast friends, though, as did John and Olivia. Still married to wife no. 2, Huston rented an apartment for their trysts and "saw a lot of Livvy, as intimates called her." Livvy found John capable of "tremendous love of a very tense order." They went on and on, and in May 1944, Olivia told Louella that she was in love with John—though the imminent marriage never jelled. By the time dear John came back from the war, Livvy was suing Warner Brothers and keeping busy with someone else. (See also HUSTON listing.)

★*LITVAK, ANATOLE* Russian-born director, nicknamed Toly, married to Miriam Hopkins at one time and an ardent pursuer of many Hollywood leading ladies. The Huston bio mentions that when John was assigned to script a film for Litvak, Toly was "currently Olivia de Havilland's beau." Anyway, he later directed Livvy in *The Snake Pit* (1948), one of her major successes.

★*McKEON, JOSEPH* The army major who was calling her Livvy, one assumes, as her romance with Huston began to fade.

MISCELLANY

★*FLYNN, ERROL* During all those movies together, Flynn evidently never scored, though not for want of trying. In her autobiography *(A Lonely Life)*, Bette Davis recalls, "it was Olivia de Havilland whom he truly adored and who evaded him successfully to the end. I really believe he was deeply in love with her." (See also FLYNN listing.)

★*HOWARD, LESLIE* When Olivia played a supporting role with him and Bette in *It's Love I'm After*, Howard was mostly after Livvy, living up to his reputation as one of Hollywood's indefatigable womanizers. Davis's latest biographer notes (in *Bette*) that pale, wan Leslie "could have given some points to Errol Flynn." Further on, "he made Olivia de Havilland's life miserable by almost literally begging her to go to bed with him." Olivia remained aloof. "If she hadn't yielded to Errol Flynn, who was also persistent, she certainly wasn't about to yield to Leslie Howard."

★*MEREDITH, BURGESS* Mentioned among the swains who "assiduously courted" her, Meredith had no mean reputation himself for Don Juanism with Norma Shearer, Paulette Goddard (whom he married), and a long list of eminent beauties.

★*STEWART, JAMES* One of her close-mouthed dates.

DIETRICH, MARLENE
(b. 1901)

German-born screen siren who became a universal sensation when director Josef von Sternberg made her synonymous with *The Blue Angel* in 1930. As the throaty, stockinged cabaret strumpet who wore a man's hat and carried a walking stick, she was on her way to becoming one of the great, gorgeous Stone Faces of modern cinema. While she never became a superior actress, she certainly became a scintillating star—the lacquered creation of makeup men, costume designers, lighting experts, and brilliant photographers, who achieved with Dietrich the apotheosis of what English critic Kenneth Tynan called "sex without gender." Beneath the surface glitter, she sometimes pretends to be just a simple German hausfrau who likes to cook, and her tireless campaigning as an entertainer for the troops during World War II helped to fix her image as . . . well, a regular guy. There was always talk about her private life, affecting mannish attire and dallying with writers, intellectuals, actors, athletes, and other women of every sexual persuasion. What ever she may be, Dietrich is indubitably one of a kind.

PRIMARY SOURCE: *The Life of Marlene Dietrich*, by Charles Higham (Norton, 1977; Pocket Books, 1978).

★*AHERNE, BRIAN* Handsome British actor. He went after a part in *Song of Songs* just so he could date Marlene. He got it all.

★*BACHARACH, BURT* Famed arranger-conductor who worked with Marlene on her nightclub act; she'd introduce him as her *amitié amoureuse*, "giving rise to gossip all over the world." When la Dietrich heard he was marrying Angie Dickinson, she snapped, "Angie Dickinson? Nobody can smile that much and for such long periods. Why not marry Julie Andrews?"

★*BRYNNER, YUL* It was Marlene, the story goes, who shaved Yul's dome and thereby helped him win the role in *The King and I*.

There were rumors of romance; it was known she "heaped him with gifts."

★*CARSTAIRS, JO* English millionairess and racing driver, famous for her "blond crew cut, Jack Dempsey shoulders and tattooed body—as well as for her wit and great charm." Though their worlds were far apart, Jo and Marlene came together often over the years.

★*COOPER, GARY* Co-starred in her first American film, *Morocco*, but she was still under Von Sternberg's spell. Again in *Desire*, when Marlene was on the rebound from John Gilbert and definitely ready for Coop, though not for long. (See also COOPER listing.)

★*CURNOW, HUGH* A young Australian reporter Marlene met on a tour Down Under in 1965. He tagged along to Paris and they began collaborating on her memoirs of the war years. The project didn't get far, and neither did the romance. By coincidence, she was back in Australia when Curnow was killed in a helicopter accident.

★*D'ACOSTA, MERCEDES* Lesbian socialite and author. They became intimate friends; in the 1930s Mercedes encouraged Marlene to wear slacks—which became "The Look." During the heat of their relationship, "twice a day florists would deliver enormous bunches of white roses to Mercedes' house." Marlene always sent flowers to her lovers.

★*FAIRBANKS, DOUGLAS JR.* They dated frequently in London in 1936, and she talked him into accepting the lead in *The Prisoner of Zenda*, which made his career.

★*FISHER, EDDIE* He was 25, she was getting her Las Vegas act together. She told him, "You know, Eddie, I am old enough to be your mother." Eddie thought she was life itself: "The nights I left her . . . I was walking on air. She was the most stimulating woman I had ever met." Finally, his manager warned Fisher, "You cannot be seen with that woman. It will ruin your career." When he canceled their next date and repeated the remark to Dietrich, she simply said, "Well, Eddie, maybe he is right." A rather sour-grapes finish but no sour Kraut. "When we met again at a party . . . she

was as gracious to me as ever." (See also FISHER listing.)

★*FORST, WILLI* Popular German actor in the late 1920s; Marlene's debonair leading man, onstage and off.

★*GABIN, JEAN* Actor sometimes called the French Spencer Tracy. One of Marlene's longtime loves, beginning in prewar Paris when she was almost 40. Marlene once told a journalist that Gabin had "the most beautiful loins I've ever seen in a man." Author Higham speculates that Marlene was drawn to Gabin's "earthy, perhaps rather stupid, but constantly alive peasant quality, his sheer manly virility."

★*GAVIN, JAMES, GENERAL* Head of the 88th Airborne Division during World War II, the youngest commander in U.S. Army. When he heard that Marlene, who was in France entertaining the troops, might be captured by the Germans, Gavin parachuted into the front lines to her rescue. They gaily drove back to Paris in a jeep and made a date for after the war. Which they kept, more than once.

★*GILBERT, JOHN* Silent star who fell on bad times after talkies came in and Garbo, his great love, went out of his life. When Marlene met "this fragile man" in 1935, "all her motherly instincts were aroused." Twice she succeeded in getting him off the bottle. But Dietrich was badly singed by the torch Gilbert still carried for Garbo; in retaliation she ran headlong into the affair with Gary Cooper. Gilbert "fell to pieces," and soon died of a heart attack.

★*GOLDBECK, WILLIS* David O. Selznick's production manager; a brief affair, just one of those things.

★*JARAY, HANS* Austrian actor, director, and playwright. Theirs was an "intimate friendship . . . enclosed in joy" and "it ended, as it began, in luminous affection."

★*KENNEDY, JOE* The father of Jack, Bobby, Ted, etc. Referred to as one of Marlene's "intimate friends" and a favorite fellow vacationer on the Côte d'Azur in 1939.

★*PHILIPPE, GERARD* For a time, Marlene was "obsessed" with the sensitive French actor, who starred in *Devil in the Flesh* (1946); she also used her influence to advance his career.

★*REMARQUE, ERICH MARIA* Writer, famed for the antiwar classic *All Quiet on the Western Front*. His attraction was intellectual, as he was reputedly a poor lover, often too drunk to achieve erection. Remarque and Dietrich shared a passion for literature, music, and pacifism. Although both were married, and both had affairs with others, each considered their own relationship a very special one. Remarque even followed her to Hollywood, which he *despised*.

★*SEIBER, RUDOLF* Marlene's one and only husband; they married in Berlin in 1924 and remained man and wife until his death in 1976. They had a daughter, Heidede (later Maria Riva, actress). Rudi followed Marlene (and her mentor-lover Von Sternberg) to the U.S. in the early 1930s, and he eventually settled down on a chicken ranch in the San Fernando Valley with his mistress Tamara Matul. Marlene was close to both of them, and even gave Tamara her cast-off clothing. Rudi and Marlene never saw the need to end their comfortably unconventional marriage.

★*STEVENS, MARTI, and PATCEVITCH, IVA* During the 1960s, her "most intimate friendships" were reportedly with this duo: Stevens, millionairess and woman of beauty, style, and wit; Patcevitch, "publisher and bon viveur."

★*STEWART, JAMES* According to Joe Pasternak, when Dietrich laid eyes on Stewart she began rubbing her hands; "She wanted him at once! He was a really simple guy at the time, in love with Flash Gordon comics." Marlene had an idea: She promised Jimmy a surprise, which turned out to be a life-size doll of Flash Gordon for his very own. "That started their romance," recalls Pasternak.

★*SYM, IGO* Austrian musician and actor, who taught Marlene the musical saw in Vienna in the 1920s. She became an expert musical-saw player, frequently entertaining her lovers and friends. Sym may be one of the few men

to whom Marlene "gave her whole heart and soul."

★*TODD, MIKE* She was fascinated by him and the way he spent money. Todd once told her they'd have to stop seeing each other or he'd fall in love; Marlene volleyed, "No man falls in love with me I don't want to have fall in love with me." She took a memorable cameo role in Todd's *Around the World in 80 Days*. (See also TODD listing.)

★*VACHON, GINNETTE* Heiress and "warm admirer in Marlene's recent years in Paris."

★*VISCONTI, LUCHINO* Italian director. While they filmed *The Monte Carlo Story* in 1957, Marlene reportedly fell in love and "longed" to marry him, homosexual or not.

★*VON STERNBERG, JOSEF* Fabled Austrian-American director who "created" Marlene Dietrich in *The Blue Angel*. He was "obsessed, drugged" by Dietrich; their relationship was "a fierce, argumentative confrontation of male virility and female energy . . . they collided, and sparks flew." When his wife Riva asked Von Sternberg why he didn't go ahead and marry Dietrich, he said, "I'd as soon share a telephone booth with a frightened cobra." In their Hollywood films she was invariably cast as a prostitute, and in their private life he often treated her like one. The bond between them finally snapped, yet years later they'd meet often as friends.

★*WAYNE, JOHN* It was in a studio commissary that Marlene first spied Wayne, says director Tay Garnett: "She swiveled on her heel, looked him up and down as though he were a prime rib at Chasen's . . . and said, '*Daddy, buy me that.*'" Their affair "got off like a fireworks display," and as usual with the men in her life, evolved into a "liaison of companionship, a brotherhood of the spirit." (See also WAYNE listing.)

★*WILDING, MICHAEL* Hitchcock directed Michael and Marlene in *Stage Fright*, and the two immediately began "a big affair," and an important one, too. His friends say that Wilding *adored* Dietrich, and was emotionally torn about leaving her to marry Elizabeth Taylor. (See also TAYLOR listing.)

MISCELLANY

★*BANKHEAD, TALLULAH* Her comment on replacing Marlene in the movie *A Very Different Woman:* "I always did want to get in Marlene's pants." Actually, they seem to have had a casual "Hollywood friendship."

★*DEL RIO, DOLORES* Marlene's "close friend." They were paired at a costume party with Marlene in white tie and tails, Dolores dressed as a bride.

★*HEMINGWAY, ERNEST* He once said he and Marlene were "victims of unsynchronized passion." At one point when *he* was ready, "the Kraut got involved with that worthless Remarque," grumbled Papa.

★*HITLER, ADOLF* His henchmen Goebbels and Von Ribbentrop made overtures to Marlene on Hitler's behalf, but "she rejected them with disgust." She later reflected ruefully, "I might have saved the lives of six million Jews. Maybe I should have gone to him."

★*O'HARA, JOHN* Novelist. He'd simply had "a boyish lech" for Marlene, nothing more, until she told him how much she loved *Butterfield 8.* Then he began to regard her "with great respect."

★*PASTERNAK, JOE* Producer. He believed she was "the sexiest woman he'd ever seen," and pursued her relentlessly. A mutual friend recalls that Marlene told Joe she'd sleep with him when Hitler was dead. In 1945, he called to mention that Hitler was now dead. "No," she said, "Hitler is alive and well and living in Argentina."

★*PATTON, GEORGE, GENERAL* When she entertained U.S. troops at the front during World War II, it was at his specific request. Patton loved her because she was "a good soldier." For Christmas 1944 he gave her a pearl-handled pistol that had belonged to his father, a gift she was later forced to surrender to U.S. Customs because of the legal ban on importing firearms.

★*PIAF, EDITH* Just close friends; Dietrich said Piaf reminded her of Jean Gabin. Piaf said Marlene gave her strength.

★*RIGHTER, CARROLL* Astrologer. "Marlene never accepted a script, took a plane or entered a love affair without his advice." And by recommending him to her friends, she made Righter rightly famous.

★*RUBBER, VIOLA* Friend of Jo Carstairs and eventually Marlene's private secretary.

★*SELZNICK, DAVID O.* Marlene had a favorite parlor game: Name the one person in the world you would not go to bed with even if your children's lives depended upon it. Marlene's answer was always the same: Selznick.

★*VERTINSKY, ALEXANDER* Russian troubadour who gained fame in his native land for songs of unrequited love. Forced to flee Russia, he landed in Hollywood, became hopelessly smitten with Marlene, and wrote a poem about it. Destiny took him back to Moscow. On a visit in the 1960s Marlene placed flowers on his grave.

Dietrich also had close relationships with *NOEL COWARD, SOMERSET MAUGHAM, DARRYL F. ZANUCK, THOMAS MANN, MAURICE CHEVALIER, JEAN COCTEAU, KENNETH TYNAN,* among others.

DOZIER, WILLIAM
(b. 1908)

Omaha boy makes good. A former talent agent with his own stable of stars, Dozier was one of the early upwardly mobile executives who escalated to the executive sweets at RKO, Columbia, and Goldwyn. As an independent producer, he made *Harriet Craig* (1953), then switched into TV production and stayed there. He and his present wife (see below) are well known as gracious Hollywood hosts.

PRIMARY SOURCES: *Joan Crawford: A Biography,* by Bob Thomas (Simon and Schuster, 1978; Bantam, 1979); *No Bed of Roses: An Autobiography,* by Joan Fontaine (Morrow, 1978; Berkley, 1979); *Veronica,* by Veronica Lake with Donald Bain (Citadel, 1971).

★*CRAWFORD, JOAN* When she needed an impressive escort for some gala, Joan often called on Dozier. He was with her the night she fell into a snit over the fact that Greg Bautzer, her longtime man, was escorting Ginger Rogers. Then Dozier had the nerve to ask Babs Stanwyck to dance. Joan left the party alone, and when Bill tried to see her later, Crawford's maid said her mistress had retired for the night. Dozier, now in a snit himself, threw a handful of gravel at her bedroom window and left. The next day *he* got flowers and an apology. (See also CRAWFORD listing.)

★*FOLEY, KATHERINE* First wife, a non-pro. Had one son, Robert.

★*FONTAINE, JOAN* He courted and proposed to Joan while she was confined to a hospital bed, then quickly whisked her off to a wedding (May 1946) in Mexico City. The Cinco de Mayo fireworks were bursting outside their window, as "Mrs. William Dozier had a wedding night to remember!" Joan and hubby Bill formed their own production company, and for a while their lives were filled with happy activity. "We traveled, entertained, chartered yachts. Bill had a Cadillac, I had a four-door Lincoln Continental convertible." However, before daughter Debbie was eight months old, Joan and Bill were going their separate ways. She was his second wife. (See also FONTAINE listing.)

★*LAKE, VERONICA* Once again, Dozier courted a lady in the hospital. Veronica had had a miscarriage; Bill brought her a gift, "cherry pie and Grand Marnier—a whimsical favorite of mine." Dozier's secretary tried to warn Veronica that Bill was not the marrying kind, but she didn't seem to care. They continued to be playmates and bedmates until Dozier got involved with Fontaine. (See also LAKE listing.)

★*RUTHERFORD, ANN* Sweetly pretty leading lady of the '40s, former child star and the apple of Mickey Rooney's eye in two *Andy Hardy* movies. Other nondescript roles before *The Secret Life of Walter Mitty* in 1947. After 1953, Ann's movies were few and far between. But she married well—Dozier.

EKLAND, BRITT
(b. 1942)

Swedish-born perennial starlet at her petulant best as a would-be Bardot in *The Night They Raided Minsky's* (1968), playing a Quaker farmer's daughter who unexpectedly invents the striptease. Britt appeared to be in on the joke, on that occasion, though few of her screen roles have provided public entertainment surpassing her liaisons with a number of famous men. It all began for Britt when she became the wife of the late comedian Peter Sellers, in 1967, and "was whisked into the heady provinces of princes and palaces." In her book, she wrote frankly about many of the palaces she has played, with or without princes, and let the world know that it was not her style to sleep with *happily* married men.

PRIMARY SOURCE: *True Britt*, by Britt Ekland (Prentice-Hall, 1980).

★*ADLER, LOU* Record mogul, film producer. Britt says she had never before run away with a stranger, but dashing off with Lou to the San Sebastian Film Festival seemed so "intoxicatingly romantic," and once there, she couldn't resist him. "Not when he removed his Mexican hat. I knew he was serious." L'affair Adler was, in fact, one of the most serious of Britt's life after Sellers, before Stewart, producing a son, Nicholai (b. 1972), but no marriage. Still, she thought her "entire future" lay with Lou at his beach house in Malibu, until she discovered he had other romantic involvements—Michelle Phillips, for one. Britt steamed: "Our relationship hit rock bottom when I decided that double standards weren't strictly a man's game."

★*AMERICAN STUDENT* Their "spontaneous romantic excursion in St. Moritz" was interrupted by a call from her parents, saying she had landed a contract at 20th Century-Fox.

★*BEATTY, WARREN* Britt just can't say enough about Warren: "The most divine lover of all. . . . Warren could handle women as smoothly as operating an elevator. He knew exactly where to locate the top button. One flick and we were on the way." The way led from a whirlwind time in London to Beatty's penthouse pad at the Beverly Wilshire Hotel. There they spent days sunbathing naked on the terrace. "Warren would drift in and out making drinks for us and occasionally taking a call from a studio to set up fresh movie deals." Years after this, Warren resurfaced in Britt's life, but the charm was gone; "Warren had made himself too available, it seemed to me that practically anyone could have him." (See also BEATTY listing.)

★*BLOND SWEDISH ACTOR* Hippiedom was at its peak and Britt suddenly thought: "What do I really know about life?" Following her "compulsive urge to become a hippie," she got involved with the blond Swede; they smoked pot and hung out. Britt doesn't say what this experience taught her about life.

★*BORIS* Britt's ballet tutor during her Swedish school days. They made love on the wooden benches in the ballet school's dressing room because "Boris, who was living in digs with the school's principal, the aging Madame Karina, could never take me home."

★*BUBBA* High-wire artist, 22, whom Britt encountered while filming *The Flying Wallendas*. He would look down from the highwire and "see her sad face" (saddened by Rod Stewart), and he wanted to make her happy again. He did. Britt loved Bubba's sense of adventure and fun, how he'd shed his clothes and walk around the bedroom on his hands. "I had taken a condominium facing the sea and in Bubba I found a fresh will to live."

★*CICOGNA, COUNT ASCANIO ("BINO")* Italian producer; he wanted Britt to be his very own star. While filming *Machine Gun McCain* for him, Britt hesitated; he was married and had two sons, after all, and she was still tied to Sellers. But once she felt "those streams of fire" flaring through her body, "there was no turning back." Bino was insatiable. "We would make love in his Mercedes, in my villa or in the hotel but he was never indiscreet." Their "hon-

eymoon" lasted through a trip around the world and a second movie, *Cannibals*. When that one proved a flop, Bino faced bankruptcy; he developed a weakness for drugs and ultimately took his own life.

★*FILM MAN* On location in Colorado, Britt embarked on an affair with him that was "a cheap and ghastly mistake that jarred my emotions." It also shook loose her relationship with Adler.

★*GIO* Gigolo to an Italian Contessa who had given him a lavish Roman apartment, a Mercedes, and "tailored him in silk and gold." Britt thought a taste of *la dolce vita* might be fun, but Gio's performance turned out to be *niente*; pity the poor Contessa.

★*HAMILTON, GEORGE* It was a madcap ten-day affair in the South of France. He proposed; he sent her flowers with the message "I did. I do. I will." Britt was then recovering from Warren Beatty, "and it was so *funny*, George did a marvelous impression of Warren." He was still talking about marriage when she literally pushed him on his plane with the airy send-off, "Just think of me as the girl you saw in the holiday brochure."

★*KJELL* Britt's first fling. A crew-cut boy from Stockholm playing drums in a jazz club by night, selling cars by day. "The first time with any man is always a disappointment." They were secretly engaged for over a year.

★*LICHFIELD, LORD PATRICK* Queen Elizabeth's cousin, noted British fashion photographer. "Funnily enough Patrick was a bit hung up that we should have slept together on our first night!" Britt never considered marrying Patrick, no matter how many times he asked. She finally had to be firm: "Don't be ridiculous, Patrick. There are a million other women in the world." It pleased her to know he later found one—Lady Leonora Grosvenor, daughter of Britain's biggest landowner, the Duke of Westminster.

★*O'NEAL, RYAN* After her split with Adler, Britt went to London and found Ryan to tell her troubles to. "The question of going to bed with him was academic." But it wasn't the mad, passionate kind of thing she'd known with Beatty, "or, for that matter, with George Hamilton." Her interlude with Ryan was "comfort and consolation," and soon over, leaving pleasant memories. (See also O'NEAL listing.)

★*PIANIST* Renowned, anonymous. They were young, in their first touring review, and sleeping together when his true love was not around. "He said I kindled the genius within him, although I would be reluctant to take credit for his fame today."

★*POLIDORI, IGI* Italian director, responsible for her first film, *Il Commandante*, and first "fulfilled" affair. In Rome she stayed in the spare room of his house, "knowing the inevitable would occur." Igi, true Italian, taught her what sexual satisfaction was all about. "I felt I had become a woman."

★*SELLERS, PETER* On their first date, in London, he took her to see *The Pink Panther*, then back to his hotel for caviar and champagne, marijuana, and kisses. Although their debut abed was not exactly awe-inspiring, they tied the knot a few weeks later, in February 1964. Sellers was 38, Britt 21. Within days, "his incredible affection had soured into an habitual jealousy" that forced her to give up her first big movie role and fly to Hollywood. In his search for the "ultimate orgasm," Britt reveals, Sellers often used amyl nitrate "poppers," a strong stimulant which *could have* brought on the series of devastating heart attacks that almost killed him that spring. He was barely out of the hospital, however, before they were at it again in the shower. A daughter, Victoria, was born in early 1965; the marriage proceeded on its stormy course until Peter literally threw Britt out of Rome's Excelsior Hotel in the middle of the night. Next day, he got the captain of his yacht, the *Bobo*, to put all of Britt's belongings on the jetty—including her three Yorkshire terriers. "I flew to London to file for divorce." (See also SELLERS listing.)

★*STEWART, ROD* When "the tartanscarved rock star" came into her life, she "rose back into the sky like a gull whose oil-soaked wings had been cleansed by a detergent." Waxing lyrical, too. Soon they were doing the deed several times a day. Rod liked her to dress in "virginal white stockings, panties, petticoat, negligee—and peel it all off like the leaves of an artichoke." They made love *ad nauseam*, sometimes "leaving our guests to chew on their spareribs" while they nipped off to the bedroom, or the backseat of the Mercedes. "Rod regarded every orgasm as his testimony of love for me. Greater love has no man!" When randy Rod hinted he might occasionally enjoy other women, Britt threatened to "chop off" his balls, and deplored the groupies on tour "kissing and groping him as if he were a sexual messiah." They spoke of marriage many times, but it never happened. Then, on returning from a holiday in Sweden, Britt ran into George Hamilton, who said, "Hey, isn't it funny that my ex-girl should be going with your ex-guy?" (He meant Liz Treadwell and Rod.) Britt did not yet consider Rod an "ex." When the break came, she sued for $12 million "palimony" but finally settled out of court. In 1979, Stewart married George's real "ex"—his former wife, Alana Hamilton.

MISCELLANY

★*ELY, RON* Barrel-chested actor who co-starred with Britt in *Slavers*, "and believed we might escalate things into real life." Britt leveled with him: "I'm in love with someone else. I had taken a stack of Rod's tapes to Rhodesia and played them all the time."

★*SNOWDEN, LORD* Photographer Snowden, aka Anthony Armstrong Jones, made some seductive snaps of Britt, standing "frocked but braless in one of Snowden's borrowed white shirts." Through Snowden and Princess Margaret, whom Sellers knew well, Britt became "very much part of the royal circle" in the mid-'60s, even visited Windsor Castle, "where the Queen poured afternoon tea like any mother in any ordinary home."

FARROW, MIA
(b. 1945)

The daughter of director John Farrow and actress Maureen O'Sullivan, best remembered as *Tarzan's* mate. Fey and frail, Mia made herself known as Alison Mackenzie during a two-year run on the TV soap opera *Peyton Place*. The rest seemed relatively easy, though her best work in films *(Rosemary's Baby*, 1968) and her worst work *(The Great Gatsby*, 1973, and the godawful *Hurricane* of 1979) have contributed less to making her a public figure than Mia's unlikely marriage to Frank Sinatra, then a second marriage to Andre Previn. Between times, some of her soul-searching has been through gurus. Though hardly sexy or beautiful by any existing Hollywood standards, it seems clear that this waif with a whim of steel has something that gets 'em. Last to be got was reportedly Woody Allen.

PRIMARY SOURCES: *Eddie: My Life, My Loves*, by Eddie Fisher (Harper & Row, 1981); *The Roman Polanski Story*, by Thomas Kiernan (Delilah/Grove, 1980); *Peter Sellers: The Mask Behind the Mask*, by Peter Evans (New English Library, 1980); *Sinatra: An Unauthorized Biography*, by Earl Wilson (Macmillan, 1976; New American Library/Signet, 1977).

★*ALLEN, WOODY* The reclusive director and very private actress have been seen a lot lately at Elaine's, New York's paparazzo paradise. Mia is also the star of two new Woody Allen films. It has even been rumored that they plan to marry. It would be her third and his third. *If.*

★*MAHARISHI, THE* The Beatles (John, Paul, Ringo and George) were absolutely scandalized when they saw the great master Maharishi Mahesh Yogi making a pass at Mia on the banks of the Ganges.

★*POLANSKI, ROMAN* She managed a "secret" and rather brief fling with the Polish-French director in London, and was looking forward to resuming their liaison during the South Seas filming of *Hurricane*. But Polanski didn't get to direct that one, as scheduled; he was held up by a rape trial in L.A., which led to his voluntary deportation. (See also POLANSKI listing.)

★*PREVIN, ANDRE* British musician and conductor; Mia evidently caused Andre to divorce singer Dory. They got married, Andre and Mia, had six children (three adopted) and a divorce.

★*SELLERS, PETER* For a fortnight or two, Mighty Mia replaced Britt Ekland in Sellers's affections. Britt noted with some irony that just after she married Sellers, he forced her to give up a role in the film *Guns at Batasi*. And who was her replacement? Right. Mia.

★*SINATRA, FRANK* He was thirty years older than his spindly, unglamorous, unsexy-looking teenage bride. They were wed in 1966, in Las Vegas, at the height of her fame as the star of *Peyton Place* and just about the time she was to discover discos and gurus and all that. Frankie was still into playing the horses and singing the golden oldies at Vegas. (See also SINATRA listing.)

MISCELLANY

★*FISHER, EDDIE* No hard evidence of a romance, though Fisher's autobio lauds her charm and humor, and declares he was "enchanted" by Mia. "We saw quite a lot of each other during one period. She and Frank were having a tiff, and, ignoring his calls, she was going out with me, or anybody else, just to make him jealous." One night after partying around Hollywood, Eddie recalls Mia wanted to drive to Mexico. Once there, she said, "Let's get married." Eddie said, "Okay," just testing. "I'll have to call Roddy for permission," she said, meaning Roddy McDowall. She didn't say why. Roddy wasn't answering when she phoned, so the wedding was off.

FISHER, EDDIE
(b. 1928)

Singer who was tops in pop during the '50s. He had tied for first place (with a lady violinist) on *Arthur Godfrey's Talent Scouts*, performed on radio, and became *the* teen idol as star of *Coke Time* on television after army service during the Korean War. Fisher's autobiography delivers, as promised, "all the familiar elements of the Horatio Alger rags-to-riches story, a fairy tale about a poor boy who grows up to sing for a princess, dine with presidents and marry not one but three Hollywood stars." Eddie also describes his years-long descent into self-destruction through heavy gambling and drugs with the help of the late, infamous Dr. Max Jacobson (also known as Dr. Feelgood). Through it all, writes Fisher, his love of an audience was matched only by the love of a woman. "And I had to have both." The memoirs bulge with effusive evidence of a good try.

PRIMARY SOURCE: *Eddie: My Life, My Loves*, by Eddie Fisher (Harper & Row, 1981).

★*ACTRESS* At 21, footloose in L.A., he went to see a play about a prostitute, then visited backstage to congratulate the actress, an "older" woman of about thirty. He was stunned when she invited him out to dinner, more stunned when she invited him to check into a motel up the coast. A one-night quickie, and young Eddie was "deeply disappointed" with himself next day. It wouldn't be the last time.

★*ADAMS, EDIE* Blond musical-comedy entertainer, widow of early TV comedian Ernie Kovacs. Edie suffered from stage fright every time she performed, and Eddie tried to help her when she was on the bill with Liberace at the Riviera. Soon they were enjoying a "very nice" romance. The relationship ended when Ann-Margret came to town unexpectedly, and Edie unexpectedly popped into Eddie's dressing room—at the wrong moment. But Edie and Eddie remained friends.

★*ANN-MARGRET* After his humiliating breakup with Elizabeth Taylor, Eddie went on the wagon, woman-wise. Then he saw Ann-Margret doing a musical number on the Academy Awards show, and recalls, "something I thought had died was coming back to life." Soon after, she came backstage after his opening at the Coconut Grove, and "it happened—boom—just like that . . . she did more than take my mind off Elizabeth." They parted when he cut short Ann-Margret's talk of marriage.

★*BOECK, RENATA* Blond German model he met through producer Robert Evans, finally dated in New York, and in one evening "lightning struck." A furious Evans said Renata was *his*, wanted to duel Eddie over her, suggested a "jury" of friends arbitrate. Meanwhile, Evans snatched her away and lodged her in a New York hideaway with her two dogs and a blind cat. Renata escaped to Las Vegas, where Eddie was performing. She won thousands at the gaming tables, later used at least some of it "to build her mom a schloss back home in Hamburg."

★*CAMPBELL, JUDY* Eddie met Judy, aka Judith Exner, through his good friend Sam Giancana, Chicago mob chieftain, who sometimes used the alias Dr. Goldberg with showbiz chums. Eddie thought she was "a wonderful woman." Not until later did he learn she had been one of JFK's girlfriends, though "Judy and I became more than just friends after she and Sam Giancana broke up."

★*DAVIS, LYN* Young attractive Californian trained in psychology and philosophy. She assisted Fisher on his book, which is dedicated: *To Lyn who arrived just in time.* "Through her eyes, I have seen my past in a new light," he concludes. "She lights up my present."

★*DELON, NATHALIE* Beautiful blond actress-wife of French star Alain Delon. She accompanied Alain on a movie assignment in Hollywood, and relayed a message to Eddie that she needed to see him, *alone.* When he arrived home, she was waiting by the pool, and without fanfare, admitted she was in love with him. What to do? She was married to his *friend*. When Nathalie propositioned him in Las Vegas, "something like a charge of electricity went through my body." Still, Eddie resisted. She finally got him at the Fontainebleau in Miami Beach, when they were unexpectedly left alone. Throughout "nine wonderful days and nights" all of his guilts resolved in a romantic haze. Later, in New York, Nathalie popped up again. More haze, more guilt, then Alain phoned Eddie and demanded he put Nathalie on a plane. Their tearful farewell disturbed him; he thought about the women in his life, "who cared too much, or didn't care enough . . . Was I too romantic, too old-fashioned?"

★*DIETRICH, MARLENE* She was preparing to do her nightclub act, and Eddie, at 25, had been doing one for years when she came to see him perform. He introduced her to songwriters, and grateful Marlene invited him up for dinner. "She was the sophisticated older woman and I was the inexperienced boy, just like in one of her own movies." And, as could be expected, Marlene knew how to make him feel like a man. That night, which was only the beginning, Eddie discovered that Dietrich's "aura of glamour and mystery" was absolutely real. (See also DIETRICH listing.)

★*EVA* Agent Kurt Frings introduced him to the young German actress in Europe while Eddie was doing a TV special. Eva agreed to meet him at a masked ball. Eddie sang "Oh! Mein Pappa" and went home with Eva. A big Deutsch bruiser burst through the door and blacked both her eyes, cursing in German. Expecting his capped teeth to be the next target, Eddie bolted and ran. Through the snow in his bedroom slippers.

★*GARLAND, JUDY* They both were performing at Lake Tahoe. On their first date, Judy passed out from the wine she'd been drinking. He took her to Sinatra's unused bungalow, where she asked for a Seconal. But instead of falling asleep she seemed to revive, "sweet and bright and funny." They spent the night together, plus many subsequent nights

in L.A., but Eddie thought of the affair as just a beautiful friendship, whereas Judy wanted more. Finally, he slept through a lunch date they'd made at his hotel in Chicago. Judy had a lavish repast wheeled in from room service, with a note: *Thanks for lunch.* Adds Eddie, even in rejection, "Judy had style." (See also GARLAND listing.)

★*INGRID* Scandinavian brought to his house one evening for a dinner. She confessed she had been warned she would fall in love with him. "What could I do but try to live up to that reputation? I pushed the button that closed the doors separating the dining room from the bedroom, and my guests had dinner without us." Later, he had a crazy idea—inspired by methamphetamines—to invite Ingrid and four other girls to Caesar's Palace in Vegas. He planned to make it with all of them. But when his estranged wife Connie Stevens showed up unexpectedly, she found Eddie reading in bed. He had "made the rounds," as he put it, but was unable to perform, apparently because of drug-induced impotence. Ingrid subsequently moved in with him until he filed for bankruptcy and found Marcia (see below), yet she later accompanied him on a junket to cure his addiction in Switzerland, by which time he had a cocaine habit costing up to $200,000 every three months.

★*MARCIA* Met Marcia at the home of Clyde, his principal supplier at the time. It was New Year's Eve 1970, and they didn't come out of the bedroom until late the next day. Then she invited him to move in. Eddie believes she saw herself as his savior. Not quite. They had a stormy live-in relationship.

★*OBERON, MERLE* Fabled star of *Wuthering Heights*, friend of Liz's and Eddie's who remained friendly to both. He was a guest with Merle at the beach house of former Mexican President Miguel Aleman, and she pensively told Eddie, "I can have anything I want but I don't have love. . . ." Later, he heard Merle scream and found her naked, frightened by a giant spider. Then they swam together in the nude, and arranged an assignation in her room that night. Eddie recalls: "Even if she was well over fifty, she was one of the most beautiful women in the world. . . . she made our night together a ceremony, as if we were performing a sacred ritual."

★*PARTY GIRLS*   Series of Hollywood love-lies recruited by fan-magazine writer Steven Brandt, whose own interest in girls didn't go beyond dancing, though he "became a sort of unpaid press agent for the ones he liked." The ones he liked for Eddie included Sue Lyon, Michelle Phillips, Sally Kellerman, Barbara Parkins. During one three-week stint at the Coconut Grove, recalls Fisher, Brandt brought a different girl to Eddie's show every night—eighteen of them. "I thanked God for Monday nights off."

★*POWERS, STEPHANIE*   Met her at the Daisy disco in L.A., and found bright, talented Stephanie more "mature" than most. Their relationship thrived until she became fanatic about dieting, for Eddie preferred her just the way he found her. "As her flesh disappeared so did my affection." Stephanie ultimately formed a long-term liaison with William Holden, plus a professional partnership with Robert Wagner in TV's *Hart to Hart*.

★*PROSTITUTES*   During a particularly low point, he moved into a house run by an L.A. madam who became his new supplier of drugs *and* sex. There was a new girl almost every night, but Eddie found something wrong about paying for sex. "More often than not we just talked . . . I became interested in these girls as human beings . . . so fascinated that I started making videotapes of them."

★*PROWSE, JULIET*   Leggy, lovely dancer. When she came to catch his act, Eddie was immediately attracted. But he knew she'd been Sinatra's girl, so he phoned Frank to check with him first about dating Juliet. "He gave me his gracious permission." Yeah, okay, but did *she?*

★*REYNOLDS, DEBBIE*   Introduced to rising starlet Debbie on a movie lot, he invited her to his next opening at the Coconut Grove, finding her "sweet and unspoiled . . . I had found a really nice girl—in Hollywood of all places." Eddie was eager, Debbie still a virgin, but they managed, and before long Louella or someone had dubbed them "America's Sweethearts." Eddie wasn't sure, noting that Debbie invariably hogged the spotlight, and their marrying often seemed to be the inevitable climax to massive publicity. They spent their honeymoon at a Coca-Cola bottler's convention in Atlanta, where blunt, practical Debbie told an assemblage of Fisher's sponsors, "I don't drink Coke. It's bad for your teeth." Later, she seemed penurious to a fault, with Eddie complaining "Debbie spent my money but saved hers." They made a terrible movie together, *Bundle of Joy,* while Debbie was appropriately pregnant with Carrie, born 1956. They were already talking divorce when Debbie again announced she was with child. Their son Tod was born in February 1958 (his namesake Mike Todd, Eddie's best friend, died in a plane crash one month later). Of course, it was Liz who finally prompted Eddie to break away. Though deserting poor Debbie and his two children damaged his public image, Fisher claims their marriage was accurately summed up in a portrait Debbie commissioned. "Debbie, dressed as a clown, dominated the picture. I was a gray outline behind her. It was symbolic of our relationship."

★*RICHARDS, TERRY*   Former Miss Louisiana in the Miss World competition, less than half his age when Fisher met her after having a face-lift and becoming chummy with his plastic surgeon. They were all on a 1975 holiday in Baja when Terry and Eddie were married "under the influence of Gatorade and vodka" in a mock ceremony of sorts performed by a mail-order minister. She wore a sheet, Eddie was bare-chested, in jeans. Later, they hoped to live the Simple Life, which meant a beard for Eddie, "feathers and white leather" for Terry. Nothing worked out. Though not sure the marriage was legal, they divorced—just to be on the safe side—in April 1976.

★*SCHELL, MARIA*   Smiling Austrian-born star who was another friend and confidante of Liz's and Eddie's, and instrumental in helping them adopt their daughter Maria, who was then named for her. When it was all over, Eddie met Schell while she was doing a play in Paris, he was in town for a few days, so "we decided to spend them together." Years later, Maria embraced Fisher publicly at a Hollywood party and told the whole room, "We had the most wonderful, the most marvelous affair!" Eddie's rueful footnote: "Maria was one of the very few women who had something nice to say about me after our romance was over."

★*SHEAN, PAT* Show girl at the Tropicana in Las Vegas, and one of his first extramarital flings during the period of discontent with Debbie. Eddie always "kept a small apartment in L.A. as a hideout." Pat later married Bing Crosby's son Dennis.

★*STEVENS, CONNIE* Eddie had just put Nathalie Delon on that plane to Paris when he ran into Connie, just divorced, in the lobby of New York's Plaza Hotel. Connie swore she'd never marry again: "I'm just going to have a relationship with a man for three months at the most. Come on, let's go have a drink." Fisher quickly rallied from his heartbreak: "I couldn't believe my ears. This was the girl for me." That's what his friends thought, too. But Connie had his baby, daughter Joely, in 1967, before Eddie could make up his mind to marry again (third time up). They finally took the plunge, flying to Puerto Rico in Sinatra's private plane. Then they turned into the Bickersons. After the fighting they made up often enough so that Connie became pregnant again ("that seemed to be one of the few things we could do well together"). And daughter Trisha Leigh was born December 1968. Divorce, of course. They had always kept crossed Italian-Israeli flags over their bedroom fireplace (Connie had Sicilian blood), as a symbol of their happy union. Which Eddie finally found "a very bad joke."

★*TAYLOR, ELIZABETH* She was Mike Todd's widow, of course, and Eddie consoled her, having been so close to Mike that columnists once dubbed them Damon and Pythias. Then one day Eddie came upon her "dressed in a flesh-colored bathing suit, dangling her feet in the pool . . . Our eyes met, and that was it . . . I was in love with Elizabeth." He sensed it was mutual. Next day they went for a drive, holding hands. "Elizabeth, I am going to marry you," Eddie announced. Not easily ruffled, Liz paused, looked up and said, "When?" In the public furor that followed, "Elizabeth was cast as the vamp, I was the villain, and Debbie the innocent victim." He and Liz stuck it out together, though, "drugged with love" and spending a lot of time in bed. Elizabeth insisted on converting to Judaism; Eddie legally adopted Mike's daughter Liza. They married, fought, made a movie together (*Butterfield 8*, for which Liz won an Oscar, Eddie won the *Harvard Lampoon*'s citation as Worst Actor of the Year), and Eddie found life with Elizabeth one crisis after another, "confusion, chaos . . . everything at fever pitch." Then came the offer for Liz to appear in *Cleopatra*. For a cool million, she agreed. They hadn't decided on a leading man, except for Rex Harrison as Caesar. "How about Richard Burton?" Eddie said. "He'd make a good Mark Antony." Liz said, *Who?* The rest, of course, is history. (See also TAYLOR and BURTON listings.)

★*TURNURE, PAMELA* Press secretary at one time to First Lady Jacqueline Kennedy, and a refreshing change from the actresses he had known. They simply fell in love. Pam joined him in Miami Beach, but later in New York she scared Eddie off a little by saying "If we don't stay together, I think I'm going to die." He didn't phone the next day or two, and within a few weeks Pam returned every gift he had ever given her—"a unique experience in my relationships with women." (See also KENNEDY listing.)

★*WYNNE, JOAN* Eighteen-year-old Copacabana cutie during Fisher's first engagement there. They stayed together, off and on, for seven years. But Eddie was "outraged" when Joanie got a job at a club in New Orleans and he heard she was dating a baldish, much older gent. "Here she had a nice-looking boy her own age with a glorious voice and a glorious future and she was going out with an old man."

MISCELLANY

★*ANGELI, PIER* The night of his first date with Debbie Reynolds, he forgot he had previously invited Pier to be his opening-night companion. She showed up but walked out, pausing to give Eddie a memento, half a gold coin on a key chain. "When you find the other half of this, you'll find love," she said, then turned and ran.

★*CRAWFORD, JOAN* Ruminating about older women after his memorable night with Oberon, "I remembered that during dinner at her house in Hollywood, Joan Crawford had made a pass at me and I got out in a hurry."

★*KELLY, GRACE* He liked her style. They were both unattached, both Philadelphians, both famous when they met at a New York cocktail party. Eddie asked her for a date. "I'd love to," said Grace with a winsome smile, "but I'm sailing for Europe tomorrow." That trip took her to Monaco. Eddie never collected his raincheck.

★*VAN DOREN, MAMIE* Eddie knew her as a showgirl in New York who disliked quiet dates in out-of-the-way places, preferred to be out in public making sure she was seen, a "star-hitcher" as he nicely puts it. Much later, they met in Hollywood when *Life* was doing a story on her—Eddie refused to be photographed with Mamie, who said, "I'm going to get you for this if it's the last thing I do."

FLYNN, ERROL
(1909–1959)

Swashbuckling leading man who became a legendary lover, boozer, and brawler, burning out fast and dead at 50. Born in Australia, Flynn traveled the world before settling in Hollywood to star in *Captain Blood, The Adventures of Robin Hood, Gentleman Jim,* etc. Vain, extremely handsome, bisexual, a dedicated satyr, Flynn clearly savored the fringe benefits of stardom but was too involved with yin and yang and yachting to take acting seriously. He claimed to have lost his

virginity to the family maid at age 12. Years later, after having his way with a number of native New Zealand girls, he contracted gonorrhea and concluded it might be best to avoid women who'd had previous sexual experience—a vow from which he often lapsed, though it explains his well-known appetite for nubile virgins. In recent years, Flynn's rollicking sexploits have taken on a more sinister tone, notably when one of several biographies (Higham's, below) spelled out his wartime activities as a Nazi spy, a persuasive but apocryphal story involving, of course, a few spies who loved him. Flynn's own autobiography, *My Wicked, Wicked Ways,* is generally discredited as a "beard," or whitewash, intended to obscure the real story.

PRIMARY SOURCES: *The Two Lives of Errol Flynn,* by Michael Freedland (Arthur Baker Ltd., England, 1978; Morrow, 1979; Bantam, 1980); *Errol Flynn: The Untold Story,* by Charles Higham (Doubleday, 1980).

★*AADLAND, BEVERLY* The 16-year-old blond actress who lived with Flynn during the last, dissipated year of his life. She starred with him in *Cuban Rebel Girls,* a quasi home movie about the Cuban Revolution, Flynn's last—and worst—movie.

★*ANDERSON, GERTRUDE* Flynn's Swedish mistress in the late 1930s. Biographer Higham reports that she was such a smooth Nazi agent that the FBI old-timers in Los Angeles still talk of her with awe—"and disgust that she escaped from them into Mexico after Pearl Harbor."

★*BAUER, ERNA* Another suspected Nazi agent, whom Flynn allegedly dated in Hawaii.

★*BOY HUSTLER* He often visited an Australian millionaire's villa in Cuernavaca when Flynn was a guest. According to a famous director, the boy told him that he and Flynn would perform fellatio on each other, and "Errol was so handsome, superbly built and passionate, that for the first time in his career as a male prostitute he was genuinely turned on by a client."

★*CAPOTE, TRUMAN* The famed writer was only 18 when he met Flynn at a New York party. Flynn first asked him to go to El Morocco, but then proposed they go straight to Truman's place. Truman demurred; he lived in a "tiny little walkup" on Gramercy Square. Errol didn't care. Years later, Higham writes, Marilyn Monroe asked Capote if he had enjoyed the experience. He shrugged. "If it hadn't been Errol Flynn, I wouldn't even have remembered it."

★*CHRISTIAN, LINDA*   They met in Mexico City; he took her maidenhead in Acapulco, then brought her to Hollywood, where he changed her name from Blanca Rosa Welter to Linda Christian and helped get her a screen test. Linda, who was to marry Flynn's "friend" Tyrone Power, has a different perspective. (See also CHRISTIAN listing.)

★*DAMITA, LILI*   French actress of great style and wit—and temper; the first Mrs. Flynn. He dubbed her Tiger Lil. They married, produced a son, Sean (b. 1941; photographer still missing in Vietnam), had lots of fights and, on Flynn's part, an untold number of affairs before they finally threw in the towel.

★*DIAZ, APOLLONIO*   Prosperous Acapulco "beach boy." Flynn had an affair with him while in Mexico ostensibly conducting an affair with wife-to-be Nora Eddington.

★*EDDINGTON, NORA*   Flynn's second wife. He spotted the pretty 18-year-old when she worked in the cigar stand outside the courtroom where Flynn's first rape case was tried. After Lili, "Flynn wanted a simple, down-to-earth sex partner and chum . . . someone who would never be sharp enough to guess that he was an enemy of America; who knew nothing of espionage or politics." So says biographer Higham, who adds that in order to bed the virginal Nora, Flynn "raped her brutally." But she was "won back with his charm," married him, bore him two daughters before the inevitable divorce.

★*ENGLISH GIRL*   As a guest of the Maharajah of Jaipur, she was ensconced in the sacred, very private, heavily guarded Maharani's quarters. That didn't stop Flynn; had his one-nighter with the girl been discovered, he would have been "shot dead."

★*GHIKA, PRINCESS IRENE*   A 19-year-old Romanian princess, nicknamed "the geek" by Flynn. They announced plans to wed, but Flynn told a reporter the decision was premature, because Irene "had not yet become a mistress of the culinary arts." They continued to be seen together around Paris, however.

★*HANSEN, BETTY ANN*   Seventeen-year-old who charged Flynn with statutory rape. Betty Ann testified in court that Errol "did it" with his shoes on. Flynn's film *They Died with Their Boots On* was being released at the time. Acquitted.

★*HASSAN, SHIRLEY EVANS*   A waitress who claimed Flynn fathered her daughter. He denied it. Or just forgot?

★*HUGHES, HOWARD*   Yes, Howard Hughes. One Johnny Meyer, who worked for both Flynn and Hughes at different times but for the same reason (as a pimp, to acquire both male and female hustlers), told biographer Higham that he actually set Flynn up with Hughes, "in a spirit of outrageousness." Meyer's story: The meeting between HH and EF was in Santa Barbara; it was late at night at a private home. Flynn arrived, looking drunk, then Hughes, "looking right and left and creeping into the house under a heavy felt hat." Later, Meyer drove off like a bat out of hell, terrified that the Feds might close in. "I have no idea whether they went to bed or not," Meyer added; "but I think it likely." (See also HUGHES listing.)

★*MARQUIS, LEE*   Nightclub singer. Flynn was named in her husband's divorce action.

★*MARSH, TARA*   An American Nazi Flynn knew in Mexico City. Tara boasted she had been to bed with Hitler, told Errol that der Führer was a normal male despite the loss of a testicle in World War I.

★*O'CONNOR, TING*   Flynn was in his late teens; fittingly, they met on a tramp steamer. She taught him the intricacies of "Oriental lovemaking," introduced him to opium, and robbed him.

★*PERON, EVA*   His yacht *Zaca* first brought Errol to Argentina, where he met Eva Peron "and she fell for him." He was still fascinated by Fascism, therefore intrigued by Evita. Flynn in his later years told a friend his affair with Eva lasted until her death in 1951, in meetings all over the world. At one point, Peron himself found out about it, and told Flynn to leave the country within twenty-four hours or he'd be "found dead in his room."

★*POTTER, PAT* Melbourne hairdresser, Flynn's first serious girlfriend.

★*POWER, TYRONE* The source here is again Johnny Meyer, via Higham. Ty was about 24, and his wife Annabella was away, when he began an affair with 30-year-old Flynn. They met sporadically and in secret at the home of director Edmund Goulding, known for his "homosexual leanings." Meyer assumed that Flynn was the "male" in the relationship, with Ty "very much the female" and very much in love. Though Errol's "ruthlessness" caused a breakup, Meyer says their sexual relationship resumed in Mexico after the war, when Ty was ending an affair with "a famous Latin lover of the screen." Again, alas, it did not last long; "Tyrone wanted things done to him Errol found repellent . . . Errol preferred oral sex with men."

★*SATTERLEE, PEGGY* Nymphet who accused Flynn of rape and testified he called her "my little strumpet . . . you know, it's some kind of English muffin." Again acquitted.

★*TIAROUINA, NAOMI* Russian princess, cited by Flynn as his introduction to sadism. She'd pummel his back with a steel brush. *After* sex.

★*VELEZ, LUPE* Actress and Errol's neighbor. The day she invited him into her bedroom, he disrobed and lay waiting on the bed. No Lupe. He was surprised to find her "kneeling in front of an altar which had an enormous crucifix on it." She prayed for a considerable time, crossed herself three times, "then went down on him."

★*WINTERS, SHELLEY* Up-front actress. Their first date lusted an entire weekend, according to Ms. W. (See also WINTERS listing.)

★*WYMORE, PATRICE* Tall, beautiful, a superb figure. With Patrice, 24, Errol at 41 felt he'd "struck gold." She was his third and last wife. At their lavish Riviera wedding reception,

he was served a writ charging him with the rape of a 16-year-old French girl. The suit was later dropped. After a few years, the couple separated, but remained legally wed through all his further adventures until Flynn's death in 1959.

MISCELLANY

★*DE HAVILLAND, OLIVIA* Demure actress who thought Flynn "the most attractive, the most charming, the most magnetic man" she'd ever met. He was also smitten. One night, during the filming of *Robin Hood*, dressed in his Robin Hood costume, he charged into Olivia's hotel, banged on her door, and loudly announced his intention to take her virginity. Help had to be summoned to remove him from the premises. De Havilland still has regrets, "If only he had known how to woo and win me." He never learned. (See also DE HAVILLAND listing.)

★*HOPPER, HEDDA* Powerful Hollywood columnist. She lived next door to Errol and Lili and frequently complained about their loud quarrels. Once, in retaliation, Flynn went to Hedda's front door, masturbated vigorously, and splattered his semen all over it. Hedda, watching from the window, laughed. To which Errol retorted: "Will you invite me to *come* here again?"

★*LUPINO, IDA* Powerful actress-director who in Flynn's group became "one of the boys." Ida says she's sorry she turned down his proposal. "You know, Little Scout," Flynn reflected, "you're the only one I've ever cried over." A mutual friend believes the deep relationship between Ida and Errol "was buoyed by the fact they never went to bed together."

★*MIAMI PROSTITUTE* In 1950, after a night with Errol and his friend Freddy McEvoy, the girl was found dead. The two men were questioned closely but released. "McEvoy never returned to the United States. Errol gave a deposition for the inquest and the girl's death was put down to a heart attack."

★*PARIS PROSTITUTE* According to Flynn associate Bill Marshall, quoted by Higham (as was the above), Flynn raped this girl with a dildo, leaving her to bleed to death. Marshall suggests it was only his great fame and his outrageous lies that kept Flynn from the guillotine.

FONDA, HENRY
(b. 1905)

Despite his plainspoken American Gothic manner, one of the unquestionable giants of stage and screen. Fonda never severed his cultural roots in live theater, as so many did when the siren song of Hollywood beckoned. After he became a major film star (with the definitive *Young Mr. Lincoln* and Steinbeck's *The Grapes of Wrath* among his masterworks), he continued to act on Broadway—first as the phenomenal *Mister Roberts* in 1948—and set the pattern for the kind of stubborn, solemn All-American good guy he came to represent. Says Peter Ustinov of Fonda: "He's got that quality of a great wine that suddenly begins to do unbelievable things as it gets older." Having two famous children, Jane and Peter, has helped to focus the spotlight of publicity on his private life. An even bigger help were his five marriages. "If I made penetration," Fonda told his biographer, "a proposal was the next step." He also claimed: "I was not a ladies' man . . . I don't kiss the way you should." Onscreen, that is. Offscreen, he admits to having had few complaints.

PRIMARY SOURCE: *Fonda: My Life*, as told to Howard Teichmann (New American Library, 1981).

★*ADAMS, SHIRLEE* Slender airline stewardess and sometime model who is Fonda's fifth, final, and favorite wife. They met at dinner with a mutual friend at a point in Fonda's life when he had sworn off marriage. After Shirlee, he allows, "I felt like a kid again. I wanted to send her valentines every day." Not much older than daughter Jane, Shirlee calls Fonda quite simply "the most attractive man in the world." They courted off and on, inde-

cisively, for several years, and spent some happy time together in the Bel Air mansion which was later the scene of the Manson murders. They married in 1965. Fonda: "After stepping up to bat five times, I finally hit a home run."

★*BLANCHARD, SUSAN* Third wife, stepdaughter of Broadway lyricist Oscar Hammerstein. They met and began an affair while he was still married and performing on Broadway in *Mister Roberts*. She was 21, Fonda 44. Following his wife's suicide in April 1950, he married Susan in December. They adopted an infant daughter, Amy. Though Fonda's children adored Susan's youth, humor, and vivacity, the marriage foundered after five years, while Fonda was filming *War and Peace* in Rome. He believes they simply drifted apart because of his preoccupation with work. Says Susan: "I felt I was being completely smothered. . . . I think there's a scream inside Hank that's never been screamed, and there's a laugh that's never been laughed."

★*BROKAW, FRANCES SEYMOUR* Aristocratic second wife, New York socialite who met Fonda on a film set in London and was known to boast, "I've always gotten every man I ever wanted." She wanted Hank. He, responding, followed her to Paris and proposed in Budapest. They married in 1936. "She was as good-looking as a model from *Vogue* or any actress I'd met, and bright as the beam from a follow spot." She bore him two children, Jane and Peter, but Hank and Frances weren't deeply compatible. She liked fancy sit-down dinners; he liked Greenwich Village jazz spots. Later, in Hollywood, she kept the books on family finances. As friend Leland Hayward observed, "Frances is interested in only two things, sex and money." Her interest in the latter waned. While Fonda was in the U.S. Navy during World War II, she became increasingly morose, unsettled, sought treatment, secretly had extracurricular romances as well as a hysterectomy. In 1950, not long after Fonda asked for his freedom to marry Susan Blanchard, Frances committed suicide in a sanitarium in Beacon, N.Y., by cutting her throat from ear to ear. The children were told she had died of a heart attack.

★*COCA, IMOGENE* Top TV comedienne of the 1950s. Colleague in the hit Broadway revue *New Faces of 1934*, the first big break for both. Enchanted by the "adorable little clown," Fonda pulled her under the grand piano at a party and said, "I've been crazy about you ever since we started rehearsing." Flattered, Imogene said she would see him later, and did. Fonda recalls, "We both felt guilty as hell. We were always afraid her mother would find out."

★*FASHION COORDINATOR* Chic photographer's assistant, an Upper East Side neighbor and Fonda's companion until shortly after he first saw Shirlee at the New York premiere of *The Longest Day.*

★*FRANCHETTI, AFDERA* Exotic daughter of a Venetian family, engaged to the heir to an Italian dukedom when she met Fonda in Rome as his third marriage was coming apart. Named for a volcano in Ethiopia, Afdera (whose "eyes seemed to hold secrets that went back to Eve and the apple," notes Teichmann) captivated Fonda. When she broke her engagement and flew to New York to become the fourth Mrs. Fonda, her brother Nanook (named for the Eskimo) beat her up. She arrived black and blue but still beautiful. They married in March 1957. Another flop. Afdera's jet-set companions bored him stiff. Fonda admits he was on the rebound, choosing "a totally unpredictable and glamorous woman" for "the craziest, most insane marriage anybody ever got into." While it lasted (until 1961), Afdera made all the gossip columns as a stylish contessa, though Fonda wryly comments, "She wasn't any more a contessa than my flannel shirt."

★*FRENCH GIRL* Family friend of Charles Boyer, she encountered Boyer and Fonda aboard the *Ile de France* in the summer of 1936. He was en route to England, where he met Frances Brokaw. The mademoiselle spoke no English, Fonda spoke no French. One evening, his biographer recounts, "she tapped discreetly on the door to his cabin, and

for the remainder of the voyage, speech was unnecessary."

★*INGENUE* Summer-stock actress who offered young Fonda a ride in her car, after a beer party. At the beach, he got out to relieve himself, returned to find his date naked in the back seat. "Get your ass in here!" she said. Which is what he did. There was a repeat performance at a friend's house the following night. This was not Fonda's introduction to sex, but successfully whetted his appetite. "Many more days like that I would have grown old before my time."

★*LADY IN AIRPORT LOUNGE* Chum George Peppard tried to pick up the attractive vacationing blonde, who didn't tumble until he mentioned Fonda's name. They were en route to Rapid City, S.D., to shoot *How the West Was Won* (1963). The blonde appeared on location, uninvited but inviting Hank to her room, which was "seven porches and seven railings" away from his. Fonda climbed over all of them to reach her, but was puzzled when she reappeared at his next location (Washington, D.C., for *Advise and Consent*). Again, he consented to go to her room. Every night. Never saw her again.

★*PROSTITUTE* His first time, noted as "a horrible experience" in a two-dollar Omaha whorehouse. "It was just wham-bam. I was repulsed. It turned me off for quite a while."

★*SULLAVAN, MARGARET* Volatile star of stage and screen, Fonda's first wife. They met in Boston when both were unknowns lucky to make $10 a week. After smoking a reefer, he got high and invited her for a moonlight swim. He walked on his hands, showed her how to do it, and "when they fell, it was into each other's arms." Their stormy marriage (Christmas 1931) lasted only four months. Back in New York, Fonda found "living with Sullavan was like living with lightning." He was "completely destroyed" to hear she was having an affair with Broadway producer Jed Harris. Though Sullavan became "hot" in Hollywood several years before he did, their professional and personal relationship continued long after the divorce. In 1936 they made a movie together, had a brief affair, and talked of remarriage. But Maggie married and divorced William Wyler, then married Fonda's friend and agent producer Leland Hayward. An apparent suicide on New Year's Eve 1959, she was the subject of daughter Brooke Hayward's bestselling *Haywire*. Another tragedy in Fonda's life, which deeply depressed him.

★*USHER* Comforted Fonda one bleak summer when he was playing small roles in stock at Mt. Kisco, N.Y., where his former wife Sullavan was resident leading lady. To usher out the blues, he borrowed the company's station wagon, equipped with "enormous lengths of heavy blue moire that made a cushy mattress."

MISCELLANY

★*ANNABELLA* French actress, his co-star in the made-in-England *Wings of the Morning*. Annabella "wanted more than his acting." He was still stalling when her French husband approached him to beg that he "stop making love to my wife." Deeply moved by his own experience with cuckoldry (Sullavan-Harris), Fonda promised to stay clear, and kept his word. Three years later, Annabella divorced the Frenchman and married Fonda's good friend Tyrone Power.

★*BALL, LUCILLE* Occasional double date, Fonda with Ball, Ginger Rogers with his roommate Jimmy Stewart. After one long night of partying until dawn ("Ginger tried to teach them the Carioca"), Ball recalls Fonda saying "yuk" when he saw her nighttime makeup in cruel daylight. The romance instantly fizzled. Fonda's comment. "Shit! If I hadn't said *yuk* . . . they might have named that studio the Henrylu, not Desilu."

★*CRAWFORD, JOAN* When they made *Daisy Kenyon* (1948) together, Joan hankered to make Hank at the same time. All else failing, she gave him a gift—a jockstrap encrusted with rhinestones, sequins, and beads. During their next scene, she whispered, "How about modeling it for me later?" Fonda supposedly turned beet-red and declined, though producer Dory Schary says, "Hank will refuse to admit the truth. He's not a kiss-well-and-tell man."

★*DAVIS, BETTE* Her sister Bobbi was "pinned" to Hank's pal, Hunter Scott, and the four spent a long-ago weekend at Princeton. It was Hunter who suggested a kissing contest. Alone with Bette, Fonda finally braved "a peck on the lips," nothing more, but in a few days he received a note from Bette saying she'd told her mother "about our lovely experience together in the moonlight . . . She will announce the engagement when we get home." Hank was stunned: "Holy Shit . . . one kiss and I'm engaged!" *That's* how naive he was, he recalls, and "that's what a devil Bette Davis could be at seventeen."

FONDA, JANE
(b. 1937)

Major movie actress, one of the best, who has obviously grown into her illustrious father's genes. From her overprivileged origins as the daughter of Henry Fonda, Jane began as a wide-eyed ingenue (in *Tall Story*, 1960, her film debut), blossomed as a continental sexpot under Vadim (chiefly in *Barbarella*), then found herself and, not incidentally, won an Oscar for *Klute* (1971). Her life and career are peculiarly inseparable, for Fonda's slowly evolving sense of commitment to various causes—antiwar, antinuclear, environmental—is often reflected in the parts she chooses, from *Coming Home* to *Julia* to *The China Syndrome*. Though she has not often been the target of malicious personal gossip, she might be said to make up for it—and then some—by taking the heat for her political activism and outspoken opinions on virtually any public issue.

PRIMARY SOURCE: *Jane: An Intimate Biography of Jane Fonda*, by Thomas Kiernan (Putnam, 1973).

★*DELON, ALAIN* Top French star who made *Joy House* with Jane in Paris in 1963.

At a pre-production press conference she said, "I will undoubtedly fall in love with Delon. I can only play love scenes well when I am in love with my partner." He was said to be taken with her outspoken American charm; she taken with his suave good looks and continental assurance. A fast take, cut to Vadim.

★*EVERETT, TIMMY* A fellow student at Lee Strasberg's Actors Studio, and "the first real love" of Jane's life. He tells how they were rehearsing a scene together at Jane's place and she asked him to stay for a drink. With the wine, music, low lights, "all of a sudden we were looking at each other in this strange way. I just got consumed by this wave of tenderness and desire, and so did she. We ran upstairs to the bedroom, tore our clothes off and stayed in bed for three days." Timmy adds, "Even today it hurts me to talk about Jane. When it was over, I tried to kill myself."

★*FRANCISCUS, JAMES* Close during the late 1950s in New York when she worked as a model, took classes at the Art Students League, and he was a struggling young actor. Then Jane joined Actors Studio, and ultimately found the relationship "sort of dull and boring."

★*GARDNER, FRED* Influential Marxist and founder of the GI movement against the war in Vietnam. He met Jane at a party, turned the page on a whole new chapter in her life. Became her teacher, guide to political activism, and, in time, her lover. Meanwhile, her marriage to Vadim foundered. Quoth Vadim: "It's very difficult being married to a Joan of Arc."

★*HAYDEN, TOM* California politician, Jane's second and current husband, who began his career as the radical leader of SDS. In 1972 they embarked on a ninety-city tour of the U.S., supporting the peace campaign, trying to defeat President Nixon's bid for a second term. During their travels, Jane and Tom fell in love, and she became pregnant. She divorced Vadim, married Hayden, and later that year (1973) gave birth to their son, Troy. Jane expressed the desire to start a truly revolutionary family. The Haydens later switched their politi-

cal focus to environmental concerns.

★*SUTHERLAND, DONALD* During the antiwar '60s they became close political chums, and took their FTA show (Free the Army) on the road. They also appeared together in the anti-establishment *Steelyard Blues* and *Klute*. Of their relationship at the time, Jane said, "When we're together, it's delightful. When we're apart, we remain friends. . . . We don't even feel the need to be physically faithful, because we know that sleeping with another person does not diminish what we feel for each other."

★*VADIM, ROGER* France's Svengali of film, famed for launching the careers, and sometimes marrying, such celebrated sex kittens as Bardot and Catherine Deneuve. Jane was initially leery of the European Casanova she had once met in Hollywood: "I thought he was going to rape me right there in the Polo Lounge." Vadim subsequently directed her in his remake of the sexy French classic *La Ronde*, married her, and starred her in the racy exploitation flick *Barbarella*. He was Jane's first husband, and the father of her firstborn, Vanessa, in 1968. Their fast life in Malibu with the likes of Roman Polanski and Sharon Tate began to pall for Jane after her friend Sharon became a victim of the Manson gang, and Jane herself began to feel the first twinges of political awareness.

★*VOUTSINAS, ANDREAS* Aspiring director who encountered Jane at Actors Studio and became her drama coach and mentor, more or less controlling her life and career for two years (totally displacing Timmy Everett). Voutsinas's domination of Jane did not please papa Henry, who called him "an evil molder of Jane's personality." Voutsinas admitted he aimed to become "the power behind the throne." He didn't get far before Jane's instinct for survival toppled him.

★*WHITELAW, SANDY* Socialite interested in the theater, who subsequently became a producer of sorts. Jane started seeing him, and other young men, in New York—after Franciscus, before Everett.

★*YALE BOY* As a Vassar girl, Jane tried to persuade said Yale boy to marry her. She quipped later, "He had the good sense to decline." According to her friend Brooke Hayward, at Vassar, "Jane had a reputation for being "easy." Another observer described her as a "sophisticated delinquent."

FONTAINE, JOAN
(b. 1917)

Prim, English-bred actress best known for *Rebecca* and her Oscar-winning role in *Suspicion*. Born in the Orient, Joan was transplanted at an early age to California, along with sister Olivia de Havilland, her lifelong nemesis. Writes Joan: "There is much in my life that might make me the envy of many . . . fame, fortune, romance, self-expression, independence. Yet I have found no lasting romance, no marriage that I could salvage."

PRIMARY SOURCE: *No Bed of Roses: An Autobiography,* by Joan Fontaine (Morrow, 1978; Berkley, 1979).

★*ADDAMS, CHARLES* Wry cartoonist. They "amused each other, were both hobbyists. . . . I'd always joked with him that he would spawn with anything that twitched," jokes Joan. "He frankly agreed."

★*AHERNE, BRIAN* "Extremely handsome" British leading man of stage and screen, Joan's first husband. Married 1939, divorced 1942. On the eve of their marriage he tried to cancel out; on their sexless wedding night he talked of his affair with Marlene Dietrich and got up to illustrate some ballet steps he had taught Marlene's daughter Maria. "With Brian pirouetting about the room, his dressing gown flapping, its tassels waving in the air, I grew increasingly numb. . . . Finally, closing the bedroom door behind us, Brian said he wished he'd remembered to pack a hot-water bottle for his sinuses." Joan spent most of the night at a window watching the fog whirl around their Nob Hill hotel. But a few nights later,

things improved, and "the bell in that 'sacred temple' rang for the first time."

★*"DOCTOR NOH"* Phony name for the "expert in tropical diseases" who once nursed an ailing Joan. He called her one day while she was playing bridge in her apartment to say he was coming right over. With barely a nod to her guests, Dr. Noh led her into another room and, without a word, put his arms around her and kissed her. "I was putty when faced with a strong man and I knew it . . . That night he returned . . . to stay in my life for eight years." During that time they traveled *everywhere*— but then, in order to keep herself interesting and the relationship exciting, Joan went back to work; first in a film, then a national tour of *Dial M for Murder.* At the end of the tour she and Doctor Noh met again for their traditional champagne reunion. She learned he had been seeing other women. "This time the champagne was lukewarm. Within days it was flat. So was I."

★*DOZIER, WILLIAM* Head of RKO Studio, and husband no. 2. They were wed in May 1946, and Joan began to have doubts while on the honeymoon. That's when she got a call from a Hollywood columnist asking if Joan knew about a "damaging episode" in her husband's past. She didn't. When she brought up the subject to Bill, he said he had figured what she didn't know couldn't hurt her. "Had I only suspected that this attitude would prevail throughout our future together." Still, they formed their own film production company, made movies together, and produced a daughter, Debbie. Before the baby was a year old, however, her parents were "estranged." (See also DOZIER listing.)

★*HOUSEMAN, JOHN* Writer-producer-actor and Joan's fiancé for a number of months in the 1940s. But she strongly objected to his overbearing mother.

★*KHAN, PRINCE ALY* Middle Eastern playboy who once wed Rita Hayworth. The day after Joan met him in Paris, he sent her the obligatory roses. Over lunch at Maxim's he gave her a small package from Cartier's. "In his

Ferrari, we dashed to his horse farms to name his foals. We raced to Deauville . . . We attended galas at the casino . . . and swam in the Mediterranean at his villa." God, those *were* the days.

★*NAGEL, CONRAD* Early film star, twice Joan's age and a Christian Scientist. While on a duck-hunting weekend in the country, Joan and Conrad were ensconced in adjoining rooms. He made a midnight visit, drawing a chair near her bed to sit and chat. But suddenly Conrad rose from his chair, threw back the bedcovers, "and before I could protest, the dire deed was done. One might say I was surprised out of my virginity. I was twenty. . . . I could only thank God that the wretched hymen was no more. . . . The whole experience had been no more than a quick surgical violation conducted with considerable modesty and no conversation. It reminded me of the time when I had to stand up in class as a child and be vaccinated." Their relationship continued for some months, but Joan finally broke it off, realizing that had she married him, "my life would have been spent playing golf with an older generation."

★*STEVENSON, ADLAI* The thinking man's politician. After their friendship became public knowledge, he explained that he still had political ambitions and could not marry an actress. She replied it was just as well, as her family would not approve of her marrying a politician. "Adlai and I both sobbed a little, professed lifelong adoration and friendship. . . . it was a heart-breaking scene which both of us enjoyed immensely."

★*VIERTEL, PETER* Screenwriter. "Poised, cool, multilingual Peter" and Joan became the best of friends, sharing houses in Switzerland, Ireland, etc. Once she stopped off to see him in Vienna, where he was working on a film. "Deborah Kerr was the leading lady. Peter had discovered her, she had discovered him. They were later married."

★*WRIGHT, ALFRED* *Life* magazine writer who once interviewed Joan and Olivia and re-entered Joan's life when she was ill. Her dependency made him feel needed. "My only major mistake was that eventually I got well." That wedding night was another bummer. "After cornflakes and milk by the library fire, we rolled into my canopied bed and I set the alarm for 6:30 A.M. Tomorrow was a workday for both of us." Alfred was frequently away on assignments, while Joan stayed home, "needlepointing everything in sight but the walls and ceiling." She suspected he was involved in some hanky-panky, which was confirmed one night when she received a call from an irate husband, wanting to know the whereabouts of both Alfred Wright *"and my wife."* "I knew another volume in my life was closing," wrote Joan. Alfred was no. 4.

★*YOUNG, COLLIER* Writer-producer and Joan's third husband. Collie was "a perennial Peter Pan, a wit and a wag," who lived with Joan several years before marrying her. They were wed in November 1952. "The year yawned by. . . . as the champagne bubbles of our union evaporated into the aridity of householding and child care. My wings were clipped. I was grounded." *Another* volume would soon close. Joan recalls that her Christmas gift from Collie had been a copper frying pan. "I would have preferred a single white rose."

MISCELLANY

★*ANDERSON, EDWARD* An American consular officer young Joan met on return from Japan. She "readily" accepted his proposal, promised to join him when she was eighteen. "Our ineffectual attempt to shatter my virginity in his cabin—a romance aborted by a knock on the door—seemed a pledge to him." Later, in Hollywood, he remarked that Joan was "only a bit of fluff." He left, brideless.

★*BURNE, RUPERT and HEWITT, A. E.* Two bachelors "from Shell Oil" with whom Joan, as a teenager, spent idyllic days in Japan. "I look back on those days as the happiest of my life. Neither man ever made a pass at me. If only time could have stood still."

★*FONTAINE, GEORGE MILAN* Joan and

Olivia's American stepfather, who used to bathe the little girls in the tub each night. Joan recalled that "the washcloth would tarry too long in intimate places. . . . Fathers and daughters, stepfathers and stepdaughters. The story is not new."

★HUGHES, HOWARD He was dating Joan's sister, Olivia de Havilland, and Joan was just about to marry Brian Aherne. Hughes told her such a step would be a big mistake, that she should marry *him*. Within months after her divorce from Aherne, Hughes tried again. But she decided to marry Bill Dozier. Hughes heard their marriage was in trouble, and again he proposed. She asked, "Why me, Howard?" He told her: "Because you know the business, because you like to travel, you like to fly. . . . We could read scripts together, play golf, see the world." When Howard called her at home, Dozier would sometimes answer and hand her the phone with a curt "God calling." On her divorce from Dozier, Joan again rebuffed Hughes, and she claims that she is "one of the girls pursued by Hughes who never had an affair with him." When she went off to Europe on holiday he threatened: "Come back immediately or I'll cut out all your closeups in *Born to Be Bad*." That didn't work either.

★JOHNSON, LYNDON, and HUMPHREY, HUBERT President and Vice President. Both danced with Joan at a White House bash, and both, she says, asked for her New York phone number.

★KELLY, JOHN "SHIPWRECK" Rich playboy with madcap ways. Impatient for her to get ready for a date, he once plunged, fully clothed, into Joan's bath.

★KENNEDY, JOE Tycoon, womanizer, and father of all The Kennedys. At a dinner party he complimented her talents as a hostess. Then he proposed moving in with her—whenever he came to California. "You can do what you like when I'm not here," he said "but there's only one thing . . . I can't marry you." Joan was stunned, seeing that "Joe had never even held my hand. I simply laughed it off,

chucked him under the chin, and returned to the table."

★MAYTAG, FRED Scion of the washing machine family. Their acquaintance began on a ship bound for Japan; she was 15, he 22. Later, in his Tokyo hotel room, "with infinite gentleness and kindness, never touching me, he explained the facts of life." He described in detail the anatomical differences between the sexes, and their *multiple uses*. "He briefly took off his robe. I had never seen a man's genitals before. Though in name only, when I returned to my room at midnight I was at last, I felt, a true sophisticate."

★NICHOLAS OF YUGOSLAVIA, PRINCE A young man who would become "a dear, platonic companion, even to sharing my apartment with me while he attended Oxford. His brother Prince Alexander often did the same."

★STEVENS, GEORGE Joan was in love with George for many years, but learned little from him as a director. His direction to her was simply, "I don't *know* what's wrong. Let's do it again!"

★WANAMAKER, TOM Scion of the department store family. Another shipboard romance, during the latter days of Joan's marriage to Aherne.

★WARWICK, THE EARL OF Joan was an overnight guest in Warwick Castle when, hark!, in the middle of the night his lordship came into her room wearing nothing but a multicolored bath towel. "Fortunately, I was reading Churchill's *History of the English-Speaking Peoples*. With cold cream on my face, my hornrimmed spectacles firmly in place, I asked him if he had trouble with sleepwalking. . . . Eventually," says Joan, "the Earl took himself off to a warmer bed."

GADLE, CLARK
(1901–1960)

The brash, hearty he-man who set the pattern for a score of imitators, of which the newest—and best—is probably Burt Reynolds. When Gable told Vivien Leigh in *Gone with the Wind* that he didn't give a damn, the whole world believed him, and that historic "first"—cursing on the screen was unprecedented in 1939—would not have sounded the same from any other actor. Gable was Hollywood's unrivaled King, but he seemed to have his mind on more manly things than moviemaking. Fishing, hunting, drinking cronies, and fun-loving women were high on his list. If he liked a girl, he was apt to call her Baby. When Judy Garland sang "Dear Mr. Gable" to him she sang for women everywhere. After World War II and the loss of his third wife, Carole Lombard, Gable never quite matched the momentum of earlier years, though his last appearance in *The Misfits* (1960) now seems an appropriately tough, typical, fond farewell.

PRIMARY SOURCE: *Long Live the King: A Biography of Clark Gable,* by Lyn Tornabene (Putnam, 1975; Pocket Books, 1976).

★*ALLAN, ELIZABETH* English beauty with a bit part in Gable's *Men in White;* his "souvenir" of the film.

★*ASHLEY, LADY SYLVIA* Gable married and divorced her before most people in Hollywood knew who she was. A former show girl, she went to England and became wife of Lord Anthony Ashley, heir to the Duke of Shaftesbury, who divorced her, naming Douglas Fairbanks, Jr., as corespondent. She was married to Fairbanks and Edward John, Lord Stanley of Alderly. Divorced again in 1948, Sylvia headed for Hollywood, met Clark at a party, and won him. In 1949 Gable said simply that it was a bad year, "and I don't want to talk about it." Sylvia was his fourth wife; she looked a bit like Lombard, his third.

★*BLONDELL, JOAN* Said Joan, the definitive saucer-eyed blond kewpie: "He affected all females, unless they were dead."

★*CHISHOLM, BETTY* Dignified, rawboned blond widow, and heiress to Jones Sausage fortune. She played a mean game of golf. His favorite partner in Phoenix.

★*CRAWFORD, JOAN* To Joan, Gable was without doubt "the most exciting actor of them all." When they co-starred in *Possessed* they were madly in love, she recalls, and in one scene, "his nearness had such impact, my knees buckled." The attraction was mutual. "You can look at any picture we made together," said Joan, "and there's something going on that is alive and can walk right out at you." Although they talked of marriage, it was a hopeless situation (he was wed to Ria, she to Doug Fairbanks, Jr.). After Lombard, however, Clark dated Joan again, on and off, but the early passion had waned. (See also CRAWFORD listing.)

★*DADOLLE, SUZANNE* French model. She looked like Lombard too. His girl in Paris.

★*DILLON, JOSEPHINE* Actress, drama coach. She convinced Gable he could be a successful actor, if he'd let her show him the way. They married in Hollywood in December 1924. He was 24, she 40. Josephine became the first Mrs. Gable, but a rather overripe one, and a source of embarrassment to him in years to come.

★*DORFLER, FRANZ* Actress, Clark's first love. Both loved the theater, dreamed of conquering it together as a married couple, like the Lunts. That was the plan. Then Franz advised Clark to study acting with the distinguished Josephine Dillon (see above). Exit Dorfler.

★*FREDERICK, PAULINE* Famous stage actress in the early part of the century; Gable's "first really big-league affair." They met when he took a small part in her *Madame X.* At the time, she was 44, lived in a mansion on Sunset Boulevard, and was considered "sexually insatiable." Pauline had had three husbands and a lover who hanged himself when she rejected him.

★GIBSON, CAROL Daughter of one of Gable's fishing buddies in Oregon. His girl on the Rogue River.

★HARLOW, JEAN Did they or didn't they? Seems likely that they did—at some point during a professional relationship that lasted through six movies. On-the-scene observers say that Gable and Harlow "got along like a pair of bear cubs." By the time they worked together in *Red Dust*, he had become accustomed to Harlow, who cursed like an army sergeant, shunned underwear, and "iced her nipples to make them show through her silks and satins." He called her Baby. (See also HARLOW listing.)

★HARRISON, JOAN An English dazzler who worked for Alfred Hitchcock. One of his girls in London.

★HAWKS, SLIM Accompanied Gable on hunting and fishing trips, after her split from director Howard Hawks.

★KELLY, GRACE He was in his 50s, she in her early 20s when they trekked to Africa to shoot *Mogambo* (a remake of the Gable-Harlow classic *Red Dust*). "Grace went on hunting trips in the bush with Clark. . . . Clark read her poetry beside the wide Kagera. They swam together in jungle lakes and watched the rhinos go by." Back home in Hollywood, they continued to see each other "fairly regularly." It was thought they might marry, but the age difference was too great, Grace decided.

★LANGHAM, RIA FRANKLIN PRENTIS LUCAS Thrice-wed Houston socialite who became the second Mrs. Gable. Like Josephine, his first wife, she was seventeen years older than Gable. To some observers, "Ria was a buyer, and Clark sold out." They were wed in 1930, stayed legally tied until he met Lombard and bought his freedom.

★LOMBARD, CAROLE There was no more perfect Hollywood couple than Gable and Lombard. He was the King, she a blond, warm, beautiful, wisecracking "man's woman." In public. In private, "She swore profusely, kept a black dildo in her dressing room, had a retinue of servants and sycophants fussing over her from head to toe." Lombard was still married to actor William Powell when cast opposite Gable (the only time) in *No Man of Her Own* (1932). Actually, the sparks between them were not ignited until years later. Within the first month of their affair, he was driving around in a white jalopy festooned with red hearts—"a wacky gift from his girl Carole." The first time Gable took her duck hunting, she asked, "What do we do?" Just sit and wait, he told her. Lombard said she could think of better things to do than sit, so they made love—twice—in the duck blind. They were married in March 1939, in Kingman, Ariz. When not involved in outdoor sports, they became the envy of their madcap crowd, giving the lie to oft-repeated jibes that Carole privately claimed Gable was a lousy lay. Says one friend: "You didn't just drop in on them. They were a very sexy couple. They were all over each other, and Sundays were for making babies." They had none, however, and on another March day, in 1942, Carole was killed in a plane in the Nevada mountains while returning from a war-bond tour. For Gable, nothing was ever the same again, though he earnestly sought passable substitutes.

★O'BRIEN, DOLLY Another beautiful blonde, a blue-eyed Palm Beach belle. "He was, in his fashion, quite smitten." In the late 1940s.

★ROGERS, MILLICENT Standard Oil heiress, thrice married and a "clothes horse" whose wild collection of costumes was recently displayed in an exhibition at the Metropolitan Museum of Art. She professed to be mad about Gable and stalked him relentlessly, but lost out to Lady Ashley.

★ST. JOHNS, ADELA ROGERS Socialite journalist-screenwriter. One of Gable's most trusted friends. A favorite Hollywood rumor had Adela mothering a child by Gable sometime in the '30s. When asked about this by Merv Griffin on a TV show in 1975, Adela answered enigmatically, "What woman would deny that Clark Gable was the father of her child?"

★TAYLOR, MARY Socialite, and a frequent date after his separation from Ria Langham. Before the plot thickened with Lombard.

★*THOMPSON, NATALIE* Daughter of Beverly Hills socialite. Gable's girl in Carson City.

★*WILLIAMS, KAY* Fifth and last wife, another lissome blonde in the Lombard mold, perhaps. Thirteen years earlier Kay had turned down a blind date with Gable because "she was being watched by her ex-husband, a mysterious South American." She was also married to millionaire Adolph Spreckels before meeting Gable in the mid-1950s. The timing judged right, they spoke their vows before a justice of the peace in Nevada in 1955. A friend observed that Kay saw her role not so much as a wife as "custodian of a national treasure." She took those duties seriously. Gable died of a heart attack in 1960, shortly after filming *The Misfits*. On March 20, 1961, Kay Gable gave birth to an eight-pound boy named John Clark, Gable's only child.

MISCELLANY

★*COLBY, ANITA* Fashion model and film-studio executive. She was the girl who said no to everyone. "At 30 she had never been wed, or laid, as far as anyone knew." When Clark dated her, they traveled with chaperons. Oh, she loved him, but was not "in love" with him. "I would no more have thought of going to bed with him than with the man in the moon." She was stunned when he proposed. "How do you say *no* to Clark Gable," she mused. She found a way.

★*GARDNER, AVA* Second leading lady in *Mogambo*. Ava was Clark's kind of "no bullshit buddy," and they might have hit it off if she had *ever* run into him between husbands. (See also GARDNER listing.)

★*GODDARD, PAULETTE* Gable allegedly found himself in the position of "fending her off." But she told Anita Loos that Clark was a "great gourmet."

★*LAMARR, HEDY* They co-starred in *Boom Town* and a comedy called *Comrade X*. But supposedly the chemistry didn't register offscreen. Then maybe it did. (See also LAMARR listing.)

★*LEIGH, VIVIEN* She Scarlett, he Rhett. Some people wonder to this day why they didn't fall in love during the five months they spent creating classic sexual tension in *Gone with the Wind*. Well, he was deeply involved with Lombard; Viv was Laurence Olivier's bride. Also, the two were locked in continuous power struggles on the *GWTW* set, and star egos prevailed over sex. (See also LEIGH listing.)

★*LOY, MYRNA* His leading lady in seven films. In recent years Loy marveled that she and Gable were never lovers. "I was like his little sister. I guess he wasn't my type."

★*LUPINO, IDA* Just pals.

★*MACDONALD, JEANETTE* Much to her chagrin, Gable totally ignored her existence, except on camera—in *San Francisco*. She occasionally broke into tears over his indifference. Clark said cryptically that Jeanette "ate too much garlic."

★*PICKFORD, MARY* She rejected Gable's attentions, and "later suspected she must have been out of her mind."

★*TIERNEY, GENE* He found her "enchanting." She found him "an old fashioned gentleman." (See also TIERNEY listing.)

★*TURNER, LANA* Although there was "an explosion of rumors" about a romance, spoiled Lana said of Gable: "Ours was a closeness without intimacy. There was a dear loving for him, but never an affair. No way." (See also TURNER listing.)

★*YOUNG, LORETTA* She says frankly, "I think every woman he ever met was in love with him." But *these two* in an affair? Doubtful, despite one durable Hollywood rumor that they were roommates up in the boondocks while making *Call of the Wild* (1935).

GABOR, ZSA ZSA
(b. 1919)

She became Miss Hungary at 15, but was promptly disqualified for lying about her age. It hardly mattered. She grew up to be either a fortune-hunter or a film star or a caricature of what European women were believed to be. and that didn't matter much either. It cannot be claimed that Zsa Zsa is one of a kind, since Mama Jolie and Zsa Zsa's two sisters, Magda and Eva, project similar images as updated courtesans—throwbacks to a time when it wasn't such a bad thing for a girl to have men marry or keep her, pamper her, shower her with diamonds, wrap her in furs, and hope no one comes along with a better offer. In fact, Zsa Zsa works hard selling the myth that she does nothing at all but look pretty and talk funny, dollink, and she talks so fast that practically no one ever contradicts her. Actually, Zsa Zsa is her own best joke—almost a spoof of Dietrich—but without believing a word of it.

PRIMARY SOURCE: *Zsa Zsa Gabor: My Story,* "written for me by Gerold Frank" (World, 1960; Fawcett/Crest, 1961).

★*BELGE, BURHAN* He was His Excellency, Press Director of the Foreign Ministry of Turkey, when 15-year-old Zsa Zsa met him in Budapest. He joked that he'd marry her when she grew up, "because you have too much spirit to be a concubine." A year later, sick of school, still breathless from her first affair and first foray into show business, she told M. Belge she was ready. She'd marry him if she could keep her dog Mishka. Burhan said, "Why not?" Papa Gabor said, "Why a *Turk?*" The newlyweds boarded a train for Turkey, and Zsa Zsa was relieved that Burhan did not slip into her bridal berth. She discovered later that the problem was Mishka. "How could I know that to a Moslem, dogs are unclean—Burhan would never sleep where a dog had lain." She was finally forced to submit to her husband's advances, as they settled into the quiet diplomatic life in Ankara. In a few years she went to visit her sister Eva in Hollywood and cold-Turkeyed—she never went back.

★*HILL, ALEXANDER* Zsa Zsa writes of Hill only as "my gallant new beau from New York." That was two decades ago. Since then she's had beaucoup de beaux.

★*HILTON, CONRAD* Hotel czar. Second husband. When she first laid eyes on him (while wearing "shimmering dark-blue satin with turquoise embroidery"), she said to herself, *This* man I could marry." Sister Eva sighed, "First a Turk, now a Texan." Connie Hilton proceeded to "courtship" Zsa Zsa in earnest; it was lunch and dinner every day, "spooning" in the car when he took her home. They were wed in the spring of 1942, in Santa Fe, in company of "a lot of Hilton Hotel managers." Then they settled down in Bel Air. Daughter Francesca was born. Nobody tried harder than she did to make a success of a marriage, says Zsa Zsa. But! He kept her on an allowance of only $250 a month—for *everything.* Also, he had peculiar habits such as kneeling in prayer just when Zsa Zsa was feeling amorous. "Damn it, go to your room and wait for me," he'd order, making her feel like "a scarlet woman." In his own memoir, Hilton wrote that his Catholic guilt for marrying a divorced woman was, "in the end, more than I could pay." The emptiness of her marriage finally drove Zsa Zsa slightly dotty, to the extent that she was sent to a sanitarium for six weeks for shock treatments.

★*KENNEDY, JOHN F.* They sometimes dated, but Zsa Zsa didn't know who Jackie was in 1953, when the future First Lady—still a roving photographer—flew back from London with her, asking beauty tips all the way ("She had kinky hair and bad skin"). Zsa Zsa says Jackie told her she'd be met by a "young man who's going to propose to me." When they got off the plane, Zsa Zsa spotted JFK, threw her arms around him, and burbled, "My darling sweetheart . . . I was always in luff with you!" Miss Bouvier was not amused. (See also KENNEDY listing.)

★*O'HARA, MIKE* Lawyer and husband no. 7, recently divorced. (Mama Jolie told Earl Wilson, "Zsa Zsa is shopping—for her eighth husband"). Husbands nos. 4, 5, and 6 were gentlemen named Hutner, Cosden, and Ryan. Number 7½ was Felipe de Alba. Their impromptu 1982 Mexican marriage, before Zsa

Zsa got her final papers from O'Hara, was supposed to be clinched by a second ceremony. Zsa Zsa impulsively called the whole thing off, saying: "He bored me. He's a playboy and I'm a hard-working actress." They'll remain friends, of course. Stay tuned.

★*RUBIROSA, PORFIRIO* Husband George Sanders had just flown off to Europe when Zsa Zsa stepped into an elevator at New York's Plaza Hotel, bumping into Rubi. She really *tried* to keep her distance, but the next morning her room was full of Rubi's roses. Next he escorted her to the premier of *Moulin Rouge*, her headiest screen triumph. "Flushed with the excitement, I said yes. So it all began." Throughout the next year Zsa Zsa felt like "a character in a play by Pirandello or Molnar or Noel Coward—I found myself rushing from George to Rubi, then rushing from Rubi to George." When Sanders filed for a divorce in 1953, Rubi intensified his pursuit, reminding Zsa Zsa that Barbara Hutton wanted to marry him, and he might do it, too, if Zsa Zsa didn't run away with him that very minute. She didn't. So Rubi tied the knot with Barbara—but only briefly. The next spring in Paris, Rubi announced his engagement to Zsa Zsa, who still harbored strong doubts. "His jealousy suffocated me." It was a good life while it lasted, though; "every night a bistro, a club, one night drunk, the next sober, one night I adored him, the next I left him. . . ." When at last he found someone else to share his life, she wished him well and hurriedly hung up the phone. "It was perfect casting, Rubi and I. . . . We had a great love." (See also RUBIROSA listing.)

★*SANDERS, GEORGE* While still Mrs. Hilton (and seven months pregnant with Francesca), Zsa Zsa saw Sanders in *The Moon and Sixpence* and announced to sister Magda that she would someday marry that man. When first they met, she told him about her crush. Sanders smiled. "Indeed," he said, in his impeccable British accent. "How very understandable." He took her home that night and stayed, announcing he would henceforth call

her Cokiline, an endearment meaning "little cookie." Married on April Fool's Day ("How delightfully appropriate," murmured George) in 1949, in Las Vegas, George forgot the ring. He also remarked that now that she was no longer the glamorous Mrs. Conrad Hilton, just the *plain* Mrs. George Sanders, he wasn't sure he could make love to her anymore. Somehow he managed. Their rocky marriage grew rockier after Zsa Zsa was suddenly discovered as a TV game-show panelist and became an instant celebrity. When they argued, George would move out—only to pop back later, asking Zsa Zsa for a sandwich and a glass of milk. "We sealed one reunion when I bought him an electric saw for Christmas," gushes Gabor. It was not until the messy affair with Rubirosa that Sanders decided to end the marriage. One night, presumably as a parting gesture, he climbed into Zsa Zsa's bedroom, where she lay abed with Rubi, and ripped up a framed photo of himself on her bureau. After the divorce they became good friends again; he even called to tell her he was about to marry Benita Colman. Sanders committed suicide at age 65, as he'd always vowed he would.

★*SCHMIDT-KENTNER, WILLI* German composer. Sixteen-year-old Zsa Zsa was making her stage debut in Vienna, and there in the first row was "a wild, passionate-looking man in his late forties, with a square Mongolian face and a great mane of iron-gray hair." His effect on her was quite physical. One day he asked, "Will you come with me to Cobenzl?" She said yes, "almost humbly." She told him many lies—namely that she had already had many men. They reached the tiny village of Cobenzl by funicular, went to a charming inn "almost lost amid the fir trees," and there, trembling and clinging to him—thinking to herself, "I am *wicked*," she surrendered her maidenhead to Willi. She was actually annoyed that he "called attention to that fact and spoiled all the fun." Later, Willi asked Zsa Zsa to run away even farther—to Rome. They were en route by train when Zsa Zsa had second thoughts, slipped away in the middle of the night and caught the next train back to Vienna. "I sat on the bench in the half darkness, thinking, 'what now?' . . . It's hard to explain these things . . . but four weeks later I was married to someone else." (That would be Belge.)

★*TRUJILLO, RAFAEL JR.* Son of the dictator of Santo Domingo, and an international playboy much like his father. Zsa Zsa was "kind" to Ramfis, as she called him, inviting him to parties where he met movie stars (including Kim Novak, whom "he should have married," says ZZ), and he was generous to her in return. Zsa Zsa didn't understand the scandal that erupted when Ramfis gave her a Mercedes Benz—and one for Kim as well. Seems the U.S. government had just given the Dominican Republic a healthy foreign-aid grant, and feared young Trujillo might fritter the money away on luxury cars for movie stars.

MISCELLANY

★*ATATURK, MUSTAFA KEMAL* "Half man, half god . . . the 'savior' of modern Turkey," she calls him. Anyway, the ruler of that country when Zsa Zsa moved there with husband no. 1. She immediately attracted Ataturk's attention. When told she had a secret admirer, someone she could meet "by taking this key, and going to an obscure address in the old city"—why, of course, she was *hooked.* Walking into the darkened rendezvous room she heard Ataturk's voice: "Woman was not made to resist temptation." She met the Turkish leader secretly in this same place on a regular basis for two years—until he died. Zsa Zsa says she and Ataturk did nothing more than talk and drink tea. "He would sit in his deep easy chair with a glass. . . . I did nearly all the talking."

★*BAUTZER, GREG* Showbiz lawyer who dated many a Hollywood beauty in the 1940s. Zsa Zsa was on his arm (wearing "shimmering dark-blue satin," etc.) when she met Conrad Hilton. (See also BAUTZER listing.)

★*DE BENDON, COUNT JOHN* Her escort in London. He was the first to point out "that absurd Rubirosa guy."

★*KHAN, ALY* They met in Paris, as his marriage to Rita Hayworth was collapsing. Aly told Zsa Zsa, "You're one of the few women in America I've longed to meet." He asked her to dine; the next morning her room was "filled with roses" *again.* Zsa Zsa thought the prince was charming, debonair, and all that. But, as they danced, "somehow I sensed that while our cheeks touched, his eyes were sweeping the room, alert for a new face, a new adventure." (See also KHAN listing.)

★*"MISTER CORD"* Zsa Zsa's fictional name for a famous Hollywood producer. At a party in Malibu he offered to pay handsomely for her favors. She fled in a huff. "How dare he! Just because he ruled *Hollywood?* I had known men who ruled *countries!*"

★*SHAW, GEORGE BERNARD* At a London luncheon with G.B. and H.G. Wells, with Zsa Zsa sitting between them, *someone* reached under the table to pinch her leg. "I like to think that it was Mr. Shaw."

★*TONE, FRANCHOT* They dated while Rubi was married—ever so briefly—to Barbara Hutton.

Other escorts mentioned in passing: *STEWART BARTHELMESS,* the *PRINCE OF HANOVER, HERBY LUTZ,* multimillionaire *BOB TOPPING* . . . "I said to myself, why do I need *GEORGE SANDERS?*"

GARBO, GRETA
(b. 1905)

Celestial Swedish film star who still rules by divine right, though she has not made a movie in forty years. If movie stardom is defined as being remote, lustrous, inaccessible, light-years removed from anything ordinary, Garbo had it all. Old photographs, film festivals, and golden memories preserve her legend, yet when she is actually *there* on screen—in *Grand Hotel, Camille, Ninotchka,* or the silent classics—she seems amazingly vivid and warm-blooded, because she *was* a superb actress as well as an image. She seldom got the man in her romantic film tragedies, and Garbo herself might have meant it when she said, "I vant to be alone." Often disappointed in the movies she made, she may have been equally disappointed in the men who fell in love with her. What they meant to her can only be pieced together from hearsay and conjecture, for Garbo remains as elusive today as she was in 1941, at age 36, when she retired and said re her future, "I don't know. I'm just drifting." As possibly the world's most famous semi-recluse and nomad, independently rich, she'd have made a fascinating companion for the late Howard Hughes.

PRIMARY SOURCES: *Garbo: A Portrait,* by Alexander Walker (Macmillan, 1980). Also *The MGM Stock Company,* by James Robert Parish and Ronald L. Bowers (Arlington, 1973).

★*BEATON, CECIL* Internationally famous photographer, one of the few men who took the opportunity to ask Garbo to marry him. He later jotted down her answer, much like the dialogue in a Garbo movie script: "But we would never be able to get along together, and you wouldn't like to see me in the mornings in an old man's pyjamas. . . . Besides, you'd worry about my being so gloomy and sad. . . . It's a funny thing, but I don't let anyone except you touch my vertebrae—they so easily get out of place."

★*BRENT, GEORGE* Her leading man in *The Painted Veil* in 1934 and, according to an enduring tale, so smitten that he begged her to marry him. Garbo was involved enough to promise she'd think about it, and give him an answer after one of her periodic family visits to Sweden. She went away, returned, never phoned, until Brent, distraught, learned she was back in Hollywood and straightaway sent a personal messenger to plead his case. Garbo listened, looked, waited two beats, and asked, "Who's Brent?"

★*GILBERT, JOHN* They became Hollywood's hottest couple on screen and off after *Flesh and the Devil* in 1927. He was her first American lover, but how well she really loved

him is another matter. Gilbert impulsively told the press he was going to marry Garbo, but their one aborted elopement turned into a screwball comedy: en route to a justice of the peace, Garbo managed to ditch Gilbert by bolting into a ladies' room, later boarding a train home. The stars were still working together in 1929 when Gilbert inexplicably married actress Ina Claire (Garbo's love rival in *Ninotchka* ten years later). Garbo and Gilbert remained close until 1930, however, when she refused Laurence Olivier as her leading man in *Queen Christina* and fought—and won—to give the role to Gilbert, whose future looked bleak with the advent of sound. The film was a success, but Gilbert *fini* in more ways than one. Said Garbo later: "God, I wonder what I ever saw in him. Oh well, I guess he *was* pretty."

★*HAUSER, GAYELORD* Health guru who became Garbo's "willing guide to the life spiritual and the body temporal." He had a certain showmanship, in common with all the men who briefly took charge (or so they thought) of Garbo's directionless life. He answered Garbo's need for flattery, reassurance, and control, and he also brought her into the international set—changing her social ways as well as her eating habits. "In short, he directed Garbo's attitude to herself in much the same way as subtle and sympathetic moviemakers had directed her in the playing of a character."

★*SCHLEE, GEORGE* Russian-born New York financier, husband to fashion designer Valentina. He was Garbo's greatest good friend for many years before he died in 1964. Schlee "directed" Garbo's life for her, as Stiller and others had done, and also provided her some of the good things in life to which she had become accustomed. Garbo moved into Schlee's apartment building on New York's East 52nd Street, often went out with both Schlee and wife Valentina—the ladies sometimes attired in identical gowns. All three were booked into the Hotel Crillon in Paris when Schlee succumbed to a heart attack. His wife refused to allow Garbo on the plane carrying his body back to the U.S. The two women are still neighbors, however, said to be carefully timing their elevator exits and entrances to avoid confrontation.

★*STILLER, MAURITZ* Swedish Svengali of films who created the Garbo image in her first great European film, *The Saga of Gosta Berling.* In 1925, they traveled to Hollywood, where Stiller should have been a success, with all his drive, his showy disposition, "his talent for seducing or bullying people into exactly what he wanted them to do." But Stiller's stubbornness and vanity worked against him; he was fired by MGM after Garbo's second film. Stiller returned to Sweden, where he died, suddenly, in 1928. Desperately in need of a friend, Garbo found John Gilbert.

★*STOKOWSKI, LEOPOLD* Virtuoso musical conductor, whom Garbo met in 1937—he was 55, she 32. Vacationing together at a rented villa in Rapallo, Italy, Garbo and Stokowski attracted hordes of reporters ordered to penetrate the tight security. What was going on in there? A gardener reported he had caught them in the act of calisthenics—Greta briskly ordering Leopold, "one-two-three-*bend!*" Stokowski, presumably in great shape, much later married heiress Gloria Vanderbilt, many years his junior. Garbo went on alone.

MISCELLANY

★*BURTON, RICHARD* One of the comeback offers Garbo turned down was *My Cousin Rachel* (1952), which starred Olivia de Havilland and Burton. A long time later, Garbo and Burton met socially and he asked permission to kiss her knee. "Certainly," said the Divine One. Burton knelt and did so, still recalls it as "an experience I'll never forget."

★*CLIFT, MONTGOMERY* He became fascinated with Garbo and hosted dinner parties for her in New York. On one of their few dates à *deux*, though, he found that kissing her was not the thrill he had imagined. (See also CLIFT listing.)

★*CRAWFORD, JOAN* No real relationship except that Joan found Garbo the most tempting reason she had ever found for becoming a lesbian. (See also CRAWFORD listing.)

★*ONASSIS, ARISTOTLE* One of the powerful, rich friends who allegedly gave Garbo financial advice—as well as privacy. Garbo was frequently a guest on the Onassis yacht, where she fended off at least one pass. (See also ONASSIS listing.)

GARDNER, AVA
(b. 1922)

Sultry, much-married movie star of generally undistinguished films, better known for those in which she played a Hemingway man's woman (*The Snows of Kilimanjaro, The Sun Also Rises*), as if to presage her own reputation as an expatriate international party girl. Her good friend John Huston describes her otherwise: "Ava today is chaste. She's become tired of passion. In a sense she always was." Born in North Carolina to an oversized, overworked family of tenant farmers, tomboy Ava slipped away to the movies to see Clark Gable in *Red Dust*, little aware that twenty years later, in 1952, she would appear with Gable in a remake titled *Mogambo.* Hers is a classic version of the American dream in which a backwoods beauty gets it all, but pays a heavy price in private woes.

PRIMARY SOURCE: *Ava: A Life Story,* by Charles Higham (Delacorte, 1974).

★*CABRE, MARIO* He played Ava's bullfighter lover onscreen and off while she was in Spain filming *Pandora and the Flying Dutchman.*

★*CHIARI, WALTER* Comic actor, an "Italian Danny Kaye" who became "obsessed" with Ava, "although when we were together I often felt I was alone."

★*DOMINGUIN, LUIS MIGUEL* Once more a matador, and among the greats. Their passionate affair, begun when she was in Italy for *The Barefoot Contessa,* became a *cause célèbre.* Ava said no to marriage.

★*DUFF, HOWARD* On the rebound from Artie Shaw, Ava met brash, uncomplicated, sexy Howard, then a young contract player. Her mercurial ways put him off, but "sexually, she had me hooked from the outset." They were among the hard-drinking, nightclubbing swingers in wild postwar Hollywood. Duff later married Ida Lupino.

★*HUGHES, HOWARD* Ava liked tall, thin, dark men; HH was into girls with "big boobies." They fought a lot, made up a lot; eventually she found his romantic attentions too much. But HH was to reappear again and again in Ava's life, "usually when I needed him." (See also HUGHES listing.)

★*ROONEY, MICKEY* Ava vowed that if she ever made it to Hollywood, she'd marry "the biggest star of them all." In 1941, that led her to runt-sized Rooney. They met during her first week at MGM. He fell, hard. "His attack on Ava was like that of a baby chimpanzee on a giraffe." He sent her roses by the hundreds, and proposed a total of twenty-five times. They married in January 1942, exactly six months after Ava landed in Hollywood. On their wedding night, Mick discovered his sexy bride was still a virgin. After eight months it was boring for both of them.

★*SCOTT, GEORGE C.* He was Abraham to Ava's Sarah in John Huston's version of *The Bible;* their offscreen relationship was on an equally epic scale. Director Huston said Scott was "literally out of his mind" over the reluctant Ava. He pursued her across continents, broke down hotel doors, physically abused her. Ava was shattered; Scott was hospitalized for a time. "That's what love did to the man," said Huston.

★*SHAW, ARTIE* Oft-married band leader. He was depressed over his disastrous marriage to Lana Turner (see Turner, below); Ava was oppressed by Howard Hughes. Artie found Ava insecure, uncerebral; "he worshiped her body but despised her brain." Intimidated into scholarly pursuits, she learned enough to dump Shaw, after ten months of marriage. Two down for Ava. (See also SHAW listing.)

★*SIDEWATER, FRED* Assistant producer on *The Bible;* claims he made it with Ava when he took some official papers for her to sign.

★*SINATRA, FRANK* Ava's star was on the rise, Frank's temporarily sinking when that ole debbil sex plunged them into *the* affair of the early '50s. He was still legally tied to wife Nancy, and Ava still felt she could roam free, which provoked Frank into public fits of jealousy. Their eventual marriage, in November 1951, was more of the same. The final split came in 1954, after his Oscar for *From Here to Eternity*—her affair with Dominguin. The lady has not been hitched since. Can't say the same for Frankie. (See also SINATRA listing.)

★*TURNER, LANA* According to one story, Frankie walked in on Ava and Lana, in bed, in dishabille. Another version: When he interrupted them, the two female friends were simply yukking it up over the sexual endowments of certain men they knew. In either case (and the first is given wider credence) Frank flew into a *fury.* (See also TURNER listing.)

★*YORDAN, PHILIP* Now a millionaire wheeler-dealer in the film world. He gave Ava her first important role, in *Whistle Stop.* Their affair was short-lived, lackadaisical on Ava's part. Yordan said she was, "quite simply, the most boring woman I have ever known."

MISCELLANY

★*BEY, TURHAN* A sometimes date in the early '40s. (See also BEY listing.)

★*CARROLL, JOHN* Ditto.

★*DAVIS, SAMMY JR.* *Confidential* magazine carried an "exposé" on Ava and Sammy, hinting she had other "bronze boyfriends." They were friends, yes; lovers, doubtful.

★*FRANCIOSA, TONY* His then wife Shelley Winters *said* there was something going on when Tony and Ava made *The Naked Maja.* The two principals deny it, and one witness said, "Franciosa and Ava *hated* each other."

★*GRANGER, STEWART* He says she tried to tempt him out of marital fidelity, while both were suffering the heat of Pakistan for *Bhowani Junction.* (See also GRANGER listing.)

★*GRAVES, ROBERT* The British poet

thought of Ava as "at once tragic and adorable." Longtime friends.

★*HEMINGWAY, ERNEST* He visited Ava in hospital in Madrid, took her gallstones as a souvenir, along with what developed into a long but platonic relationship.

★*HUSTON, JOHN* They've worked together, drunk together, played together; a profound friendship, but probably nothing more.

★*HYAMS, JOE* Journalist assigned to interview Ava in Palm Springs, wound up driving her to Mexico to buy tequila. Once there, she suggested they stop over in a "cheap and seedy" hotel. Despite his admitted "wild attraction" to her, Hyams remained ever the discreet professional, and subsequently married Elke Sommer.

★*LAWFORD, PETER* A frequent companion in the early MGM days.

★*TRABERT, TONY* Australian tennis star who invited Ava to his matches while she was Down Under filming *On the Beach*. Rumors of an affair, but "nothing could have been further from the truth."

★*VIERTEL, PETER* Screenwriter who adapted Hemingway's *The Sun Also Rises*, in which Ava played Lady Brett. Theirs was believed to be more of an "intellectual" relationship.

★*WALKER, ROBERT* A sometimes date in the '40s.

GARLAND, JUDY
(1922–1969)

The trunk she was born in turned out to be a Pandora's boxful of bad vibes for Judy, a heartbreak kid if Hollywood ever had one. She was magical in person, dynamite on film from the very beginning when she sang "Dear Mr. Gable" and brought down the house. Few performers experienced such intense highs and lows as Garland, who was exploited by her mother, her husbands, movie moguls, directors, managers. Records and movies are her monuments: *The Wizard of Oz,*

Meet Me in St. Louis, A Star Is Born, name your favorite. Sometimes, in later comeback years, the voice cracked or her strength faltered, but everybody knew the troubles she'd seen, and (unless they couldn't stand her) loved Judy even more for them. That incredible spontaneous talent nearly always burst through when she'd launch into her repertoire of golden oldies sung—a dumbstruck critic once wrote—"as if she were inventing them on the spot." When the houselights went up, the rest of her life often looked to her like a yellow brick road going nowhere.

PRIMARY SOURCES: *Judy Garland: A Biography,* by Anne Edwards (Simon and Schuster, 1974); *Judy,* by Gerold Frank (Harper & Row, 1975); *Little Girl Lost: The Life and Hard Times of Judy Garland,* by Al DiOrio, Jr. (Arlington, 1973).

★*COOPER, JACKIE* Child star who grew up with Judy. They enjoyed kissing games, puppy love in their teens, but went the distance one memorable night as adults. (See also COOPER listing.)

★*DEANS, MICKEY* Judy's fifth and last husband, twelve years her junior. Deans was manager of the popular 1960s New York discotheque Arthur. They'd meet there and talk through the night, then shop for groceries at five in the morning. "Judy, as tiny as she was, would sit in the basket as Deans pushed her around the all-night market." They decided it would make sense to marry; the ceremony took place in London on March 15, 1969. "Wearing a blue chiffon dress, too short and too sheer . . . she was a very unusual-looking bride." At the time, Judy's health was deteriorating rapidly, but she went on yet another concert tour—to Scandinavia. It was on June 22, just after her 47th birthday, that Judy died in the London townhouse she shared with Deans. He found her "in a sitting position, her head collapsed onto her breast, like a small brown sparrow with a broken neck."

★*FINKLEHOFFE, FREDDIE* New York scriptwriter, wit, and horseplayer. His gambling instinct drove him to propose to Judy: "I'm strictly a long shot in marriage, right?" Judy scratched Freddie, but came in on the money

Ingrid Bergman and Roberto Rossellini: All she could say in Italian was *ti amo*. *(Wide World Photos)*

Tallulah Bankhead and almost-husband, Count Anthony de Bosdari: She called off the wedding and took off the necklace. *(Wide World Photos)*

Elizabeth Ashley and George Peppard: George should have phoned first. (See Ashley re Nardini.) From *The Carpetbaggers*, Avco-Embassy, Joseph Levine, A Paramount Release. *(Cinemabilia)*

Warren Beatty with Joan Collins and Princess Margaret: Old flames with a possible royal flush. (See listings for all.) *(Wide World Photos)*

Warren Beatty with Julie Christie *(Columbia Pictures)*

Marlon Brando and France Nuyen: Expecting? Was she or Movita the mother of Miko? *(Wide World Photos)*

Above: Montgomery Clift and Elizabeth Taylor: One of her four-letter words was *love.* From *A Place in the Sun. (Cinemabilia) Right:* Elizabeth Taylor and John Warner: After *The Little Foxes,* pffft. *(Wide World Photos)*

Richard Burton and Genevieve Bujold: They had fun filming while Liz fumed. *(Universal Pictures)*

Richard Burton and Sophia Loren: She said all they played was Scrabble. *(Wide World Photos)*

Richard Burton and Elizabeth Taylor: The movie was *Boom!*, the marriage was bust. *(Universal Pictures)*

Above: Richard Burton and Elizabeth Taylor: Heigh-ho the glamorous life. *(Wide World Photos) Below:* "What do the papers say about us now?" *(Wide World Photos)*

Patricia Neal and Gary Cooper: Love sprang in *The Fountainhead. (Cinemabilia)*

Top above: Clara Bow and Gary Cooper: The "It" Girl lured him off his horse. From *Children of Divorce,* 1927. *(Cinemabilia) Above:* Marlene Dietrich and Gary Cooper: Making it in *Morocco. (Cinemabilia)*

Joan Collins and Anthony Newley: She got tired of musical beds. From *Can Hieronymous Merkin Ever Forget Mercy Humpe and Find True Happiness? (Universal Pictures)*

Bette Davis and William Wyler: Unlucky in love, with her second Oscar (for *Jezebel*) as consolation. *(Cinemabilia)*

Bette Davis and Gary Merrill (at piano): Maritally, Gary was her swan song. *(Davis collection)*

Marlene Dietrich and Jean Gabin: Fit to fiddle, and she loved his loins. *(Wide World Photos)*

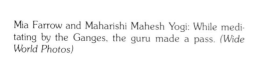

Mia Farrow and Maharishi Mahesh Yogi: While meditating by the Ganges, the guru made a pass. *(Wide World Photos)*

Left: Eddie Fisher and Debbie Reynolds, wife #1. *Right:* Eddie Fisher and Terri Richard, wife #4. *(Wide World Photos)*

Left: Errol Flynn and Olivia DeHavilland: One leading lady he never knew how to woo. *(Cinemabilia) Above:* Errol Flynn and Beverly Aadland: As time flew, the girls grew younger. *(Wide World Photos)*

Clark Gable and Carole Lombard: Bored with bird-watching, they did it twice in the blind. *(Wide World Photos)*

Greta Garbo and George Schlee: Shielding Swedish chic. *(Wide World Photos)*

Above: Judy Garland and David Rose, husband #1. *(Wide World Photos) Right:* Judy Garland and Mickey Deans, last husband *(Wide World Photos).* From husband #1 to #5, getting happy always came hard.

Ava Gardner, Lana Turner, and Fernando Lamas: Glamour galore—and only Sinatra knows for sure. *(Wide World Photos)*

Stewart Granger and Jean Simmons wedding (with Michael Wilding): After the wedding, to bed with a book. *(Wide World Photos)*

Stewart Granger and Deborah Kerr: Long before *King Solomon's Mines*, the lady made the first move. From MGM's *King Solomon's Mines*. *(Cinemabilia)*

Jack Nicholson and Michelle Phillips: Once she met Warren, Jack became the boy next door. *(Wide World Photos)*

Cary Grant and Sophia Loren: Close, but slightly out of step in the clinches. *(Wide World Photos)*

Jack Nicholson and Candice Bergen: The movie was called *Carnal Knowledge*. *(Cinemabilia)*

with his friend Sid Luft. At least for a time.

★*FISHER, EDDIE*   They'd met before. Both were performing in Tahoe in 1962, after he and Elizabeth Taylor had parted. He spent a night with her in Frank Sinatra's bungalow after she'd passed out in the ladies' room on their first real date. "Here's the lady I had secretly been in love with for years." She had so much love to give, Eddie recalls, and so many people loved her. "But for Judy that was never enough." (See also FISHER listing.)

★*FORD, GLENN*   Judy was 12 and still singing with the Gumm sisters; Glenn was 18 and stage manager at the Wilshire Theater in Santa Monica. "From then on he was her slave." And she his. However, it would be many years later, in her 40s (in 1963, to be exact), before they'd enter into an adult affair. She was then riding high not only in romance—hinting that she and Ford might marry—but also in her new career on television. But Judy's series and her interlude with Ford ended at roughly the same time.

★*GREEN, TOM*   A publicity man for the Luft group, and briefly betrothed to Judy. "This is the first time I've known what real happiness is," she proclaimed. When she needed to pay medical bills she asked Tom to pawn some rings for her, but three weeks later had him arrested for stealing the jewelry. The charges were dropped. So was Green.

★*HERRON, MARK*   An actor in his late 20s when first involved with Judy in 1964. The three Garland biographies give conflicting reports of her marriage to Herron. Edwards says that in 1964 they went through a mock ceremony in Hong Kong (in Chinese, yet), which could not have been legal because Judy was still legally Mrs. Luft. The real wedding did take place in Las Vegas in November 1965, and the newlyweds moved to London, hoping to find happiness. Judy found only that Mark was traveling a lot. "He conducted our relationship from a moving telephone booth." They were separated after six months.

★*LUFT, SID*   Judy claimed that with Sid, it was love at first sight. A former William Morris agent, Luft took charge of Judy's life at about the time she was making her first "comeback"—at age 28—knocking 'em dead at the London Palladium. "I love Judy," Luft proclaimed; "I want to protect her from the trauma she once knew." And she claimed to be *desperately* in love, too, plunging into her third marriage (on June 11, 1952) with a rare abandon. Shortly after the birth of Lorna, in December of that year, Judy's mother died—precipitating one of the star's worst and longest breakdowns. Luft soon engineered another "stunning comeback" for his wife, the film *A Star Is Born*. "By that time Judy was irrevocably rehooked on pills, and her love for Luft had turned to . . . a grave sense of betrayal and rejection." Judy gave birth to her third and last child, Joey, the same night she *didn't* win the Oscar she expected for *A Star is Born*. In 1960 she got a new manager and left Luft, who—*after* their divorce—persuaded Judy to sign a contract that made her mere "chattel" to a group of investors she did not even know. Author Edwards charges that Judy was shamelessly exploited by Luft and his partners in the last months of her life.

★*MANKIEWICZ, JOE*   Writer-producer-director. With Joe's wife in a psychiatric clinic, divorce would have been unseemly—if he had indeed *wanted* a divorce and *intended* to marry Judy. Which is doubtful. Judy seemed to be quite in love with him—for a time, at least—and took his advice in seeking psychiatric help of her own. When she told him she thought she might marry Minnelli instead, Judy recalled that Mankiewicz reacted with "shock—and a certain relief."

★*MINNELLI, VINCENT*   Director, mostly of musicals; worked with Judy on *Meet Me in St. Louis*. "She trusted this man with the big eyes and the promise of soul buried there." Later she was to suspect he was a "company man" watching over her for L.B. Mayer—and her mother. They were wed on June 15, 1945; daughter Liza was born in March the next year. Judy's marriage and her finances and her health all went to hell at approximately the same time, and in July 1947, Louella Parsons reported: "Judy Garland is a very sick girl and has suffered a complete nervous collapse." Her confinement in a sanitarium included shock treatments to help cure her addiction to pills.

★*POWER, TYRONE* Judy was 17 and had just won an Oscar as the "best juvenile performer" of 1939; Tyrone was young and beautiful, one of the fastest-rising stars in Hollywood. L.B. Mayer sent word out that no public mention was to be made of the Power-Garland liaison, "and Louella obeyed." The biographers who write of Garland and Power have different versions of how serious the affair became. Hers indicate it was a "brief romantic interlude"; his say it was a great love affair which caved in under pressure brought by MGM—and the trauma of an abortion when Judy became pregnant. Two biographers assert the couple had nevertheless vowed to marry when Power returned from the Marine Corps. Instead, he came home and began dating Lana Turner. "It was the ultimate blow to Judy's ego." (See also POWER listing.)

★*ROSE, DAVID* The handsome 30-year-old bandleader came into Judy's life about the same time she was seeing Tyrone Power. Rose gave Judy an engagement diamond for her 18th birthday—even though he was not yet divorced from Martha Raye. L.B. Mayer had fits. David and Judy promised to wait a year before they eloped. And they did, then married in Las Vegas on July 26, 1941. She soon became pregnant by Rose, a condition not welcomed by her husband, her mother, or Mayer at MGM. The studio physician performed an abortion; press reports had it that Judy suffered a "tonsil flare-up." Judy won her divorce from David Rose in February 1943.

★*SINATRA, FRANK* At one point, après Minnelli, before Luft, Judy was convinced she was mad for Frankie. But then he stood her up at an intimate dinner for two, and their fling was flung. (See also SINATRA listing.)

MISCELLANY

★*BAILY, EDWARD, II* He was a young man on the edge of despair when he saw his first Judy Garland concert at New York's Palace Theater in 1967. After that, he never missed a performance, traveling to wherever she was, "pledging himself to remain close to her, to cheer and protect her." In one year's time, adoring fan Baily sent Garland $100,000 worth of roses.

★*KELLY, GENE* He gave Judy a shoulder to cry on about her marriage to David Rose. Kelly's own union with Betsy Blair was still sound, and he gave Judy no indication he could offer her more than friendship, though she continued to fantasize he might. She insisted Kelly co-star with her in *For Me and My Gal*, her first musical away from Rooney.

★*MAYER, LOUIS B.* MGM's studio head had a penchant for young girls, and gossip linked Mayer with many of the very young players at MGM. "It must always remain in the area of speculation whether or not Mayer's intentions toward Judy were honorable and paternal, or either." The talk about them persisted for years, beginning when she was not yet 15. And his "godlike influence" over her lasted for the seventeen years in which she "worked, slept, ate, appeared in public, dated, married and divorced at his command."

★*ROONEY, MICKEY* They were co-stars in any number of MGM musicals, fellow students at the MGM school—where they swapped mash notes, "such bright and original things as 'I love you,'" recalls Rooney. Their love of fun was real, their "love affair" was not. When asked why he never married Judy he said, "I couldn't, it would have been like marrying my sister."

★*SHAW, ARTIE* Seventeen-year-old Judy had a terrific crush on the twice-married, twice-divorced bandleader. They would have secret dates, using Jackie Cooper as a "beard." (See also COOPER and SHAW listings.)

GRABLE, BETTY
(1916–1973)

She was *the* pin-up girl during World War II, her shape and million-dollar legs and over-the-shoulder smile so familiar that GIs in basic were taught the grid system of map-reading with the famous Grable poster under those crisscross lines of north-south-east-west coordinates. A kind of ultimate chorus girl in flashy Fox musicals from *Down Argentine Way* (1940) to *Sweet Rosie O'Grady* (1943) and *The Dolly Sisters* (1946), in 1945 Betty was the highest-paid star in Hollywood, two years later the highest-paid woman in the U.S.A., at $325,000 per annum. She married big-band maestro Harry James during the golden years, and had two children by him during their two hit-and-run decades together. She is called a "reluctant" movie queen in her bio because it was mother Lillian, not Grable, who wanted fame and fortune so much. On her own, Betty was just an easygoing girl who loved to gamble and swap ribald jokes. By 1953, she was co-starring with Marilyn Monroe in *How to Marry a Millionaire*, and it became clear that a new Big Blonde had taken over. She performed *Hello, Dolly* on tour when there were no more movie roles, and finally met the love of her life, a man twenty-seven years her junior—a happy ending that never would have worked for a Betty Grable musical.

PRIMARY SOURCE: *Betty Grable: The Reluctant Movie Queen*, by Doug Warren (St. Martin's, 1981).

★*COOGAN, JACKIE* The child star of the 1920s. Earned millions before coming of age and fully expected to claim his fortune at 29. (He didn't, and the suit against his mother resulted in the Coogan Law, guaranteeing that child actors—and *not* their parents—were entitled to most of their earnings.) When young Jackie met young Betty, both were living high. She threw a famous costume party, for example, attended by *tout* Hollywood, at which all the guests came dressed as babies. Coogan

and Grable were the media darlings of 1937, the year they married, the first time for both. Betty's career was blazing, his was waning, so they lived off her earnings while he battled his mother in court. Grable already had another romantic interest (see Shaw, below) when she won her divorce from Coogan in November 1939.

★*DAILEY, DAN* Song-and-dance man, teamed with Grable in four '40s musicals. They clicked—onscreen and off. Stories persisted that Harry James walked into Betty's dressing room to catch Betty and Dan in the act. Fisticuffs ensued. "All rumor," notes her biographer. "The only certainty is that Betty *somehow* came up with a black eye." Dailey's mounting problems included a troubled marriage and possible public disclosure of his transvestism—the compulsion to dress in women's clothing. (Once at the Daileys', a drunk comedian headed for the bathroom but literally stumbled into a closet, pulling Mrs. Dailey's dresses on top of him. When discovered by Dan, the comedian said, "Well, Dan . . . I found *your* closet, now can I see Gwen's?") Dailey and Grable remained close friends for life.

★*JAMES, HARRY* Popular big-band leader and trumpet player. Betty's second (and last) husband, father of her two daughters, Victoria (b. 1944) and Jessica (b. 1947). They met while appearing in *Springtime in the Rockies*, and at first both denied rumors of romance because Harry still had a Mrs. She was persuaded to get a Mexican divorce and on July 5, 1943, Betty married Harry in Las Vegas. When he wasn't on the road with the band (and with his dozens of other women, to her chagrin), Betty and Harry spent a lot of time at the racetrack. Horse owners themselves, they gambled away a considerable fortune. Grable held the marriage together until late 1965.

★*RAFT, GEORGE* Late in life, Raft insisted that Betty Grable was the only woman he ever loved. To Betty, "The velvet-voiced gangster type was excitement personified." Their affair was as well known as the fact that Raft's devoutly Catholic wife would never, ever grant him a divorce. The couple's mutual frustration caused friction and fights. When Betty started seeing Harry James, Raft was so jealous he had her followed. Throughout their long relationship, Raft lavished gifts upon Grable—jewels, furs, at least one racehorse. Some say his investment never paid off: "There were kisses, hugs, laughter and good times—but sex? Maybe not." Aw, come on.

★*REMICK, BOB*   He was a "gypsy" dancer in the road company of *Hello, Dolly!* in which Betty toured in the mid-'60s. He was 22; she was 49—and Remick reportedly accepted the age difference more readily than she. Said Betty: "Can you imagine me at *my* age, and I've got a twenty-three-year-old trick?" Blond, handsome, devoted Remick was considerably more than that; he lived with Betty, and cared for her, the last seven years of her life.

★*SHAW, ARTIE*   On the rebound from Coogan, Betty fell hard for the marriage-minded bandleader. Because he was in New York, she took a role in Ethel Merman's *Du Barry Was a Lady*, on Broadway, and became "overnight . . . the toast of the town." Artie and Betty lived it up all over New York that fall of 1939. Came New Year's Eve, he said he had a gig on the West Coast; on January 2, Grable read in the newspapers that Shaw and Lana Turner had eloped to Las Vegas. (See also TURNER and SHAW listings.)

MISCELLANY

★*ARNAZ, DESI* Performing on Broadway in *Too Many Girls* while Grable was in *Du Barry*. She'd sometimes join his table at Dinty Moore's. "It was impossible to sit next to Betty and not want to know her a little better." A "little better" was as far as Bobalu got.

★*CALHOUN, RORY* Betty made a couple of films with Rory, and co-starred with him in a short-lived London musical, *Belle Starr*, by Steve Allen. On her return to New York, Betty was greeted by reporters informing her that Rory's wife, Lita Baron, had filed for divorce listing Grable as one of the seventy-eight women with whom Rory had committed adultery. Betty's reaction: "Rory *Calhoun?*"

★*LEVITT, MICHAEL*   Betty's greatest, certainly her closest lifelong fan. He'd been corresponding with Grable for years. When *Hello, Dolly!* came to his hometown, Chicago, she looked him up. He remained with her through thick and thin, and was at her bedside when she died. Once, when she'd been drinking too much, Betty puckered up for a kiss-kiss and nastily bit through Levitt's upper lip. He still has the scar.

★*MATURE, VICTOR*   Caused a lot of talk when they spent four days together aboard a coast-to-coast train. And later, around New York. Betty introduced him to all her friends, and he landed a lead in the musical *Lady in the Dark*, with Gertrude Lawrence, thereby reviving a sluggish career. They were probably just friends, but Vic was grateful.

★*PRICE, CHARLES*   He was a 14-year-old drummer in Ted Fio Rito's band, Betty was the 16-year-old singer. When she became "enamored," her mama put a stop to it.

★*THOMPASON, ALEX* New York playboy—"he owned, oh, Lord, *everything*"—whom Betty dated during the *Du Barry* days.

GRANGER, STEWART
(b. 1913)

He's as close as the British Commonwealth ever came to providing a successor to Errol Flynn. His real name was James Stewart, which had to be changed for obvious reasons. He didn't quite make it to superstardom despite his good looks and a lot of costumed swashbucklers in the vein of *Scaramouche* (1952) or such memorable adventure-dramas as *King Solomon's Mines* (1950). Long married to Jean Simmons, Granger's pretty-boy air may account for the rumor—once published in a book by Hedda Hopper—that he and Michael Wilding were a romantic "item." (Wilding sued for libel and settled out of court for an apology and an undisclosed sum from Hedda.) *Au contraire,* Granger's rollicking autobio discloses that he and Wilding were close buddies and avid men-about-town, on the make in many a town. Both chose acting careers, Granger discloses, "for the fun, the money and the birds . . . later, we were destined to marry two of the most beautiful girls in the world." Wilding's beauty, of course, was Elizabeth Taylor.

PRIMARY SOURCE: *Sparks Fly Upward*, by Stewart Granger (Granada, London, 1981).

★*FRENCH FRIEND* Actually a friend of Granger's first wife, Elspeth. Her visit to his hotel room related to a personal matter, she said. When he asked what it was, "She calmly put down her glass, started untying my dressing gown and told me she wanted to make love to me. . . . I was raped." Later, experiencing ominous physical sensations, Granger discovered he had contracted a virulent dose of gonorrhea. "Dear God," he thought, "what kind of friends does Elspeth have?" His wife had to be told, and at first she found the situation hilariously funny. On second thought, suddenly aware that she herself might be infected, she hissed, *Disgusting!* To think that you could give your wife the *clap!* Stewart hissed back: "I didn't. *Your French friend did.*"

★*JOSETTE* French prostitute. Young Granger went to Paris to play rugby and encountered some foreplay as well. At the first *boite de nuit* he entered, a "dishy" lady smiled up at him, soon enticed him to a room in La Paradis Hotel. Granger had to admit to "Josette" that he was still a virgin. "With shrieks of delight she started ripping off my clothes. She did it with humor and tenderness and I shall always be grateful to her. "The next day Granger played excellent rugby, and that night his initiation with Josette continued. She cried when they parted, Granger recalls, which led him to think he hadn't been bad. "In fact, I don't think I was *ever* as good again in my life."

★*KERR, DEBORAH* The lady made the first move. They were returning home from a film premiere in a chauffeured limo when Deborah suddenly threw her arms around Granger and gave him a big kiss, then con-

fessed she'd been dying to do that all evening. " 'Come over here,' she said. And I was lost. I'd never felt anything like this in my life." In the "exhilarating months" that followed, both tried to be discreet. But when Vivien Leigh told him that everybody—except possibly his wife—knew about the affair, he decided to confess to Elspeth (again) and moved out. But Deborah and Jim (James Stewart is his real name) discovered they could not remain insensitive to the gossip, the feeling of guilt. He went back to Elspeth. The former lovers later co-starred in *King Solomon's Mines*.

★*LAMARR, HEDY* With his buddy Michael Wilding, Granger attended a party in Hedy's hotel suite in Paris, and she invited him to tarry after the others left. Alone with the glamorous star, Granger didn't know quite what was expected. Lamarr stared at him in astonished outrage: "My God. I don't believe you don't want to! Kings want to. Heads of studios want to. Presidents want to. Why don't *you* want to?" Granger protested that he *did* want to. She advised him to hurry, then, she had a hairdresser's appointment. He undressed and approached her naked body on the bed. It all could have turned out okay—if Hedy had only stopped ordering him around. "I was starting to become aroused when she instructed, *Now don't come too fast, will you?* That was it." Granger beat a hasty retreat, and lived to regret it, says he: "I mean—*Hedy Lamarr!*" (See also LAMARR listing.)

★*MARCH, ELSPETH* Actress in the Birmingham Repertory Group when Granger became the new leading man. He had a letter of introduction from another actress, advising Elspeth that the bearer was "sexy as hell." "With that Elspeth gave me a cool look. . . . Three years later we were married." They tried desperately to have a child, and with Elspeth finally pregnant, but confined to her bed, Granger began to feel "stifled." "As a male chauvinist pig, naturally I thought *she* should be fulfilled by the very fact she had *me*." The couple had a son Jamie, and daughter Lindsay; but their domestic situation grew worse. At the time in England, adultery was the only acceptable legal grounds for divorce. So Granger and a female chum arranged to be "caught" in bed by Elspeth's hired photographer, then asked the shutterbug to join them for lunch—but he was on his way to do another couple. Divorce granted.

★*MINOUCHE* Famous French actress who liked to be called that by her intimates, of which she had many . . . said to include Errol Flynn, Baby Pignatari, Rubirosa, Aly Khan. Unnerved by such stalwart competition in the sack, Granger took three Benzedrines, "having heard from a fighter pilot that these keep you awake and up to the mark." Later in his flat, Granger reports, "even Minouche was staggered as I made my assault. . . . I pounded away all night, Minouche finally pleading with me to stop." He slept for three days after she left.

★*SIMMONS, JEAN* Granger was 34 and divorced, Simmons 18 and the most sought-after young actress in England when their "flirtation" began. They made a film together *(Adam and Evelyn)* and tried to be discreet about their private Eden. As Granger notes, Jean was the darling of the press, and "I could imagine their reaction to her first love being old swashbuckling Granger." Their engagement was announced on a visit to Hollywood, and it was Cary Grant who suggested his buddy Howard Hughes might be able to arrange a romantic private wedding for the couple. Suddenly they were being whisked to Tucson in Hughes's private plane, and Michael Wilding was whisked in from New York to be their best man. The ceremony was conducted by a justice of the peace in the home of Hughes's lawyer; Jean giggled, got hysterical, and choked on her champagne. That night Stewart climbed into bed with a book . . . and she fell asleep. "That was a big mistake. . . . I would live to regret it." It was not the wedding of Jean's dreams. Another regret turned out to be the newlyweds' involvement with Howard Hughes—who bought up Simmons's contract and wouldn't let her work for anyone else (thus she lost *Roman Holiday* to Audrey Hepburn). Convinced that "the S.O.B.

was propositioning her," Granger got drunk one night and even planned how to murder the billionaire. Instead, they settled their differences through legal action. So did the Grangers, pulled apart by acting assignments, frequent separations, economics, incompatibility. They were married ten years, had a daughter, Tracy. After their 1960 divorce, Granger left his Southern California ranch and returned to England. Jean subsequently married director Richard Brooks. That didn't work, either.

★*VITTORIA* An exquisite Spanish girl Granger met in Spain at the Fiesta of the Bulls in Pamplona. She took charge of his days and his nights, and even began discussing marriage, though he actually preferred her mother. When he left she promised to wait for him. He learned later that Vittoria *had* waited, until she heard the news of his marriage to Jean Simmons.

MISCELLANY

★*DUKE, DORIS* During a summer when Granger and Mike Wilding were pretending to be international playboys on the French Riviera, they occasionally took Doris to dinner and "flirted with her outrageously. . . . We realized that she was rather naive and could be swept off her feet quite easily."

★*GARDNER, AVA* While on location in Pakistan for *Bhowani Junction*, Stew and Ava were naturally seeing a lot of each other. But Granger always retired alone to his bachelor quarters. About 2:00 A.M. one night Ava burst into his room and demanded to know why he didn't find her attractive. "Ava, you're probably the most attractive woman in the world, but I'm married . . . to Jean." "Oh, fuck Jean," Ava answered. "I'd love to, darling," Granger retorted—and they both started to laugh. "Here I was with the sheets pulled up to my chin like a frightened virgin and here was Ava looking ravishing." She teased him a lot about being a faithful husband. (See also GARDNER listing.)

★*KENDALL, HENRY* Older English film star during Granger's early days at Margate Studios. He invited the young man on a seaside holiday, all expenses paid, with Granger acting as his chauffeur. Granger jumped at the chance, and as they drove along, "Suddenly I felt his hand on my thigh. . . . Why hadn't I realized? Whoever got a job like this for nothing?" When Granger confessed he was "not one of those," Kendall called him a prick. Granger offered to drive him back to London, but Kendall said, oh, well, they might as well enjoy the holiday. "He never referred to the subject again, bless him."

★*MANNIX, TONI* A very luscious lady of a certain age, and wife of an MGM executive. She was Granger's "date" at a dinner in a Polynesian restaurant. They were knocking back the rum punches when Stewart noticed the lady groping his fly. "I mean, there's a time and place for everything, but while eating with chopsticks was not the time." Later that night Mrs. Mannix staggered into his room, muttering, "Let's take up where we left off." When Granger feigned innocence, she snarled, "What's the matter kid, can't you get it up?" "No, madame, not with you," he countered. "Fucking pansy," she shouted—and flounced out.

★*OBERON, MERLE* "One of the most beautiful ladies" Granger ever encountered, "with the most attractive voice. . . . I realized that conversation can be as important in a relationship as sex." Merle rebuffed Granger's passes, but offered to introduce him to a fetching friend.

GRANT, CARY
(b. 1904)

Breathes there a man with soul so dead that he has never secretly yearned to be Cary Grant? Probably not. His cleft chin, his surprised look, his perpetual bounce and slightly goofy charm are all part of the secret formula that makes him one of the best movie actors of all time. Yet, Grant never took home an Oscar—until 1970, when a special prize was given him "for just being Cary Grant." He started out as Archie Leach from Bristol, England; running away with an acrobatic troupe at 16, he got into vaudeville, and by 1930 became one of the most promising leading men on Broadway. On film the effortless art he brings to *I'm No Angel* (1933) with Mae West works just as well (let's face it, better) with Katharine Hepburn in *Bringing Up Baby* (1937) and *The Philadelphia Story* (1940). Grant's volatile chemistry with the women he married, on the other hand, has been much less successful, despite his frequent attempts to settle down—which usually end with settling up, coasting a while, starting over. It may be a thought for the day that life is seldom like a Cary Grant movie, even for Cary Grant. However, he seems to be quite happy, thank you, with his current wife, the former Barbara Harris.

PRIMARY SOURCES: *Cary Grant: An Unauthorized Biography,* by Albert Govoni (Regnery, 1971); *The Lives and Loves of Cary Grant,* by Lee Guthrie (Drake, 1977).

★*BROOKS, PHYLLIS* She was Grant's long-running romance between wives Cherrill and Hutton. A budding but soon wilting actress; their affair intrigued film-colony gossips for a couple of years.

★*CANNON, DYAN* She might have been one of the few women alive in mid-twentieth-century America who didn't consider Cary Grant Mr. Wonderful. Her image of perfection, "my dream man," was Lee J. Cobb. After a five-year courtship, Dyan came to her senses and said, "I do." That was July 22, 1965. She was 27, Grant 61. When asked if they really intended to have children, as announced, Grant replied with a twinkle: "A man can do anything he sets out to do—if he applies himself diligently." The couple's daughter Jennifer, Cary Grant's only offspring, arrived prematurely in February 1966. About two years later Dyan's divorce suit cited Cary's "cruel and inhuman treatment," charging that he was "an apostle of LSD," had "yelling and screaming fits" and physically abused her. Friends reported that the dissolution of his fourth marriage was the "absolute nadir of Cary Grant's life." He has since rallied, has a new wife (Barbara Harris), "and basks in the attentions of his adoring, quite beautiful teenage daughter, Jennifer."

★*CHERRILL, VIRGINIA* Chicagoan Virginia married at 18, divorced at 20, was promptly "discovered" by Charlie Chaplin—to play the blind girl in his *City Lights*. She next made news with her scheduled wedding to New York socialite William Rhinelander Stewart aboard the Astors' yacht. The yacht put out to sea, but returned to port with the ceremony called off and the engagement kaput. Footloose in Hollywood again, Virginia went to a party at the bachelor pad Cary Grant shared with Randolph Scott. Grant remembers that the fog that night made her hair curl. "I fell in love with her the minute she walked in." They were married in February 1934, in London. Grant was 30 years old when he first took a wife, roughly the same age when the wife took a powder. By summer there were rumors of a rift; in September Virginia walked out. The courtship lasted longer than the marriage.

★*DRAKE, BETSY* Tall, aristocratic actress, granddaughter of the founder of Chicago's Drake Hotel. From their first shipboard lunch —aboard the *Queen Mary* sailing from England to the U.S. in late 1947—Cary was fascinated by Betsy. She took his advice and moved to Hollywood, landing her first film role opposite Grant in *Every Girl Should be Married*. On Christmas Day 1949, he married her, flying to Arizona for a simple wedding ceremony with Grant's best friend Howard Hughes as best man. Newlywed Betsy relished the fact that Cary always woke up in fine humor, "bounding out of bed and dancing around the room. . . . the sight of Cary doing a jig clad only in his pajama top left Betsy helpless with laughter." Her acting career abandoned, Betsy delved into things occult—experimenting with hypnotism and using her powers to help Grant give up cigarettes. Grant's own self-help search led him into "therapy" with LSD, which, he says, made him feel born again, and the attendant revelations ultimately led him to give up Betsy. They were separated in 1958, did not divorce until 1962.

★*HUTTON, BARBARA* She was either the first or second richest girl in the world (vying for the title with Doris Duke) and already had two titled husbands behind her when she met movie star Grant in 1940. Their frequent dates became "delicious grist for the Hollywood gossip mill," but Grant saw to it that the wedding itself was a private, unheralded affair. In early July 1942, he legally changed his name to Cary Grant (from Archie Leach), became a U.S. citizen, and drove up to Lake Arrowhead, Calif., to take Barbara as his bride. (It was little known or noted that gallant Cary signed a prenuptial agreement waiving all rights to Hutton's vast fortune.) Three years later Barbara testified at the divorce hearing that Cary didn't like her friends and she didn't like his. Incompatibility. Divorce granted, but their relationship would be long and friendly. (See also HUTTON listing.)

★*LOREN, SOPHIA* The two biographies of Cary Grant make light of his romance with La Loren. *Her* autobiography, however, reveals that their love affair was serious enough to almost divert her from marrying the love-of-her-life Carlo Ponti. Sophia fails to mention that while she and Cary were romancing on the plains of Spain (co-starring in *The Pride and the Passion*), he was still very much married to Betsy Drake—who for reasons of her own, left Spain for the U.S., via the S.S. *Andrea Doria* on its ill-fated voyage in July 1956. When the *Doria* went down in the Atlantic off Nantucket Island, Betsy was rescued and dispatched a cable to Grant assuring him she was okay. When the cable reached him thirty-six hours later, Grant was greatly puzzled, unaware the ship had sunk and just then living in a world of his own with Sophia. (See also LOREN listing.)

★*NOVAK, KIM* Cary led Kim through "an intense whirl at the Cannes Film Festival of 1959. . . . They were seen and photographed *everywhere*." Well, nearly.

★*OTASEVIC, LUBA* Yugoslav women's

basketball star who once worked as a double for Sophia Loren. And looked a great deal like the Italian star. That was almost good enough.

★*ROGERS, GINGER* After Grant's divorce from Virginia Cherrill, he and Ginger had a brief but "bona fide" romance.

MISCELLANY

★*BERGMAN, INGRID* Their teaming in *Notorious* marked the beginning of one of Grant's "most cherished friendships." When Ingrid left Rossellini (causing almost as much of a brouhaha as when she married him), Grant was the good friend who met her at the London airport and stood by her side to face a barrage of hostile reporters.

★*BOURON, CYNTHIA* A former employee of 20th Century–Fox, who, in 1970, filed a paternity suit against Grant, naming him the father of her seven-week-old daughter. In Grant's countersuit, Ms. Bouron failed to bring her baby in for a decisive blood test. Case dismissed.

★*BRIAN, MARY* Slow-fading screen charmer, big in the '20s, whom Cary dated in the '30s.

★*KINKAID, GLADYS* A dancer, and Cary's first crush. He was 18, and so smitten he bought the object of his affections a costly coat-and-scarf set for Christmas. She was grateful but perplexed; until then, Archie Leach had been too shy to even speak to her. And after Christmas, well, she moved on.

★*MACDONALD, JEANETTE* The star soprano of *Boom-Boom* on Broadway, in which Grant had his first featured role. One critic noted, "Archie Leach and Jeanette MacDonald proved to be a star-spangled combination," though Jeanette was destined to wind up opposite Nelson Eddy. She and Cary took their first screen tests together, and off she went to Hollywood. He didn't, not yet. Jeanette would always be one of his dearest friends.

★*WEST, MAE* In Hollywood to make her first movie and alighting from her limo on the studio lot, Mae saw this *sensational-looking* young man. "Whooo is *that?*" West whistled softly. They told her his name was Cary Grant and he was now making *Butterfly* with Sylvia Sidney. Replied Mae: "I don't care if he's making Little Nell . . . if he can talk, I'll take him." And she got him—as her leading man in *She Done Him Wrong*, the comedy smash of 1932. Few can forget her come-on line to Grant in that film: "Hello there . . . warm, dark and handsome." Both mum as to whether he went up to see her sometimes. (See also WEST listing.)

★*WRAY, FAY* King Kong's true love was an old friend of Grant's from his stage days in New York. She helped him pick his movie name—choosing Cary from a character in a play they'd done together. An executive at Paramount added the Grant. Thus, the birth of a legend-in-his-own-time.

HARLOW, JEAN
(1911–1937)

There had never been anyone quite like her when Harlow took Hollywood in 1930, as an English tart in *Hell's Angels*. Betty Grable and Marilyn Monroe became *the* blondes of the '40s and '50s, but they were something else—sexy as well as sweetly vulnerable. Harlow was pure '30s, the kind of dame who called her guy a "big lug." She talked tough, she walked tough, she picked 'em up and dropped 'em like hot potatoes, according to her mood, and in that she seemed an extremely modern, new kind of sex symbol who knew how to handle herself, buster, in a man's world. In her life offscreen, Jean was considerably less secure, and made some wrong choices, which led to disaster on at least one occasion. When she died at 26, of uremic poisoning, rumors persisted that she had had an abortion, and there was even mad speculation that the Platinum Blonde had been poisoned by the stuff she used on her hair. In the mid-'60s, two filmed biographies (Carroll Baker as *Harlow*, then an Electrovision quickie starring Carol Lynley) portrayed her crudely as a short-circuited sex machine with no moving parts.

PRIMARY SOURCE: *Harlow: An Intimate Biography*, by Irving Shulman (Geis/Random House, 1964).

★*BERN, PAUL* At 42, he was Irving Thalberg's top aide at MGM, "a slight, balding man who resembled a frightened waiter." No one would have picked Bern as a likely consort for Hollywood's 21-year-old blond bombshell. Harlow said she took an immediate liking to him because he talked to her about books and music and "didn't look at my knockers." They were married on July 2, 1932. That night Jean phoned her agent Arthur Landau urging him to come rescue her. Landau found Harlow's back covered with bloody welts and teeth marks on her stomach and inner thighs. And Jean shouting, "That little bastard's a maniac, a rotten goddamned sex fiend!" Bern lay in a drunken stupor, naked. "Paul Bern had the sack and penis of an infant boy. Potbellied, hairless . . . Paul had hips that were finely rounded, proportioned for a woman." Bern's pitiful explanation to Landau: "Every man I know gets an erection . . . just by talking about her . . . didn't I have the right to think Jean could help me at least that much?" Bern suffered from chronic impotency (he denied being a homosexual, as often rumored), and when his sex-goddess wife failed to cure his problem, he grew to hate her. One night, just two months after their wedding, Paul strapped a large flesh-colored dildo to his body and danced wildly around the room—it was so sick, Jean began to laugh until they both collapsed in tears. That night Bern shot himself in the head, setting off a historic Hollywood scandal. His brief suicide note to Jean expressed "abject humiliation" and closed with "you understand that last night was only a comedy." The beating he had given Jean probably damaged her kidneys and contributed to her death by uremic poisoning five years later.

★*McGREW, CHARLES* Jean was still in boarding school, only 16 in March 1927, when she eloped with McGrew, a Chicago boy. She was expelled from school, Charles retrieved by his parents, and the marriage annulled. Distraught over McGrew's attempt to make love to her on their wedding night, Jean told her mother, "Chuck seemed to like it, but I thought it was awfully messy. A nothing. But Chuck says it takes time before it feels good. He isn't full of hot air?"

★*POWELL, WILLIAM* Debonair leading man, also a sympathetic listener and probably the only mature lover Jean Harlow ever had. It was Powell who advised her to make a clean break with her crazy mother, Mama Jean, but Harlow never managed to do so (a fatal mistake, since Mama Jean's fanatic belief in Christian Science deprived Jean of the surgery that might have saved her life). Powell and Jean denied marriage plans although they were constantly in each other's company, and she accepted a huge sapphire ring from him in an "unofficial" engagement. Devastated, he was at Harlow's bedside when she died.

★*ROSSEN, HAL* Cameraman who worked with Harlow on *Bombshell*, and eloped with her to Yuma, Ariz., where they married just before dawn on September 10, 1933. In December 1934, Jean filed suit to divorce Rossen, her principal charge being that Harold read in bed until very late, "much to the detriment of her art as an actress, for the next day, after losing sleep, she was unable to play her role to the best of her ability." She also said he was gloomy around the house, rude to her friends, sullen and irritable. No alimony was asked.

★*SALESMAN, TAXI DRIVER, ETC.* After her brief, bitterly tragic marriage to Paul Bern, Harlow seemed determined to find either fulfillment or further degradation in sex. She began disguising herself, going out alone to pick up men where she could. One such pickup, a salesman, told her she needed to learn the fine points of screwing, but might be able to get a pretty good job in a whorehouse since she *was* good-looking, with "a sexy body and remarkable nipples." Harlow allegedly hoped to become pregnant by one of these men, in which case she'd go away, have the child, get a false birth certificate, and announce on her return to Hollywood that she had had Paul Bern's child. But as much as she tried, she did not conceive. Shulman concludes: "Bitterly, she realized that she could be sexually promiscuous and never worry about human consequences. . . . As a goddess, she could be indiscriminate, flagrant, outrageous, and it would not matter because she was sterile. Therefore, she could never really be a citizen in the community of women."

HARRISON, REX
(b. 1908)

Civilized drawing rooms seem to be Harrison's natural habitat, and he thrived as never before in the book-lined study where he played *My Fair Lady* on stage and screen. During a long career unevenly divided between movies and theater, Harrison has done his best, which is very good, to keep sophisticated comedy alive. He has also managed, between gigs, to marry three excellent actresses—further evidence of his impeccable taste, though he may be naturally deficient in constancy. In retrospect, most of the films he has made probably attain whatever they have of worldliness and wit from sexy Rexy.

PRIMARY SOURCE: *Rex: An Autobiography,* by Rex Harrison (Morrow, 1975).

★*HARRIS, ELIZABETH* The fifth and current Mrs. Harrison, former wife of actor Richard Harris, who gained a "son" by marrying Rex. She had previously had three by Richard. It was toward the end of 1969 that "this new light began to shine for me in the person of Elizabeth." Harrison said he had always thought, before, that actors should be married to actresses. "Absolute rubbish—actors should be married to *wives*." Of course he's happy that Elizabeth knows the theater, "but happier still that she is not ashamed to

have housewife written on her passport." Elizabeth and Rex produced two more children, Simon and Harriette, and live in a big house in the South of France. When he's not being Professor Higgins somewhere.

★*KENDALL, KAY* While co-starring on stage in *The Constant Husband* in 1954, Harrison found Kendall "easy, full of fun, beautifully inconsequential, flirtatious, impertinent and rakish. . . . I felt strangely desolated whenever she disappeared." Kay lived a totally mad life, changing apartments every week, engaging in "fisticuffs, runnings away, reconciliations and incessant hectic activity." She was 26, Rex 46 when they fell "deeply in love." Within a year after the historic Broadway opening of *My Fair Lady,* in 1956, Rex learned that Kay was suffering from incurable leukemia. He decided to keep the news from her. Divorcing Lilli Palmer, he married Kay on June 23, 1957. After two years in New York they went to Portofino, then Switzerland, finally home to England, where Kay died in 1959. "At that moment my philosophy of tomorrow left me. For me, there were no tomorrows, there was only yesterday."

★*LANDIS, CAROLE* Harrison was just beginning to make it in Hollywood in the late '40s, and found a kindred spirit in Landis, who shunned tinsel town's party circuit in favor of picnics on the beach. Before long, "we both knew something rather alarming was happening to us." When the affair between Rex and Carole "showed no signs of abating," his wife Lilli left town. Then Rex signed for an important part on Broadway as Henry VIII in *Anne of a Thousand Days.* Carole agreed it was a fascinating play, marvelous part. "She seemed a little down, but I was so high myself on the idea of getting back into the theater, that I'm afraid I didn't notice the extent of her downness." That night Carole committed suicide; he discovered her body. Shattered, Rex said he had "no warning" of how she felt. While still grieving he was forced to face "innuendoes against me that were scarcely credible. . . without quite saying so, it was implied I had been responsible for Carole's suicide. After that terrible week in July, 1948, I had no great desire to see Hollywood again."

★*PALMER, LILLI* Austrian-born Lilli emigrated to England in the late 1930s to escape the rise of Nazism. Lilli and Rex met in the theater, and he found her "steadfast, reliable, stalwart . . . not overburdened with our particular English sense of humor, but she had other sterling qualities." With the outbreak of World War II, Rex joined the RAF, his first wife (Colette) filed for divorce, and, on leave, he and Lilli became one . . . well, two. Then three, with the birth of a son, Carey. After the war, Hollywood beckoned to both of them, and their careers flourished until the Carole Landis tragedy. Later, reunited, the Harrisons discovered the Italian fishing village of Portofino, where they built their dream villa and entertained the greats and near-greats from the worlds of entertainment, politics, and European nobility. Except for the predictable star wars between two highly theatrical temperaments, life seemed normal. Until Kay Kendall. Rex writes: "I was bitterly unhappy for Lilli who had done nothing to deserve her plight." She agreed to a Mexican divorce so Rex could marry Kay. In no time she found Carlos Thompson, an old friend from South America, and is now Mrs. Thompson.

★*ROBERTS, RACHEL* Harrison says he never believed that political commitment contributed to enjoyment in the theater, "so it is obvious that Rachel and I had many differences of opinion. . . . if our minds had been clear we would have seen from the first we were totally unsuited. Most of the blame, I'm sure, is mine." She became the fourth Mrs. Harrison in 1961; it ended in 1968.

★*THOMAS, MARJORIE* Alias Colette; the first Mrs. Rex, mother of actor-director Noel. They were young and poor, the relationship was stormy. When he got a Broadway offer, Colette wasn't keen on moving to New York. "She had fallen in love—not with me, I hasten to say, but with another supporting actor of the day." With his career picking up, the marriage "was slipping fast." When war came to England in 1939, Colette "went off to join the Red Cross . . . and I hardly ever saw her again. I suppose we both knew it was no go."

MISCELLANY

★*BARRY, CHRISTINE* A pretty young actress whom Rex took home to meet the folks. "She was adopted, and her real mother was said to have been a very handsome woman, dangerously fond of pear cider, and her father a blueblooded lord." Alas, they parted.

★*LEIGH, VIVIEN* They were co-stars in the movie *Storm in a Teacup.* "I loved Vivien. Although we never as much as held hands, I cannot say my love was platonic; it was more exciting than that." After she married Larry they all became "great friends."

★*MORGAN, PRIMROSE* Another young actress; she "staggered" young Rex on agreeing to go out, staggered him again when she came home for a drink. "I was mildly embarrassed to tell my parents that there was an actress called Primrose Morgan staying in the spare room." Quite innocent, he insists.

★*"SHEILA"* The first line of Harrison's autobiography: "I felt my first romantic urge when I was about six." The urge was for Sheila, a year older, Rex's partner in summer afternoons of skinny-dipping. They had "an idyllic time, running about the cornfields and jumping stark naked into the tadpole-infested ponds." They were found out.

HAYWARD, SUSAN
(1918–1975)

Suffering was her stock in trade; that's how she got a 1955 Oscar as Lillian Roth, the alcoholic thrush in *I'll Cry Tomorrow.* She also played a crippled soprano, a condemned murderess, and innumerable raging neurotics. Her private life seldom made headlines because Susan was much too busy being a star. Once she worked her way up from playing distressed damsels in costume dramas, she found some chewable contemporary scenery and went at it voraciously. Re her reputation for being difficult, Brooklyn born Susan responded: "I had to fight my way up in a town called Hollywood. . . . the only way I knew how to protect myself was to scare people before they scared me." Hayward might have been wonderful in *All About Eve* (the title role). Offscreen, her own story was somewhat less tumultuous but included the requisite number of surefire scenes.

PRIMARY SOURCE: *Susan Hayward: Portrait of a Survivor,* by Beverly Linet (Atheneum, 1980).

★*BARKER, JESS* Susan was 26, probably still a virgin when she met 29-year-old Broadway actor Jess Barker, at the Stage Door Canteen. Two weeks after their first date she knew she would marry him, and insisted he see her *exclusively.* Soon the pattern began: Their battles were over everything and nothing. One day Susan tossed a gold cigarette lighter, given him by a former girlfriend, into the ocean. One night he poured all the perfume he'd given her down the sink. The stormy affair endured nine months; it came as a shock to her friends that when she married Jess, in July 1944, "prim and proper Susan was *pregnant.*" Within two months she was talking to her lawyers about divorce—which she'd do many times before finally getting one in 1955. The couple had twins, Timothy and Gregory, more or less "mothered" by their father, whose career hit the skids while Susan's talents were increasingly in demand.

★*BARRY, DON "RED"* Popular star of B westerns. In his twilight years Barry claimed that "every man alive should experience one Susan Hayward in his lifetime." He thought she was the "most wonderful and exciting experience" of his life. Must have been exciting the night Jill Jarmyn, one of Barry's former girlfriends, walked in and found Susan there in bed with him. Jarmyn testified that Susan pushed Don out of the way, demanded, "Who is this girl?" and without waiting for an answer, punched Jill in the jaw. Jill also claimed that Susan came at her with a wooden clothes brush and a lighted cigarette, knocked her down, and started ripping the buttons off her blouse. Jarmyn settled out of court to avoid further embarrassment for "Susan's children." Barry said: "What's the fuss? I just invited both girls to drop in for coffee sometime." His statement prompted Marlene Dietrich to murmur, "That Red Barry must make *some* cup of coffee."

★*CARROLL, JOHN* Slick-looking musical-comedy star, and a noted mustachioed sexual swordsman. They met on *Hit Parade of 1943,* and it was the only time Susan became romantically involved with a leading man. For certain scenes, Carroll was "embarrassed to find himself with a perpetual erection," and Susan suddenly became more "communicative" between takes. They were an *item.* Just before he shipped out with the air force, Carroll popped the question, telling Susan to pick out her own engagement ring. She chose a 4.5-carat whopper; he expressed dismay at the price. She called off the engagement and presumably retained her virginity (some say that Carrol's proposal was only a ploy to get her into bed), but bought the ring anyway. Told everyone it was a Christmas present from her mother.

★*CHALKLEY, FLOYD EATON* When they began dating he was a mystery man variously described as an FBI agent and an Atlanta used-car salesman. In fact, Floyd had worked for the FBI and *did* own a car dealership in Georgia. When Susan eloped with Chalkley in February 1957, Hollywood was bowled over. Especially when the new Mrs. Chalkley announced she was retiring from films to live in a big Georgia farmhouse. (But when they offered her the lead in *I Want to Live,* it was goodbye farmhouse and hello to her second Oscar.) Chalkley was every inch the southern gentleman, good-looking, charming, etc., but had a drinking problem and evidently some expensive hidden vices; shortly after he died of cirrhosis in 1966, Susan was heard to say, "If Eaton had lived a couple of years longer, I'd have gone bankrupt." He was her second and last husband.

★*HAYES, HAL* Charming, rich businessman; Susan was only one among "a number of Hollywood women in love with him." He once followed Susan to New York, but the rendezvous was brief. Earl Wilson reported that "Hal Hayes is wearing some scratches on his nose given to him by Susan Hayward during a little disagreement they had."

★*HUGHES, HOWARD* Their first date was the pits. Said Susan's former agent Ben Medford: "She cooked him a chicken dinner. He disliked her intensely. She disliked him. That was all." Well, not quite. Years later, he picked Susan to co-star with Robert Mitchum in *The Lusty Men*, and shortly after (following her separation from Barker) Hughes began to court her. She introduced him to her twin sons as "Mr. Magic." His magical powers failed him the New Year's Eve he arranged simultaneous dates with three women—Susan, Jean Peters, and an unidentified starlet—and brought each to a different private room at the Beverly Hills Hotel. Susan blew the bizarre evening by walking in on Howard and Jean, then walking out. After filming *The Conqueror* for Hughes, she tried to revive the relationship. But he was then set to marry Miss Peters. (See also HUGHES listing.)

★*MEYER, DR. FREDERICK* Identified by Louella Parsons as a professor of philosophy, the columnist continued: "He may be the man Susan has been looking for all these years. He's certainly in love with her and they are together every night." Dr. Meyer was never mentioned again.

★*NELSON, RON* A young, bespectacled bachelor who made friends with Hayward in her retirement years in Ft. Lauderdale. He became head of the local Heart Association, an organization Susan supported. Her son Timothy thinks that Nelson "moved himself into my mother's life because he needed something from her. She in turn needed something from him."

★*WHITE, GORDON* British publisher. They met at the Cannes Film Festival in 1956. It got heavy. He gave her a Yorkshire terrier, promised to meet her in Hollywood in a few weeks. But the trip was delayed. Several times. When he finally turned up, he was turned down.

MISCELLANY

★*CALLOW YOUTH* They were in drama school, and decided to run away together—to get married in Gretna Green, Md. He wired home for money, but his father showed up, in person, to ask his son if he really loved this girl. When the son hesitated, Susan took her suitcase and went home. *Her* father berated her, wanted to know if she had made any "mistakes," with the young man. "She assured him she hadn't—and *wouldn't*—and he never brought up the subject again. But she never forgot it. It colored her relationships with men for years."

★*CHANDLER, JEFF* As Ira Grossell, he was a classmate of Susan's at a Brooklyn public school. They remained lifelong friends, occasionally dating in Hollywood, never a real romance.

★*ELLIS, LARRY* Young actor who reentered her life in 1973, around the time Susan's cancer was diagnosed. Larry took her places, tried to be flippant; "Susan would say I was the funniest guy she had ever met."

★*GABLE, CLARK* The studio tried to spread rumors of a real-life romance between the stars of *Soldiers of Fortune*. There was nothing to it, even onscreen; "Gable and Hayward together for the first and last time received about as much enthusiasm as the Hong Kong flu."

★*GUINLE, JORGE* Chairman of the Jockey Club of Rio de Janeiro, and Susan's host during that city's heady Sweepstakes Ball. When he flew to California to see her, both knew the ball was over.

★*REAGAN, RONALD* Susan and Ronnie and Jane Wyman, among others, were on tour during World War II with Parsons's Flying Stars (columnist Louella Parsons was the emcee). Susan did a comedy skit with Reagan in which she had to smack him hard, and she seemed to enjoy it a lot—yet there were rumors about them getting along fine between scenes. Reagan's fiancée, Jane Wyman, did not care for Susan.

★*WAGNER, ROBERT* His first important role was a memorable bit with Susan in *A*

Song in My Heart, in which she played singer Jane Froman. She was just terrific to him, says Wagner, but it was strictly a professional relationship. The gossip items pairing them off he calls "just a lot of bull."

★*ZANUCK, DARRYL F.* Actress Susan and 20th Century–Fox studio chief Zanuck did not get along. At all. A studio publicity woman thinks it was because she kept turning him down. "Susan was always contemptuous of girls who slept around. . . . She never stooped to between-take 'quickies' in her dressing room, or to sleeping with men to advance her own career."

HAYWORTH, RITA
(b. 1918)

Her parents were a Ziegfeld girl and a Spanish dancer, and somehow or other she happened to be a cousin of Ginger Rogers. Thus she was naturally nimble as a Latin starlet named Margarita Cansino. After they lifted her hairline and changed her name, Rita Hayworth was something else. In *Only Angels Have Wings* (1939), she began to display that elusive glamour that one Hayworth expert called "flesh impact" on the screen. It worked like a charm throughout the '40s in a series of splashy musicals (two with Fred Astaire) as well as in *Gilda* (1946), where her steamy rendition of "Put the Blame on Mame" put Rita on top of the heap. Her penchant for apparently impulsive marriages (to Orson Welles, Aly Khan) made her still more famous, though not always in helpful ways. The lush life left Rita looking ravaged before her time. Sadly, she began playing faded old broads on the screen, while in real life she was plagued by alcoholism, engaged in embarrassing public outbursts, and was finally—a few years ago—declared legally incompetent to manage her own affairs. Sadly, Hayworth had always had a problem doing that.

PRIMARY SOURCE: *Rita Hayworth: The Time, the Place and the Woman,* by John Kobal (Norton, 1978).

★*COHN, HARRY* The Columbia Studios chief who had a way, usually his way, with women. Not all of them especially liked him, nor did Rita. Yet insiders believed he actually proposed to her, and many years later Rita said of her relationship with her boss of twenty years, "You want to know something about him? I think if he could ever have been in love with anyone, he was secretly in love with me." Rita signed her contract with Cohn at 18, and he felt he created her. He was highly possessive—allegedly going so far as to bug her dressing room—and was devastated when she gave up a contract paying nearly a quarter of a million dollars a year to marry her playboy prince Aly Khan. Cohn's relationship with Rita was never the same again.

★*FORD, GLENN* Their first movie together was *The Lady in Question,* in 1940, but it was not until *Gilda* in 1946 that the chemistry between Rita and Glenn ignited. Ford recalls that yes, indeed, "Rita and I were very fond of one another, we became very close friends—and I guess it all came out on the screen." Hayworth at the time was divorcing Orson Welles.

★*HAYMES, DICK* Band singer and another of the marrying kind. In 1953 he was just divorcing his third wife, Nora Eddington Flynn, when he met and married Hayworth. One month later he was arrested for being delinquent in his alimony payments to his second wife, actress Joanne Dru. Then the IRS started attaching his earnings. It was, to put it mildly, "one marriage that was predestined to failure before the ink was dry." Haymes immediately intervened in Rita's life and career, suggesting he not only produce but co-star in her upcoming film, *Joseph and His Brethren.* As it turned out, *Joseph* was abandoned, and so was Dick, her fourth husband. Divorce granted in December 1955.

★*HILL, JAMES* Producer, and long one of Hollywood's most eligible bachelors. Rita met him during the making of *Pal Joey* in 1957 and married him shortly after. He was a partner in the Hecht-Hill-Lancaster production firm for which she made *Separate Tables,* her first "freelance" film away from Columbia. Although she was filled with fresh hope, the marriage to Hill soon ended in divorce. Number five. Rita has never remarried. Asked once about her marriages, she said, "I didn't want five husbands, but that's how it ended up."

★*JUDSON, EDWARD C.* A middle-aged former car salesman when he met 17-year-old Rita and told her he knew what was best for her. He began advising her on what clothes to wear and the best places to be seen. Under Eddie's direction, she began the electrolysis treatments that would widen her brow, changing her from a rather full-blown Latin type to a classic beauty. After dating for a year, Judson asked Rita to marry him. She said yes, feeling he had her best interests at heart. He was 40, she 21, at the 1939 wedding in Las Vegas. During their first year of togetherness, there wasn't enough money to buy furniture, so their living room had only an electric train set, "to play with when Rita was bored." She became more and more bored with Judson as her career in movies boomed. Rita's first marriage lasted five years.

★*KHAN, PRINCE ALY* Rita spent the summer of '48 in seclusion on the Riviera, weary of it all after her divorce from Orson Welles. Then her friend Elsa Maxwell implored Rita to come to a very special party: "Come in white and come in late. Make a grand appearance. It will be good for your morale." On the appointed evening, "Aly was talking with Elsa when, suddenly, he jerked upright and pointed like a bird dog: 'Who *is* it?' he demanded. 'That's your dinner partner,' Elsa answered." Thus began one of the most highly publicized romances of the mid-twentieth century. Before long, Rita moved into Aly's chateau in Cannes; it was the only place to escape the photographers. Khan was completely khrazy about Rita, who even won over his disapproving father, the Aga. Columbia's Harry Cohn was the only party aggrieved by Rita's marriage, and when she failed to report for work, he fired her (the *Hollywood Reporter* headlined: "From Cohn to Cannes to Khan to Canned!"). The lavish wedding took place May 27, 1949, on the Côte d'Azur. Aly's wedding present to

the bride: an Alfa Romeo. Orson Welles sent her a spaniel puppy named Poogles. On December 27 of that year Aly and Rita's daughter Yasmin was born. And "two years after the wedding the fairy tale was over." After several attempts at a reconciliation, Rita won a divorce in January 1953, on grounds of "mental cruelty." (See also KHAN listing.)

★*MATURE, VICTOR* Rita's constant escort while they co-starred in *My Gal Sal.* Rita had just separated from first husband Judson, and the Hun, as Mature had been dubbed, was one of the hottest leading men in Hollywood. But Uncle Sam put a halt to the romance when Mature was called up for service with the Coast Guard. Hayworth didn't wait; she had too many other ships coming in.

★*MERRILL, GARY* One of Rita's more serious affairs after her fifth and last marriage to James Hill.

★*WELLES, ORSON* Rita was dazzled by the creator of *Citizen Kane.* They were immediately referred to as the Beauty (hers) and the Brain (his). He guided Rita on an extensive program of self-education—part of which included listening to *him.* Welles and Hayworth eloped in September 1943. Daughter Rebecca was born in December 1944. Her parents announced plans for a divorce at the end of 1945, but did not actually obtain one until the end of 1947. During the interim, Welles directed his wife and himself in *The Lady from Shanghai.* Rita says she knew the film was a classic while they were making it. Critics and film scholars still debate whether Orson, in a fit of misogynism, patterned the leading character after Rita, "a lady of ice masquerading as fire. She slips emotions on and off like rings, adept at playing with feelings, because she has none of her own till she is exposed as a spider lady trapped in her own net all sticky with lies."

MISCELLANY

★*ASTAIRE, FRED* They made two films, became fast friends, and *Time* magazine called Rita "the best dancing partner he ever had."

★*TOMLIN, PINKY* Her first "screen romance," and first studio-arranged date. Pinky didn't know that 17-year-old Rita didn't drink. They went drinking, she got bombed, then sick. Pinky was puzzled: "I got to thinking that if her father was a Spanish dancer, he was probably a knife-thrower too."

In Rita's Hollywood heyday, her regular escorts were known to include *TONY MARTIN, DAVID NIVEN, ERROL FLYNN, HOWARD HUGHES, STAVROS NIARCHOS*, singer *ROBERT SAVAGE*, and bullfighter *LUIS DOMINGUIN*.

HEFNER, HUGH M.
(b. 1926)

Founder and guiding spirit of *Playboy* magazine, its related clubs and hotels, and his own Playboy Philosophy extensively outlined in print. Sex without guilt and personal freedom in the broadest sense are the gist of it, summed up by the precedent-shattering publisher, who has characterized himself as "an indoor boy and an incurable romantic" (which social historian Gay Talese interprets as "a sex junkie with an incurable habit"). Either way, the *Playboy* lifestyle presaged and contributed substantially to the present permissive society—and not simply by popularizing centerfold tits-and-ass. One of the most celebrated night people anywhere, Hefner spends a lot of time in silk pajamas. In recent years, he has moved from Chicago to L.A., and his Holmby Hills estate (the Mansion, to insiders, described by biographer Brady as "a 30-room Xanadu") has become more famous for splashy social and charitable events than for the rumored orgies with willing Bunnies on demand. Despite modest published speculation that he has slept with more than two thousand women, the list here constitutes but a token sampling of the busty battalions supposedly booked into Hefner's famous round bed wired for sound and light and instant replays. HMH continues to thrive, his reputation as a legendary cocksman threatened only by creeping respectability and swiftly changing social standards.

PRIMARY SOURCES: *Hefner: An Unauthorized* Biography, by Frank Brady, (Macmillan, 1974); *Thy Neighbor's Wife*, by Gay Talese (Doubleday, 1980).

★*ARNSTEIN, BOBBIE* Girl Friday, Hefner's longtime confidante and secretary, whose romantic attachment, Talese writes, "had ripened into a deep and special friendship." Like her boss, Bobbie came to prefer lovers a bit younger than herself. Through one of them, she was arrested, charged, and convicted on a trumped-up drug rap by Chicago prosecutors. Pressured from without and within, emotionally distraught, she committed suicide early in 1975, a personally painful episode in his life which was publicly denounced by Hefner as "a politically motivated anti-*Playboy* witch hunt."

★*BENTON, BARBI* She was bouncy, green-eyed Barbara Klein, a UCLA co-ed, when they met at the first taping of Hefner's *Playboy After Dark* TV show in 1968. Just months before, with her spectacular body and ultra-bright smile, Barbi had been a high school cheerleader and Miss Teenage America contestant. When Hefner asked for a date, she hesitated, "I've never gone out with anyone over twenty-four." Hefner's riposte: "That's okay, neither have I." After a courtship longer than usual for him, Barbi became his live-in lady at the newly acquired L.A. mansion, also accompanied him on a 1971 round-the-world trip aboard the big black Bunny jet. Barbi thought she and Hef might marry. She moved on and up in her show-business career, solidified her unhappy position in a love triangle with Karen (see below). After nearly ten years, Barbi moved out, eventually married someone else. Hefner moved on—as usual.

★*CHRISTY, KAREN* Bosomy Texas blonde discovered in a Dallas "Bunny hunt" in 1971, she spent the first night of her first day at *Playboy* in Hefner's circular bed and stayed around for a couple of years. It'd be Christmas with Karen in Chicago, New Year's Eve with Barbi and the gang at Mansion West, and Hefner tried hard to keep it that way, according to Talese's detailed account, loving Barbi "for her vitality and blithe spirit," reluctant to lose Karen because she was "uninhibited in private. . . . he had never known anyone who could surpass her skill and ardor in bed." Karen also wanted an exclusive on Hef's attention. By the time she slipped back to Texas, mightily peeved, he had given her an emerald ring, a 5-carat Tiffany diamond, a full-length white mink, a Matisse, a Mark IV Lincoln, and a Persian cat. Talese reports that in Dallas she was soon wearing a new beau's gold chain with an unusual pendant, "—a 14-carat price tag on which was printed: 'Sold.'" Karen later married Ed Simonini, linebacker for the Baltimore Colts.

★*CYNTHIA* Another green-eyed 18-year-old, but Cynthia had *red* hair. When queried about his predilection for younger women, Hefner once explained, "I simply find them more attractive than women my own age." Cynthia was attractive enough to adorn the cover of *Playboy* five times. Started out as a secretary-receptionist at the magazine, quickly became what Brady calls "queen consort of Hugh Hefner." She was "deeply in love" with Hef, later told a *Life* interviewer that they spent a lot of their time together watching Chaplin movies and listening to Jeanette MacDonald–Nelson Eddy records. "I don't know how real it was, but it was beautiful just sitting there sighing," sighed Cynthia after she was replaced by Mary (see below).

★*JOYCE* An 18-year-old Floridian with *black* hair and dark eyes. Hefner met her in 1958, she did her first *Playboy* cover that year, was uncovered as a centerfold in December 1958. Marriage was the last thing he had in mind, much to her surprise. HMH sent Joyce off on an all-expense European vacation and took up with Cynthia.

★*LOVELACE, LINDA* The celebrated star of *Deep Throat* apparently became the center of attention at one memorable "orgy" at Hefner's mansion. That evening, in the pool, she gave Hef his anticipated "thrill and chill," and reports that he was one of the few who

didn't request a demonstration of her "deep throat" technique. This was before Linda woke up to find that her life as a porno queen had been a horrible dream. (See also LOVELACE listing.)

★*MARY* A regal "Grace Kellyish" blonde, intelligent and friendly, who smoothly slipped into her role as Hefner's hostess and chatelaine. Their five years of domestic harmony were shared with a huge St. Bernard that Mary christened Baby, while she was Mommy, Hefner Daddy. Friends thought marriage was a sure thing this time. And for Mary, it was—six months after leaving Hefner's mansion, she married a surgeon.

★*NURSE* A girlfriend in Chicago while his marriage was winding down, his magazine had not yet got started. They made a sex movie together in a friend's apartment, Talese reports, "a private venture that he did strictly for the fun and experience of doing it." Seems young Hefner had a hunch that his future would be somehow tied up with sex.

★*PILGRIM, JANET* In 1955, she became the first traditional girl-next-door type (as opposed to the cantilevered super-bimbos à la Jayne Mansfield) to appear as a Playmate centerfold. Her real name was Charlaine Karalus, a statuesque 20-year-old who worked for *Playboy*, processing back orders and subscriptions. She went to the bossman one day to ask for a new addressograph machine. "Tell you what," said Hef, "if you become our Playmate for July, I'll get you that addressograph." Charlaine said okay. They changed her name to Janet Pilgrim to protect her from cranks, etc., and she became one of Hefner's steady companions for a time. The man in her centerfold shot, wearing a tuxedo, back to camera, is HMH himself.

★*THEODORE, SONDRA* Lissome blonde, recent no. 1 girl at Mansion West and a member of the vocal group the Singing Playmates. They plan to get their act together and take it on the road, according to *Playboy*.

★*TWEED, SHANNON* Blond Canadian-born model, current Playmate of the Year and believed to be Hefner's personal favorite.

★*WILLIAMS, MILDRED* Hefner's first and *only* wife. Still wearing bobbysox, she was a classmate of Hef's at Steenmetz High in Chicago. They kept their romance alive in letters when he enlisted in the army at 17, continued their courtship after his 1946 discharge. "At the manly age of 22, Hefner had not yet slept with a woman," but not for lack of trying. Talese notes that Mildred's Catholic upbringing made her resist intimacy beyond "heavy petting in his father's Ford," then mutual masturbation and a memorable Greyhound bus ride during which "he urged her to perform fellatio on him right there at their seat, under a blanket." Soon after, "she experienced her first orgasm, through cunnilingus" and let Hefner take nude pictures of her. They became lovers in the spring of 1948, married in June 1949. Before the wedding, when Millie confessed to another affair with a faculty member in the town where she was attending school, Hefner was *aghast*, but not turned off by the fringe benefits of her sexual awakening. The couple had two children, Christie Ann in 1952, David in 1955. By that time, Hefner was dedicated to nurturing his *Playboy* empire at any cost, and the marriage deteriorated. They separated legally in 1957, and divorce followed two years later. Still friends.

★*YOUNG MAN* Hefner has admitted to a homosexual experience on at least one occasion, notes biographer Brady, waxing poetic to add that "a lone sparrow does hardly a spring make." Seems he met the Young Man in a near North Side bar while out drinking, and decided to "experiment." The act was consummated at the Young Man's apartment. Talese ascribes the incident to Hefner's self-voyeurism: "Once he allowed himself to be picked up by a homosexual in a bar, more to see than to enjoy sex with a man."

MISCELLANY

★*BUNNY* Of the many Bunnies cited by Brady, one recalls specifically the time she was summoned to Hef's private apartment late at night, how she found nine or ten girls already there drinking, turning on, with Hefner the only man in sight. The girls took turns masturbating him, continues Bunny Tattletail. "But he was getting his kicks not from being masturbated, but from the fact that we were all *watching* him being masturbated."

★*PLAYMATES, BUNNIES, STARLETS, PORNO STARS, & GIRLS GIRLS GIRLS* There have been quite a few, usually part of the *Playboy* "family."

HEPBURN, KATHARINE
(b. 1907)

The one and only invincible Kate has turned out to be among the greatest American actresses of this or any time. Time was when they didn't much like her in Hollywood—too affectedly Bryn Mawr, too Yankee, too sexy in an odd way unlikely to be understood by any man west of Connecticut. Well, the moguls were right, in a sense. When Hepburn made *Bringing Up Baby* and *Holiday* (both 1938) and *The Philadelphia Story* (1940), those classic American comedies with Cary Grant never quite established her as a box-office bonus baby. The public warmed to her more after *Woman of the Year* in 1942, first in a series of winning romantic comedies she made with Spencer Tracy, who became as important in her personal life as he was significant to her career. While Tracy lived, his affair with Hepburn was politely ignored by most journalists, and Kate's youthful romantic escapades rarely made headlines— she just didn't seem to be that kind of girl. Though apparently ageless, she's now one of the sexiest septuagenarians around, a *grande dame* of stage and screen with four Oscars to keep her warm. The last in 1982 for *On Golden Pond*.

PRIMARY SOURCES: *Kate: The Life of Katharine Hepburn*, by Charles Higham (Norton, 1975); *Tracy and Hepburn: An Intimate Memoir*, by Garson Kanin (Bantam, 1972).

★*HAYWARD, LELAND*   Dashing Hollywood agent. "In the parlance of the time, he was a 'capital beau,' full of gossip, wisdom, toughness, engaging treachery, a *man*." He was also a snappy dresser, drove a Rolls-Royce, piloted his own plane, and made lots of long distance calls—at a time when few people knew how. Hayward's clients included his mistress Margaret Sullavan as well as Hepburn. Kate was shocked to learn of Hayward's marriage to Sullavan, but her Yankee spirit rallied and she sent the bride a congratulatory telegram (which Sullavan tore to shreds and threw away). Summing it up for Hepburn: "She loved him for the time he was hers. That was all."

★*HUGHES, HOWARD*   She found him *fascinating*, and *enormously attractive*. An individualist, a loner, an adventurous aviator who'd dip his wings in fly-bys over her house, Hughes was also a hypochondriac—which brought out the nursemaid in Kate. Their affair rushed along like a whirlwind, they were "always dodging in and out of cars, trains, planes in an attempt to avoid publicity—which, of course, resulted in an excess of it." Hughes would follow Hepburn on tour, and fly in for lunch whenever she was on location. Brian Aherne recalled one such time when Howard sat between Kate and director George Cukor, talking in "that high pitched voice deaf people have. Kate and George would say, *sotto voce*, 'Pass the bread, please,' right in front of him, and they'd roar with laughter as he strained to understand them. Hughes didn't know what they were up to!" Hepburn never, ever considered marrying the billionaire, and eventually grew bored with him. (See also HUGHES listing.)

★*SMITH, LUDLOW OGDEN*   "Luddy," Katharine Hepburn's one and only husband. She persuaded him to call himself Ogden Ludlow, so appalled was she at the prospect of having to call herself Kate Smith. She was 19, he was Philadelphia Main Line, and the marriage was disaster. Kate *hated* domesticity, *hated* giving up her barely budding Broadway career, and realized that "marriage was totally incompatible with her need for absolute freedom of thought and action." Within three weeks the couple separated, although they remained legally wed for several years—"clearly a defense against having to face marriage again." In time, Kate and Luddy became the closest friends.

★*STEVENS, GEORGE*   Hepburn and director Stevens had severe artistic and temperamental clashes on the set of *Quality Street*, but soon after—and after Kate's madcap fling with Hughes—they began dating. Some observers thought George and Kate were deeply in love, but there's no substantiating evidence from either of them. They were to work again, harmoniously, on *Woman of the Year*.

★*TRACY, SPENCER*   The first meeting of these two born-for-each-other actors and lovers took place quite by accident in a corridor outside the studio commissary when both had been signed for their first film together. Kate looked him up and down and said, "I'm afraid I'm a little tall for you, Mr. Tracy." Legend has it that Tracy then said, "Don't worry, I'll cut you down to size." Bystander Joe Mankiewicz claims *he* was the one who joked about Spence cutting Kate down to size—which may be true, for Tracy never gave any indication he found Hepburn less than perfect the way she was. As Higham writes, theirs was an attraction of opposites: "Kate was edgy, assertive, brilliant, stylish; Tracy was a subdued, slow-moving, retiring grizzly bear of a man—impatient with fuss, simple, direct." They acted together in nine movies, classics such as *Adam's Rib* and *State of the Union*, and for twenty-five years kept their love affair untouched by scandal—an unspoken pact with gossip-mongers not to embarrass them because Tracy was irrevocably married, and a Catholic. Their relationship rested on a high regard for each other's talent, a mutual generosity, and complete lack of possessiveness. "And, perhaps more than anything else, a gloriously shared sense of humor." Also, Kate adds, "A tiny thing about Spencer: He made the best cup of coffee in the world." The couple's last film together was *Guess Who's Com-*

ing to Dinner, in 1967, which showed an aging Tracy ravaged by alcoholism and disease. He died shortly after. Hepburn has said, "I'll miss him every day as long as I live."

MISCELLANY

★BARRYMORE, JOHN The legendary actor (and lover) was Hepburn's co-star on her first film, Bill of Divorcement. The first day on the set he invited her into his dressing room. Once there, without warning he flung off all his clothes. Kate was astonished and shrank against the wall. "My dear," Barrymore said, "any young girl would be *thrilled* to make love to the great John Barrymore." Kate replied, "Not me. My father doesn't want me to make babies."

★FAIRBANKS, DOUGLAS JR. He fell "head over heels" for Kate, repeatedly begged her for a date. When she finally agreed to dinner, the evening was cut short by her "sick headache." Fairbanks drove Hepburn home and was still sitting outside her house thinking about her when another car pulled up. Kate ran out and jumped into it. The man at the wheel was probably Leland Hayward.

HOWAR, BARBARA
(b. 1934)

Southern belle who moved to Washington, D.C., in 1957, got a job as a Congressman's secretary, and climbed the capital social ladder chum by chum. Close to the Johnson family, a virtual chaperon/companion to young Luci, Howar's priorities were seldom ambiguous, and were summed up by "a color photograph of me in *Time* in a six-hundred-dollar dress dancing cheek-to-cheek with a man I helped elect President of the United States. For me, happiness was national exposure. . . ." Unceremoniously dumped by the Johnson team when her name came up in one too many potential scandals, Howar divorced her husband and landed a job as a TV personality, for a time

on the short-lived *Joyce and Barbara Show* with Mrs. David Susskind. That didn't work out. Evidently, Susskind wanted her to be sexy on the air; Barbara wanted to be brainy. She wrote a book.

PRIMARY SOURCE: *Laughing All the Way*, by Barbara Howar (Stein & Day, 1973; Fawcett, 1974).

★DARIN, BOBBY The pop singer. Howar was his escort when he came to Washington for a telethon. "I know it would be better reading to report that I began thinking of the world's problems through an exposure to John Kenneth Galbraith, or, at least, Paul Newman, but it was Mr. Darin, the teen-rage of the fifties, who led me through the maze of bigotry in which I lived . . . and made me *care*." When they became "the best of friends," Barbara began following Bobby on the nightclub circuit. "We ate greasy hamburgers and talked race with Flip Wilson in Philadelphia, discussed censorship with Tony Franciosa in Puerto Rico," etc. Bobby Darin, says Barbara, "did fine things for my soul."

★HOWAR, ED First (and only) husband. They met at a cocktail party; he was a swarthy young man, son of "America's richest resident Arab." He was also "handsome, educated, quiet, and possessed of the patience I knew was required of a husband for me." They married in 1959 in a civil ceremony, a compromise between his Moslem religion and her abandoned Catholicism. The couple had two children, and she had at least two notably sticky affairs (see Senator and Trusted Friend below) before Howar finally turned nasty, sent detectives after Barbara, and threatened exposure of all her sins if she did not come back to him. She did, for a while. But they divorced in 1967.

★SENATOR, U.S. Barbara thought she could handle the trauma of being 30 by going to Harry Winston and buying herself a diamond necklace. "When that didn't prove sufficiently rejuvenating, I had an affair. . . . and I went right to the highest quarters for a lover: the United States Senate." Guess who. Barbara says that Washington will always be a city for extracurricular romance and undercover trysts, "because it's a town where women are more easily tolerated if they dabble with politicians rather than politics." She and the Senator were novices, both had families, and "however happy we were, we understood all along that there was no future in our liaison." His ambitions pulled them apart, but no regrets: "Nothing is better for the spirit or body than a love affair. It elevates thoughts and flattens stomachs. . . ."

★TRUSTED FRIEND AND ADVISER TO THE PRESIDENT This was during the Lyndon Johnson regime, and "what had begun as a campaign flirtation turned into a full-fledged love affair at Inaugural Headquarters." People talked, but Barbara didn't mind, she was feeling "happy, free and very, very reckless." She told husband Howar all about it and asked for a divorce. Although he was hurt, Barbara felt he understood. Barbara and Trusted Friend and Adviser took off for a holiday in Jamaica. Their romantic idyl was interrupted by five private detectives dispatched by her husband, who also had had her under surveillance in Washington. She was given no choice: either surrender everything, including her two children, or Howar would file for divorce naming as corespondents a United States Senator and an adviser to the President. Trusted Adviser said, "Look, Barbara, the country doesn't need this right on top of the Walter Jenkins and Bobby Baker affairs." She decided not to fight and reconciled with Ed Howar for the time being. Barbara's bitter postscript: "In her lifetime as a Madame, Polly Adler never received as many propositions as I got in the six months before my red-hot reputation cooled down."

MISCELLANY

★DOBRYNIN, ANATOLY Russian Ambassador to Washington. At an embassy party, Barbara challenged his statement that Russian women could hold their liquor better than Western women. There followed a drinking contest; when Barbara had downed six ounces of straight vodka, "I wiped my mouth with the back of my hand and smashed the goblet in the fireplace. . . . The room fell silent. Dobrynin and I fell into each other's arms, laughing and clapping one another on the back." At future parties Barbara noticed that the portly Mrs. Dobrynin steered her husband away from "both me and the vodka."

★JOHNSON, LYNDON Through her role as "lady in waiting" to the Johnson daughters, Barbara became part of Johnson's at-home circle. Often she would watch the President's favorite spy movies with him in the White House theater, while he stroked her hand. Barbara never knew whether to make a positive or negative response—or which one would be worse. "Before any choice was offered, LBJ would fall asleep in his chair while still holding my hand. I will never forget the discomfort of my paralyzed left arm tingling from lack of circulation, afraid to move for fear of awakening the man and his interests." There were other incidents requiring "adroit footwork" to keep the President at bay "without incurring his rage or damaging his pride." Barbara does not blatantly suggest that the thirty-sixth president of the United States was a dirty old man, "but I would not bet the rent money that he was not."

★KISSINGER, HENRY Democrat Barbara "dated" Republican Kissinger for four years, and writes that she'd like to be *above* a dissertation on the relationship. But . . . "Ridiculous! To ignore Dr. Kissinger is unthinkable." Although the good Dr. K. may wish she had. To begin with, says Barbara, there was "an absence of carnal knowledge between me and Henry." She goes on: "Henry Kissinger does not truly qualify as a sex symbol. . . . For all the Jill St. Johns, he is a ladies' man in appearances only. . . . He is power and ego oriented, not sex-driven." So there. (See also KISSINGER listing.)

★MCCARTHY, GENE Former Senator, former Presidential candidate. He drove Barbara home from a party and they sat and talked until "early morning." She thought he seemed bored but not unhappy, and "less a cold man than a private one." When he left, "unlike him, I was not tired of Gene McCarthy." Purely platonic.

HUGHES, HOWARD R.
(1905–1976)

Billionaire business tycoon, movie producer, aviator. The famed, filthy-rich eccentric was known in his final years as a recluse who seldom left the shuttered penthouse suites where he spent his time gorging on medicine and movies (his favorite seemed to be *Ice Station Zebra*, a frigid 1968 Cold War drama starring Rock Hudson). It wasn't always so. Back in the '30s and '40s when he wasn't involved with aviation—TWA was his baby—Hughes was usually up to his eyeballs making movies *and* movie stars. Busty women obviously tantalized him, at least professionally. He directed *Hell's Angels*, which made Jean Harlow a star in 1930, and his controversial *The Outlaw* made Jane Russell's cleavage a momentous national issue in 1943. He later took over RKO Studios. Probably a true romantic, although a deeply neurotic one, Hughes was rumored to be impotent. Some evidence suggests otherwise, yet Hollywood never had a more assiduous pursuer of its beauties; he married one (Jean Peters, who divorced him in 1971) and chased them all quite dashingly. What happened when he caught them may never be fully known, so many of Hughes's so-called conquests must end with a question mark. Did he or didn't he? As in the great Clifford Irving hoax of the '70s, which never brought him out of hiding, HRH remains elusive as ever.

PRIMARY SOURCES: *Empire: The Life, Legend and Madness of Howard Hughes,* by Donald L. Bartlett and James B. Steele (Norton, 1979); *The Real Howard Hughes Story,* by Nelson C. Madden (Manor, 1976). Also, autobiographies by Ingrid Bergman, Joan Fontaine, Stewart Granger, Veronica Lake, Otto Preminger, Gene Tierney, and Shelley Winters; and biographies of Bette Davis, Errol Flynn, Ava Gardner, Jean Harlow, Susan Hayward, Katharine Hepburn, Elizabeth Taylor and Lana Turner.

★*BERGMAN, INGRID* So enamored was Hughes, he told the Swedish star that he bought RKO Studios—just for her. Ingrid failed to understand Howard's charm, but she did recognize his power and wealth; when she and Roberto Rossellini wanted financing for their infamous film, *Stromboli,* she went to Hughes to find the backing. Later, Hughes quite calculatingly informed the press of Bergman's pregnancy via Rossellini. He thought the scandal could help the picture. (See also BERGMAN listing.)

★*BOARDMAN, ELEANOR* Possibly the first Hollywood actress to receive Howard's attentions. In 1925, she found him "very attractive, very shy, hard of hearing, difficult." Hughes's money was insufficient incentive for Boardman, one of the reigning queens of the silent screen, who was to marry director King Vidor.

★*BOND, LILLIAN* One of the many actresses Hughes dated in Hollywood in the '30s.

★*DARNELL, LINDA* In his autobiography, *Preminger,* Otto tells about Hughes's pursuit of the sultry, dark-haired actress who said she didn't *need* to know Hughes, because she was a married woman and she had a good contract at 20th Century–Fox. Hughes didn't give up; he followed her to the golf course one day and insisted he take her to lunch. She finally said okay, if her agent could come too. Hughes then piled Linda *and* her agent into his very own Constellation and flew them to San Francisco. Lunch was at the Fairmont Hotel—on a high floor overlooking the bay—while a small orchestra played. Slow fade. Preminger says, "I don't know exactly what happened, but a few months later Linda divorced her cameraman husband."

★*DAVIS, BETTE* Her most recent biographer, Charles Higham, claims that Bette and Howard were caught in bed by her husband

Ham Nelson, who told the startled pair he had been tape-recording their pillow talk. Hughes offered Ham $70,000 to destroy the tapes, and Bette eventually paid back every cent of it. Her affair with Hughes was comparatively brief, coming during a hiatus in his pursuit of Katharine Hepburn. (See also DAVIS listing.)

★*DE HAVILLAND, OLIVIA*   Only 21, Olivia had to ask her mother for permission to date Hughes. Their on-again-off-again affair sometimes found Hughes courting Olivia, sometimes her sister Joan Fontaine. De Havilland has only fond memories of Howard, recalling his boyish charm, his inner loneliness. She also remembers the way he danced: "He rocked very slowly and occasionally walked to the music." (See also DE HAVILLAND listing.)

★*DOMERGUE, FAITH*   She was just another starlet at another yachting party when Hughes zapped eyes on her. Some of his friends thought it was real love. Within a few days, Hughes bought out Faith's contract, put her on salary, and enrolled her in acting classes. In a towering rage she once publicly accused him of holding back her career. So Hughes promised she could choose her own script. Her choice was *Vendetta*—it cost over a million, and was one of his biggest flops.

★*DOVE, BILLIE*   A Ziegfeld girl on Broadway at 16, Billie was just beginning to bedazzle Hollywood when Marion Davies introduced her to Hughes. She became the golden-haired Cinderella to his Prince Charming. When she took rides in the country, Hughes would "trail her in his plane, waving and showering her with flower petals." Billie once had a rendezvous at the Ambassador Hotel with her old flame George Raft; fortunately, Raft's friends in the lobby called to say that Hughes was on his way. Raft beat a quick exit via the service elevator, and later said, "The last guy in the world either of us wanted to cross was Howard Hughes."

★*FALCONI, AIDA*   A cantina girl in Nuevo Laredo, Mexico. "In the late '40s Aida was rumored to have been a favorite of an American pilot with a Texas accent who fitted Hughes's description." She became pregnant,

and although her financial resources had always been extremely limited, she suddenly came into a lot of money. Three months before her child was expected, she flew to Mexico City. "She was never heard of again." At least not in Nuevo Laredo.

★*FLYNN, ERROL*   Yes, Errol Flynn. Howard and Errol had at least one secret date, according to Johnny Meyer, the man who regularly acted as pimp for both of them. Meyer said he saw both Flynn and Hughes go into their Santa Barbara "love nest," but adds he has no idea whether "they went to bed or not." He thinks they did. (See also FLYNN listing.)

★*FONTAINE, JOAN*   She devotes an entire chapter (albeit a short one) to Hughes in her autobiography, *No Bed of Roses*. When he took over RKO Studios in 1948 he got Joan's contract too. He'd already been proposing to her "for over ten years," and popped the question again. "Why me, Howard? Why *me*?" Joan whined. He also tried to install her in a house he chose, and discussed how she'd divorce her husband William Dozier. Fontaine insists she's one of the few girls pursued by Hughes "who never had an affair with him." (See also FONTAINE listing.)

★*GANLEY, GAIL*   One of Hughes's "forgotten starlets." She was an 18-year-old UCLA student when approached by a "talent scout" who said his client, a famous man, wanted to take pictures of her. The photographer wore a Van Dyke beard (Howard Hughes in disguise?). Soon, the young lady was being whisked by limousine to an expensive drama coach, one known to work for Hughes, and for two years she received regular paychecks—from *someone*. In 1962, Gail sued Hughes for $553,000 for the "misuse of her time." It was settled out of court. She never made a movie.

★*GARDNER, AVA*   When they met in 1943, Howard was "a spindly, delicate six foot three inches, 158 pounds, and terrified of physical injury or illness." But then, Ava *liked* thin, dark men; and Howard awakened her motherly instincts. Ava also liked the way he would make things easy for a lady; "He presses a button and there's a plane ready to take you anywhere in the world . . . He's just the ticket for a girl like me, from the Deep South and lazy." They fought a lot, made up a lot, and Hughes was always there when Ava needed him. (See also GARDNER listing.)

★*GAYNOR, MITZI* Movie and musical star. One of the lovelies Hughes promised to marry. So she said.

★*HARLOW, JEAN* She was his creation, one of the *great* sex symbols. Yet, by most accounts, there was no sexual relationship at all between Harlow and Hughes. When he saw her first screen test he said, "She's a nix." When her agent argued that Harlow was a good kid who deserved a break, one of Hughes's henchmen, knowing his boss's lust for big breasts, said, "We don't want a good kid, we want a pig." Nevertheless, Harlow got the role in *Hell's Angels* and was an overnight sensation, the "blond bombshell" of 1930. But to Hughes, she remained a mere commodity. (See also HARLOW listing.)

★*HAYWARD, SUSAN* Soon after her breakup with husband Jess Barker, a mysterious stranger began calling on Susan; she introduced him to her children as "Mr. Magic." He sent her flowers and expensive trinkets, and asked her out for New Year's Eve in 1953. Howard had three dates that night, one with Susan, another with Jean Peters, the third with an anonymous starlet; each was installed in a different room at the Beverly Hills hotel. Susan discovered the ruse and walked out. She tried in vain to reestablish contact a couple of years later, but Hughes was already preparing to marry Jean Peters. (See also HAYWARD listing.)

★*HEPBURN, KATHARINE* Howard and Kate were a serious item—she was one of the two people he kept in touch with on his record-breaking round-the-world flight in 1938. "Hughes and Miss Hepburn, both lanky and angular, both golfers and pilots, made a handsome pair—and he pursued her diligently." Once when she was touring in a stage production, Hughes followed in his own plane, never missing a performance, and sent an emerald

to her dressing room every night. She was "enormously attracted," but much too independent for him. Eventually exasperated, she despaired of getting angry at him, "because he couldn't hear what she was saying anyhow." Kate got "very bored" with Hughes about the time she met Spencer Tracy. (See also HEPBURN listing.)

★*LAKE, VERONICA* Included herself among Howard's "favorites," and often had him over for casual dinners. He'd reciprocate by calling at 5:00 A.M. and asking her to drive him to the airport. Veronica denies a romance. (See also LAKE listing.)

★*LOMBARD, CAROLE* Evidently a brief affair, while he was still seeing Billie Dove.

★*LUPINO, IDA* She says he used to take her—*and* her mother—dancing. "Howard loved music and was a good dancer." They also spent weekends in Palm Springs. According to Ida, just pals.

★*MARSH, MARIAN* A lovely blond actress, another frequent date in the mid-1930s.

★*MONROE, MARILYN* Their names were "linked." It had to be.

★*MOORE, TERRY* In 1952, when she left her football-hero husband Glenn Davis, Hughes was involved. But she and Hughes were dating before her marriage to Davis—as well as after. Within the last few years, Ms. Moore has come up with the rather bizarre story that she and Howard were actually married in 1949, on board a ship, and that the marriage records were somehow swept overboard. She adds that she gave birth to Hughes's child in Munich, Germany, in 1951, but that the premature baby died within twenty-four hours. So said Ms. Moore in filing her claim to the Hughes estate.

★*PAGET, DEBRA* Actress. For a while in the early 1950s the dark-haired Debra, who was then queen of the costume epics, sported a huge diamond on her left hand. It was identified (by her) as an engagement ring from Howard.

★*PETERS, JEAN* They met in 1946, when she was a starlet; in one of their "off" periods, Jean married socialite Stuart W. Cramer III, and shortly afterward divorced him. On January 12, 1957, in Tonopay, Nevada, Hughes took Jean Peters as his second wife. She was 30, he 51 (he had vowed he wouldn't marry again until after 50). Hollywood hailed it as the perfect union; Jean was his kind of All-American beauty. However, the couple did not begin to live under one roof until four years later. Their marriage was flawed by Hughes's eccentric demands for privacy; eventually Jean had to go through his aides, using the code name "Major Bertrandez," in order to see him. When she filed for divorce, Jean had not managed an appointment for over three years.

★*RICE, ELLA* Howard Hughes's first wife. Ella was the daughter of a wealthy Houston businessman, niece of the founder of Rice Institute. Their marriage lasted from the summer of 1925 to December 1929, when he took up residence in Hollywood—and fell victim to the glamour, excitement, and beautiful women thereof.

★*ROGERS, GINGER* Another who thought Howard was "a very good dancer." And Ginger ought to know.

★*ROGERS, MARY* An actress, a frequent Hughes date in the early 1930s.

★*RUSH, BARBARA* She found him "kind and intelligent." They drank tea "and talked mostly about medical matters, since he knew that my uncle had developed the Rush pin for hip operations." And Barbara knew of the Hughes Medical Foundation, his only major philanthropy, about which he cared deeply.

★*RUSSELL, JANE* It was Hughes who came up with the ad slogan "How would you like to tussle with Russell?" for his sexy western, *The Outlaw*. According to one judge who banned the film from his city, "Jane Russell's breasts hung over the picture like a summer thunderstorm spread out over a landscape." Jane, a sometimes Sunday-school teacher, was mightily embarrassed by it all, and denies there was *ever* a romance between herself and Hughes. In fact, Russell bitterly claims that after *The Outlaw*, Hughes totally ignored her, and let her career languish for years.

★*SHUBERT, YVONNE* Attractive young actress, a frequent favored companion in the late 1950s. Her code name was "The Party."

★*SIMMONS, JEAN* It was Cary Grant who thought of having Howard Hughes arrange some privacy for Jean's wedding to Stewart Granger. Hughes had not yet laid eyes on her, but when he did, he bought up her contract and refused to let her work for anyone else. Granger was convinced Hughes's only motive was to get Jean in his bed. In a drunken moment, ole Stew even thought of pushing Howard over a cliff. A sticky wicket which ended, finally, in a lawsuit to get Jean out of the Hughes contract. (See also GRANGER listing.)

★*TAYLOR, ELIZABETH* "He was an out-and-out bore," said Liz, and she not the least tempted by Hughes's offer of one million big ones to marry him. (See also TAYLOR listing.)

★*TIERNEY, GENE* She thought Howard "sweet," her mother thought he'd be a "good catch," and husband Oleg Cassini thought he was being cuckolded by Hughes. Cassini once caught Hughes bringing Gene home, leaped out of hiding, and hit Howard in the face. When next they met at a party, Hughes locked himself in a bedroom until his henchmen rushed to the rescue. (See also TIERNEY listing.)

★*TURNER, LANA* They were supposed to announce their engagement after a madcap transcontinental flight—with Hughes at the controls, naturally. No one knows what happened up there in the wild blue yonder, but when Lana and Hughes touched ground, they weren't speaking, and the engagement was off. Lana later complained that she'd already had her linens monogrammed "HH"; Hughes said, succinctly, "Go marry Huntington Hartford." (See also TURNER listing.)

★*WINTERS, SHELLEY* Their first date was a dinner in an abandoned restaurant, a movie in an abandoned theater. Shelley thought him nice, though weird, and will always be grateful for the favors he granted her over the years. For once, no word from Shelley on what favors she returned. (See also WINTERS listing.)

HUSTON, JOHN
(b. 1906)

Celebrated director-writer-actor, involved with more than sixty pictures including such all-time greats as *The Treasure of the Sierra Madre* (1948), *The Asphalt Jungle* (1950), and *The African Queen* (1952). The son of actor Walter Huston, John is a lover of horses, strong drink, fine art, and fine women. Throughout his illustrious career, women have generally responded to his deep caramel voice and intelligence combined with a kind of roughneck charm. Marilyn Monroe (he directed her last picture, *The Misfits*) once remarked that she didn't see how any woman could be around John without falling in love with him. Writing about himself, but by no means telling all, Huston nevertheless boasts of "Five wives; many liaisons, some more memorable than the marriages."

PRIMARY SOURCES: *An Open Book: An Autobiography*, by John Huston (Knopf, 1980); *John Huston: A Biography*, by Axel Madsen (Doubleday, 1978).

★*BLACK, LESLEY* Second wife, willowy Irish beauty on her first visit to the U.S. when Huston met her in Chicago, and proposed fifteen minutes later. John was 28, an actor playing Abe Lincoln in a stage production. Lesley, he recalls, "was right out of the Arthurian legends—a Lily Maid." They were married in 1937, but by 1941 Abe and his Lily Maid were nearly kaput. Huston attributed the breakup to her depression over the death of a newly born child. Madsen's bio adds the thought that "John had never stopped behaving as a bachelor . . . never stopped seeing other girls he picked up at huge, star-studded parties where he was always welcome." Anyway, Huston went off to the war in Europe, and Lesley filed for divorce.

★*CECE* Nickname for Celeste, Huston's fifth wife, who remains entirely nameless in his own book. She was the daughter of a Beverly Hills car-rental executive, "a tall, slim divorcée with doe eyes, nervous manners, and a fast, with-it patter." Cece started out as John's production secretary on a film. She was 31, Huston 66 when they married in the summer of 1972. Madsen notes, "Cece was many things to John—carnal surprise, social tonic, contemporary flutter, and even a lover of fast horses." Even his children liked her, but the marriage lasted just three years. Snarls Huston while vaulting over the episode: "I survived—but barely."

★*DE HAVILLAND, OLIVIA* Oscar-winning actress, sister of Joan Fontaine. He fell in love while directing *In This Our Life* (1942), with "Livvy" and Bette Davis. He was still married to Lesley Black, but Olivia accompanied him to New York in 1943 when he was headed overseas for war service. By 1945, however, their announced marriage plans were a casualty. Again, curiously, de Havilland is not acknowledged in the text of Huston's autobiography except for one brief entry about their working together on a film. Yet the book includes two snapshots of the couple, arms entwined, and a caption: *With Olivia de Havilland on a 1941 fishing trip.* (See also DE HAVILLAND listing.)

★*FITZGERALD, MARIETTA* Socialite known in later years as Marietta Tree, then married to Desmond Fitzgerald. She was a granddaughter of the founder of Groton. A war-weary Huston returned to New York after shooting *The Battle of San Pietro* in Italy, and quickly fell in love with Marietta, whom he calls "the most beautiful and desirable woman I had ever known." Huston anticipated their wartime romance leading to marriage after her husband was told the simple truth. Fitzgerald came back from the Far East, but agreed to a divorce only if his wife would undergo psychoanalysis first, to be sure she knew what she wanted. While Marietta was being analyzed, wayward John met Evelyn Keyes.

★*FLON, SUZANNE* French actress. She played the lost love of Toulouse-Lautrec in Huston's 1953 epic *Moulin Rouge*. But for once, Huston did not forget her. He writes,

"Her affection over the years has been my blessing on earth."

★*HARVEY, DOROTHY* First wife, actress he'd been smitten by after seeing her in a school play. "The first girl to whom I had ever made love that I had any feeling for other than carnal," Married when Huston was 20, they rented a beach shack in Malibu—and John adds, "As a result of that euphoric experience, I recommend young marriages to everyone." A few years later, they moved to town, started drinking too much. "Our marriage had become conventional. . . . I began having affairs. There were so many pretty girls." Nothing serious, he notes, "until Dorothy entered a room at the wrong moment." He sued for divorce in 1933, charging Dorothy with extravagance.

★*JOHANN, ZITA* Stage actress, wife of actor-producer John Houseman and Clark Gable's statuesque, sensual co-star in *Machinal* on Broadway. An RKO movie contract brought her to Hollywood, alone, and she began dating Huston, then still married to Dorothy. They went everywhere openly, says Madsen's bio, by all accounts a spectacular couple. After Zita suffered damage to her face in a 1933 auto accident, Houseman learned of it through a headline blaring: BEAUTY MARRED. It wasn't *that* bad, though Huston was booked for drunken driving, got off with a $30 fine. His book never mentions Zita.

★*KEYES, EVELYN* Third wife. Movie actress and author of autobiography titled *Scarlett O'Hara's Younger Sister*. They met at a postwar dinner party where Evelyn was seated between Huston and Errol Flynn. She slept in John's guest room on their first date, but that was only the beginning. Up to the very end, their exchanges were always cryptic. Evelyn proposed they get married during a dinner at Romanoff's restaurant. After a pause, John said, "Why not?" And they eloped that night. However, she was not fond of his friends, his habits, nor the menagerie at his ranch (Evelyn was allergic to fur), especially his pet chimpanzee. Finally she put it to him straight: "John darling, I'm sorry. One of us has to go

. . . it's the monkey or me." Once more, John paused briefly: "Honey . . . it's you." Before their divorce, Huston already had wife no. 4 waiting in the wings seven months pregnant. As part of the settlement, Evelyn took half of Huston's valuable pre-Columbian art collection. Years later, she won the other half when he challenged her to toss a coin for it. (See also KEYES listing.)

★*SALLIS, ZOE* Anglo-Iranian beauty, mother of Huston's second son, Danny, born in Rome out of wedlock in 1962, during his separation from his fourth wife, Ricki Soma. Zoe was at his side during the frenetic location filming of *The Night of the Iguana* (1964) and played a handmaiden in *The Bible* (1966).

★*SOMA, ENRICA "RICKI"* Fourth wife, a *Life* cover girl and daughter of popular Manhattan restaurateur Tony Soma. A family friend, Huston had known her since Ricki was a budding 9-year-old ballerina. With Huston in his mid-40s, Ricki in her teens, her parents were not pleased at the outset. Neither was third wife Keyes, who asked herself: "Is there something appealing about a girl-child growing up to a fuckable age under your nose? Probably." Ricki and John married in February 1950, one day after his divorce from Evelyn; their son Walter Anthony was born in April that year, daughter Anjelica a year later while Huston was shooting *African Queen* in the Congo. Daughter Allegra was born in London in 1964 while *The Bible* was in post-production, during Huston's legal separation from Ricki. En route to see John in Rome—accompanied by a young male friend—Ricki was killed in an auto crash in 1969.

MISCELLANY

★*"HATCHET FACE"* John was in his early teens, attending military school and hankering to have a go with "an absolutely hideous girl" all the lads pursued. He told her she was beautiful, took her to the beach, where virtue triumphed. "We got sand on our private parts—and that was the end of that."

★*NURSEMAID* The beginning had already

occurred, at home. Some time before 1912, she provided his "introduction to sex" in the classic manner. His mother fired the wench.

★*POTTER, PAULINE* Once head designer at Hattie Carnegie in New York, a longtime intimate and lifetime confidante, who later became a celebrated European hostess as Madame Philippe de Rothschild. Huston says, "There was no idea of a romance . . . she was simply the closest woman friend I've ever had."

HUTTON, BARBARA
(1912–1979)

Rudy Vallee sang at her coming-out party in 1930, during the depths of the Depression, with forty million unemployed. What the world needed then, it seemed, was a costly, lavish social debut for the Woolworth heiress—a poor little rich girl who was going to inherit $45 million tax-free. Her mother had committed suicide at age 35 in a suite at the Plaza Hotel after learning about one of her husband's love affairs, and young Babs found the body. That was one of the earlier lessons in her lifelong process of learning that money isn't everything. Her biography notes correctly that Babs Hutton "was as famous in the '30s and '40s as Hemingway and Hitler." She did everything expected of a girl in her position—spent millions on jewels and parties, married a movie matinee idol plus several titled European noblemen who were passionately in love with her money, and ended up in splendid, sickly solitude.

PRIMARY SOURCE: *Million Dollar Baby: An Intimate Portrait of Barbara Hutton*, by Philip Van Rensselaer (Putnam, 1979).

★*FRANKLIN, LLOYD* Very handsome Englishman whom Barbara met in 1960, when he was 20 and she was nearly 50. He was playing guitar and singing in a bar in Tangier, and she wanted him bad. Got him easy. Their affair spanned four years, Europe, the U.S. mainland, and Hawaii. Then Barbara heard that Lloyd was having an affair with an Indian maharanee in Deauville, where he was playing polo. She locked him out of her house for keeps. Lloyd, like her first husband, Alexis, was decapitated in an auto accident.

★*GRANT, CARY* Third husband, the one Barbara said she loved the most, and who wouldn't? "He was so sweet, so gentle. It didn't work out, but I loved him." She also admired superstar Cary as one of the few men she knew who worked for a living—and liked it. She believed he could "save" her. He did make her happy for a while after they married in 1942. (They were known in the press as "Cash and Cary.") But eventually Barbara grew bored with Hollywood, yearned to return to Europe, and became depressed over her deteriorating health. After their 1945 divorce (by mutual consent) Barbara vowed to reporters, "I'll never marry again." (See also GRANT listing.)

★*MDIVANI, PRINCE ALEXIS* First lover, first husband. International playboy whose brothers, Serge and David, became famous for draining the wealth of their movie-star wives, Pola Negri and Mae Murray respectively. Alexis was dark, good-looking, married, and very dangerous. When 19-year-old Barbara got him, she gleefully allowed, "Father would have a fit." When they married in 1933, she was still ecstatic; "It's going to be *fun* being a princess." A week after the wedding the prince slapped the princess on her naked bosom and admonished, "Look at your breasts! They're too fat!" With that, Barbara Hutton began her lifelong, anorexic dieting. Her new slimness and new blond hair delighted her husband, and their sex life became quite active. "He's tireless," said Barbara. Tireless too were their travels abroad, spending lavishly on the finer things of life. It was just too, too much. Prince and Princess divorced in 1933. Shortly after, he was decapitated in an auto accident.

★*REVENTLOW, COUNT KURT* Her second husband, second title. As a blushing bride (1934) Barbara swore she was happy at last. "My search is ended, I know this is safe and sure." It was neither; Reventlow turned out to be the cruelest and greediest of Barbara's husbands. After she had repeatedly denied him a husband's rights, he tried to inspire greater responsiveness in his wife by taking her to a cheap sex show in Paris. Babs was disgusted, Kurt horny. The divorce, maintaining custody of her son Lance, born in 1936, cost Barbara her American citizenship and a cool $4 million. The only advice forthcoming from her favorite aunt, Marjorie Hutton, was: "If you're contemplating marriage again, Barbara, dear, just remember to rotate your hips. It makes things more pleasant for the man."

★*RUBIROSA, PORFIRIO* Dominican diplomat and playboy extraordinaire. Elsa Maxwell told Barbara that Rubi would make her well again; "He's so healthy, so vigorous. . . . They say a woman isn't the same after a night with Rubi." On their wedding night (December 20, 1953) Rubi proved so amorous Barbara had to run into the bathroom to escape him; she fell and broke an ankle. Later she reported that the sight of Rubirosa naked was absolutely "appalling." Rubi didn't care; he was still carrying on with Zsa Zsa Gabor, who gave more press conferences than Barbara did to reveal her feelings about Rubi. Said Zsa Zsa: "Rubi loves me, I love Rubi, but who loves Barbara?" The marriage, Barbara's fifth, ended after seventy-three days. Yes, Rubi went back to Zsa Zsa. (See also GABOR and RUBIROSA listings.)

★*SWEENEY, BOBBY* American golfer with whom Barbara had an affair for several years, during and after her marriage to Reventlow. Little Lance once stated flatly, "I like Mr. Sweeney better than Daddy." Babs broke up with Bobby when she met Cary.

★*TROUBETZKOY, IGOR* Of Lithuanian royalty—in other words, without funds. But Igor, handsome and romantic, was the champion bicycle rider of France. He came in fourth among Barbara's husbands in 1947,

just about the time Barbara started having severe medical problems. Regarding their eventual divorce, Barbara observed, "A man can't feel very romantic when you're always in the emergency room."

★*VINH NA CHAMPASSAK, PRINCE DOAN* An artist of obscure origins. Like all of Barbara's husbands, he was a good-looker. She had him elevated to his majestic title when she met him in Tangier. They married in 1964, divorced in 1966. He was to remark: "She gave me more than four million. She gave me love." Doan was Barbara's seventh and last husband.

★*VON CRAMM, GOTTFRIED* Number six. A German baron who kept insisting, "I'm mad for you, darling Barbara." He used her money to restore his brother's and his mother's castles in Germany. Still, his family didn't like Barbara and spoke German in front of her all the time. The couple lived separate lives for years before their divorce in 1961.

JOPLIN, JANIS
(1943–1970)

Texas-born white soul singer who succumbed to a lethal overdose of hard drugs and liquor at age 27. Joplin stomped and shouted onstage, often brandishing a bottle of Southern Comfort, and her gut-wrenching performances were matched by the frenetic style of her private life—a series of funky scenes not unlike those played by Bette Midler in *The Rose,* filmed fiction with a hard edge of actuality. When she was the liberated pre-punk queen of '60s youth, Janis said: "People aren't supposed to be like me, sing like me, make out like me, drink like me, live like me; but now they're payin' $50,000 a night for *me* to be like me."

PRIMARY SOURCES: *Going Down with Janis,* by Peggy Caserta (Dell, 1974); *Janis Joplin: Her Life and Times,* by Deborah Landau (Paperback Library, 1971).

★*BRYCE* First name only, the second husband of Joan Baez's older sister Paulene, according to Caserta, in description of a scene at the Fifth Avenue Hotel, Greenwich Village: "She was balling the second of four guys who happened to be calling on her that day— Bryce. She'd already balled another guy, and there were two waiting in the lobby."

★*CASERTA, PEGGY* California boutique owner, author of bio chronicling her lesbian love affair with Joplin, at its best when both were high on heroin. "Balling Janis, particularly when she was drunk or stoned, could be an all-night affair," says Caserta. Graphic details pepper this self-absorbed biographer's tome, which includes such trivia as the fact that Caserta attended grade school with Lee Harvey Oswald.

★*CAVETT, DICK* TV talk-show host. After appearing on Cavett's show, Janis told Caserta she had balled him. And, "You'd never guess it, but Cavett has a much bigger cock and is a better lay than Namath." Caserta wondered if Janis wasn't making it all up.

★*COHAN, PETER* Sometime assistant to rock entrepreneur Albert Grossman, Joplin's manager. On at least one occasion played super-satisfying second diddle with Joplin and Caserta in a three-way sexual sandwich.

★*HELL'S ANGEL* An unidentified stud on wheels, but off long enough to seduce Janis, she insisted, "by cracking a fucking whiskey bottle over my head."

★*HELMS, CHET* Manager who hitchhiked with Janis from Austin to San Francisco, and urged her to get serious about her singing.

★*KRISTOFFERSON, KRIS* Composer-singer who became one of moviedom's top romantic leads. Peggy Caserta's problem: "We were in love with, and occasionally balling, the same silver-tongued devil of a man."

★*L'IL ABNER* Teenaged fan taken for a joyride by Janis, who spent four days enjoying his "crowbar" before she admitted he was just too young.

★*MACDONALD, COUNTRY JOE* Leader of musical group Country Joe and the Fish. Janis couldn't hook him for very long at a time, a constant source of frustration. At that point, quoth Caserta: "Nothing was going to convince me that Janis was anything but a straight little chick who wanted a man, almost any man, to love her."

★*MELVIN, MILAN* Performer with The Committee, satirical revue, and a former husband of Joan Baez's sister Mimi. Joplin called him "a magnificent fuck . . . not much for preliminaries, but the rest of it is sensational."

★*MITCHELL, VINCE* Equipment manager for Joplin at Woodstock. Pulled on his undershorts and left the room when he learned that Janis's other love was a lady.

★*MORGAN, SETH* Favorite male at the time of her death, who made her so happy that Janis was thinking seriously about marriage. Janis told Caserta that in love making, "Seth does the strangest thing. Every time I get ready to come, he hauls off and slaps me on the ass real hard. Man, I can't tell you how good that makes me feel."

★*NAMATH, JOE* Football star and man about town. As a lover, Joplin reportedly found him laughable: "Poor old Broadway Joe. He was a disaster." (See also CAVETT'S listing above.)

★*NEUWIRTH, BOBBY* Well-to-do rock star follower, one of Janis's companions during the pandemonium of Woodstock.

★*NIEHAUS, DAVID* A pickup and fellow traveler collected on a junket to Brazil. In love again.

★*POLLARD, MICHAEL* Actor who rose to prominence briefly for his supporting role in *Bonnie and Clyde*. Occasional date while Joplin was on a celebrity kick.

★*RIVERS, TRAVIS* Friend sent by Helms to bring Janis back from a trip home to Port Arthur, Texas. "He just threw me down and whoooo, baby! I think it had been about a whole year since I'd been laid. Who the hell you goin' to fuck in Port Arthur?"

★*"SUNSHINE"* Temporary live-in girlfriend, dismissed by Caserta: "One of those star-struck little chicks who gets their kicks just being around someone like Janis."

★*WAILEY, PAUL* Small, thin, pimply, and

married. Something borrowed, briefly, from a group called Blue Cheer.

MISCELLANY

★*BLACK GIRL*   Brief fling during first trip to San Francisco in early '60s.

★*SUCCESSION OF GUYS, GROUPIES, HANGERS-ON*   Mostly nameless companions in pursuit of pleasure, pursuant to Joplin's professed philosophy: "If it feels good and doesn't hurt anybody, do it."

KEATON, DIANE
(b. 1949)

Wistful but strong-willed actress known chiefly as a former girlfriend and favorite leading lady of Woody Allen's, with a 1977 Oscar for *Annie Hall* among her souvenirs. Keaton has recently been personally and professionally involved with actor-producer Warren Beatty, co-starring with him in *Reds* and scoring a personal triumph that may outrank anything she has done heretofore. Keaton got her start in the Broadway company of *Hair*, one of the featured few who did *not* appear nude. Surprisingly, she has exposed her private world in other respects by the long liaison with Allen, playing the *fey goyish* girl of his fantasies, though she proved in *The Godfather* (I and II) and in *Shoot the Moon* (1982), with Albert Finney, that she is a subtle, forceful dramatic actress who does not need the man in her life to support her claim to stardom.

PRIMARY SOURCE: *The Diane Keaton Scrapbook*, by Suzanne Munshower (Tempo Star Book/Ace Books/ Grosset & Dunlap, 1979).

★*ALLEN, WOODY*   She was performing in *Hair* on Broadway and only 22 when she met cabaret comedian Woody, then 33 and three quarters of an inch shorter than her five feet seven. Keaton has appeared in five films directed by and/or co-starring Allen, playing characters that are usually more dizzy than brainy—with the notable exception of *Interiors*. Like Annie Hall, Diane *is* a kooky WASP California chick, and Allen *is* a neurotic Jewish New York intellectual. (Remember that scene in the movie in which he tells his analyst that he and his girlfriend hardly make love at all, "not more than three times a week," and she claims to her shrink that her boyfriend can't get enough sex—demanding it three times a week!) Anyway, what Allen and Keaton had together was obviously great while it lasted. And it lasted, more or less, until Beatty came along. Gushes Munshower, "They aren't lovers, but they're more than just friends." Meanwhile Allen's found a new lover in much-married Mia Farrow.

★*BEATTY, WARREN*   He's Mr. Handsome, also shrewd and talented and perhaps one of the swingingest bachelors in Hollywood, now or ever. Beatty had a variety of liaisons with lovely ladies (see his own listing) before he became *the* man in Diane's life. According to Munshower, again, "On the surface these two might *seem* an unlikely pair, but in reality, Diane and Warren have a lot in common. Like Diane, Warren moved to New York shortly after high school to pursue an acting career . . . he took odd jobs . . . he also got his start on the Broadway stage and made the transition to movies." Also, this analysis concludes, Beatty is "a very private person, and has every intention of remaining that way." Actually, Diane and Warren weren't seen together much after the filming of *Reds*, but recent reports indicate they're still a viable team.

MISCELLANY

★*GOULD, ELLIOTT*   A friend. He says that Diane "has the personality of an Amish groupie."

KENNEDY, JOHN FITZGERALD
(1917–1963)

Thirty-fifth President of the U.S.A., assassinated in Dallas, Texas, before concluding his first term. His well-earned reputation as a ladies' man when he was a U.S. Senator abated somewhat, if only temporarily, following his 1953 marriage to Jacqueline Lee Bouvier. Despite persistent rumors that their marriage had foundered, the Kennedys were a stylish, pace-setting President and First Lady. Not until years after JFK's death and his widow's remarriage did the rumors, gossip, reminiscences, and skeletons of old scandals begin to emerge from the Kennedy closets, often quite soundly substantiated.

PRIMARY SOURCES: *Jackie Oh!*, by Kitty Kelley (Ballantine, 1979); *Jackie: A Truly Intimate Biography*, by Freda Kramer (Grosset & Dunlap, 1979). Also *Zsa Zsa Gabor: My Story*, "written for me by Gerold Frank" (World, 1960); *Ecstasy and Me: My Life as a Woman*, by Hedy Lamarr (Bartholomew, 1966); *Finding Marilyn: A Romance*, by David Conover (Grosset and Dunlap, 1981); *Gene Tierney: Self-Portrait*, by Gene Tierney (Wyden, 1980).

★*ARVAD, INGA* Scandinavian beauty, married, and a very good friend in the early years, though old Joe Kennedy objected to his son's relationship with a woman—albeit she worked for the *Washington Times-Herald*—who reportedly had once chummed around with Hitler. The FBI thought she might be a Nazi spy. Ever nonchalant, Jack called her Inga Binga.

★*BOUVIER, JACQUELINE LEE* Wife, First Lady, mother of Caroline and John-John, later married to Aristotle Onassis. Supposedly irreverent and playful, enjoyed gossip about other people's sexual indiscretions but became less and less amused by her husband's chronic infidelity. Known to have said, "I don't think there are any men who are faithful to their wives." (See also JACQUELINE KENNEDY ONASSIS listing.)

★*DICKINSON, ANGIE* Durable Hollywood bombshell and top-ranking TV star, former wife of composer Burt Bacharach. Speculating on Kennedy's decision to marry Jackie, family friend Betty Spalding said: "He was going to be President, and he certainly couldn't take Angie Dickinson to the White House with him." Biographer Kramer makes clear reference to a "lovely blond actress, later to become the wife of a celebrated composer, who excited Jack's interest for a time."

★*EXNER, JUDITH CAMPBELL* Girl about town who subsequently talked profusely about her liaisons with JFK, Frank Sinatra, and such unsavory Mafiosi as Sam Giancana. J. Edgar Hoover warned Kennedy to cool it, and he did.

★*FIDDLE AND FADDLE* Nickname for White House employees described by Senator George Smathers as "a couple of dogs . . . those two girls were the ugliest things I've ever seen." According to George, a woman did not have to be beautiful to win JFK's favor.

★*GABOR, ZSA ZSA* Hungarian-born actress and manhunter. "Jack used to take me out quite often . . . he was a sweetheart." (See also GABOR listing.)

★*GRAHAM, NOEL NOEL* Widow of Philip Graham, onetime editor of the *Washington Post*. Old flame who recalls JFK "wasn't bad" in bed, and had "a great sense of fun out of it." He was seeing her while courting Jackie, whom she strongly advised him to wed. "We were in Europe together, and after we made love in Italy I told him I was going to send him home to propose to the girl he should marry."

★*LAMARR, HEDY* Viennese-born glamour girl, a top film star during her brief encounter with young John Kennedy in Paris during the war. (See also LAMARR listing.)

★*MEYER, MARY PINCHOT* Beautiful blond socialite, (Vassar '42) longtime friend of JFK's and reportedly a frequent guest at the White House pool. Confided to friends that she smoked pot with JFK in his bedroom, and he promised to get some cocaine. In early '64, a few months after Kennedy's death, Mary was murdered—a bullet wound in the head—while jogging on a Georgetown towpath.

★*MONROE, MARILYN* Legendary Hollywood sexpot cum laude. After both JFK and MM were dead, columnist Earl Wilson reported numerous secret meetings between them during Kennedy's White House years. And a new version of the story comes from someone close to Marilyn. (See also MONROE listing.)

★*MYSTERY WOMAN* Unidentified guest of the Joseph Alsops who "went upstairs" with JFK on the night of his inaugural gala after Jackie had gone home to bed. Kelley reports Alsop's tactful "Well, the President was hungry, and so I fed him terrapin."

★*PURDOM, ALICIA* Wife of actor Edmund Purdom. J. Edgar Hoover's files yielded documents relating to an Italian magazine story that Alicia had been engaged to JFK, circa 1951, jilted when Papa Joe interfered. An alleged $500,000 payoff settled the case.

★*TIERNEY, GENE* Beautiful '40s film actress, starred in *Laura*. A long, serious relationship, though JFK's political ambition made marriage to a movie star impractical—particularly to a divorced, non-Catholic movie star. On a week's holiday at Cape Cod, where she met his family, Tierney recalls, "Jack met me at the station wearing patched blue jeans. . . . I thought he looked like Tom Sawyer." On another occasion, "It was for Jack that I first wore one of the ankle-length New Look dresses made famous by Dior." JFK's reaction was, "Good God, Gene, what's *that?*" Her rueful reminiscence notes that Jack just shook his head when she talked about high fashion. "He later married a very stylish lady, but I think it's fair to say that clothes were not his weakness." (See also TIERNEY listing.)

★*TURNURE, PAMELA* Became Jackie's press secretary in the White House, with a personal recommendation from the President. Her occasional late-night meetings with JFK were taped by Pam's Georgetown landlords, Mr. and Mrs. Leonard Kater, in 1958. They even tried to get a snapshot of Kennedy slipping away in the wee hours, but he merely laughed and drove off. Staunch, outraged Irish Catholics, the Katers later tried to use taped and photographic evidence to keep Senator Kennedy from becoming President. They often showed up at rallies or public occasions to state their case, but found the press uncooperative. Pam stayed on.

MISCELLANY

★*NIVEN, HJORDIS* Kennedy crony Senator George Smathers told of JFK's disappearing with Mrs. N. below decks of Presidential yacht for ten minutes or so during his 43d birthday party. While he draws no conclusions about *that* incident, Smathers describes JFK colorfully as "a rooster getting on top of a chicken real fast and then the poor little hen ruffles her feathers and wonders what the hell happened. . . . Jack was something, almost like a Roto-Rooter."

★*SIMMONS, JEAN* Former husband Stewart Granger, in his autobiography, recalls the time Jean came back from location shooting in Boston for a movie called *Home Before Dark*. "She told me of this very attractive Senator who had wooed her with flowers and eventually ended up practically breaking down her bedroom door." With a grin, Jean added that he "had such a lovely smile I nearly let him in." Bridling, Stewart asked if she knew his name. "Yes, he's a very important senator called John Kennedy." Adds Granger: "I'd never heard of him."

★*OTHER WOMEN* Secretaries, stewardesses, desk clerks, hatcheck girls, etc. Giddy romps in and out of the White House reported by Kelley, who found most interviewees unimpressed by Kennedy's sexual performance. Said one, typically, "I was fascinated by him at the time, but our lovemaking was so disastrous that for years I was convinced I was frigid. . . . he was terrible in bed." What's more, "he did not perceive women as human beings, or even as objects of affection."

KEYES, EVELYN
(b. 1919)

The perennial dewy-eyed starlet, who went from high school in Atlanta to the Studio Club in Hollywood, and first gained recognition as Suellen in *Gone with the Wind.* After numerous mediocre movies and four foul-to-middling marriages, Keyes wrote a novel *(I Am a Billboard)* and made a comeback on the stage, heading a road company of the musical *No, No, Nanette.* As a lady who had more often said yes, Keyes quite probably wrote every word of her effusive memoirs, in which she reveals she "took up with the man of the moment—and there were many such moments."

PRIMARY SOURCE: *Scarlett O'Hara's Younger Sister, or My Lively Life in and out of Hollywood* (Lyle Stuart, 1977).

★*ARGENTINE DIPLOMAT* Minor adventure following marriage no. 3. Name not given, though they fell in love in Paris, broke their brief engagement during Evelyn's subsequent visit to Buenos Aires. So far there had been "no hanky-panky." So they undertook, in her hotel room, "a reasonable facsimile of the sex act. A futile gesture, and empty for us both. He got up, punched his fist through the door, and left. The end."

★*BAINBRIDGE, BARTON* He seemed a "mature" businessman—he was 27 when 17-year-old Evelyn met him while staying at the Hollywood Studio Club. He introduced her to bars and sloe-gin fizzes, but sex still held no magic. "I had to be the world's lousiest lay. But then, so was Barton." Evelyn got pregnant, went for an abortion—and Barton went back for "another vasectomy" while she got her first diaphragm—and they were secretly married before the 1939 premiere of *GWTW.* After their stormy, unsatisfying mismatch, Barton committed suicide by shotgun just as World War II was warming up. He left her his new blue Packard convertible, then "spewed his brains all over the inside of my old white Pontiac."

★*"BILL"* The anonymous young man, 20 or so, to whom Evelyn lost her virginity in Atlanta in her teens. She met him at a dance studio between pirouettes. He had great teeth, and his style was loose, with great legs and knees, and "she had this thing for knees." His foreplay was pretty loose, too—an experience so intense Evelyn had to switch over to third person to describe it: "His tongue filled her mouth, he opened her blouse and sucked at her breasts, pulling at the nipples until they rose in hard little knobs. . . ." By the time they got into a motel, she was too scared to follow through. The second time worked, but Bill lacked finesse. "What a disappointment . . . all pain and blood, and not an ounce of ecstasy as promised." Having had enough of "that nonsense," she decided to be a movie actress in Hollywood and go to UCLA in her spare time.

★*BLACK SINGER* Name not given. Between marriages, Evelyn saw him performing at a party and in her "exuberance," invited him over to her place. Being a southern girl, she wasn't sure what to expect, but describes his superstud reputation as "the black man's burden." Though his color was no problem, her passion cooled when she found he wore a hairpiece. "The soft woolly stuff gave way under my clutching hand. . . . the thrill was gone."

★*DOUGLAS, KIRK* Their affair lasted four months. *The Champion* had made him "the hottest star in town" when she met him while dating Farley Granger during her estrangement from John Huston. Captivated by his hair, his dimple, his jaw, Keyes reveals Kirk was "in and out—in more ways than one," while parted from his wife and undergoing psychoanalysis. He'd pace up and down her living room (or bedroom), crying, "A ragpicker's son, facing the world, cock in hand!" She credits Kirk with getting *her* to a shrink.

★*FRENCHMAN* A brief fling in Paris, sandwiched between swimming and French lessons. At this point in her life, Keyes was appalled to find he was uncircumcised, declared herself totally turned off by "that untidy foreskin."

★*GUINLE, CARLOS* Wealthy Brazilian, one of the younger Guinle brothers. Who were the Guinles? "Rich is who they were . . . very rich indeed." Keyes spent two months in Rio as his guest after an encounter at a film festival in Punta del Este. Lots of rumba, samba, and cha-cha-cha. When she got home to her analyst, she discontinued sessions after he questioned the frequency—and brevity—of her affairs. Evelyn was listening to her own council: "At fifty dollars a throw . . . why should I be subjected to that shit?"

★*HUSTON, JOHN* Eminent director and husband no. 3, lover of horses, women, and himself. "His lovemaking was sure, with authority, and cool as always. 'Isn't this an amusing thing we're doing?' was the tone of the action. And then he fell asleep." Evelyn was even less amused by John's cronies and his macho interests. He later referred to a hunting trip as "the best part of our life together." She never got over how he'd goaded her into killing a deer, and had the head mounted on the wall at their ranch, "to haunt me until the place was sold." Huston also wanted to have a child, but couldn't seem to get Evelyn pregnant. He had better luck with 18-year-old Ricky Soma, whom he had known since she was 9—and who liked horses. Also, "I guess she would show me a thing or two about sperm," Evelyn muses. By then, of course, the end was nigh. (See also HUSTON listing.)

★*NEAL, BOB* Rich "splendid" young Texan whom Evelyn "took up with" after Ricky's visits prompted her to call it quits with Huston. Neal gave Keyes five fur coats and a gray Cadillac with a telephone in it . . . with her initials in bright red on the side. "John didn't like it at all. He said it was vulgar." Still under her errant hubby's influence, Evelyn gave everything back.

★*NIVEN, DAVID* Popular, dashing British actor. A one-night stand. Keyes found him "darling, a marvelous sense of humor, delicious as French pastry." Niven was single then—"ripe for plucking." But she was still

hung up on John. Later, she suggested David to Mike Todd for the plum role he landed in *Around the World in 80 Days*. (See also NIVEN listing.)

★*QUINN, ANTHONY* Durable leading actor. Both were contract players at Paramount circa 1937 when she was won by his "startling black eyes and intense manner." Keyes recalls that Quinn proposed marriage and thought they'd become a famous acting couple "like Lynn Fontanne and Alfred Lunt." She was still single, still sexually unschooled, but Tony wanted to consummate their togetherness. "So I tried the thing again. And was disappointed—again. The earth stood perfectly still."

★*SHAW, ARTIE* Clarinet-playing band leader and husband no. 4. Consummating *their* affair, in Paris on a second date, seemed "as natural as the morning dew." The freshness began to fade soon after their marriage. Shaw, citing the failures of Lana Turner and Ava Gardner—two former mates—set out to instruct Evelyn how to be a good wife. Artie ran a tight ship, and told her "someone has to be the captain." Guess who? Which meant filter tips facing the right way in his cigarette box, pillows fluffed just so. Six years of hypercriticism and close-order domesticity left Evelyn nothing more to dew, so she decamped again. (See also SHAW listing.)

★*SPANIARD* A handsome jai-lai player she met in Mexico post-Huston, "Our affair was Erica Jong's zipless fuck." It was all sunswept and beautiful, and he could play the piano, too. When his team moved on, she "took another lover, and another." It was never the same zip.

★*TODD, MIKE* The flashy film producer, subsequently married to Elizabeth Taylor. Evelyn got him to shave the hair off his back. A fast mover, Todd would phone her from the airport to say "SIB"—Stay in bed. He'd be reaching for the phone before they quite finished making love, but not without whispering a quick preview of what they might do the next time. Evelyn calls him "Future-shock in person." Their hectic off-again-on-again romance was troubled by Todd's uncontrollable jealousy, which got worse when she confessed sleeping with a black man (see above). Thereafter, every time they watched a black singer— or went backstage to hug Sammy Davis— there'd be a battle royal. Then Todd fell in love with Elizabeth; Keyes met Shaw. (See also TODD listing.)

★*VIDOR, CHARLES* Hungarian-born director, Evelyn's second husband, who later became known for glossy Rita Hayworth vehicles (particularly *Cover Girl* and *Gilda).* Evelyn met him while making *The Lady in Question,* and discovered that Vidor had all the answers. In sex with him, she recalls, "my body shuddered to life" and she achieved all the anticipated special effects for the first time. Cunnilingus did the trick; "buzzing rockets burst in brilliant explosion and shot me out into space." When she came down, she told Vidor she never knew it could be like that. "Of course not," he said, "you have never known a Hungarian." They married after Barton's suicide, and it was four years before all the giddy voluptuousness turned to goulash. "He got his best kicks by having sly little affairs behind his current wife's back."

MISCELLANY

★*COHN, HARRY* Powerful movie executive who ruled Columbia Pictures with an iron hand, a stern Big Daddy to most of his stars. Keyes recalls being unsure when Cohn stepped over the line that separated business from "that little degree *more* that means—I want to lay you." Though she vows he never did, he was obsessed with grilling her in his office about her sex life, and once went a few steps beyond that: "His belly touched mine. His hand reached between my legs. He rubbed. *Save that for me,* he whispered, *I'm going to marry you."* It gave her chills. Evelyn gave little in return. And, Cohn later said in his quiet, forceful way, "You'll never be a bigger star than you are now. I'll see to that."

★*HAYDEN, STERLING* Tall, blond, outdoorsy actor described by Keyes at the time "as a very serious young man bent on saving

the world." Their first date established a wide cultural gap. "He wanted to hang around my apartment that evening and read the *Communist Manifesto* aloud to me . . . I insisted on going dancing at the Mocambo." Next day, with their picture in the paper, Evelyn was again summoned by Harry Cohn. "Did you let him go all the way with you?" Calling her "worse than a whore, you give it away," Cohn dropped her contract.

★*MARCH, FREDRIC* Top film actor and the lead in her first picture, *The Buccaneer* (1938), for Cecil B. De Mille. After C. B. had reduced her to tears on the set, March took Evelyn to his dressing room and offered reassurance. "Then, in the gentlest way, he took my hand and placed it over the bulge in the front of those tight white pants. My first movie-star erection, in person." A moment later, an assistant knocked to say: "Ready when you are, Mr. March." Evelyn got out, fast.

KHAN, ALY
(1911–1960)

Globe-trotting playboy prince, son and heir of the Aga Khan, spiritual leader of millions of Moslems. Officially known as His Highness Prince Aly Salomone Khan, Aly became so notorious for his affairs and misadventures that he was bypassed in the royal succession, his own son ascending to the old Aga's title and prerogatives (one fringe benefit was the annual custom of paying the resident Aga his weight in jewels). Unmindful Aly went his merry way, until his death in a Paris auto accident in 1960.

PRIMARY SOURCES: *Linda: My Own Story,* by Linda Christian (Crown, 1962); *No Bed of Roses: An Autobiography,* by Joan Fontaine (Morrow, 1978); *Zsa Zsa Gabor: My Story,* "written for me by Gerold Frank" (World, 1960); *Rita Hayworth: The Time, the Place and the Woman,* by John Kobal (Norton, 1978); *Gene Tierney: Self Portrait,* by Gene Tierney (Wyden, 1980); *King Cohn,* by Bob Thomas (Putnam, 1967).

★*CHRISTIAN, LINDA* They traveled in the same international jet set, the group that summers on the Côte d'Azur, winters in Switzerland. It's possible but not bloody likely that Aly and Linda were no more than just very good friends; he invited her to stay at his Chateau Horizon in Cannes while she grieved over the death of her lover, race driver Fon Portago. (See also CHRISTIAN listing.)

★*FONTAINE, JOAN* In Paris, in 1951, Joan got the full treatment from Aly. First there was "a roomful of roses," then lunch at Maxim's, with a small present from Cartier's. Then, "We raced to Deauville, where we galloped along the beach on hacks . . . attended galas at the casino . . . and swam in the Mediterranean at his villa." (See also FONTAINE listing.)

★*FURNESS, LADY THELMA* She might have married the Prince of Wales (later Edward VIII, later still the Duke of Windsor—who married Wallis Simpson and made her the Duchess). But Lady Thelma fell for Aly. And the course of history changed.

★*GABOR, ZSA ZSA* It was in Paris, approximately the same time that Khan gave Joan Fontaine the big rush, that Aly shook hands with Zsa Zsa and said, "You're one of the few women in America I've longed to meet." The next day, she had the obligatory roomful of roses. They went out, but Zsa Zsa had the strange feeling that while he was dancing with her, his mind—and his eye—was on other conquests. (See also GABOR listing.)

★*GRECO, JULIETTE* An international beauty and actress who was a favored companion of Khan's in his later years.

★*GUINNESS, JOAN* Wife of Loel Guinness, noted businessman and member of Parliament, until she met Aly. She became his first wife, had two sons, Karim (the inheritor of the title) and Amyn.

★*HAYWORTH, RITA* Elsa Maxwell introduced them at a party on the Riviera, while Rita recovered from Orson Welles. Smooth-talking Aly charmed her, though she didn't know who he was. Neither Rita nor Aly was as yet divorced, and Columbia Studios boss Harry Cohn began fuming when they went to Mexico together, reporters close behind.

Cohn sent an emissary to Rita, who bitterly complained about their total lack of privacy. "It's your fault," said Cohn's rep, "you wanted to be a movie star." Then to Aly: "And it's your fault too. You're not exactly John Doe!" Ever possessive, Aly demanded of Rita, "Who is this John Doe?"—suspecting he might be a former lover. Arguments availed nothing. Rita forfeited her $248,000 salary and married Aly in France on May 24, 1949. Two years later she returned to Columbia, poorer but only marginally wiser, and then married singer Dick Haymes. (See also HAYWORTH listing.)

★*NOVAK, KIM* She was to say other men seemed only "half alive" after Aly.

★*TIERNEY, GENE* On being introduced to him in Argentina, Gene was singularly unimpressed. "I labeled him a man of trivia. Nor was I taken with his looks. He had a soft face." She changed her opinion of Khan a couple of years later, as she recovered from a nervous breakdown. He was very kind to her, "never forcing himself." And they spent a lovely summer, swimming, sailing, partying, etc. Gene saw him as the answer to her troubles. However, as he had just divorced one movie star (Hayworth), she was not the answer to his. (See also TIERNEY listing.)

KILGALLEN, DOROTHY
(1913–1965)

The pampered daughter of a famous newspaperman, James Kilgallen, she became an intrepid girl reporter and an influential Broadway columnist—though Dorothy is probably better known to the TV viewing public as a longtime panelist on *What's My Line?* Exclusive stories were her line, and Kilgallen's syndicated column featuring gossip, publicity, blurbs, and murder (she wrote a book, *Murder One*, about famous trials she had covered) made her a media celebrity of sorts. A heavy drinker, she was discovered dead on November 8, 1965, death attributed to "too much pills and liquor," though biographer Lee Israel hints at a conspiracy "to obfuscate the truth," implying a possible link with "another exclusive" due from Dottie on Kennedy's assassination. Her friend Joan Crawford had the best last word. The night after Kilgallen's death, the Big Blackout hit, with the lights going out along the entire Eastern Seaboard. Simultaneously grieving, boozing, and gazing out her window, Joan was heard to exclaim: "What a wonderful tribute to Dorothy."

PRIMARY SOURCE: *Kilgallen*, by Lee Israel (Delacorte, 1979; Dell, 1980).

★*GALLICO, PAUL*   Top New York sportswriter and novelist. Dorothy met Gallico through Daddy and dated him frequently enough to make news. From Walter Winchell's column: "Paul Gallico . . . confides to intimates that if Dorothy Kilgallen would have him, she's the one he'd like to Love, Honor and O, Boy!" However, Gallico was twice divorced (a no-no for the Catholic Kilgallens) and much too old for Dorothy.

★*KOLLMER, RICHARD*   Actor and entrepreneur, Dorothy's *only* husband. Richard, 'twas said, was "one of those rare laughers who actually emitted the sound *ha-ha.*" He probably wasn't laughing when he married Dorothy in 1940 in a *high* nuptial mass that one guest compared to "a four-day Guatemalan street festival." His "whoring" began soon after. Conveniently, when Kollmer ran a restaurant called the Left Bank, he kept an apartment upstairs to which he brought "conquest after conquest." Dorothy ignored these dalliances, as he tried to ignore hers (see Ray, below). To the public they were the deliriously happy couple of the *Breakfast with Dorothy and Dick* radio show, the most popular program of its kind. Dorothy and Dick had two sons, Richard Thomas and Kerry, eventually settled for separate quarters in their East Side New York brownstone. They were still man and wife when Kilgallen died in 1965.

★*OUT-OF-TOWNER*   He was a newspaperman whom Dorothy met on a European press junket to the location shooting of *The Sound of Music* in Austria. They junketed together again later that year, and soon were meeting in *their* room at New York's Regency Hotel. "She was like a little girl after her first date," said a friend; "going on about how marvelous he was, the moonlight and the clouds and the poetry he recited." A great deal of mystery still surrounds the relationship, according to biographer Lee Israel; to wit, the mystery of whether or not the out-of-towner saw Dorothy the night she died.

★*RAY, JOHNNIE*   The sob singer, whose breakthrough hit was "Little White Cloud That Cried." He was the "mystery guest" on *What's My Line*, and panelist Dorothy had a clue. She was 44, he not yet 30, and theirs was a strange affair. "Dorothy taught Johnnie to eat snails. . . . She bought him gifts from Bergdorf's and Cartier. . . . He sent her lavender roses. . . . At El Morocco, he took her shoe off and kissed her foot." Their very physical displays of affection—anytime, almost anywhere—became the talk of the town. At the parties at his place every Sunday after her TV show, Dorothy would invariably drag Johnnie into the den to "do it" on a long leather couch. Recalls one observer: "We used to go over to the keyhole and look into the room. It became a joke." Dorothy was aware of the men in Johnnie's life, but attached no significance to them, though he was generally acknowledged to be bisexual. After one terrible scene with husband Richard (he *hated* Dorothy's necking with Johnnie in his nightclub), she begged Johnnie to take her away with him. Years later, Ray recalled he convinced Dorothy that if she walked out with him she'd lose not only her husband, but her kids, her career, *everything.* He added: "Henry Luce [sic] and Marion Davies are one thing—*but Johnnie Ray and Dorothy Kilgallen!*"

MISCELLANY

★*BAGLEY, BEN*   Entrepreneur and record producer. He was Dorothy's frequent escort to Broadway plays.

★*POWER, TYRONE*   They met during Dorothy's short stint as a Hollywood columnist, and continued to see each other there—

"lunching, nightclubbing, laughing a good deal." He became her notion of "Mr. Right," and Dorothy wrote a short story fantasizing about a character like Power who "sweeps her off her feet into the sunset as his wife." They had one date in New York just before he announced his plans to marry Annabella. (See also POWER listing.)

★*SINATRA, FRANK* When Frankie first hit the bigtime, Broadway columnist Kilgallen was one of his most vocal fans. Then, inexplicably, she began to pester him, in print, about his arrogance, his obsession with Ava—and Ava's rumored involvement with Lana Turner. (One Kilgallen headline read, "Lana, Ava having gay time in Mexico.") Dorothy may have been the root cause of Sinatra's well-known animosity toward the press, and he began to strike back, telling nightclub audiences what an "ugly broad" Kilgallen was. He likened her face to a chipmunk's, and he may have coined the cruelest term for D. K. as "the chinless wonder."

★*VON EPP, GENERAL RITTER* Governor General of Bavaria, one of Hitler's most trusted friends. Dorothy met him on the airship *Hindenburg* (1936) and he offered to take her to lunch with Hitler. She declined—in order to continue her twenty-one-day round-the-world race, in which she was the only female competing with three other New York journalists.

KISSINGER, HENRY A.
(b. 1923)

Former Secretary of State under Presidents Nixon and Ford, brilliant German-born political pundit sometimes known to his detractors as Dr. Strangelove. Lured to Washington from the groves of academe at Harvard by Nelson Rockefeller, who thought Henry was just what the country needed, Kissinger remains an influential elder statesman in foreign affairs, with or without portfolio. Before his marriage, was also known to have a predilection for pretty ladies if they were rich or famous, and preferably both. He habitually appeared at the more frivolous public functions with a ravishing creature on his arm, though there's a substantial body of opinion (and some first-person testimony) that when all's said and done, Kissinger is more concerned with staying power in the political arena than on the merry-go-round of love.

PRIMARY SOURCES: *Kissinger: The Adventures of Super-Kraut*, by Charles R. Ashman (Lyle Stuart, 1972; Dell, 1973); *Dear Henry: A Confession*, by Danielle Hunebelle (Gallimard, 1972; English translation, Berkley, 1972).

★*BROWN, JUDY* Well-stacked starlet with leading roles in X-rated movies such as the Danish classic *Threesome*. Henry said the "Brown affair" lasted for three dinner dates, but Judy claims her Kissinger affair lasted over a year, and that Henry kept her "in a closet," while he dated more *acceptable* girls. She told him he couldn't have his cake and eat it too, to which he replied, 'Well, then, I guess I won't have my cake." Judy then held a press conference to reveal how "hurt" she was seeing Kissinger written about with so many other women. "I've got an ego, too," Judy said. Kissinger pointed out that she also had a press agent, and charged Judy with being "a publicity maniac."

★*FLEICHER, ANN* Kissinger's first wife. The marriage lasted from 1949 to 1964 and produced two children, Elizabeth and David.

★*GABOR, ZSA ZSA* It was allegedly President Nixon and wife Pat themselves who gleefully "set up" Henry Kissinger with dinner partner Zsa Zsa. Some thought it would be a terrible mismatch—egghead and bubblehead. But the lady fooled 'em, holding her own in discussions of world affairs. "Henry found Zsa Zsa refreshingly bright after his tours of duty with the gushy starlet set." Zsa Zsa thought he wasn't much to look at, "but after he opens his mouth . . . he's Cary Grant." She put down all the rumors: "He'll never marry me, dahling.

. . . He thinks I am too much woman for him." Henry was not at ringside when Zsa Zsa opened her new act in Las Vegas (because he was in Paris for secret peace talks), but he sent roses. (See also GABOR listing.)

★*HOWAR, BARBARA* Being older, smarter, married, and a *Democrat*, Barbara did not fit the pattern of Henry's glamour-girl dates. After her divorce she landed her own TV show, shown locally in Washington, on which Kissinger made his first TV appearance—exposing at last his teutonic Dr. Strangelove accent. Barbara and Henry dated for four years. She said they shared nothing more than friendship (see also HOWAR listing.) Maybe so. Howar, always ready with a quip, got off two of her better ones re Kissinger. To his face: "Henry, would that you could get in and out of Hollywood as quietly as you did Peking." To reporters: "After all, if you're with Golda Meir all day you don't need Mrs. Gandhi all night. You want Jill St. John!"

★*HUNEBELLE, DANIELLE* French journalist who, late in 1969, began interviewing Presidential Adviser Kissinger for a French TV special. She obviously developed an enormous crush on Dr. K. and continued to find excuses to see him again. *Dear Henry*, the book she wrote about her "affair" with Kissinger, gives no evidence at all that he returned her affection, or that they ever enjoyed intimacies beyond sitting on a sofa in his office holding hands. Mme. Hunebelle's book, in fact, is an embarrassment revealing little more than the author's own romantic fantasies and frustrations.

★*MAGINNES, NANCY* Author Charles Ashman mentions Nancy only as one of Henry's "legitimate ladies," on call to accompany the Secretary of State to high-class diplomatic affairs. Nancy was a New Yorker and had worked for Governor Nelson Rockefeller when Kissinger was also on the Rockefeller payroll. Kissinger, of course, married Nancy, the current Mrs. K., long after Ashman wrote his book.

★*OSMER, MARGARET* CBS News producer, a beauty as well as a brain, and for a while another one of Kissinger's "respectable" dates. Some indication of serious stuff here. Again, only for a while.

★*ST. JOHN, JILL* One of the first—and flashiest—of Henry's Hollywood women. She was dating Frank Sinatra when they met, and "only in America could a kinky-haired, horn-rimmed college professor steal a date from Sinatra." Over the next months, "Jill showed up all over California with Henry, and Henry showed up all over Jill in Washington, D.C." Miss St. John is known to be an intelligent companion, as well as smashingly beautiful. One of her more enigmatic remarks about the long association with Kissinger was that she enjoyed him as a chess partner much more than she enjoyed Sean Connery. "I don't know why. He's just more fun to play with."

★*STEINEM, GLORIA* She told the press: "I am not now, nor have I ever been, the girl friend of Henry Kissinger." Then, at a "Salute to Congress" dinner in 1972, Henry himself announced: "Gloria Steinem is not now and has never been my girl friend. But I am not discouraged. After all, she did not say that if nominated, she would not accept or if elected, she would not serve." And, author Ashman writes (circa 1972): "Gloria Steinem has become maybe the most important filly in Kissinger's life—perhaps because he has been totally unsuccessful in getting her into the hay." Their meetings—whatever kind of social or political intercourse they involved—were always carefully guarded secrets.

★*THOMAS, MARLO* They were seen dining together, jogging together. She confided to friends that she found Mr. Kissinger "terribly charming, extremely intelligent, and lovely company." They denied any plans to marry. To marry each other, that is. Ms. Thomas is now Mrs. Phil Donahue.

★*TOMPKINS, ANGEL* Tall, blond actress featured in *Playboy* and who was picked out by an advance man for Kissinger, "whose hobby was finding sweet young things whom his boss could appreciate." Kissinger kept the wraps on this romance. If there was one.

LAKE, VERONICA
(1919–1973)

Petite blond sylph from Brooklyn whose career burgeoned in wartime, often opposite Alan Ladd (beginning with *This Gun for Hire*, 1942). Her long, silky peek-a-boo hairdo became so popular and prevalent that female defense workers risked their lives imitating Lake, and the government requested she be given a role with her tresses *up* (she was then cast as a gallant nurse in *So Proudly We Hail*). Her fame was waning by the late '40s, her private life was no less a shambles, and she had a chronic peeve against Hollywood as "one giant, self-contained orgy farm . . . with every male in the movie business on the make." Few made her happy, however. Veronica decamped, and was rediscovered working in a New York restaurant in 1962.

PRIMARY SOURCE: *Veronica*, by Veronica Lake with Donald Bain (Citadel, 1971).

★*DETLIE, JOHN* Sophisticated 33-year-old Metro art director who "energetically" courted virginal 17-year-old Veronica. He called her "Mousie," she called him "Pops." He brought her luck (her first film, *I Wanted Wings*); she brought him a case of "hot pants." In 1941 they eloped, and after experiencing the "most beautiful" moment she'd ever known, Veronica fell asleep fingering her wedding ring, "a tiny panda with a diamond. . . . John knew I loved pandas." Their first child, Elaine, arrived exactly nine months later. The second, in 1943, died a few days after birth. John said it wasn't his; Veronica said nothing. They were divorced by year's end.

★*DE TOTH, ANDRE* ("Bandi") Hungarian director. Once belted Veronica and then offered her a knife "to cut out this unworthy Hungarian heart." She declined, noting she had made a lot of mistakes in her life. Her next one was marrying De Toth in 1944. Their first big problem was sex: "Whoever made up that line, wham-bam, thank you, ma'am, must

have had Bandi in mind." Problem no. 2: He *hated* being called "Mr. Lake." No. 3: He helped put her into bankruptcy. When she split in 1951, she *really* split, hibernating alone on a mountaintop for three months. Then, collecting her kids (by now a son, Mike, and second daughter, Diana, by De Toth), she said, "Fuck you, Hollywood," and headed for New York. She returned to the film capital only once more, in 1952, to collect her divorce papers.

★*DOZIER, WILLIAM* Film producer. He was one friend who offered comfort after she lost her baby, bringing her cherry pie and Grand Marnier, "a whimsical favorite of mine." After they decided to stop seeing each other, he married Joan Fontaine. (See also DOZIER listing.)

★*ELICKSON, ANDY* Merchant seaman, possibly Veronica's last great love. Down and out in New York, she was working as a waitress, he was a regular customer. She liked the way he "held his glass lovingly in hamhock hands." She waxes rhapsodic about Andy's "large, coarse body, his entrance, his throbbing moment of release . . . our miraculous and simultaneous detonation." She'd fly to meet him wherever he pulled into port, often staying over aboard his ship. They had a few good years before his death in 1965.

★*HAKIM BROTHERS* Powerful Egyptian film family. Tantalizingly, Veronica confides that she dated *all* the numerous Hakim brothers, but only slept with *one*. She enjoyed them en masse, however, "eyeing each other for some glint of a hint" as to which one it was.

★*MCCARTHY, JOE* Songwriter. Ronni thought they were two of a kind, so she married him in 1955 in Traverse City, Michigan, while touring with *Affairs of State*. They moved into a Greenwich Village brownstone and toured the local pubs *every* night, sometimes all night. "God, how we fought." Joe became violent, the courts ordered him to stay away from her. Another divorce.

★*NEGULESCO, JEAN* Film director. She was faithful to Jean "during the time we dated." He told close friends that her gaze embarrassed him: "I always think my fly is open when Ronni looks at me."

★*ONASSIS, ARISTOTLE* During the war his ships always got through, and he kept Veronica supplied with perfume, steaks, good wine, and nylons. "It was like getting a weekly Greek Care Package."

★*PERLOW, NAT* New York writer, onetime editor of *Police Gazette*. In 1961, one of her really bad years, he was Veronica's "shining knight," often paying the bills and showing up with bags of food.

MISCELLANY

★*FLYNN, ERROL* He struck out in getting Veronica into his "infamous" bed. He kissed her, smiled, said, "As you wish, Miss Lake."

★*HUGHES, HOWARD* A regular at Veronica's informal "kitchen parties." She liked him, was proud to be "one of his favorites," though she denies a romance. He would amaze her by calling from the White House, or at 5:00 A.M. asking her to take him to the airport. "His luggage was a corrugated Scott Tissue carton tied with heavy cord. A strange man." (See also HUGHES listing.)

★*LADD, ALAN* Frequent co-star. Veronica thought they were a good match; "We were both little people." They were also business-like, indifferent to the publicity that hinted they were lovers.

★*MANVILLE, TOMMY* Many-times-married eccentric millionaire. Veronica received a telegram in which he offered her $100,000 to marry him: "PROMISE DIVORCE WITHIN THREE REPEAT THREE DAYS STOP REQUEST ANSWER STOP THANK YOU." Ronni was broke at the time, and tempted.

★*MARCH, FREDRIC* Serious actor. They made one film, *I Married a Witch*, and, for her, the experience was like "being imprisoned in a Charles Addams tower." There was no other actor for whom she "harbored such deep dislike . . . and it's strictly personal." And Freddie was famously ready.

★*MOXLEY, TOM* In Florida high school, she dated him out of pity, because he was so homely and fat. Years later, she ran into this dreamboat, the same Tom. "If only girls could look into the future beyond the baby fat and acne."

★*PRESTON, ROBERT* The giver of Veronica's first onscreen kiss, an event that filled the next day's gossip columns. Gallant Bob went through innumerable retakes, and called it "the luckiest day of my life."

★*PRIEST* A friend of the family who took special interest in the problems of adolescent girls. He invited Connie (as she was called then) to sit on his lap while he told her a story. "But his voice changed, it was hoarse now, and breathy." He suddenly put one hand around her breast, the other up her skirt. In a flash, she was up and running.

★*PRODUCER* One of the biggies. She thought her appointment was to talk about movies. But! He stood, unzipped his fly, "and laid his penis on the desk," asking if she'd ever seen one before. "*Fun,* that's what we need more of," he joked. Nimble Veronica reached for a nearby dictionary and threw it. Her aim was true. Other than this incident, Miss Lake concluded, "making the rounds proved pretty tame."

★*RENTZ, FRANKIE* High school football hero. Hers was a fierce, unreciprocated crush. She *knew* that Frankie could bring her to "the heights of which women dream." Her fantasies of him were so vivid, "I'd sit in class and contract my pelvic muscles, forcing a tingle or two."

★*TUFTS, SONNY* "Good old laughable, lovin' Sonny," that's how Ronnie describes her old friend who used to set fire to Jack Warner's drapes. Also cites a "whole gang of perverted women who *claim* that Sonny had bitten them on the thighs." Toward the end of her own book, the late Veronica Lake mused that someone should write a book about dear Sonny. Sonny *Tufts???*

LAMARR, HEDY
(b. 1913)

Breathtaking Viennese beauty whose name was Hedwig Kiesler when, still in her teens, she appeared naked in *Ecstasy* (1932) and began what proved to be a lifetime of erotic revelations. At her first meeting with Louis B. Mayer, he thought she was too blatantly sexy for American audiences, but she became an overnight sensation in *Algiers* (1938) opposite Charles Boyer. Candidly describing herself as a nymphomaniac, and frankly bisexual, Hedy acknowledged the importance of sex in her life, and her autobiography noted that her men "have ranged from a classic case history of impotence, to a whip-brandishing sadist." Later, she impulsively sued her own ghost writers for $21 million. At the zenith of her career, rival studios tried to revamp Joan Bennett and countless would-be Tondelayos in the smoldering, exotic Lamarr image, seldom with much success. The low point came in 1966, when she was arrested (later acquitted) for shoplifting.

PRIMARY SOURCE: *Ecstasy and Me: My Life As a Woman,* by Hedy Lamarr (Bartholomew, 1966; Fawcett, 1967).

★*AUMONT, JEAN PIERRE* French matinee idol of the '40s. On meeting Hedy in Paris he dropped any formal greeting and went right to "I'm in love with you." His phone calls began with "Will you marry me?" Hedy was intrigued, and Aumont almost became husband no. 5.

★*BOIES, LEWIS J.* A lawyer colleague of Jerry Geisler, famed Hollywood legal eagle. A casual date, he "suddenly" began begging her to marry him. As Mrs. Boies, she spent two years listening to him talk about law and football. At their divorce trial, she accused L. J. of threatening her with a baseball bat, and complained that together they had gone through half a million dollars of *her* money. The union, her sixth, lasted from March 1963 to June 1965.

★*CHAPLIN, CHARLIE* When he and Tim Durant lived at Hedy's house they had loads of fun "playing charades and ESP games," racing around in foreign cars. He sent her pink roses, but Lamarr considered herself "too tall" for Charlie. (See also CHAPLIN listing.)

★*FATHER OF BEST CHILDHOOD FRIEND* Her friend was "upset," but Dad was so handsome she couldn't resist. Their "moments," as she calls them, were always out-of-doors. "With this mature lover, I had uncountable orgasms."

★*FLYNN, ERROL* Hedy attended many a bacchanalian bash at Errol's house, and knew all about the dressing rooms with two-way mirrors for voyeurs. She even joined Flynn and the gang for a little look-see fun. Although dubious about his sexual indiscretions, she found Flynn "cultured and fascinating." (See also FLYNN listing.)

★*GABLE, CLARK* She swears she never met the man until he entered her dressing room to offer some Hollywood-spun philosophy and a foot massage. Lamarr's autobiography mentions Gable only incidentlly thereafter, though she does write that "Hollywood's most popular leading man" escorted her to the premiere of *Algiers*, her first major Hollywood film. After, they celebrated her triumph at his Malibu hideaway. "We drank lavender sherry under a full moon. . . . What a night!" Next morning, in pajamas, he went out for the newspaper reviews, returned shouting "Geronimo! You did it!" After reading the raves, "we went right back to bed—and stayed there." Hedy later co-starred with Gable in *Boom Town* and *Comrade X*.

★*GARDINER, REGINALD* English light comedian. Hedy's first Hollywood beau. Reggie took her to the parties, introduced her to the stars. She felt sure they would become man and wife. He didn't match her confidence.

★*"GARY"* A director, and married. He and Hedy held frequent trysts, had thoughtful talks which helped her "get a clearer picture of myself." In the late '30s.

★*"GEORGIA"* A roommate at Swiss school.

She started slipping into Hedy's bed. On just one occasion, innocent, adolescent Hedy asked: "Why are you *doing* that, Georgia?"

★*KENNEDY, JOHN* "I've met all the great ones," Hedy boasted. Young Kennedy was in postwar Paris, so was she. He called for a date, she said sure, but only if he'd bring some oranges. (Wartime food rationing was still on.) "An hour later he was climbing my steps with a brown paper bag full of oranges." After Kennedy delivered, Hedy recalls, they had a wonderful time.

★*LAUNDRY MAN* He twice tried to rape 14-year-old Hedy in family home—and once succeeded. It was in analysis many years later that Hedy brought forth this painful memory.

★*LEE, HOWARD* Houston oilman, Hedy's fifth husband, now married to Gene Tierney. He approached her with an offer to help finance a film; on his second drink he announced he'd soon ask her to marry him; on the third, she invited him to stay the night. Wed in December 1953, they made it stick for six years, with Hedy honestly trying to be a hausfrau. The divorce was a wild one, with charges and countercharges; Hedy, awarded a $500,000 settlement, claims she "never got a penny of it."

★*LODER, SIR JOHN* British actor, Lamarr's second husband. Their decision to marry (in May 1943) was somewhat impromptu. Returning home from a party, she expressed doubt that any man could "do it" nineteen times in one weekend, as a mutual acquaintance had just boasted. Cool, confident John said, well, if she'd marry him immediately, they'd have the coming weekend to find out. Hedy loved a challenge. After achieving intercourse eight times on the first day of their honeymoon, they abandoned the Olympic goal. "Actually, it wasn't such a bad start, but what a terrible finish." The Loders had a daughter, Denise. Hedy simultaneously announced her second pregnancy (resulting in son John Anthony) and asked for a divorce. "John blinked. 'Well, a regular Louella Parsons—*two* exclusives in one night.'"

★*"LOLLY"* Studio wardrobe woman. Fol-lowed Hedy into her dressing room, tore off her own clothes, then Hedy's. When the star protested, Lolly said, with a surly tone, "You're not talking to a wardrobe mistress, you're talking to a girl-lover. Just like you." Though due on the set in half an hour, Hedy asked herself, what could she do?

★*MAN OF INFLUENCE* She went to him to help her get that part in *Boom Town*. He asked if she was "willing to pay the price." When told that she just couldn't perform in bed "for business," he decided to help her get the part anyway. "Five years later I had an opportunity to return the favor. He was very grateful."

★*MANDL, FRITZ* "Munitions King" of pre-war Europe, very powerful, very rich, Lamarr's first husband. She was an 18-year-old novice actress, who had just made the landmark skin flick *Ecstasy*. Mandl spent the next two years trying to buy up every available print—lest all the world should see his wife's *tuchis*. They lived in ultra-grandeur, with twenty servants, an apartment in Vienna, a palace in Salzburg, and seven cars. "Every luxury but freedom" for Hedy, literally held prisoner by Mandl. She finally managed an escape to Paris, a divorce, and an unexpected meeting with L.B. Mayer.

★*"MARCIA"* An MGM starlet who was posing, scantily clad, for publicity stills on Hedy's very first day at the studio. Hedy caught herself sneaking glances at Marcia's "semi-erect nipples, the charming derrière with its lush, creamy contours." No action that day, but months later, Hedy proposed a lunch-hour drive. In the front seat, cuddling, Marcia whispered, "I need you." Suddenly, her hands were all over Hedy, "and I let her do what she wanted. . . . This was always the solution to my ills."

★*MARKEY, GENE* Screenwriter, husband no. 2. He was strolling through the New York street-scene set on the MGM backlot, feeling horny and homesick, when along came Hedy. He asked her to go to the beach next day; but meant a beach in Mexico. In Tijuana, he said, "Hey, let's get married and really make it a full day." The ceremony was over in six minutes, "and the marriage lasted about the same amount of time, although we didn't get a divorce for almost a year." Markey had already been married to Joan Bennett, was later to wed Myrna Loy.

★*"MARTY"*   Another starlet, whose dressing room was next to Hedy's. Marty's friends had their own version of a naked lunch (playing poker in the buff), and asked Hedy to join them. She seldom said *nein*.

★*MOG, ARIBERT*   Leading man in *Ecstasy*. Hedy admits that he had that ole "Actors Studio realism" in their steamy love scenes. "His vibrations of actual sex proved highly contagious. . . . I ended up 'winging it' too."

★*MONTGOMERY, GEORGE*   Actor-director-furniture maker. Everyone thought they'd marry, including Hedy. But when he donned the khaki to go fight World War II they realized they weren't "sure enough." Shortly thereafter, sure enough, George married Dinah Shore.

★*"PIERRE"*   An artist, Hedy's paramour at the time she wrote her autobiography. He was younger than she, good-looking, and, like her, broke. They shared a house without electricity or gas or locks on the doors. But love helped them survive. "When a woman is over fifty and can say her love affair with a new man is the most satisfying of her life, you can be sure it's close to the truth."

★*RETTY, WOLFGANG ALBA*   Actor in Max Reinhardt's troupe, the first man to give Hedy "that clean, happy feeling." She was very, very young. He later fathered Romy Schneider.

★*"SAM"*   A Hollywood mogul who remains anonymous for obvious reasons. His jealousy was such that he tried to shoot a diamond earring off her ear because another man gave it to her. Yet he once tied Hedy to the bed and, after making love, called a friend, "a fat, ugly one," to also have his way with her. "Sam" was responsible for what Hedy calls one of the most shocking episodes of her life. He commissioned, at great expense, a life-sized rubber replica of Hedy, complete with the necessary anatomical parts. She was forced to watch him "make love" to it. "He *kissed* those lips. . . . He said 'thank you, darling, I hope I didn't muss your hair.'" Hedy notes that a friend (?!) years later sent her a newspaper clipping about the merchandising of "life-sized party dolls." It made her sick all over again.

★*STAUFFER, TED*   Restaurateur and hotel owner, onetime orchestra leader. Hedy flew to Acapulco for a rest and met Teddy instead. She remembered that at one time he had been "all over with Rita Hayworth." A few months later she walked down the aisle once more. "Everybody loved Teddy. . . . the trouble is, I loved him for the same reason everybody else did. There was nothing *special*." He was no. 4; the year was 1951.

★*"STEVE"*   Assistant director, who remarked that Hedy looked tired, and probably needed a good "boff." He provided same, then and there. "I did feel better and stronger later that evening."

★*VON HOCHSTATTEN, RITTER FRANZ*   Son of one of Germany's most prominent prewar families. When Hedy refused to give up her budding career to marry him, he killed himself.

★*WANGER, WALTER*   Director. Hedy refers to him only as "an early friend." He was at the center of a scandalous fracas years later when he shot and wounded, in a parking lot, agent Jennings Lang, whom Wanger saw as a rival for the affections of his wife Joan Bennett, the *most* famous Lamarr look-alike.

★*WHITNEY, JOHN HAY ("JOCK")*   "His name and his money were magic everywhere," Hedy recalled. After she made *Ziegfeld Girl*, they flew to Bill Paley's place on the Riviera, where Hedy met Anthony Eden. And others, presumably.

★*YOUNG MAN*   Hedy was 15, her girlfriend was in love with him, but Hedy insisted he loved *her*. To prove it, and to save her friend from a horrible fate, she let the man "go all the way." From then on they went steady and she didn't see much of the girlfriend.

MISCELLANY

★*"ARTHUR"* Rich Texan and self-proclaimed "swinger." He offered Hedy $100,000 to go to bed with him; she said she didn't take money but might be won by flowers, wine, and sweet talk. "This charming young man *did* romance me, *did go* to bed with me—and was *impotent!*" Hedy notes, in all humility, that few men had that problem with her. Arthur again offered the $100,000 payment; Hedy told him to keep it.

★*BEAUTIFUL LEADING MAN* She adored his beautiful muscles, loved the idea of boarding a private plane with him for a skiing weekend in Aspen. But Hedy *loathed* the smell of liquor on his breath, and checked into her own room in the ski lodge. "It was sad, because we never made it again."

★*BIT ACTOR* Alone with Hedy in a studio screening room, he whispered that this was a chance for them "to tear off a matinee piece." She slapped him, he grabbed her arms, and in a flash they were on the floor fighting like cats and dogs. She was *determined* not to be raped. Fortunately, there was a break in the film they were watching, the house lights went up, the bit actor hissed, "Bitch," and dashed out of the room.

★*BOY WHO LUSTED* "The mistake I made was saying yes to him *once*," then she often had to say no. He begged her to see him just once more, and when she arrived at his castle (his parents were rich) he was hanging out the window by a belt. "It was a terrifying sight, he almost died." This taught Hedy not to toy with a boy's emotions.

★*BOYER, CHARLES* At a party he stood behind her and whispered that from the sight of her hair, her figure, he was sure that she must be an extraordinarily beautiful woman. When she turned around, he sighed, "Ah, it's so heartening to have snap guesses confirmed." He then asked if she'd like to do a picture with him. It was *Algiers*, which made Hedy a star.

★*CHAPLIN, CHARLIE JR.* While shipmates on a fabulous yachting party, he said, "I love you, Hedy." She told him she wasn't surprised; his father had, too.

★*COHN, HARRY* Head of Columbia Pictures. He wanted to know how many men Hedy had slept with, and what they had done for her. "That's what's wrong with your career," he said. "Sleep with one right man—me—and your future is assured." Hedy walked out without signing a Columbia contract.

★*DE MILLE, CECIL B.* Colorful director who worked with Hedy in *Samson and Delilah*. He said her other pictures had made every man in America want to marry her; this one would make them want to go to bed with her. He had a theory about women, that they really wanted to be "taken, ruled and raped"; Hedy couldn't bring herself to disagree. She had a few public dates with De Mille, lunches in the dressing room, probably nothing more.

★*GRANGER, STEWART* Their one aborted rendezvous in her hotel room in Paris went askew, Stew recalls, when Hedy started telling him *exactly* what to do. (See also GRANGER listing.)

★*"HARRY"* One of her shrinks. At the time, she was so mixed up, being in love with George Montgomery *and* John Loder and now Harry. She wanted Harry to stop blinking his limpid brown eyes at her, or "if my problem was that I needed love, to give me what I needed. He never did."

★*HOPE, BOB* He got Hedy to play Mata Hari opposite him in *My Favorite Spy*. She claims Bob was the only man she'd ever met who left her in doubt whether he was on the make or not. "I have no real evidence, but I'm still not sure."

★*HUSTON, JOHN* Hedy harrumphs at the notion that John Huston is Hollywood's best poker player. "I've beaten him head to head, as they say."

★*NIVEN, DAVID* An "escort" aboard the Douglas Fairbanks, Jr., yacht. (See also NIVEN listing.)

★*RITCHIE, BOB* The American agent who brought Hedy to L.B. Mayer, way back then in Paris.

★*SINATRA, FRANK* After his divorce from Ava Gardner, Hedy spent many evenings listening to his troubles. When she noticed that Frank had a beautiful china chess set, she asked him to play. "But he didn't know how. He just cried on my shoulder saying he didn't understand women." Hedy never had a romantic "thing" about Frankie, but in a jam, there's no one she'd rather turn to. (See also SINATRA listing.)

★*VIDOR, KING* Director. Talked Hedy into starring in *H. M. Pulham, Esq.,* which many critics believed was her best.

Among the "world's greatest men" that Hedy met, in addition to previously mentioned *JOHN KENNEDY* and *ANTHONY EDEN,* were *WINSTON CHURCHILL, DWIGHT EISENHOWER, CHARLES DE GAULLE;* and as the wife of Fritz Mandl, she socialized with *ADOLF HITLER* ("posturing") and *BENITO MUSSOLINI* ("pompous").

LEIGH, VIVIEN
(1913–1967)

Major British actress whose place in film history is assured by her portrayal of Scarlett O'Hara, chosen after every possible American candidate for the role had been tested and rejected, and filming of *Gone with the Wind* (1939) was already under way. Leigh won an Oscar for that, and for *A Streetcar Named Desire* in 1951, as a very different kind of southern belle. Though a glittering star of London theater as the wife of Laurence Olivier—during the two decades of their marriage, there was no more famous acting couple in the world—Leigh was often envious of his reputation as *the* great actor. She was known for her remarkable beauty but limited range, and her movie career suffered because of severe emotional instability—worse as the years went by—and generally delicate health. Despite an impressive record of achievement, Leigh is another tragic example of the truth that beauty, fame, talent, and loving friends are not always enough to keep the bluebird on your windowsill.

PRIMARY SOURCES: *Vivien Leigh,* by Anne Edwards (Simon and Schuster, 1977; Pocket Books, 1978); *Sir Larry, The Life of Laurence Olivier,* by Thomas Kiernan (Times Books, 1981).

★*FINCH, PETER* The Oliviers "discovered" Peter Down Under, and encouraged him to bring his acting talents to England. He did, and quickly established himself in the British theater's inner circle. In 1954, restless Vivien suddenly became "flirtatious" with other men—especially Finch. Soon Peter and Viv were seen strolling hand in hand, right under Olivier's nose. Nothing was said. "An aura of Victorian forbearance pervaded . . . and everyone was impeccably polite." Vivien, very much on edge, impulsively decided to run away with Peter, but once on the train she had second thoughts and pulled the emergency cord. That didn't end the Finch affair, which continued sporadically over the years. Finch was with her when she had her first nervous breakdown—on the set of *Elephant Walk.* Young Elizabeth Taylor took over in Viv's role.

★*HOLMAN, HERBERT LEIGH* Vivien's first husband; a businessman who was forever tolerant of his wife's acting ambitions. He remained the perfect English gentleman when Vivien met and fell madly in love with Olivier, and demanded a divorce. Vivien had a daughter, Suzanne, by Holman, and she took his middle name as her stage name. They continued to be very close.

★*KORDA, ALEXANDER* Legendary theatrical and film producer and, the evidence suggests, "a legendary womanizer." Viv's chum Maureen O'Sullivan, an earlier Korda discovery, confided to her that Korda "made it a practice to try to sleep with every actress he put under contract . . . It's something he feels they owe him." Korda certainly knew how to make points with Viv—by promising to make Laurence Olivier her next leading man. But first, said the flamboyant Hungarian, he himself wanted to "get to know" Vivien a little better. "You mean . . . ?" "Yes, my darling," Alex is said to have replied. It was a brief affair, though, "two or three times is all," said one of Vivien's intimates, until the young actress's passion for Olivier was finally consummated—without the promised intro from Korda.

★*MERIVALE, JACK* With Olivier now asking for a divorce—to marry Joan Plowright—Vivien arrived in New York in 1960 to appear in *Duel of Angels*, co-starring her old friend Jack. "Olivier's rejection had robbed her of self-esteem . . . but here was an attractive, talented, intelligent man who from the first moment of their reunion showed signs of being *dazzled.*" In time he was also confused, sorrowed and numbed by Vivien's sporadic seizures of madness. But he loved her, and stayed with her the last seven years of her life.

★*OLIVIER, LAURENCE* For romantic anglophiles and inveterate theater buffs, there never, ever again will be as dashing, handsome, and talented a couple as Olivier and Leigh. The first time she saw him onstage, Vivien—then a young wife and mother—confided to her best friend, "Someday, I am going to marry Laurence Olivier." He, too, was married at the time, to actress Jill Esmond, but on meeting Vivien he was dumbstruck. "Olivier thought her the most beautiful woman he had ever seen." Throughout their breathless affair and the ecstatic early days of their marriage, the luminous couple—known to their intimates as Larry and Viv—often acted together. On film in *That Hamilton Woman*, on the stage in *Hamlet, Macbeth, Caesar and Cleopatra,* etc. Vivien's recurrent schizophrenic illness, their terrible fights during those periods, and Olivier's need to find peace and stability finally eroded the marriage (but not her love), and drove him into the arms of Joan Plowright. Vivien always kept his photo, framed in silver, on her nightstand. The couple had no children together. The marriage lasted from 1940 to 1960.

★*PURDOM, EDMUND* The young British actor came to New York with Olivier and Leigh in their flashy tandem productions of Shakespeare's *Antony and Cleopatra* and Shaw's *Caesar and Cleopatra.* An American member of the cast recalls a lot of coolness between the married co-stars, and, "It was clear to just about everyone that something was going on between Purdom and Vivien. Vivien was the one who pursued it—not Purdom—in fact, I'd say he was embarrassed by it."

MISCELLANY

★*STRANGERS IN THE NIGHT* When Vivien suffered the worst spells of her sickness, one of the symptoms was an uncharacteristically promiscuous behavior. She would go to bars, or simply roam the streets looking for a pickup. The memory of these nights helped drive her deeper into madness.

LOEW, ARTHUR JR.
(b. 1926)

Heir to a substantial Hollywood fortune as grandson of film pioneer Marcus Loew, a co-founder and controller of Metro-Goldwyn-Mayer. During the '50s he belonged to a B unit of producers made up almost entirely of the sons of MGM executives. His major achievement was producing *The Rack* (1956), with Paul Newman's starmaking role as a POW. Though movie production was his birthright, young Loew spent a good deal of his youth—and family money—pursuing for personal pleasure many of the cinematic love goddesses his forebears had pursued largely for profit. Isn't that the American Dream? Hard-working immigrants arranging for future generations to have a bit of fun?

PRIMARY SOURCES: *Joan Collins: Past Imperfect*, by Joan Collins (C.W. Allen, England, 1978); *Bittersweet*, by Susan Strasberg (Putnam's 1980); *Elizabeth Taylor: The Last Star*, by Kitty Kelley (Simon and Schuster, 1981).

★*COLLINS, JOAN* She knew his reputation as a playboy; nevertheless . . . "We fell in love. Or did we fall in *like?*" Still smarting from her hapless marriage to Max Reed, she moved in with Arthur, who seemed the best cure for her problems (though Loew urged her to consider psychotherapy as well). Then one day, she really looked at Arthur, sprawled on the couch of his elegant living room: "He was as bad as the others. He had me. . . . I bought all my own clothes and furs. I paid for my airfare when I went to London. I was young, beautiful, desired by many men . . . successful. Why should he have all this for nothing?" She thought they should marry; he didn't go for it. That was *not quite* the end. Arthur later visited her for a jolly reunion on the set of *Sea Wife* in Jamaica. When some member of the crew asked, "Where's Joan?" another quickly replied, "She's laying Loew." Considering Arthur's reputation, it sounded like an old joke. And nearly their last laugh. (See also COLLINS listing.)

★*GROVES, REGINA* Second wife, married 1968. Still smiling, presumably.

★*POWER, DEBORAH MINARDOS* Young widow of Tyrone Power, pregnant when Power died in 1958, seven months after their marriage. Some of Ty's intimates had disapproved of Deborah (see POWER listing), but Loew approved her heartily. After their 1959 marriage, he legally adopted her infant son, Tyrone Power IV. The couple called it quits in 1963.

★*STRASBERG, SUSAN* Susan thought she and Arthur "hit it off well . . . a pleasant relationship, emotionally undemanding," and she liked his sense of humor, the parties he took her to. They took one romantic trip to Mexico, which was ruined when Susan got violently ill. On their return to Hollywood, she learned Arthur was still seeing old flame Joan Collins. Susan threw an ashtray at Arthur. Missed. But, Loew and behold, came to the conclusion that her own relationship with him "was not intense enough for me to work up any real indignity" about his dalliance. Excelsior. (See also STRASBERG listing.)

★*TAYLOR, ELIZABETH* They dated when both were quite young; he reappeared in her life again after Liz's husband Mike Todd died in a plane crash. It was more than romance. The pair was so close, in fact, Taylor asked Arthur to take care of her children while she

flew off to Europe for a month of rest and relaxation on the Riviera. At the time, Elizabeth entertained thoughts of marrying Loew, but Eddie Fisher moved faster. So much faster that the Liz-Eddie love saga started beside Loew's swimming pool. (See also FISHER and TAYLOR listings.)

LOREN, SOPHIA
(b. 1934)

Lush Italian beauty who has been a major international star for more than a quarter of a century. All that warmth and humor and high-spirited glamour never entirely hide Sophia's earthy peasant origins. Americans really discovered her when she did a pizza-tossing turn in *Gold of Naples* (1954), and got to liking her even better in the sunny, homegrown Italian comedies she made with Mastroianni for Vittorio de Sica (who also directed her 1961 Oscar-winning role in *Two Women*). Loren's romantic life, as covered by the press, has seemed largely an Italian-style saga about her struggle to marry and have children by producer Carlo Ponti. Only in her bestselling autobiography—and in a TV special where she portrayed both herself and her mother—did Sophia allow a peek into some other family closets, one containing, of all people, Cary Grant. Small world.

PRIMARY SOURCE: *Sophia Living and Loving; Her Own Story*, by A. E. Hotchner (Morrow, 1979; Bantam, 1979).

★*GRANT, CARY* He was a superstar in his 50s, she a relatively unknown 22-year-old Italian actress when they met on a plain in Spain for the filming of *The Pride and The Passion* in 1956. They were constantly in each other's company, "and such wonderful company Cary was! We dined in romantic little restaurants on craggy hilltops to the accompaniment of flamenco guitars, drank the good Spanish wine and laughed . . . and we fell in love." But *mama mia*—Sophia was also in love with long-time "fiancé" Carlo Ponti, who had been unable to get a divorce. What future was there for Sophia in being his mistress? "And here was Cary Grant, ready to renounce everything for me." She returned to Italy to think about Grant's proposal of marriage, but was soon summoned to Hollywood for a film called *Houseboat*—with *Cary Grant*. Nervous Ponti also appeared on the scene and surprised Sophia by coming up with a legal solution to their marital status—a proxy divorce in Mexico followed by a proxy marriage uniting Carlo and Sophia as man and wife. It was not the wedding of her dreams. Sophia had only one more scene in *Houseboat*, showing her marrying Cary—in full bridal regalia. "It was *precisely* the wedding I had always dreamed of . . . a very unkind quirk of fate." Graciously accepting defeat, Cary whispered, "I hope you will be very happy, Sophia." (Never does Loren's as-told-to autobiography mention the fact that in 1956–57, Cary Grant was still married to Betsy Drake.) (See also GRANT listing.)

★*PONTI, CARLO* The portly 38-year-old Italian producer spotted 15-year-old Sophia in a crowd in Rome and urged her to enter a beauty contest in which he was a judge. She came in second. During the next few years Ponti arranged screen tests for Sophia, got her small film roles. Later, as she became an Oscar-winning international star, he would produce many of her movies. Sophia and Carlo became romantically involved when she was 19, waiting "until I felt the strength of his love and my deep need for him as my father figure." They were married twice—once by proxy in 1957, and in person in France in 1966. To those who wonder about her relationship to Ponti, Sophia says: "Our ages are too far apart. Our looks are too different. We defy the system. . . . I admire Carlo's intellect, his tenderness. . . . He is, above all else, a helpmate, not just a mate. I cherish Laurence Durell's observation: 'A helpmate surpasses a lover, and loving kindness surpasses love, even passion.'" The Pontis have two sons: Carlo Jr. and Eduardo. There are recent reports of Ponti's severe illness and an estrangement between the couple, and Sophia has been seen in the company of a handsome French doctor.

MISCELLANY

★*BURTON, RICHARD* Sophia tells her version of what happened when Burton came to Rome to co-star with her in *The Journey*. He was in agony over his first announced separation from Elizabeth Taylor. When lonely Richard asked to stay at the Ponti villa, the answer was yes. Sophia and Richard spent long hours playing Scrabble (she claims she beat him consistently, "causing Burton to howl to the heavens. That he could be beaten in his native language by an illiterate Italian peasant!"). And she listened to him pour out his troubles re Liz. "My role was that of psychiatrist, comforter and ego masseuse. . . . I had become genuinely fond of Richard." Richard was also fond of Sophia. (See also BURTON listing.)

★*DE SICA, VITTORIO* Late great Italian director, who worked with Sophia on fourteen films, beginning with *Gold of Naples*. "He became a force in my life. I liked him. I loved him. I admired him, and our 'love affair' was to last for twenty years."

★*MASTROIANNI, MARCELLO* In eight generally memorable films, Marcello and Sophia became one of the most successful romantic comedy teams ever. Sophia thinks "There is no hyperbole too extravagant for describing the cohesion we have before the camera." Off-camera, she relishes his dry, off-beat sense of humor. Like the time she and Marcello were on Dick Cavett's TV show, and Cavett pressed him for details about his rep as a Latin lover. Said Marcello, "Well, to tell you the truth, Dick, I'm not a great fucker." Sophia quickly interjected: "Marcello really doesn't understand English very well." Marcello stared at her: "No," he insisted, "I'm *not* a great fucker." Cavett finally caught his breath and said: "Do either of you have any hobbies?"

★*SELLERS, PETER* Sophia reveals that of all the men with whom she acted, other than Cary Grant, "two had very special appeal to me—Peter Sellers and Alec Guinness." There's no incontrovertible evidence of a romance between Loren and Guinness. but Sellers never tried to hide the fact that he was "round the bend" about Sophia when they made *The Millionairess*. (See also SELLERS listing.)

LOVELACE, LINDA
(b. late 1940s)

Retired porno performer, whose extraordinary erotic talents made her the first hardcore superstar in *Deep Throat*, the landmark sex film released in 1972. Though the film was tried and convicted on obscenity charges in New York by a judge who called it "a nadir of decadence" (JUDGE CUTS THROAT, WORLD MOURNS went up in lights on the marquee of the World Theatre), Linda became an overnight media darling. Now settled down as a Long Island housewife, Linda has recanted her wicked ways in a tell-*all* autobiography charging that in those exhibitionist years, her "mentor" and husband Chuck Traynor virtually kept her a prisoner in prostitution (and various other perversions), so drugged that she seldom knew *what* she was doing, either in *Deep Throat* or in all those 8mm quickies where she had to work with animals and a lesbian's toe. The *new* Linda claims to be a prude. "If people can keep it between themselves and their mates, that's just fine. But lovemaking should be a two-person proposition. No more, no less. It's just nobody else's business." That's from Linda's highly publicized best-seller.

PRIMARY SOURCE: *Ordeal*, by Linda Lovelace with Mike McGrady (Citadel, 1980; Berkley, 1981).

★*CHICKLET* Linda's fellow model in first session posing for dirty pictures. It was a day of firsts. "The first photographs. The first sex with another woman. And there was still another first to come . . ." The fat photographer

came up with a prop for Chicklet: "My first dildo."

★*DAVIS, SAMMY JR.* When Linda Lovelace became a *star* via *Deep Throat*, she and Chuck Traynor got the full Hollywood treatment—including a night out with Sammy Davis and his wife Altovise. "Sammy and me. Chuck and Altovise. It would become more in time, more than just a seating arrangement." What it became was mostly Linda and Sammy. He explained to her that his code of marital fidelity included anything except having normal intercourse, "because that, the act of making love, would be cheating on his wife." What he wanted her to do was "deep throat" him. Linda claims Sammy actually considered divorcing Altovise to marry her—and to prove his intent, they had *normal* intercourse. But within a few days after that, Linda left Chuck Traynor, Sammy, and "that whole way of life."

★*DOCTORS* Traynor had the brilliant idea of exchanging Linda's services to cover their medical expenses. There were several such setups. In addition to the proctologist, Linda made regular visits to a dermatologist and, when Chuck developed eye trouble, he added an optometrist to the list. "I found it absolutely amazing that so many professionals would be so willing to trade services. And I also found myself praying that Chuck and I stayed in good health."

★*DOG* Linda herself puts an end to the speculation; for a porn movie, she *was* forced to have intercourse with a dog. Afterwards, "I was in the deepest valley I'd ever been in, devastated, wanting only to die. I looked up and saw Chuck . . ." This new degradation only made her more docile, says Linda, and more a victim of Chuck's power. "Now I felt totally defeated. . . . He would use it against me forever." From then on if Linda didn't do something he asked, he'd bring her a pet—a dog.

★*GOLDSTEIN, AL* Editor of *Screw* magazine, he conducted *Screw*'s infamous interview with Linda, and afterwards was asked by Chuck if he wanted a free sample of Linda's deep-throat technique. "The editor of *Screw* almost tripped over his own feet racing over to the bed." Linda says there was one more "interview" like the one with Goldstein, but most journalists were decent people who did not respond to Chuck's invitations. "I realized that interviews didn't all have to be bad."

★*HEFNER, HUGH* Linda was shocked to discover that, although their styles were completely different, Hefner and Chuck Traynor had a lot in common: They liked to talk about kinky sex. "Chuck's primary goal was to bring Hugh Hefner and myself together sexually. He saw this as the beginning of a great palship." On an "orgy night" at Hefner's California mansion, Chuck was performing a few tricks with Linda in the pool: "It reminded me of those old Fred Astaire movies where all the other dancers suddenly stopped what they were doing and formed a circle around Fred and Ginger." And everyone applauded, just as in the old movies. "Hefner finally got himself aroused enough to approach me . . . so he came up behind me and entered me in the backside. That was his big thrill and chill and that was that." Months later, when someone told Hefner that Chuck had forced Linda to do everything she did against her will, "he was very upset about it."

★*JASON* Undertaker who overtook her during her early days of prostitution. "The only trick I could ever have a decent conversation with . . . He was a gentleman and he wasn't into anything too weird, unless bringing me flowers and calling me 'sweetheart' could be considered weird."

★*MANDINA, PHIL* Traynor's lawyer. Linda disliked him on sight, and later grew to hate him. With Mandina's girl, Chuck and Linda played games like seeing who could make who come first. Although she despised the lawyer, "it had to be done, and done well . . . If I didn't satisfy Mandina, then I'd be in for a beating."

★*MICHELLE* As punishment for trying to run away, Chuck took Linda to a party hosted by Michelle, who, with Linda and a large dildo provided the floor show. Linda wound up making an emergency visit to the proctologist. Traynor accused her of ruining the evening with all her bleeding and cries of pain. Later, he *loved* recalling that night with Michelle. "Remember that night we were over at her house with that fucking dildo? God, that was some night."

★*PERRY, LOU* One of the producers of *Deep Throat.* Linda was required to visit him every day at his office. "As I was doing what I had to do, he went on fussing with the papers on his desk. Then he suddenly stopped, leaned back in his chair and looked up at the ceiling." After the deed was done, he'd tell her to get out of there. He was a *little bit* nicer about it all when *Deep Throat* became a big hit.

★*REEMS, HARRY* Porn superstar, and Linda's leading man in *Deep Throat.* Linda liked him, speculates that he became *the* male superstar of pornographic movies because he is intelligent and he has a good sense of humor. "Harry's strongest appeal to me, however, was the fact that Chuck did not like him at all."

★*ROB & CATHY* More porn performers. Linda made over a half-dozen 8mm movies with Rob, including some with his wife Cathy. She thought Rob *adorable,* tall and blond and cute. "How could a guy who looked like that do what he did for a living? I will never understand that."

★*TRAYNOR, CHUCK* At first he was a perfect gentleman, taking her out in his flashy car, lighting her cigarettes, opening car doors, etc., and "never once coming on to me sexually." Then she moved in with him; in a very short time he had her turning five tricks at a time in a nearby Holiday Inn. It was through hypnotism to help her relax the muscles in her throat that Chuck taught Linda how to "deep throat," as she puts it. He also forced her to marry him, so she couldn't testify against him in future. Although Linda tried several times to escape Chuck's grasp, he always found her—and threatened to kill her or those closest to her if she ever tried that again. "Every day I either got raped, beaten, kicked, punched, smacked, choked, degraded, or yelled at. Sometimes, I got all the above. . . . There was no love, no affection, no normal sex with anyone from the day I met Chuck Traynor until the day I finally got away. I did not have a single orgasm for six or seven years, I never had any enjoyment from any of it at all." When she finally did break away from Chuck, he found an apparently more agreeable soulmate and sex partner in porn queen Marilyn Chambers, who is still Mrs. Chuck Traynor. No public complaints have yet been heard from Marilyn. (See also CHAMBERS listing.)

★*WINTERS, DAVID* Flamboyant choreographer and producer who began working with Linda on a nightclub act—which never reached the footlights. "He habitually wore stretch pants and boots, a loose chemise with puffed sleeves, and a pocketbook with jingling little bells on it. . . . I took one look at David Winters and decided he was wonderful. Chuck took one look at David Winters and decided he was a fag." Nevertheless, it was in David's arms that Linda landed upon leaving Chuck. She says: "He helped me get back the self-respect that Chuck had stolen." He also helped her get rid of her money—fast. Linda began to feel used again, with David outlandishly padding a version of her sexual memoirs, *The Intimate Diary of Linda Lovelace,* and arranging for her to do another classier porn movie. "As the movie was coming to an end, so were David Winters and myself. And it was not an easy end. It was, in fact, violent. . . . My love for David was a perfect bubble, but bubbles do burst."

MANSFIELD, JAYNE
(1932–1967)

More blondeshell than bombshell, she was a Bryn Mawr girl, though the antithesis of a Bryn Mawr type—she just happened to have been born there. As leading contender in Hollywood's hopeless quest to

uncover another Marilyn Monroe, Jayne was said to be so hungry for publicity that she would attend the opening of a supermarket to get her picture in the paper. Typical of her technique with interviewers: "When I was told about sex, first I laughed and then I cried. . . . I couldn't see the point. Fortunately, I changed." Her dippy diligence paid off, for she became a star of sorts after appearing on Broadway in *Will Success Spoil Rock Hunter?* and then repeating her role in the movie version. Mansfield's slow rise and abrupt decline in the Hollywood firmament spanned a mere five years, though she continued to grab some space in the columns by changing husbands, making movies, and doing her hotsy-totsy nightclub act to the very end—in a grisly auto accident en route to another gig.

PRIMARY SOURCE: *Jayne Mansfield and the American Fifties,* by Martha Saxton (Houghton Mifflin, 1975).

★*BAUTZER, GREG* Hollywood lawyer and escort to the stars. Jayne noted he was "a regular standby—always there to take a girl to the most elegant parties." Yet he made a girl feel she was something *special,* said Jayne. Re Bautzer on Mansfield: "I liked her because she was flat-assed-out-honest . . . and I say that in the affectionate sense. . . . There was something overblown about her figure, something not sexy but pathetic. I would rather have gone to bed with Agnes Moorehead." (See also BAUTZER listing.)

★*BOMBA, ENRICO* Italian producer of Jayne's 1962 film *Panic Button.* A friend recalls that "only constant excitement held Jayne's attention; Bomba lasted as long as he did because he was exciting." Mansfield was still married to Hargitay when she took Bomba as a lover, and sometimes Mickey went along on their dates. The night Jane and Bomba were doing the twist and her dress fell off, Mickey was not amused. Jayne said: "I just happened to be wearing a loose-fitting dress. Occasionally it came apart." If Enrico had divorced his wife and married Jayne (which he gave no indication of doing) she fancied that he would become "Carlo Ponti to her Sophia Loren."

★*BRODY, SAMUEL* Lawyer who worked with Jayne to win custody of the son she had with Matt Cimber. The last love of her life, and probably one of the most intense. His friends were amazed that Sam got mixed up with Jayne. "His practice went to hell after he met her. He chased all around the world with her. She must've been a very romantic girl to have attracted a guy as sweet as Sam." He *was* totally infatuated, wanted to marry Jayne. "She's a good mother, a good cook, highly provocative and very intelligent—an IQ of 163—that's enough to make any man a super wife." And Jayne fully intended to marry Sam, though the relationship had rough moments when he slapped her around. "She provoked him partly to keep him on his toes, and partly because she saw violence as a demonstration of love." Sam Brody was driving the car that night in 1967, and ran into a truck on a foggy highway—killing both himself and Jayne, who was decapitated.

★*BYRON, JIM* Press agent who helped launch Jayne's Hollywood career by thinking up wilder and wilder publicity stunts. Jayne and Jim had a "halfhearted sort of affair" for the first six months they worked together; he described the period as one of "gigantic closeness and romance." Jim remembers that Jayne "never felt she had enough time to do everything. It expressed itself in eating. She would devour her own food . . . and mine. She did everything that way, she even made love that way." Jayne soon started dating other men, but remained friends with Jim; "She would regale him with stories about losing her diaphragm at inopportune moments."

★*CIMBER, MATT* Director and Mansfield's third husband. He directed her in a production of *Bus Stop* in Yonkers, N.Y. She adored his physique, "the most beautiful I have ever seen, aesthetically speaking." At 28, Cimber had never married—and he went through with it with Jayne simply because "we woke up one morning and thought, why not?" He was then her manager, and Jayne admired his forceful-

ness, arrogance and cynicism, his IQ of 165, "two points higher than Jayne claimed for herself." She saw him as an Arthur Miller to her Marilyn. The marriage wasn't a great romance, Cimber says, but they made each other laugh. "For a long time before we got married, we weren't even making it. I'd come back from a date at four in the morning, we'd meet someplace and compare notes and *laugh.*" Matt gave Jayne a red Ferrari and a townhouse in New York. "It won't have anything pink or heart-shaped except me," Jayne said. (See Hargitay, below.) The couple had a son, Anthony Richard, in October 1965, and divorced after a bitter custody battle.

★*COCHRAN, STEVE* He-man actor, a "fling" for Jayne. She liked him because he was *casual* at all times.

★*HARGITAY, MICKEY* Hungarian bodybuilder and former Mr. Universe. Jayne's second husband. Jayne saw herself and Mickey as the perfect couple, "a matched set of astounding bodies. A heroic couplet." And she made sure that their bodies were seen everywhere. They even took to making love at parties. Mickey adored her, and tolerated every crazy thing she did. After their marriage in 1968, they occupied an enormous pink house that had a heart-shaped swimming pool with "Jayne loves Mickey" written on the bottom. And, of course, they slept in a pink, heart-shaped bed. The Hargitays had three children, Mickey Jr. in 1958, Zoltan in 1960, and Mariska in 1964. His selfless idolization of Jayne finally became a bore. He wanted to erect a huge marble statue of her in the entranceway of their pink palace, to which she said, "Oh, Mickey—*come on!*" After the divorce Jayne told an interviewer that although she had been attracted to Mickey, she really liked hairy men, "and he didn't have a single hair on his chest." Also, she added, he was not a man with whom she could have "an intellectual attachment."

★*MANSFIELD, PAUL* He was 20 and the "the handsomest boy in our crowd." Jayne was 16 and precocious. They got married "and nine and a half months later I had a little baby girl." That was Lisa Marie, born in 1949.

Paul was drafted in 1952 and Jayne accompanied him to the army camp in Georgia, where she began performing in shows, displaying her figure to the soldiers. When Paul came home from Korea, Jayne insisted they move to Hollywood, where she intended to become a movie star. After several tumultuous years of Tinsel Town, they divorced in 1956.

★_NOONAN, TOMMY_ He was star and director of the movie _Promises, Promises_, in which Jayne and Hargitay appeared. Noonan, described as the kind of guy "who could talk an Eskimo into buying a refrigerator," not only convinced Jayne to pose for _Playboy_, but talked Mickey into letting Jayne go to Palm Springs with him, "to promote the picture." Their affair sizzled along for about four weeks.

★_OLIVARES, DOUGLAS_ A 20-year-old Venezuelan Jayne met and fell in love with and brought back to Hollywood in 1965. She introduced him to her children as their new father. Matt Cimber arrived one day to talk about their son Tony and found Jayne drunk, sitting on Olivares's lap, ordering the older children to serve her drinks.

★_ROBERTSON, ROBBY_   Airline pilot. Jayne listed his assets: "He's six feet tall with dark brown eyes and charcoal gray hair. I feel so companionable and safe with him." She claims she took one look at him walking down the aisle of the plane and thought, "I've got to have this." Also, he was "the only man in my whole life I ever gave my phone number to the first time he asked for it." When they started seeing each other regularly he took a sincere interest in her career. "He wanted me to be the biggest thing since Jean Harlow." But Jayne finally felt he was trying to exert too much control, telling her that some of her pinup pictures were in bad taste. Things like that. Robby later married Linda Darnell.

★_SARDELLI, NELSON_   Brazilian singer with whom Jayne shared the bill at a supper club in Biloxi, Miss. He told reporters he was deeply in love (although married to someone else), and to prove it, he would frequently kiss Jayne—on her _ankles_. Jayne thought Nelson

had "a beautiful heart and mind and body—and he's got dimples too." He also had a sense of humor. On accompanying Jayne to Juarez, Mexico, where she hoped to get a divorce from Mickey Hargitay, Sardelli quipped, "Boy, I wish Hargitay were here to help with the baggage." Jayne's ex-husband Matt Cimber has said that Sam Brody and Nelson Sardelli may have been the only two men in Jayne's life who really loved her.

MARGARET ROSE, PRINCESS
_(b. 1930)_

English Princess, sister of Queen Elizabeth II, daughter of George VI. Called P.M. by her friends, her highness has been more familiarly known to the London disco crowd by the code nickname Yvonne. Her illustrious sibling Lilibet's long shadow always brought out the rebel in Margaret, who went through a madcap girl-about-town period in early adulthood, then had an ill-fated romance, an unhappy marriage, an unseemly divorce, and sundry escapades which fostered her reputation for being "spoiled and selfish." In Brough's bio, one local constable reported Meg phoning for squad cars in the pre-dawn hours to shine their headlights on the croquet lawn at Blenheim Palace, because she and her chums "wanted a game before beddy-bye." Since the not quite hushed-up scandals of recent years, another critical observer has offered the harsh judgment "You occasionally see faces like hers alone in a bar, staring at a tumbler of gin as though it were an hourglass."

PRIMARY SOURCE: _Margaret: The Tragic Princess_, by James Brough (Putnam, 1978; Avon, 1979).

★_ARMSTRONG-JONES, ANTHONY_ "Don't you think he's really rather extraordinary?" Margaret asked her friends after she'd become acquainted with Tony, the photographer chap who thought about life as "super" and "terrific." After the final solution to the Townsend affair (see below), it became urgent to find a husband for Margaret, and Tony, with distant royal lineage and good connections, fit the bill. Tony introduced Margaret to mod, swinging London; with his help she even escaped from the palace to his secret hideaway on the banks of the Thames for some blissful premarital moments. The wedding took place May 6, 1960; Queen Elizabeth made Tony the Earl of Snowdon, Viscount Linley, just before the birth of the couple's son—who now has the second half of that title. Meg also bore a daughter, Lady Sarah Frances Elizabeth. And, for a while, Tony and Meg "made a sparkling pair, as engaging as a little bride and groom on top of a wedding cake." In time, though, their clashes could no longer be concealed. At a party Tony might put up with Margaret's jibes for so long, then snap, "Oh, God, you *bore me.*" In an effort to spare the children—and the royal image—the Princess and Lord Snowdon stayed together until 1976—when both found new interests (for hers, see LLEWELLYN, below).

★*LLEWELLYN, RODDY* Son of wealthy businessman Harry Llewellyn, "Roddy could have been a cousin of Tony's, eighteen years younger, an inch or so taller. They had the same lithe build, lean cheeks, and quick bright smiles." Middle-aged Margaret would discover that young Roddy, like Tony, preferred wearing blue jeans and sandals to more formal garb—"but Roddy opted to wear a silver stud in his left ear." At first, he was seen only as one of Meg's amusing companions, fun to have along on a country weekend. Then he began staying overnight in the spare room at Kensington Palace, traveling with Margaret to the Caribbean. A friend tried to explain the relationship: "They have turned each other into happy people. They have saved each other's lives. They are both emotional, and if they feel like having a bloody good blab, they sit down and have one." Roddy reportedly still sees Margaret, despite the bad press and public abuse their relationship has brought to the scandal-prone princess.

★*TOWNSEND, PETER* A trusted equerry at Buckingham Palace, his duties brought him into direct contact with Princess Margaret during her adolescent years. It was to Townsend she turned in grief over the death of her father, King George VI, and the subsequent "loss" when her sister Lilibet became every inch the Queen. Peter might have made the perfect mate for Margaret, except that he was nearly 20 years older and, worse still, divorced. He had married young and in haste, to a woman with whom he actually spent little time. "Ridiculous, wasn't it?" Peter said ruefully. British law held that until she was 25, Margaret had to ask the Queen's permission to marry. She might have gotten it, too, had not Winston Churchill, "defender of the faith and protector of monarchies," advised Her Majesty against a divorce-tainted marriage in the royal family. After a decisive private audience with Elizabeth and Prince Philip, Margaret sadly summoned Peter. "There could be no hysterics, no melodramatics." There was only a short announcement on October 31, 1955, beginning, "I would like it to be known that I have decided not to marry Group Captain Peter Townsend." However, Peter continued to drop in for tea with Margaret and the Queen Mother, and in a few years found a bride in Marie Luce Jamagne, a 21-year-old girl who belonged to his riding club.

MISCELLANY

★*BEATTY, WARREN* The Princess reportedly asked her good friend Pete Sellers to fix her up with Warren, and he did. Or, so the story goes. They started out a threesome—the Princess, Pete and Warren—until, back at Kensington Palace, Sellers made a timely exit. (See BEATTY listing.)

★*DALKEITH, EARL OF* A prime contender in the who'll-marry-the-Princess sweepstakes. He was one of Grandmama's godsons. Dalkeith lost, or won, depending on how you look at it.

★*DOUGLAS-HOME, ROBIN* To the aristocracy born, and a man of "delicate sensitivity." He developed a severe crush on Margaret, offered her his sympathy and friendship in the wake of the Townsend affair. Margaret began to write Robin that she would come away with him, as in a Victorian novel. When he realized the truth—that Margaret had other interests—he was devastated and mortified. "The following year, he carried the plot of the neo-Victorian melodrama to its curtain and killed himself." Most of Margaret's letters to Robin were recovered and destroyed, but at least one embarrassing missive showed up in print in a German newspaper.

★*LICHFIELD, LORD PATRICK* Margaret's distant relative, and like Tony a photographer. He became one of the men-about-London who consoled Margaret during the bad days of her marriage to Tony. Some elfin overseer seemed to arrange that they never showed up with their respective dates at the same disco. "While Tony and his partner patronized Chez Maggy, Margaret was out with Patrick Lichfield at Raffles." Oh, what a mad, mad whirl.

★*SELLERS, PETER* England's late great comic actor, and one of Margaret's frequent escorts when Tony was away. Sellers privately claimed there was more to the relationship than just doing the town, and, in fact, some of the Princess's intimates suspected some royal hanky-panky between P.M and Peter. "Whenever the subject of Sellers arose, it was handled urbanely by the more roseate chroniclers of life within the family. He was, wrote one of them, 'particularly good at making a straight-faced threesome.'" (See also SELLERS listing.)

★*TENNANT, COLIN* He was a schoolboy at Eton when he met Margaret during her wartime "incarceration" at Windsor Castle. Welcomed into her adult set, Tennant was thought of as a possible mate—but married one of Meg's friends, Lady Anne Coke. It was at their wedding that Margaret met Tony Armstrong-Jones.

★*WALLACE, BILLY* One of the few Americans even remotely in the running for the young Princess's hand. He was a millionaire, even in British pounds sterling, and his uncle happened to have a home in Sussex. All in all, though, Billy didn't add up.

Margaret's other suitors, either rumored or real, included: SIMON PHIPPS, MARK BONHAM-CARTER, TOM EGERTON, LORD OGILVY, SONNY BLANDFORD, JULIAN FANE, MICHAEL TREE, DOMINIC ELLIOT and DEREK HART. They know who they are.

MARVIN, LEE
(b. 1924)

Seasoned in TV on "M Squad," Marvin began to make it big on film as an easy-going tough guy in the Bogart tradition, then hit the top playing a gloriously drunken cowboy opposite Jane Fonda in *Cat Ballou* (1965). He's been one of moviedom's main macho men ever since, looking increasingly battered in a wide variety of roles from *Point Blank* (1967) to the musical *Paint Your Wagon* (1969) to *Big Red One* (1980). Meanwhile, Marvin was earning a reputation off-screen as a hell-for-leather roustabout who'd rather drink and/or fight than take his career seriously. Probably more serious than movie-goers realize, in recent years he has seen his fame as a performer overshadowed by his extensive press coverage as defendant in a historic lawsuit to establish the principle of "palimony" for common-law wives. Lee looked happier, it seems, in his popular public image as the kind of lout whose best friend was a palomino.

PRIMARY SOURCE; *Marvin, The Story of Lee Marvin*, by Donald Zec (St. Martin's Press, New York, 1980).

★*EBELING, BETTY* Marvin's first wife, mother of his three children. They spotted each other at a Hollywood party; Betty, tall, slim and auburn haired, "had the kind of elegance that made the male guests guard their language." She was a recent music major from UCLA, he was gaining a reputation in Grade B thrillers. On their Las Vegas wedding night (in early 1951), they weren't able to find a hotel room so Lee got soused and on the way home to L.A. picked up a hitchhiking, drunken soldier. "I was getting a most fascinating debut," Betty recalls, "as Mr. Marvin's ever-loving wife." Despite their different interests ("Lee's were booze, boats and bikes, Betty's art, music and the peaceful life"), the couple had a relatively tranquil union for the first seven years. The next seven saw Marvin's stock skyrocketing while his drinking bouts became more outrageous. It was during the filming of *Ship of Fools* that Betty finally said life with Lee was "just too much." Part of the excess was "the arrival on the scene of a petite, frisky young singer named Michelle Triola."

★*FEELEY, PAMELA* She was only 15, Lee 21 when they met in his hometown of Woodstock, New York. After a few dates Lee went off to the Big Apple to study acting, then on to Hollywood. Twenty-five years later, in 1970, toward the end of his relationship with Triola, Marvin returned to Woodstock, encountered Pamela, and to everyone's surprise, married her within the week. His attractive brown-haired bride had been wed three times before, had four children. She's still hitched to Lee, though, and he's boasted: "We've got a damn fine thing going."

★*MOREAU, JEANNE* Everyone on the set of *Monte Walsh* expected antagonistic fireworks when Marvin and Moreau met. Instead, "the effect was like a sudden commotion in Heaven. A hint of angels singing, violins playing. The two stars stood face to face, measured each other to their mutual satisfaction. . . . and Marvin was hit amidships by his delectable co-star." The lady told interviewers that Marvin was "more male than anyone I have ever acted with. He is the greatest man's man I have ever met and that includes all the European stars I have worked with." When the filming was done, Jeanne invited Lee to her villa in Saint Tropez, from where, theoretically, they might launch "a whole new world together." One of Marvin's close friends summed it up later: "He found Jeanne Moreau as intoxicating as anything he'd ever drunk in his life, but sipping cognac on the Left Bank or queuing to get on to Sam Spiegel's yacht at Cannes was not for Lee Marvin."

★*TRIOLA, MICHELLE* A singer who hit it big in the Las Vegas casinos, Michelle broke into movies with a bit part in *Ship of Fools*, starring Lee. Their mutual attraction soon grew intense, and Michelle recalls, "I knew we were in some kind of trouble." Before long, she had divorced her mate, he his, and Michelle became "resident mistress" at Marvin's Malibu beach house. Marriage, which Marvin calls "a stumble into the big ditch," *was* discussed. Michelle felt the need to legally change her last name to Marvin and reportedly remarked while on location with Lee in Tokyo, "I don't want the Emperor of Japan to think I'm a hooker." The relationship was on the rocks some time before Marvin abruptly married Pamela Feeley, but shortly thereafter, when he stopped support payments to Michelle, "posses of lawyers were galloping head-on towards each other in what may well become the suit of the century." Author Zec rather grandly refers, of course, to Michelle Triola Marvin's famous "palimony" suit against Lee Marvin. With attorney Marvin Mitchelson pleading her case, Michelle claimed she was entitled to the rights of a legally divorced wife. She'd always felt like a Mrs., she said; "I washed the dishes and Lee put out the garbage." The suit was rejected in lower courts, but the "rights for mistresses" were eventually upheld by the California Supreme Court. Michelle sought a settlement of $1.5 million, her estimated share of his earnings during their time together in the 1960s. But the court awarded her only $104,000 for "rehabilitation purposes." Both sides claimed victory, and Michelle declared magnanimously, "Lee is a good guy. I say 'Gung Ho' to him just as he says 'Gung Ho' to me." Because of Michelle Triola, countless nervous gents have been saying "heave-ho" to live-in lovers who won't sign a pre-connubial agreement regarding their "shared" assets.

MISCELLANY

★*"BLACK CLOUD"* The wife of one of Marvin's pals, she got her nickname because she looked like an Indian. Lee was "kind of fond" of her, and word got around that her husband, Lee's pal, was going to kill Lee. One day he came close—when he arrived at his Malibu beach pad, "and under the house I find Lee and Black Cloud with a whole bunch of wine." Lee was passed out drunk, of course, and Black Cloud's mate recalls, "we all had a good laugh over it."

★*OPERA STAR* She was both pretty and well endowed. Lee was standing next to her at some formal affair, when he "happened to notice this lady had quite inadvertently allowed her right breast to pop out of her extremely low cut dress. . . . Before she could do anything, Lee ·upped to the rescue with 'May I, dear lady?' and very delicately elevated her breast, reseating it neatly into its little nest." One observer insists that the diva's simple "thank you" ended the affair.

MONROE, MARILYN
(1926–1962)

There are at least a half-dozen extant biographies of Marilyn, the original Golden Girl described by Norman Mailer as "every man's love affair with America." Vulnerability was the essence of her sex appeal. Behind the glowing movie-star facade, even in a mediocre film, it's possible to see what playwright Arthur Miller saw, "her spirit shining through everything she does." He was married to her, though not for long, after her marriages to a young policeman and a Hall of Fame baseball hero. Few who worked with her found the going smooth. During the stormy production of *Some Like It Hot* (1959), one of MM's best films, though far from her favorite, director Billy Wilder made unflattering remarks about her in an interview and received an angry response from Miller, reminding him that Marilyn was "the salt of the earth." Wilder straightaway shot a message back to tell Miller that "the salt of the

earth just told an assistant director to go fuck himself."

PRIMARY SOURCES: *Marilyn Monroe Confidential,* by Lena Pepitone and William Stadiem (Simon & Schuster, 1979; Pocket Books, 1980); *Finding Marilyn: A Romance,* by David Conover (Grosset & Dunlap, 1981); *Norma Jean: The Life of Marilyn Monroe,* by Fred Lawrence Guiles (McGraw-Hill, 1979); *Marilyn: A Biography,* by Norman Mailer (Grosset & Dunlap, 1973).

★*BOLANOS, JOSE* Mexican movie producer who, according to Pepitone, was Marilyn's secret—and last—lover. Marilyn heard that he made lousy movies, but "What do I care? . . . He's the greatest lover in the whole wide world." Bolanos asked Marilyn to be his wife, but she didn't have a chance to think about it; she died shortly after the relationship began.

★*BRANDO, MARLON* In his novel-biography, Mailer refers to MM's "curious innocence about sex—once after going to bed with Marlon Brando she said next morning to Milton Greene, 'I don't know if I do it the right way.'" But then, muses Mailer, "which of us does know?" (See also BRANDO listing.)

★*COHN, HARRY* Head of Columbia Pictures. "For him, women were slaves. . . . he wasn't even the kind who said hello first. He just told you to get in bed." Quite a different version of the Cohn-MM combo is set forth by cautious biographer Guiles, who claims that Cohn was hardly aware of Marilyn's presence, "except for one audition in his office—made comfortable by their mutual interest in Christian Science." However, it was Cohn who first got Marilyn's name up in lights—with second billing in *Ladies of the Chorus* in 1949, which MM often called the greatest thrill of her life. She sang a song in it called "Every Baby Needs a Da-Da-Daddy."

★*CONOVER, DAVID* Army photographer who took pictures of defense worker Norma Jean Dougherty in 1945, and told her she ought to be doing something more with her life. He offered to help her become a model. Soon, Norma Jean and David were romping in the Mojave Desert for an entire week, his camera clicking as she tossed her curves and smiled that famous, tremulous Marilyn smile. They slept in the same motel room, writes Conover, but never touched one another until the night "she dropped the big white beach towel around her breasts and put her arms around me and kissed me and whispered, 'Let's do what comes naturally.' We did." Their junket over, Conover was shipped out. After the war, he moved to British Columbia—and it was *years* before he learned that *his* Norma Jean was Marilyn Monroe. Reestablishing contact, they became friends—never again lovers, although Marilyn evidently did not hesitate to tell him details of her sex life, which he prudently jotted down in a diary for all the world to know.

★*DIMAGGIO, JOE* Legendary baseball star for the New York Yankees. He was actually more famous than MM when they married, she for the second time. Fans of both Joe's and Marilyn's viewed this as a perfect All-American love match. Whatever they had in their stormy and very brief marriage (from January to October 1954), it was nothing compared to the loving closeness they enjoyed after the divorce—right up to the day she died. Marilyn often told Conover about Joe's secret "sleepovers" at her place; and the whole world knew how he cared for her when she was sick, comforted her when she was depressed, always got her out of trouble. Marilyn called Joe "the greatest love of my life." To this day, MM's crypt in Westwood has fresh red roses ordered by DiMaggio in perpetuity.

★*DOUGHERTY, JIM* Marilyn's first husband. Her aunt wanted the 16-year-old Marilyn out of the house and out of mischief. Jim was literally the boy next door, the only man she knew. "He was not my choice, but I never had a choice," Marilyn recalled ruefully. She always thought highly of Dougherty, even though their life together was brief. When he went overseas during World War II, she moved to L.A., got a job in that defense factory. Years later, as an L.A. cop, Dougherty was assigned at least once to control the crowds at

a Monroe premiere. But Marilyn didn't show.

★*FOSTER FATHER* As a child and adolescent, with her mother unable to care for her, Norma Jean was shuttled from one foster home to the next. At 15, possessed of precious little information about the facts of life, she was raped by a "foster father." "At first it was nice to be held and kissed. No one ever kissed me. But then . . . he wouldn't stop. It hurt a lot at first, then I didn't feel anything. I just lay there. I just cried." The assault resulted in pregnancy. She gave birth to a boy and relinquished him for adoption, according to Pepitone's book.

★*HYDE, JOHNNY* Top Hollywood agent who had previously helped Betty Hutton and Rita Hayworth up fame's ladder, and engineered Marilyn's breakthrough roles in *Asphalt Jungle* and *All About Eve*. Marilyn felt gentlemanly Johnny was the kindest man in the business; they became lovers and constant companions, but Marilyn could never quite go overboard. "I love him but I'm not *in* love with him," she told a friend, and repeatedly rejected his marriage proposals even after Hyde's wife filed for divorce because of Marilyn. "Even when he offered me his fortune, I still refused. It was the hardest thing I've ever done. Then he died of a heart attack. I felt partly to blame, and I cried for days. He was like a father. . . ." Though she was urged not to attend the funeral, she went, anyway, and Johnny's young son Jimmy recalls "Marilyn screaming my father's name over and over again. It shook everyone."

★*JOHNNIE* Italian chauffeur. He looked a little like Rudolph Valentino, hence her nickname for him, "The Sheik." Marilyn would invite Johnnie over, says Pepitone, and "they'd spend a whole afternoon locked up in her room, eating caviar and champagne, squealing and laughing. Marilyn never said anything about Johnnie to me. She just winked when he left, and I winked back."

★*KARGER, FRED* Vocal teacher at Columbia Studios. The only man Marilyn loved who didn't love her back, though his mother hoped he would marry her. "Still, we remained friends. He taught me how to sing, and for that I'll always be grateful." After they parted, Karger went to the altar with Jane Wyman, Ronnie Reagan's ex.

★KENNEDY, JOHN F. David Conover gives direct attribution where mostly rumor had existed before. He writes that Marilyn called him one night in early 1962 and announced breathlessly, "I did it! I did it! . . . I made it with the Prez." Conover asked, "Who?" "She giggled. 'You know, silly—President Kennedy.' " She said this was something she had planned and dreamed about. The "historic event" (Conover's words) took place, she told him, in Palm Springs. "At Bing Crosby's desert house. Sometime between midnight and 2:00 A.M., we were walking together in the moonlight across the sand dunes. It happened so suddenly. . . ." She sounded thrilled and happy, Conover reports. He advised Marilyn to "play it cool."

★KENNEDY, ROBERT The relationship here was a little heavier, once again Conover quoting Marilyn. She claimed Bobby said he loved her and wanted to marry her—when he got a divorce. "Then the bastard ran out on me. I can't get hold of him at the Justice Department, or anywhere. He just won't return any of my calls." Marilyn thought he was avoiding her because she had told him she was pregnant, although she'd already had it "taken care of." Conover again preached caution, and advised her that Bobby Kennedy's silence could be an attempt to avoid scandal and/or blackmail. That was Conover's last conversation with Monroe. Ten days later she was dead. His epilogue hints at dubious evidence that Marilyn Monroe was murdered as some kind of sacrificial pawn in a "vicious battle between union leader Jimmy Hoffa and Bobby Kennedy." Conover's lurid version of the RFK episode is covered more coolly by Mailer, covered with an alias by Guiles, who simply calls him "the Easterner . . . a lawyer and public servant" with close contacts in Hollywood, probably dallying with MM but finally scared off by fear of a scandal.

★MIDDLE-AGED MAN IN BAR The first of a string of men Marilyn made it with for money when she first came to Hollywood. He offered her $15 to leave the bar with him, and she didn't honestly know what was going on. But she went to a hotel with him and, as instructed, took off her clothes. "I thought that was a pretty good deal for $15. At the beach I was almost naked—for *nothing.*" Marilyn was horrified when he wanted to do more than *look* at her. But she let him. "It didn't bother me much. So what was the difference?"

★MILLER, ARTHUR Major American playwright, Marilyn's third husband. It was a mating of Beauty and the Brain. MM, weary of her "dumb blonde" image, imagined marrying Miller would bring her into a heady intellectual climate, New York, the Actors Studio, all that. He gave her a gold wedding band inscribed *"A to M, June, 1956. Now is forever."* Then Marilyn discovered that she still liked to live it up a little oftener than Arthur—who valued his solitude. She sometimes referred to him as old Grouchy Grumps. Her miscarriage, when she'd wanted so much to have his child, was another setback to the marriage. The gulf widened in London—Marilyn was making *The Prince and the Showgirl* with Olivier when she discovered a page from Miller's diary, a secret indictment endorsing Olivier's view of her as "a troublesome bitch. What a waste of love! All you want is a flunky . . . well, I'm not up to it, damn it. I'm not your servant." Marilyn filed for divorce at the end of 1960, shortly after filming *The Misfits,* her last movie, screenplay by Arthur Miller. In 1964—as a final posthumous sting—he also wrote the controversial autobiographical play *After the Fall,* about a blond psychotic superstar slut named Maggie.

★MONTAND, YVES French superstar, husband of equally prestigious French cinemadonna Simone Signoret. Marilyn thought Yves looked like Joe DiMaggio, and they became lovers while filming *Let's Make Love* in Hollywood. "The pair made no effort to be secretive; on the contrary, they posed for photographers, flaunting their romance." Miller went home to New York, Simone took off for France, and there was brief speculation that Montand and Monroe might eventually marry. All it amounted to, for M'sieu Montand, was l'amour the merrier. When Marilyn went to the airport to say *au revoir* to Yves, they shared a bottle of Dom Pérignon in the back of her limousine. "He kissed my cheek and all that. But he said he couldn't possibly leave Simone and that we should forget about each other." *Fini.*

★*SCHENCK, JOSEPH* One of the founders of 20th Century–Fox, had the reputation of being able to "buy" any woman in Hollywood. He was around 70 when Marilyn met him; she frequently dined at his house. "After dinner he told me to take my clothes off and he would tell me Hollywood stories. I would listen to these tales about John Barrymore, Charlie Chaplin, Valentino, everybody—and Mr. Schenck would play with my breasts." Then he started asking her to "kiss him—*down there.*" Sometimes she would spend hours servicing him thusly, and he'd often fall asleep. On awakening, "He'd pat my head, like a puppy, and thank me. All the other girls thought I had it made. Ha! But I kept going back. At least the food was good."

★*SINATRA, FRANK* He had been Joe Di-Maggio's best buddy; started dating Marilyn casually after her divorce from Joe. Mailer notes that it probably remained casual until after her divorce from Miller, when she stayed with Sinatra in his Waldorf suite and told a friend they had trouble keeping the twin beds together. The friend asked if he'd been any good, to which Marilyn cracked, "He was no DiMaggio." Maybe things got better. Conover reports that seeing Sinatra always gave Marilyn a lift. "After one night with Frankie, I don't have to see my analyst for weeks." They were to remain close chums. (See also SINATRA listing.)

MISCELLANY

★*CLIFT, MONTGOMERY* Marilyn said he was the only person she knew in worse shape than she was. Their empathy for each other was immediately apparent on the set of *The Misfits.* She said they'd talk about what kind of drugs they had to take to get to sleep. Marilyn once tried to seduce Monty, and reported he looked confused at first. He then gave her a teasing slap on the rear end, saying, "You've got the most incredible ass," pecked her on the cheek and left. (See also CLIFT listing.)

★*CURTIS, TONY* Marilyn had a lot of fun in her kissing scene with Tony while shooting *Some Like It Hot,* but he reportedly described it publicly on the soundstage as an ordeal, "like kissing Hitler." After taking in this remark, Marilyn said she wasn't going to waste her affections on someone who was against her.

★*GABLE, CLARK* When she was a child being shunted between foster homes, little Norma Jean carried a picture of Clark Gable, pretending he was her long-lost father. Gable's interest remained paternal, and they got along famously. Working with him in *The Misfits* was, for MM, a dream come true. Marilyn was "absolutely crushed" over his sudden death less than a month after the shooting ended.

NICHOLSON, JACK
(b. 1937)

As a nonconformist and outsider, the loner who does for contemporary audiences something akin to what Bogart used to do, Nicholson truly became a star after *Easy Rider* in 1969, then consolidated his image with *Five Easy Pieces* the following year. It was mostly smooth going uphill from there to his 1975 Oscar for *One Flew over the Cuckoo's Nest.* Few remember that Nicholson was writing, directing, and acting in low-budget B movies for a good dozen years before *Easy Rider.* Famous today for his "killer grin," and for flashing it on so many attractive women that no biographer could stay abreast of him ("He's a male nymphomaniac," says one buddy), he travels in the fast lanes with an international movie crowd streaking from European pit stops to New York and Malibu.

PRIMARY SOURCE: *Jack Nicholson: The Search for a Superstar*, by Norman Dickens (New American Library/ Signet, 1975).

★*ANSPACH, SUSAN* She played the girl who was too good for Jack Nicholson in *Five Easy Pieces*, and says "what was in the film is very much what was between us in real life. . . . Jack and I had great electricity for each other." At the time, however, he was in a "rough period" with Mimi Machu (see below) and Jack and Susan "were not totally trusting of each other's way of life." She *really* loves him, though, Susan insists.

★*HUSTON, ANJELICA* Actress-model, daughter of director John Huston. Their relationship began in 1973, at last word is still going. (Anjelica had a small part with Nicholson as the lion tamer in the 1981 version of *The Postman Always Rings Twice*.) He once described her as "a creative lady who has a big bold style. . . . she's the only girl I know who has a reasoned head, considering who she is."

★*KNIGHT, SANDRA* Beautiful, dark-haired actress. Nicholson's first (and to date only) wife. They married in 1962, co-starred in Roger Corman's *The Terror* in 1963, and that same year she gave up her career when daughter Jennifer was born. The union ended in 1966. Jack has said that, "the secret inner pressure about monogamy" was too large a burden for him to bear.

★*MACHU, MIMI* Tall, gorgeous actress who was billed as I. J. Jefferson in Nicholson's films *Hell's Angels on Wheels* and *Head*. "Mimi Machu is a name that sounds like a tropical storm, which about summarizes the relationship. . . ." She was his old lady for about three years.

★*PHILLIPS, MICHELLE* Actress-singer, former wife of both John Phillips and Dennis Hopper (her leap with Hopper described as "a marriage that lasted for about a week"). Michelle soon moved in with Jack. Again, this rela-

tionship lasted roughly three years. (See also PHILLIPS listing.)

★*TRUDEAU, MARGARET* In the second volume of her life story, Ms. Trudeau recalls meeting Nicholson in London while she was writing Volume I. After a "mad episode" in the back seat of his chauffeured Daimler, Margaret more or less moved into Jack's digs although he was still emotionally involved with Anjelica Huston. When Anjelica showed up in London, Margaret "felt crushed . . . a fool." Some time later, in Hollywood, Maggie again met Jack at a party and was moved to confide in him about her "rather sordid affair" with Ryan O'Neal. "I whispered to Jack that I had to speak to him. 'Certainly, my darling,' he said, and led me off to the men's washroom, where I perched up on the toilet seat so that no one would be able to see my legs." Margaret doesn't reveal what Jack then said about Ryan. Drat. (See also TRUDEAU listing.)

MISCELLANY

★*EASTMAN, CAROLE* Screenwriter, and a "close friend" of Jack's, with whom he shares "all-night rap sessions."

★*KALLINIOTES, HELENA* Actress who appeared with Nicholson in *Five Easy Pieces*; she lives next door to him (or did) and "manages some of his affairs."

★*KELLERMAN, SALLY* Kinky actress, an early pal and acting classmate. She used to sit on Jack's lap and pour out her heart to him about her troubles with men. She calls him a true friend.

Nicholson has been known to have "short term" relationships with *CANDICE BERGEN, FAYE DUNAWAY,* and *JONI MITCHELL,* among many many others.

Jill St. John and Henry Kissinger: I wonder who's Kissinger now? *(Wide World Photos)*

Rita Hayworth and Orson Welles: Was *The Lady from Shanghai* the real Rita or Orson's revenge? *(Cinemabilia)*

Barbi Benton and Hugh Hefner: Flying high with Hef. *(Wide World Photos)*

Princess Margaret with a Peter Sellers cutout and Spike Milligan and friend: "And keep that hand off the Princess's knee." *(Wide World Photos)*

Marilyn Monroe with John F. Kennedy: She told a friend it happened in Palm Springs. *(Wide World Photos)*

Above left: Roman Polanski with Sharon Tate: Mod, mod bride on a Roman holiday. *Above:* Roman Polanski with Nastassia Kinski: Love in bloom, but he dedicated *Tess* to Sharon. *(Wide World Photos)*

Peter Sellers and Liza Minnelli: Their clairvoyants couldn't agree. *(Wide World Photos)*

Tyrone Power and Gene Tierney: Ty's time was up when JFK came along. From *The Razor's Edge. (Cinemabilia)*

Porfirio Rubirosa and Zsa-Zsa Gabor: And Zsa-Zsa picked up another Rubi. *(Wide World Photos)*

Lana Turner and Tyrone Power in Mexico: Spontaneous combustion, south of the border. *(Wide World Photos)*

Frank Sinatra and Ava Gardner *(left)* . . . and Mia Farrow *(below)* . . . and Barbara Marx (below left). Ole Blue Eyes keeps goin' till he gets it right. *(Wide World Photos)*

Jean Seberg and Jean-Paul Belmondo: *Breathless* and luckless in French beds. From *Breathless*. (Cinemabilia)

Barbra Streisand and Omar Sharif: Repercussions from Egypt—and you shoulda heard her Aunt Rose. *(Columbia Pictures)*

Barbra Streisand and Jon Peters: She only knows her hairdresser for sure. *(Wide World Photos)*

Shelley Winters and Farley Granger: Unzipped again. *(Wide World Photos)*

Right: Margaret Trudeau and Prince Charles: Her cleavage caught his eye. *(Wide World Photos)*

Britt Ekland and Rod Stewart: What price palship? (*Steve Schapiro/Sygma*)

Brigitte Bardot and Jacques Charrier: Husband #2—and then they were three. (*Sygma*)

Top: Charles Chaplin and Virginia Cherrill: And then she married Cary Grant. (From *City Lights*) *Above:* Yves Montand and Marilyn Monroe: Cheek to cheek while Simone sweated it out. (*Twentieth Century Fox*)

Howard Hughes and his women: Maybe getting there was *all* the fun. *(Private collection)*

Above right: Elvis and Priscilla Presley: The bride went thataway. *Above:* Elvis Presley and Ann-Margret: A couple of swingers quickly cooled. *(MGM)*

Right: Lauren Bacall and Humphrey Bogart: Lighting the way to a great love. *(Museum of Modern Art/Film Stills Archives)*

Katharine Hepburn and Spencer Tracy: The class act among secret lovers. *(Museum of Modern Art/Film Stills Archives)*

Errol Flynn and Tyrone Power: Together again in *The Sun Also Rises. (Twentieth Century Fox)*

NIVEN, DAVID
(b. 1910)

Urbane British leading man and author of two brightly anecdotal memoirs. Niven won an Oscar for *Separate Tables* (1958), and played Phileas Fogg in *Around the World in 80 Days* (1956). During a long career that began when he was signed by Goldwyn in 1935, his trademark—on screen as well as on the printed page—has been unflappable charm, wit, and amiability.

PRIMARY SOURCES: *The Moon's a Balloon*, by David Niven (Coronet, London, 1971); *Bring On the Empty Horses*, by David Niven (Putnam, 1975).

★*CLAUDE* Paris model, later mistress of an industrial tycoon and installed in apartment house in Paris where the tycoon's family lived one flight up. Niven had to visit on the sly, making love in whispers, the couple with handkerchiefs stuffed in their mouths to still their cries of passion. The game was up the night Claude gave Niven an alcohol rub with eau de cologne, spilled it, "and most of the contents went straight up my behind."

★*EUNICE* Wife of signal officer on a destroyer who invited Niven, then frustrated in service with the British army at Gibraltar, to warm her bed while her husband's ship was away. Hubby came home unexpectedly during "some far from routine thrashing-around." After a narrow escape, Niven was "impotent for days."

★*GBS* Nameless Great Big Star of 1936 and his companion on an erotic ten-day cross-country motor trip from New York to L.A., interrupted by urgent—and mostly ignored—telegrams from Samuel Goldwyn. While Niven indulged in the idyll with his GBS, Goldwyn waited with role for him in *Wuthering Heights*.

★*THE GREAT DANE* Tall flaxen-haired Danish beauty described as "a nymphomaniac of heroic proportions." In London, a comic wartime telegram announcing his arrival with secret weapon evoked some concern from Military Intelligence until Niven explained:

"That's not code—that's fucking."

★*KEYES, EVELYN* Described in her own book as "a one-night stand," when she was having bad problems in her marriage to Huston. Of Niven, she said, "My partner was darling." During the Mike Todd years, when Todd was casting *Around the World in 80 Days*, Keyes notes: "It was I who suggested David Niven for Phileas Fogg. The ex's right under Mike's nose—and he never knew." (See also KEYES listing.)

★*LAMARR, HEDY* She says David was her "escort" aboard a cruise on the Fairbanks yacht (see Shipmates below . . . also see LAMARR listing.)

★*NESSIE* Fetching teenage prostitute in Piccadilly who introduced him to sex when he was 14, remained his frequent date and confidante through schooldays at Sandhurst. Always described herself, wrote Niven, as "an 'ore wiv an 'eart of fuckin' gold."

★*NIVEN, HJORDIS* Second wife, top Swedish model who became (and remains) Mrs. Niven after whirlwind ten-day courtship, returned to U.S. and appeared on *Life* cover as one of Hollywood's ten most beautiful women.

★*NIVEN, PRIMMIE* (née ROLLO) Beloved first wife, wartime WAAF and daughter of a famous London divorce lawyer. Bore two sons, David Jr. and Jamie; subsequently died in California at age 25 after a freak accident, falling down flight of stairs in the dark during a parlor game called Sardines, discovered unconscious by Tyrone Power.

MISCELLANY

★*MARY LOU* Beautiful would-be starlet who ultimately found happiness with a lesbian named Bobbie at classy Hollywood brothel run by the Baroness, but remained Niven's friend until the Mob muscled in.

★*SHIPMATES* Series of girls invited by Niven and Flynn on weekend jaunts to Catalina aboard Flynn's infamous yacht *Sirocco*. The guys brought booze, gals brought food, except for "one lady whose contribution consisted of nothing but a loaf of bread and a douche bag."

OLIVIER, LAURENCE
(b. 1907)

Widely acknowledged as the world's greatest living actor for his stage performances, Lord Olivier is a titled superstar whose screen career has been as colorful and erratic as his private life. Once a romantic leading man, after divorcing his first wife he married Vivien Leigh to form a legendary acting team (although their only major film together was *That Hamilton Woman* in 1941). Not until he set feminine hearts aflutter as Heathcliff in *Wuthering Heights* (1939) and the brooding hero of *Rebecca* (1940) did Olivier become a figure in world cinema. He went on to make such Shakespearean film classics as *Henry V* (1945) and *Hamlet* (1948), for which he won two Oscars as director and star. Since his 1964 marriage to Joan Plowright, he has continued to be a royal theatrical personage in England, while esthetically slumming over here in TV commercials or overwrought character roles in such epics as *The Betsy* (1979) and *The Jazz Singer* (1980). Regarding his work, his life, his loves and hates and ill health—all subjects of gossip and controversey for half a century—he is reported to be at work on an autobiography in which Sir Larry himself will have the last word.

PRIMARY SOURCE: *Sir Larry: The Life of Laurence Olivier*, by Thomas Kiernan (Times Books, a division of Quadrangle/New York Times Book Co., 1981).

★*ESMOND, JILL*   Larry, 21, sought a bit part in a play called *Bird in Hand*, just to be near ingenue Jill, for whom "he fell hard." Descended from a noted theatrical family, Jill became Olivier's teacher, giving him a new perspective about his work. At the time they married, in 1930, she was a bigger name in London's West End, and a more in-demand performer than Larry. Only a year later in New York when they were co-starring in Noel Coward's *Private Lives*, their turbulent relationship became apparent to all. But the marriage held together until the birth of their son Tarquin, and through the first troubled years of Olivier's affair with Vivien Leigh. After international fame came to the illicit lovers (to Viv through *Gone With the Wind* and to Larry in *Wuthering Heights*), scandal-shy Hollywood moguls began putting pressure on the reluctant Jill and Viv's husband Leigh Holman to divorce their respective spouses so they could legally become man and wife. One observer felt the seductive Miss Leigh was not directly responsible for the break-up between Larry and Jill; "That marriage got off on the wrong foot and never quite recovered."

★*GARSON, GREER*   She too was an ingenue, "a young, beautiful redheaded actress from Ireland," who had a small part in Olivier's *Theater Royal* (English title for the American play *Royal Family*). At the time, he was "constantly at odds with his wife Jill." Sources won't confirm whether Larry's "infatuation" with Greer turned into a genuine love affair, but most speculate that it did. It was said that Olivier decided to produce and direct a play called *Golden Arrow*, with Greer in the lead, solely because "he desperately wanted her close to him." The play closed after ten days, though, and with it, apparently, went Larry's yen for Greer. Within a few years Garson would become Mrs. Miniver and one of Hollywood's hottest stars.

★*LEIGH, VIVIEN*   Beauteous Vivien, destined to be Scarlett O'Hara now and forever, set her sights on Olivier long before they met. After seeing him onstage, Viv told a friend that she intended to become his wife—although she was then Mrs. Leigh Holman. Her subsequent affair with Olivier was a cause célèbre. Their twenty-year marriage (1940–1960)—remarkable for both physical passion and theatrical poetry, great triumphs and heartbreaking tragedies—was plagued from the beginning by Vivien's periodic manic-depressive episodes which, at best, turned her into a shrew and at worst led her into self-destructive promiscuity. Olivier stood fast by his second wife, even though, says biographer Kiernan, "he was falling out of love" with Vivien as early as 1945.

In the late 1950's, as he reached the zenith of his career and the nadir of his marriage, Olivier found consolation with Joan Plowright, while Vivien found Jack Merivale. One of the great theatrical romances of the century had come to an end. (See also LEIGH listing.)

★PLOWRIGHT, JOAN Olivier chose the young actress to play his daughter onstage in *The Entertainer*, but not just because of her acting ability. "Joan, for all her plainness, was dark complexioned . . . and projected the sensuous look of a gypsy." Olivier later remarked that she reminded him of his mother. They first became lovers when they took the play to New York in 1958; after their respective divorces (he from Vivien, she from actor Roger Gage), they were wed in Connecticut in 1961. Joan was 32, Larry 57. She has since given him three children, and he became a dedicated, late-blooming family man. "More than anything else, that became Larry's greatest pride and joy. It gave him something to live for that was more important than acting." But Olivier has also admitted that his children have given him a reason to continue his career. "He wants them to remember him as a vital old boy who, when he went down, went down acting."

★SIMMONS, JEAN She was only 18 when she played Ophelia to Olivier's *Hamlet* in his historic film. Kiernan notes: "Some say that Olivier became enamored of Miss Simmons and fell into a brief affair with her . . . Others insist that his attachment to her, intense as it was over the several months of filming, was purely professional." Whichever, Vivien Leigh suspected the worst, confiding to a friend, "Well, I shouldn't be surprised. I was barely out of my teens when Larry started fucking me."

★WELSH, JANE Yet another young actress, who was Olivier's "first genuine romance." It was a very English affair, conducted in "fits and starts" during 1927, until Larry met Jill Esmond.

MISCELLANY

★BADDELEY, ANGELA Famed in recent years for playing Mrs. Bridges, the irascible cook in TV's *Upstairs, Downstairs*, Angela was an appealing but very married young actress when the very young (19) Olivier "became like some soppy-eyed basset hound trailing around in her wake." She rejected "his kisses, his pantings and his declarations of love . . . with dignity."

★BLOOM, CLAIRE Mrs. Olivier, Vivien, had coveted the role of Lady Anne in Larry's film of *Richard III*, which went instead to Bloom. Once again Viv believed *the worst*, and her anger at losing the role "turned into jealous rage." Only Claire's hairdresser knows for sure.

★HEWITT, MURIEL Yet another actress, who "aroused stirrings of desire" in the young actor. He was chagrined to learn that the object of his affection was married to another young member of their theatrical company— Ralph Richardson.

★OBERON, MERLE Larry's co-star in the memorable *Wuthering Heights*. She had not-so-subtly let Larry know that she was "available to him if he wanted her." He didn't want, and they reportedly wound up bitter enemies while portraying the impassioned but doomed lovers, Heathcliff and Kathy.

ONASSIS, ARISTOTLE
(1906–1975)

Greek shipping magnate, one of the world's richest men in his lifetime. Aboard his yacht *Christina*, Onassis played host to heads of state, tycoons, superstars, and Beautiful People ad infinitum. He started out with a cigar in his mouth at age 11, working in the office of his father, a tobacco merchant. At roughly the same time, Ari developed a lusty interest in the opposite sex, and his biography related that he was once caught by his father with an uneducated nubile laundress "on a pile of soiled bed linen, about to tamper with both his and the girl's virginity." His father didn't object to Ari's impulses, only to his choice of partners. He advised his son, "Never become involved with someone who can make you lose stature if the relationship becomes known. . . . sleep *up.*" Clearly, Onassis *fils* listened to Onassis *père*, thus it was that the man who had everything would one day make history by marrying the beautiful young widow of an American president.

PRIMARY SOURCE: *Onassis: An Extravagant Life,* by Frank Brady (Prentice-Hall, 1977).

★*BALLET DANCER*   A Russian dancer with Anna Pavlova's Swan Ballet Company which toured South America in the mid-1920s. Onassis, settled in Buenos Aires, was on his way to his first million in the tobacco import business, and "had a strong flavor of impending success about him that some women found intoxicating, almost aphrodisiacal." The ballet dancer was so intoxicated she refused to go home with the troupe. The affair lasted about a year; there were rumors she had a child by him, for whom Onassis provided support.

★*CALLAS, MARIA*   One of the grandest divas of grand opera, and, like Onassis, a Greek. She was approaching the apex of her career, and was married to Milanese industrialist Meneghini (30 years older than she) when Onassis invited the pair aboard his yacht for a cruise around the Mediterranean. The attraction between Maria and Ari was immediate, and apparent for all to see. Meneghini called Onassis "a moral leper." Tina Onassis said nothing until months later, in the U.S., when she filed for divorce. Callas and Onassis had a long, very close, and very public relationship, and it was thought they'd eventually marry. Until Jackie Kennedy came along. Even in the Jackie era they remained close friends.

★*CONSTANTINESCO, MARIA*   A known German spy with whom Onassis had a brief wartime affair. Investigated by the FBI, she was convicted and sent to prison.

★*DEDICHEN, INGEBORD*   Beautiful, rich, sophisticated Norwegian woman, a few years older than Ari. They met on a ship to Europe in 1934, and she took a liking to the short,

barrel-chested man who was "uncommonly reserved for a Greek, but unschooled in the etiquette of the genteel." She taught him everything he needed to know; it was from Ingebord that Onassis "gained culture and acceptance into international society." They were also deeply in love, sharing a life together for twelve years. "Why they never married has never been quite clear."

★*FRENCH TUTOR*   Ari was an eager adolescent of 12, she was "an attractive and buxom girl in her 20s." She was also his first lover. "For a period of about one year, each French lesson was accompanied by a session in bed. Onassis later revealed that his French improved markedly."

★*KENNEDY, JACQUELINE*   Onassis had known the Kennedys for years, so there was nothing untoward when he offered Jackie the use of his yacht, the *Christina,* to help her recover from the death of her infant son, Patrick, in early summer 1963. Sister Lee Radziwill would be on board, and it was Jackie who insisted that Onassis join the cruise. America's First Lady and Greece's gift to women got along "famously; at the end of the cruise, Ari gave Jackie a mammoth diamond and ruby necklace." Just a few months later, John Kennedy was assassinated, and Onassis became one of the only outsiders invited to stay at the White House during the funeral. During the next five years the President's widow met Onassis frequently, usually in private. She'd spend long weekends in his Paris apartment. It was the assassination of Bobby Kennedy that made Jackie forfeit her role as America's most respected heroine by deciding to marry Onassis, who was 62 to her 39—a foreigner, a womanizer, and a non-Catholic. But he was also very rich. Ted Kennedy reportedly took the lead in arranging a marital contract nicely taking care of Jackie's needs. The wedding took place in 1968. By the early 1970s there were rumors of a rift provoked in part by her extravagant spending. After Onassis's only son, Alex, was killed in an air crash in 1973, "Suddenly, he could no longer abide Jackie." During the last year of his life he allegedly investigated the possibility of a divorce. Onassis died in March 1975, after making provisions in his will to cut back his widow's share of the Onassis fortune. (See also the JACQUELINE ONASSIS listing.)

★*LAKE, VERONICA* Blond film star of the '40s who claims that Onassis kept her supplied with nylons and other goodies during World War II. (See also LAKE listing.)

★*LIVANOS, TINA* One of the two daughters of Greek shipowner Stavros Livanos, who at first was "outraged" that 40-year-old Onassis wanted to wed 17-year-old Tina, rather than his eldest daughter, Eugenie (who later married Stavros Niarchos, Onassis's lifelong nemesis). Tina became Ari's bride in December 1945, gave him two children, Alexander and Christina. While he roamed the world having well-publicized affairs, she had one of her own, with Renaldo Herrera, a Venezuelan millionaire. Within a year after she divorced Ari, she married the Marquess of Blandford for a relatively short stretch; she divorced him, and after her sister Eugenie died, Tina stepped into her shoes by marrying Ari's archrival.

★*PERÓN, EVA* Onassis's Argentine connections—primarily Eva Perón—led some observers to speculate that he was pro-Nazi. Also, "There was even a heavily circulated rumor that Onassis was conducting a clandestine affair with Madame Perón."

★*RADZIWILL, LEE* Jackie Onassis's sister. Before Onassis set his sights on Jackie, Lee was one of his favorite cruise mates. Kitty Kelley's *Jackie Oh!* quotes a former Kennedy aide who claims that Bobby "got all upset when Lee Radziwill started playing around with Aristotle Onassis and was supposedly going to divorce her husband to marry him. . . . he told Jackie to put a stop to it." Some sibling rivalry may have grown out of the triangle later, but the Bouvier girls managed it, as usual, with Lee moving to a back seat.

★*SIMONE, SIMONE* Controversial French film star who was said to distribute gold house keys to all the men she favored. Onassis spent "much time" with her in Hollywood during the war years.

MISCELLANY

★*GARBO, GRETA* The elusive star was known to become "very gay in Onassis's presence." For many years, they spent holidays together on his yacht *Christina,* with Greta making a discreet exit if another woman entered Ari's life. "Only once, after he had had too much to drink, did he suggest that they become lovers. 'Go to sleep,' Greta said. 'Don't ruin our friendship.' "

ONASSIS, JACQUELINE KENNEDY
(b. 1928)

Widow of U.S. President John F. Kennedy and Greek tycoon Aristotle Onassis. Born Jacqueline Lee Bouvier, a society girl with good connections and instinctive style but little money, who suffered many grievous private losses, yet learned along the way to become a conspicuous big spender. Once told a friend that "the kind of men who fascinate me are men like Dr. Christiaan Barnard, Henry Kissinger, Prince Philip, Alistair Cooke, General Westmoreland, and Cary Grant." For the most part, those are exactly the kind of men she has had, either as intimate friends or escorts. Her relationships have provoked gossip rather than scandal, and stories of heavy involvement are often carefully called apocryphal, though some seem less so than others.

PRIMARY SOURCES: *Jackie Oh!* by Kitty Kelley (Ballantine, 1979); *Jackie: A Truly Intimate Biography,* by Freda Kramer (Grosset & Dunlap, 1979).

★*GILPATRIC, ROSWELL* Under Secretary of Defense during the Kennedy years, close to Jackie before she married Onassis. In 1970, an autograph dealer prepared to auction Jackie's letters to Gilpatric, many of which were published, much to the chagrin of Onassis and to the third Mrs. Gilpatric—who soon asked for a legal separation, later described her husband's relationship to the former First Lady as "very, very close." While she was dating Onassis in 1968, they made a widely publicized trip together to see the Mayan ruins in Yucatan.

★*HAMMILL, PETE* New York Irish columnist, believed to be Jackie's best friend and lover—as well as surrogate father to her children—after Onassis. Their liaison reportedly wrote finis to Hammill's longtime romance with Shirley MacLaine. Privacy was a problem, for photographers dogged the couple's footsteps, prompting Hammill's brother to remark that a date with Jackie was like "taking out a big bright red fire engine."

★*KENNEDY, JOHN FITZGERALD* First husband, 35th U.S. President, father of daughter Caroline and son John. "In the beginning, Jackie was enamored of him," said a friend of the couple's imperfect marriage. "She learned later." (See also KENNEDY listing.)

★*MARQUAND, JOHN P. JR.* Novelist's son, named by old family friend of the Bouvier sisters as the lad who may have claimed Jackie's virginity way back then. As the story goes, she bluntly remarked afterward: "Oh, is that all there is to it?"

★*ONASSIS, ARISTOTLE* Second husband, Greek shipping magnate who wined, dined, wooed, and won the U.S. President's widow in one of the great—and certainly the most widely publicized—romances of the century. The trip from Camelot to Skorpios initially cost her some public esteem when she married Onassis in 1968. After Ari's death in 1975, Jackie recouped with a final settlement of $20 million from the Onassis empire. It all began when the former First Lady defied JFK and accepted an invitation to a cruise on the Onassis yacht. Kennedy, if not jealous, was politically embarrassed and phoned to say, "I don't care how you get off that yacht. But get

off, Jackie. You're a good swimmer." She stayed on.

★*TEMPLESMAN, MAURICE* Millionaire diamond merchant, already married but still a frequent escort. Re this relationship, Jackie is quoted as telling friends: "I admire his strength and his success. I hope my notoriety doesn't force him out of my life."

MISCELLANY

★*HUSTEN, JOHN G. W. JR.* Wall Street banker. Engaged to Jackie when she was 23 and employed as an inquiring photographer for the *Washington Times-Herald*. Then she met JFK.

★*ORMSBY-GORE, DAVID, LORD HARLECH* Old friend who accompanied Jackie on a trip to Cambodia in 1967, thereby increasing speculation about a budding "romance." A story that reportedly gave sister Lee Radziwill the giggles. "Are you kidding?" she said. "Have you *seen* him?"

★*OTHER MALE COMPANIONS* Probably platonic for various reasons: *JANN WENNER* (of Rolling Stone), *SKIP STEIN* (investment banker), *TRUMAN CAPOTE* (writer), *ROBERT MCNAMARA* (former Secretary of Defense, and head of World Bank), *ANDRÉ MAYER* (financial adviser), *FRANK SINATRA* (singer), *LEONARD BERNSTEIN* (conductor), *MIKE NICHOLS* (comedian and director), *ADLAI STEVENSON* (politician), *GEORGE PLIMPTON* (writer, jack-of-all-trades), *ANTHONY QUINN* (actor), *JOHN GLENN* (astronaut and senator), writers *ARTHUR SCHLESINGER, JR., RICHARD GOODWIN*— and more.

O'NEAL, RYAN
(b. 1941)

Though often put down as a bland leading man, Tatum O'Neal's handsome dad set hearts aflutter in TV's *Peyton Place* and has been very effective in romantic comedies since *What's Up, Doc?* with Streisand in 1972. His credentials as a light-heavy-weight actor range from *Love Story* (1970) to *Barry Lyndon* (1975). O'Neal is known to enjoy spending his free time playing Frisbee and pursuing pretty ladies, occasionally taking a punch at a photographer because he does not like to be photographed at games.

PRIMARY SOURCES: *Joan Collins: Past Imperfect,* by Joan Collins (W.H. Allen, London, 1978); *True Britt,* by Britt Ekland (Prentice-Hall, 1980); *The Greatest Star: The Barbra Streisand Story,* by Rene Jordan (Putnam, 1975).

★*ANDRESS, URSULA* She was a "house-guest" for several weeks at Ryan's Malibu pad, and, with her wet T-shirts and bikini bottoms, created quite a stir on the beach, according to eyewitness Britt Ekland.

★*COLLINS, JOAN* The sexy British actress thought that Ryan "had it all going for him in the looks department—and he wasn't lacking in the charm and humor department either. Or the dancing department, or the sex-appeal department." However, Joan gave it a pass on that first meeting with Ryan. Later, however, when hubby Tony Newley was out of town on her birthday, she celebrated with Ryan. She said he was exactly what a girl deserved for her birthday—the *best*. (See also COLLINS listing.)

★*EKLAND, BRITT* Alone and lonely in London, tattletale Britt found Ryan a good shoulder to cry on about her busted-up affair with Lou Adler. They shared "an understanding of one another's problems," and, of course, a bed. That was "academic," says Britt. It was a pleasant interlude, but not gang-busters. (See also EKLAND listing.)

★*FAWCETT, FARRAH* Former Charlie's Angel having hit-or-miss movie career, but by all reports enjoying unqualified success as Ryan's newest, brightest, and hottest flame amid persistent rumors there's a marriage in the offing.

★*LIPTON, PEGGY* Starlet and frequent companion.

★*MCGRAW, ALI* Ryan's co-star in *Love Story,* his first major success. According to one source, producer Robert Evans pretended not to notice when Ryan and Ali "got together for some unscheduled love scenes." Which meant nobody had to say "I'm sorry." Ali's next leading man was Steve McQueen, whom she left Evans to marry after *The Getaway.* Prophetic titles.

★*MOORE, JOANNA* Actress of the early '60s, appeared in *Walk on the Wild Side* ('61). O'Neal's first wife, and mother of daughter Tatum and son Griffin.

★*STREISAND, BARBRA* He was the season's Prince Charming, the Prize Catch, and Barbra could not resist. Ryan was then still married to Leigh Taylor-Young, she to Elliott Gould, so the romance had an extra element of scandal. By the time they got to San Francisco to film *What's Up, Doc?* the fireworks had fizzled. Ryan explained the original attraction: "We were able to share a kind of shyness."

★*TAYLOR-YOUNG, LEIGH* Beautiful rising star who appeared with Ryan in *The Big Bounce* (1968). Also married him, but just for a while.

★*TRUDEAU, MARGARET* It was, says the lady, "one of the shortest-lived, most exciting, and absurd of affairs." It lasted just about a week, ending when Margaret, who was refused entrance to Ryan's place because his son was visiting, hitched up her skirt and *climbed* over the garden wall. At that point, Margaret writes, she was imagining herself "as some kind of female Errol Flynn." In conclusion, though, the fling was too far over the wall—or maybe off-the-wall—for either Margaret or Ryan to handle. (See also TRUDEAU listing.)

★*WOOD, LANA* Another Hollywood beauty and frequent companion. Natalie's sister.

PHILLIPS, MICHELLE
(b. 1944)

Singer turned actress, she started out with the Mamas and Papas musical group, at that time was married to John Phillips. Generally, she has been cast as a kind of contemporary femme fatale—well, not so contemporary in *Valentino* opposite Nureyev—in such indifferent films as *Bloodlines* (1979). Phillips so far seems to be more memorable for the music and the men in her life than for any screen achievements, though there is evidence she's improving.

PRIMARY SOURCES: *True Britt*, by Britt Ekland (Prentice-Hall, 1980); *Eddie: My Life, My Loves*, by Eddie Fisher (Harper & Row, 1981); *Jack Nicholson: The Search for a Superstar*, by Norman Dickens (New American Library/Signet, 1975).

★*ADLER, LOU* The recording mogul and film producer *(Cheech and Chong*, etc.) had been living with Britt Ekland, and, indeed, went to London to be with Britt at the birth of their son in June 1973. Shortly after, mother and son returned to Adler's Malibu house, where Britt learned that Michelle Phillips had moved in during her absence. Michelle moved in again when Britt moved out.

★*BEATTY, WARREN* They were so close, they shared a big house on Mulholland Drive —along with Michelle's daughter Chyna, from John Phillips. This was one of the few recorded instances where Beatty lived with a girl *after* she'd lived with Jack Nicholson. (The boys have a friendly sort of competition going as to who's on first—according to the Nicholson bio.) (See also BEATTY listing.)

★*BIRCH, ROBERT* Television executive. Michelle married him on May 21, 1978. Didn't last long.

★*FISHER, EDDIE* He says that Michelle was one of the girls introduced to him for brief encounters during his "party period," when he was the musical man of the moment from the Coconut Grove to the Copa. (See also FISHER listing.)

★*HINES, GRANGER* Actor, fourth and current husband, father of Mark, born in March 1982.

★*HOPPER, DENNIS* She lived with the enigmatic actor-director for three years, then married him. The marriage lasted for about a week. Dennis introduced Michelle to Jack Nicholson and reportedly told Nicholson, "You'll probably be living with her in three months." He was right on.

★*NICHOLSON, JACK* They also lived together for about three years—before she "broke Jack's heart" by moving on to Warren Beatty. But she liked Jack so much she moved into the house next door to him. (See also NICHOLSON listing.)

★*O'NEAL, RYAN* He and Michelle dated for a while when Ryan wasn't busy with Anjelica Huston, who also loved Nicholson but returned to Ryan for a while after the Polanski brouhaha, then Anjelica went back with Jack and . . . oh, never mind.

★*PHILLIPS, JOHN* He was a papa and she a mama in the famous 1960s folk group the Mamas and Papas. After their divorce Michelle hopped over to Hopper's bed.

POLANSKI, ROMAN
(b. 1933)

Polish-French director presently in exile from Hollywood because of charges pending against him (see below). While away, he has had his biggest commercial success since *Chinatown* (1973) with *Tess*, a sumptuous 1979 film version of Thomas Hardy's *Tess of the d'Urbervilles*, which made an international star of Natassia Kinski. Born in Paris but brought up in Poland during the war, Polanski lost his parents in death camps (his mother died at Auschwitz) and makes movies which are a unique blend of horror, eroticism, and rather sophisticated black humor. His first major success was the Polish-made *Knife in the Water* (1962). As a jet-setting world citizen, Polanski's lifestyle began to come under public scrutiny after the Manson murders. Some morbid curiosity about him continues to the present time, though it seems a safe bet that his directorial talent will outlast the gossip.

PRIMARY SOURCE: *The Roman Polanski Story,* by Thomas Kiernan (Delilah/Grove, 1980).

★*ANONYMOUS 13-YEAR-OLD GIRL*   Polanski was arrested in Los Angeles on March 11, 1977, on charges of (1) furnishing Quaaludes to a minor; (2) child molesting; (3) unlawful sexual intercourse; (4) rape by use of drugs; (5) oral copulation; (6) sodomy Charges were brought on behalf of a 13-year-old girl. Both parties admitted that sexual relations had indeed taken place—after she had posed semi-nude for picture-taking for Polanski at Jack Nicholson's home. Polanski pleaded guilty to unlawful intercourse. The other charges were dropped, and Polanski spent six weeks in prison for "psychiatric observation." *Then* he learned he might face a much longer prison sentence—or deportation. On January 31, 1978, with only the clothes on his back, Polanski boarded a plane for England and France. He has not returned to the U.S. since; is still facing prosecution.

★*DENEUVE, CATHERINE*   Elegantly beautiful French actress. Gained her first international fame as a murderous psychopath in Polanski's *Repulsion,* made in London in 1964. Within days after the start of filming, Deneuve became a regular visitor to Polanski's flat in Knightsbridge. She remembers two sides to his character: "On the set he was a brutal tyrant, he would scream the most outrageous, obscene things . . . at night, the most endearing words came from his mouth."

★*ENGLISH BEDMATE NO. 1*   "I have no use for the way Roman deals with women on a personal level. He gives nothing and takes everything. . . . Once he's conquered a woman, which means gotten her to bed with him, it's all over."

★*ENGLISH BEDMATE NO. 2*   "The quintessential male chauvinist pig . . . he treats women like objects, like toys, like his latest pet car."

★*ENGLISH BEDMATE NO. 3*   "When I see him coming on to some young girl, I want to say to her she should give this guy a wide berth."

★*ENGLISH BEDMATE NO. 4*   Referring to Polanski and certain male friends in showbiz circles in London: "They've spent their lifetimes in sexual overindulgence, so they can no longer relate sexually to ordinary women. . . . With these fellows it has all become a matter of sexual engineering. They are obsessed with so-called tight or virgin vaginas. And where are you most likely to find these? Among little girls, of course."

★*EVA*   When Polanski, a ten-year-old Polish Jew, hid from the Nazis on a farm during World War II, he boasted to 13-year-old Eva that he could fashion a foreskin on his penis by using warm candle wax. (It was called the Polanski Prick by his circumcised Jewish chums, who used it effectively at least once to get through a "strip and search" by Nazi soldiers.) Roman took Eva to the barn one day to *show* her his invention. He lit a candle and as one thing led to another, he was soon being seduced by the girl. In a "frenzy of newly discovered sexual passion," neither one noticed they had knocked over the candle and set the barn on fire. In the hubbub that followed, Eva admitted to her family they were harboring a Jew, and Roman was turned out to fend for himself. One friend feels that because of this incident, Polanski was "sexually traumatized . . . and always associated sex with getting caught at something."

★*FARROW, MIA*   When Polanski went on trial for "unlawful intercourse" in L.A., Mia was one of the many who sent the judge a character reference. Polanski was supposed to be directing her next film, *Hurricane* (he didn't). According to author Kiernan, "she had had a brief secret romance with Polanski in London the year before and looked forward to renewing it in more tropical surroundings."

★*FRENCH BEDMATE*   One of the things she remembers clearly about Roman: "He felt inadequate because he was—well, it seemed to me, an ordinary size. But he was, in my opinion, ashamed to be looked at unless he was aroused."

★*HUGOT, MONIQUE* French actress, one of Polanski's "steadies" during his early days in Paris. "Sometimes he was like a serious, dull old man, oftentimes like a giggling child. . . . I do not think he really liked women. Oh, he liked bodies . . . but he did not like what was inside them."

★*KINSKI, NASTASSIA* German actress, daughter of actor Klaus Kinski, and an Ingrid Bergman look-alike. She was 15 when she first became involved with Polanski; he directed her in *Tess* two years later. When Natassia left Polanski in mid-1979, she landed in the arms of Czech director Milos Forman. Kinski has recently been working in Hollywood, with major roles in Francis Coppola's *One from the Heart* and a new version of *The Cat People*.

★*LASS, BARBARA* Fellow drama student at Lod Film school in Poland. When he graduated, the aspiring actress "rewarded Polanski by allowing him to go to bed with her." In love, he begged her to come with him to Warsaw, promising to find film roles for her. Shortly thereafter Polanski learned that being married would keep him out of the Polish military draft—so Roman and Barbara made it legal just before Christmas 1959. The marriage dissolved when he moved to France in the '60s.

★*SONYA* Polish acting student "with a wild look in her eye," who had stabbed two lovers before she met Polanski at Lodz. She was not overly attractive, and stuttered, but "had this awesome sexual agility. She knew more positions than the *Kama Sutra*." He was once again in love. Then it happened—she tried to stab him as he slept. Sonya was finally carted off to an institution. One friend from those days says that when he sees some of Polanski's films, "the ones with the crazy women, like *Repulsion* . . . I think of his experience with Sonya."

★*TATE, SHARON* Sharon was known in Hollywood as a one-man woman who often got mixed up with the wrong man. Her first serious affair was with an unemployed French actor who beat her up. She then moved in with hair stylist Jay Sebring, "notorious within the film community as a secret leather-and-chains sex freak and a prodigious drug user." In 1966, she met Polanski at a party in London and didn't like him much. When he directed her in *Fearless Vampire Killers*, she began to see that "this small and not terribly good-looking man was *totally* in charge of her." She liked it. Tate moved in with Polanski in 1967, they were married in early 1968; soon after, several observers say, "Roman . . . went off the deep end. He was down on Sunset Boulevard almost every night, haunting the strip clubs and picking up girls in his car. . . ." Sharon got pregnant; Polanski left her behind in Hollywood when he flew to London to plan his next film. She was talking over her Polanski problems with ex-lover Sebring on the night of August 9, 1969, when they and three others were murdered by the Manson gang. At the time, Polanski was reportedly in bed with an English stewardess.

POWER, TYRONE
(1913–1958)

Romantic leading man whose good looks all but obscured his considerable talent, displayed in such epics as *Suez, Lloyds of London, Jesse James*, etc. Son of a theatrical matinee idol whose name he bore, costume dramas were his forte, and time out for a wartime stint with the U.S. Marine Corps proved no setback to his popularity. Power had many well-documented affairs with women outside his three marriages, and apparently had a number of sexual relationships with men, much to everyone's surprise, though these were carefully kept from the public during his lifetime.

PRIMARY SOURCES: *The Secret Life of Tyrone Power,* by Hector Arce (Morrow, 1979; Bantam, 1980); *Tyrone Power: The Last Idol,* by Fred Lawrence Guiles (Doubleday, 1979; Berkley, 1980).

★*ABBOTT, EVIE* Onetime actress, first woman to whom Power proposed. They were touring with Guthrie McClintic and Katharine Cornell when they fell in love. She recalls that young Tyrone "would absolutely defy you not to like him." But Evie didn't *love* him enough to put up with being the wife of a movie star. "I saw too many women falling down over him. He was too attractive to too many people." Evie chose to marry her other suitor, actor Keenan Wynn. Years later, she divorced him to marry Van Johnson. At which time Power sent her a telegram saying: "I'm glad you didn't want to marry a movie star."

★*ANNABELLA* French actress, Power's first wife and co-star in *Suez*. A few years older than Ty, Annabella was the epitome of European sophistication. Darryl Zanuck, Ty's boss at 20th, didn't consider her a suitable date for the studio's newest glamour boy, thus Ty and Annabella were coy with reporters about their travel arrangements. ("You don't say? *She's* staying at the Hotel Pierre too?") The games were over when they married in April 1939, but the pressures had just begun for Ty. "He was very much under Annabella's thumb," observed one female co-star. By the end of 1941, the marriage was over. "The problem was that she'd become more matronly in his eyes, as younger and more exciting competitors came along." Among them was Judy Garland.

★*CHRISTIAN, LINDA* Described by Arce as "a Madame Du Barry born two hundred years too late. All her life she'd been trained in the arts of pleasing a man." Linda had already pleased Ty's good friend Errol Flynn (see below). Her first meaningful encounter with Ty was in Rome. A year or so later they would return there to marry, on January 27, 1949. Flynn reportedly said, *"He's marrying her?"* Back home in Hollywood, Ty and Linda joined what was termed a "morally liberated group," and their famous Mexican brunches often evolved into orgies. In time, both sought sex partners elsewhere. Linda found sympathy from Edmund Purdom, Ty played the field. During their marriage, which lasted until 1953, the couple had two daughters, Romina and Taryn. (*See also* CHRISTIAN listing.)

★*CULHANE, WELDON ("TY")* In 1953 he skipped his own high school graduation to see Tyrone Power in a touring company of *John Brown's Body*. Afterward, he found the star backstage. They had a pleasant chat, and Ty made a point of telling Culhane he'd be leaving from the railroad station at 10:00 the next day. Culhane showed up with a suitcase. "I thought you'd be here," said Ty, buying an extra ticket to Chicago for the young man. Nothing much happened the first few days, Culhane remembers, but on the third night, Ty simply walked into his room, lay down on Culhane's bed, and asked him to join him. "I felt warm and close and needed. He liked to cuddle." It was a lasting romance, resumed whenever Ty and Weldon were in the same vicinity. And when Culhane decided to go into acting, it was Ty who suggested he use his first name. "I wanted his name. I wanted *him*. It was exactly what I wanted him to say. It helped my fantasy world," says Ty Culhane.

★*DAY, DORIS* She's noted in passing in one Power bio, just an item that the dawning Day "spent a lot of time in Ty's dressing room." (*See* DAY listing.)

★*EKBERG, ANITA* Voluptuous Scandinavian actress who had a bit role in *Mississippi Gambler* and took up with Ty. Linda had a fit. Anita was taken off the picture—but her number wasn't taken out of Ty's little black book. And Anita would go on making Linda have fits.

★*FLYNN, ERROL* Arce reports mere "rumors" that Flynn and Power had a sexual affair, but a more recent biography of Flynn makes it quite explicit, even suggesting who was "the male" and who "the female" in their relationship, and who did—or would *not* do—what to whom. (*See also* FLYNN listing.)

★*GABOR, EVA* Bubbly Hungarian actress, younger sister to Zsa Zsa. She and Power enjoyed a fun-filled interlude.

★*GARLAND, JUDY* She was an impressionable 19, just divorced from David Rose, and mad for Ty, then a wartime marine entering Officers Candidate School. MGM tried to keep the affair secret, to protect Judy's wholesome image, and tried to convince her that she had fallen in love with "the cover of *Photoplay*." But both Judy and Ty were incurable romantics, and "totally in love." The Arce book makes no more of their affair than that, though biographer Guiles reports that Judy became pregnant by Ty, "which led him to seek (but not obtain) a divorce from Annabella." After a quickie Mexican abortion, he writes, the affair ended bitterly. "She had been able to satisfy Tyrone as few women had. . . . She would never love anyone again as deeply as she loved Tyrone." (See also GARLAND listing.)

★*GIRL IN* CONFIDENTIAL   A discarded mistress who told *Confidential* magazine that she had sexually "worn out" Ty. He retorted, "Why should I kill myself to satisfy a nymphomaniac?"

★*GIRL ON DOORSTEP*   During a location filming, she camped out on Power's doorstep every night. "Go on home," he'd tell her. "I just don't have the time." One night the camp follower insisted she *had* to see him, she'd been *saving herself* for him. "The girl wound up being one of Ty's more enduring affairs."

★*GRABLE, BETTY*   The gossips said they had a brief fling while working together at Fox.

★*HANSEN, SMITTY*   One-time male prostitute and procurer in Hollywood. He was 18 and training to become a paratrooper; Ty was in marine flight training. "He was a sweetheart, a gentleman. We were friendly and saw each other until he died . . . He was always a trick," said Hansen. He resents the statement in Kenneth Anger's *Hollywood Babylon* that Power was into coprolagnia. "Ty was never way out in what he wanted to do. If there's such a thing as normal gay sex, that's what he was interested in."

★*HART, LORENZ*   Hart was noted for "catering to amenable young men." Evidently young Tyrone was among the group frequenting Hart's place, although there's no hard evidence that the famed lyricist was anything more than "kind to him."

★*HENIE, SONJA*   Pert Norwegian-born ice-skating star, and Ty's leading lady in *Thin Ice*, etc. It was a happy, light-as-cotton-candy affair—for Ty, anyway. At the height of it, they bought matching Cord convertibles—hers white, his black. No one knows for sure what went wrong between Sonja and Ty, but she took it hard.

★*JURADO, KATY*   Mexican actress. She interrupted Power's affair with Mai Zetterling. Just for a bit.

★*LAUGHTON, CHARLES*   His widow Elsa Lanchester, having always accepted her husband's homosexual interests, says, "He didn't gossip about his affairs, and I wasn't faintly interested. . . . I know Charles adored Tyrone Power as a beauty." Although she suspected Power was bisexual, Lanchester adds, "Charles protected him on that score, completely." Regarding all this, Elsa says only one thing bothered her—when Charles gave a painting that was a special favorite of hers to Ty. "He knew I liked that painting better than anything in the house. Looking back, perhaps there was a reason Charles gave it to him."

★*MINARDOS, DEBORAH*   Young actress who bore a strong resemblance to Linda Christian—and to Ty himself. She became his third and last wife. His friends couldn't explain what he saw in her—after all the sophisticated women he'd known. Debbie prattled on in her Mississippi accent about how much she *adored* Elvis Presley, and "Ty would noticeably cringe at her gaucheries." But one friend muses, "Debbie must have done something that pleased him." They were wed in May 1958, and he died of a massive heart attack in Spain in November of that year. She later bore Ty's son, Tyrone IV. And later still, Debbie married millionaire Hollywood playboy Arthur Loew, Jr. (See also LOEW listing.) She *must* have been doing something right.

★*THOMAS, ROBIN*   An actor, handsome stepson of John Barrymore, son of writer Michael Strange. Flamboyant, free-thinking Strange thought it smashing that her son and Ty lived together; "She understood and fostered the relationship." Robin's half sister Diana Barrymore wrote that Robin and Ty were the two most beautiful people together that she had ever seen. "They showed their affection openly." When she walked into a room she'd find them embracing, with no secret or apology. This was during Power's heady days on Broadway in the mid-1930s. Robin didn't follow Ty to Hollywood, and he never got his life together after his lover left. According to Diana, he literally destroyed himself with booze and pills, dying in his sleep at age 29.

★ *TURNER, LANA* Hedda Hopper told the story that Lana was alone in a booth at Romanoff's when Ty appeared. She smiled and patted the empty seat beside hers. "Ty sat next to Lana—and combustion set in." Lana was the pursuer in this very serious affair, and she fully expected to be the second Mrs. Tyrone Power (after Annabella). They certainly were a perfect physical match: "People gasped at their beauty whenever they walked into a restaurant. . . . Lana, to most men, was the embodiment of profane love; Ty, to many women, represented its sacred incarnation. . . . They were tremendously drawn to each other, and they called it love." She botched it, though, by having a publicized fling with Frank Sinatra while Power was away (in Rome, as a matter of fact, getting it on with Linda Christian). Until then, Ty had refused to believe the stories about Lana's promiscuous ways. He told Hedda Hopper once: "You don't know the real Lana, I'll bring her to your house and show you." The visit never took place. Lana was later to tell Hedda, or one of those ladies, "No man in my life except Tyrone Power took the time to find out I was a human being."

★ *WEBB, J. WATSON JR.* New York scion, related to the Vanderbilts, striking out on his own in Hollywood when he met Ty. This tall, patrician looking young man (two years younger than Ty) became his close friend and confidant. "Annabella welcomed Watson as both an ally and as the necessary male companion Tyrone needed to keep the drives within him in balance." At Ty's death, Watson arranged for a "memorial bench," inscribed

with the familiar "Good night, sweet prince" quotation from *Hamlet*.

★ *YOUNG ACTOR* He was being groomed as a possible replacement for Ty at 20th, and became an almost daily visitor to Power's dressing room on the set. "As much as he had tried, Ty realized that he could not give up having sex with other men, noble as his ambitions had been when he married Annabella." The lesser Power never made it big. In the movies.

★ *YOUNG, LORETTA* Their brief affair was another of those that made studio bosses nervous. Wrong casting.

★ *ZETTERLING, MAI* Swedish actress. "Ty found her as sensual as Linda and as strong as Annabella." She was also smart and sophisticated, and for the first time since his divorce from Linda, he was deeply involved. "His affair with Mai Zetterling might have approached talk of marriage if it hadn't been for the complete turnabout in their relationship. She was the dominant one, and he was the one treated as the pretty plaything—and not a particularly bright one at that."

MISCELLANY

★ *COWARD, NOEL* A "durable friendship" developed between the two. Except for frequent opportunities and their well-known proclivities, there's no evidence Noel and Ty were lovers.

★ *DIETRICH, MARLENE* She was infatuated, as usual, with her leading man (in *Witness for the Prosecution*), and heaped gifts upon him. "If he said he liked a particular wine, she'd send a case of it the next day." Director Billy Wilder recalled that *everyone* developed a crush on Ty. He did too. "As heterosexual as you might be, it was impossible to be totally impervious to that kind of charm."

★ *EVANS, MAURICE* Someone who knew them both way back when wrote to author Arce to state emphatically that "Ty was *never* the lover of Maurice Evans." No one had said he was.

★ *MCCLINTIC, GUTHRIE* Director-producer and husband of actress Katharine Cornell. The McClintic union was "a marriage of convenience, for each had lovers of the same sex." And, evidently, on their road-show tours they liked a company of players around them who would, well . . . be suitable backstage companions. There's no proof that Power was one of the young actors McClintic took as a lover. At any rate, "McClintic's affairs seem to have been of fairly short duration, ending without rancor or unpleasantness."

PRESLEY, ELVIS
(1935–1977)

His swiveling pelvis as much as his singing set the music industry on its ear and created a pop phenomenon like nothing after Frank Sinatra, or before the Beatles. Strangely, Elvis's movies—a couple dozen in all—were little more than profitable but routine promotional epics to help sell the records his youthful fans would have snapped up anyway. In most of them, from *Love Me Tender* in 1956 until 1970, when he stopped making films, he was presented as a simple, down-home fella being square to the point of somnolence. The real Elvis, we have learned since, was an overweight egomaniacal redneck addicted to guns, nubile girls, and incredible quantities of drugs and liquor. And his fabulously successful career might have been ruined, not made—as legend would have it—by his flamboyant agent-manager Colonel Tom Parker. If his biographers are to be believed, and so far the evidence looks depressingly persuasive, Elvis's own films are bound to be outnumbered one day by movie bios in the tacky tradition we may have to call *Presley Dearest*.

PRIMARY SOURCE: *Elvis*, by Albert Goldman (McGraw-Hill, 1981).

★*ALDEN, GINGER* She was a Memphis girl, whose mother brought her to the Gates of Graceland as a toddler. When she was 5 he patted her head and took her on a roller coaster ride. At 20 she moved in with him. When asked how it had been to meet Elvis for the first time, Ginger exclaimed, "Well, you expected trumpets or something." Ginger proved to be one of the few women in Elvis's life who did not bend to his every whim. It drove him crazy, yet Presley decided to marry her, and popped the question on January 27, 1977, giving her a $70,000 diamond ring—in his bathroom. He had her sit in the leather reading chair next to the toilet, then sank to his knees. "His speech was more touching than any he had ever delivered in his many movies." She said yes. ("Maybe that's why I was put on earth. . . . If I could make Elvis happy, I would have served my purpose.") Their wedding never took place. On the afternoon of August 15, 1977, Ginger awoke alone in bed, then opened the bathroom door to find Elvis doubled over on the floor. "His face had become a grotesque mask, purple with engorged blood, his teeth set in his lolling tongue." He had died at 42, of polypharmacy, "the lethal interaction of a number of drugs taken concurrently."

★*ANN-MARGRET* Today a superstar, in 1964 an up-and-coming musical performer and co-star with Elvis in *Viva Las Vegas*. It was the only "authentic romance" in Elvis's long career of dating Hollywood starlets. Presley was so infatuated with Ann-Margret he broke his strict rule that women had to come to him, and would spend up to a day or two at a time at her place. To make it more comfy, he gave her a huge, round, pink bed. Then the affair abruptly ended. Ann-Margret said she hadn't the faintest idea why.

★*BEAULIEU, PRISCILLA* Presley was in the army in Germany in August 1959 when he first met Priscilla Ann Beaulieu, his 14-year-old "teen angel," stepdaughter of an army captain. He liked her immediately because she was poised, beautiful, not tongue-tied in his presence. Spending every free moment with Priscilla, he dispatched a driver to pick her up every day after school. Were the Beaulieus concerned to see their teenaged daughter whisked away in an expensive Mercedes to spend the evening with a notorious sex symbol? Well, when Priscilla was sixteen, they let her go live with Presley (nominally under the care of his father, Vernon). Four years later, Priscilla's father called Elvis to say it was time he did the right thing by the girl. Elvis reluctantly set a date, and Presley's manager, Colonel Tom Parker, took charge of the wedding plans—a garish Las Vegas affair held on April 29, 1967. Almost nine months to the day, on February 1, 1968, Priscilla gave birth to Elvis's only child, Lisa Marie. Neither his marriage nor his child curbed Presley's orgiastic lifestyle, and within four months of becoming a mother, Priscilla herself began a new romance with a Hawaiian karate instructor—for whom she eventually broke up her marriage. That was 1972; she told Presley the truth, that she was leaving him for Mike Stone. Until the end of his life Presley was fixated on Stone, threatening his life, once going so far as to suggest that one of his henchmen get out a "contract" on him. According to biographer Goldman: "All of Elvis's intimates agree that the fatal decline that ended in his death began during the period of conflict with Priscilla over her affair with Mike Stone."

★*BLACKMER, JOAN* Actress, 18 when she met Elvis while working on the Paramount lot in 1957. He came cruising by in the hot rod he drove in *Loving You*, took one look at Joan and said, "Hey, you—c'mere!" After getting to know him, she concluded Elvis was scared of women; he seemed quite content to leave her as he found her—a virgin. They were in a couple of films together, no real romance. Years later, Joan ran into Elvis backstage in Las Vegas. "He looked at her, obviously stoned, and said, 'You had your chance.' That became a standard line with Elvis."

★*BUERGIN, MARGRIT* Sixteen-year-old German girl, a typist, who dated Elvis steadily until he discovered Priscilla. For Christmas he gave Margrit, his "Little Puppy," a gold watch studded with diamonds. She also got a lot of abuse from the press and Presley's jealous fans. "American women hysterically called Margrit a 'whore' and a 'tramp.' The Germans used a more complicated expression that translates 'plaything of the occupying American prick.'"

★*GIRL WHO ALMOST DIED* Pretty teenager who spent the weekend with Presley in Palm Springs. One night they went to bed and drank quantities of "Hycodan, a blood-red, cherry-flavored cough syrup with a narcotic base." Next morning she was found unconscious, turning blue and breathing heavily in what sounded like a death rattle. An ambulance rushed her to the hospital, where she came out of the coma and spent a long recuperative period. The girl's mother, a fan of Elvis's, refused to take a penny from him for her daughter's extensive medical treatment. One of Presley's "guys" saw the girl again about a year later, and said she did not look or act the same as before. Doctors had warned that there could be brain damage.

★*"KIT"* A dancer with a "body that would make you clutch for digitalis." Yet at 24 she was still a virgin, though she did have a steady boyfriend whom her friends nicknamed King Kong. Presley was smitten—"as always it was love at first sight"—and began showering her with expensive presents. King Kong was so incensed he held a press conference about Presley's stealing his girl. Elvis left beauty to the beast.

★*LEIGH, BARBARA* Beautiful brunette actress who was then deeply involved with MGM president James Aubrey. Although it violated his "code of macho ethics" to attempt to seduce another man's woman under that man's very nose, Elvis got away with it this time. Barbara became one of Elvis's favorites during the next year, traveling with him on tour, staying with him at his homes in Memphis and L.A. As usual, he gave her a Mercedes. Eventually the affair faded because Barbara believed Elvis would never leave Priscilla.

★*LOCK, DIXIE* The first girl with whom Elvis had a serious affair. It was 1954, he was 19, she 15. They met at the Rainbow Rollerdome in Memphis with Elvis wearing a pink suit with a black stripe down the trouser seam—a car hop's outfit. Nevertheless, they started going steady, he even took her home to meet the folks. Then came fame and out went Dixie.

★*PAGET, DEBRA*   Presley's co-star in *Love Me Tender*; her cold-shoulder treatment made his pursuit more intense. Most of their dates were at Debra's home, supervised by her strict mom. Debra today admits that Elvis asked her to marry him, but her family didn't like the idea. She remembers him as a "sweet, simple person," who would ride off into the night on his motorcycle.

★*PRETZEL, THE*   Contortionist who worked at a nightclub in Germany. Elvis was fascinated enough to ask the lady out. "The Pelvis never divulged what sort of relationship he enjoyed with the Pretzel."

★*SINATRA, NANCY*   Co-star in *Speedway*, and always an adoring Presley fan. They engaged in lots of physical pranks and rough-housing on the set, and came very close to having an affair. On their parting at the end of filming, he gave her a *real* kiss, and she kissed him back. He told her it was goodbye. "He gave me a big, brotherly hug and off I went. That was the last romantic moment. I treasure it dearly."

★*STEFANIAK, ELISABETH*   Another German girl. They met at the movies. To keep her close at hand, he had Elisabeth come to work for him—answering fan mail and such, for which she was paid a grand $35 a week. Elisabeth was riding with Elvis's father Vernon one day when his car skidded off the road. In shock, injured, Elisabeth was taken to the hospital, where Elvis later came to visit. "His face bore that ugly, distrustful expression so characteristic of him," and without asking the girl how she felt, Presley hissed at her: "What were you and my daddy doin' that caused that wreck?" He lost Elisabeth on that one.

★*THOMPSON, LINDA*   In early July 1972, as he entered into divorce negotiations with Priscilla, Elvis met Linda, "with whom for over four years he was to enjoy one of the most fulfilling relationships of his life." Linda was

another Memphis girl. Miss Tennessee of 1972 and still a virgin, "the only real evidence Elvis could have of a woman's essential goodness." He sooned learned that Linda was also amusing, attentive, intelligent, and faithful, and for about a year he didn't see any other women. Even later, Linda would go out with Elvis and a new girl and give him her personal appraisal. Linda saved Presley's life on several occasions; in particular the time he nodded off during a meal from a drug overdose, and fell over, submerging his face in the dish. "If she hadn't pulled his head back, he would have earned the doubtful distinction of being the first man in history to drown in a soup bowl." Eventually, Linda began to see the hopelessness of her situation. Meanwhile, Elvis bought her a house; he had already given her over a quarter of a million dollars in jewelry and an extensive wardrobe. The termination of the relationship in 1976 was not entirely amicable, with Linda hitting up Elvis for a $50,000 shopping spree and European vacation with a girlfriend. Linda is now the wife of decathlon champion and would-be actor Bruce Jenner.

★*WALLEY, DEBRA*   Co-star in *Spinout*, in 1966. Presley was on his spiritualist trip when he gave Debra the romantic whirl; he not only wanted her body. "Elvis had decided to blow Miss Walley's mind as only a great Master can affect a hungry and adoring disciple." Through Elvis's guidance, Debra became "a cosmic flower child," dropping acid and a variety of other drugs. By the time of the Monterey Pop Festival, Debra became "the perfect freak . . . sitting in the front row gonged to the gills, her hair out like Struwwelpeter, bells around her neck and the world's biggest grin." After a nervous breakdown, and subsequent hospitalization, Debra resumed her life, is now a writer.

★*WOOD, ANITA*   Singer and actress, Elvis's steady girl from 1957 to 1962, when Priscilla showed up. She was 19 and hostess of a teen-age dance show on local TV in Memphis. She was not an Elvis Presley fan, but even less so after their first date—which consisted of cruising by the movie theater showing his latest movie. But then—she fell in love with him. Elvis helped her get a Hollywood screen test, then urged her to return to Memphis. "Come home, Little," Elvis urged, "Just come home right now." Their affair was still unconsummated when, in 1961, Anita announced she was going to leave him. Elvis let her go, remarking that he could do better. That's when he called for—and got—16-year-old Priscilla.

★*WOOD, NATALIE* Elvis was on the rebound from sultry Debra Paget when he met Natalie, "a pixieish teenager in pedal pushers and babushka." Elvis was Mr. Wrong, and she was fascinated. Natalie accepted an invitation for a week's visit in Memphis "chaperoned" by Nick Adams. Every day was the same routine, Elvis signing autographs, eating ice cream, cruising the streets, and signing more autographs. When she asked Elvis why he put up with such an invasion of privacy from his fans, he said that he owed his success to his fans . . . it was his duty. Natalie found him strange, and went home to L.A.

MISCELLANY

★*GLORIA, HEIDI, and FRANCES* The Three Musketeers. These three teenagers spent a lot of nights with Presley at Graceland, having pillow fights and eating ice cream, etc. "There was a lot of playing around, but there was no boogeyin'"—as Anita Wood would put it.

★*THE ORGY CROWD* These events were usually at Presley's house in Los Angeles or in Las Vegas. The participants were Elvis, his "Guys," and various show girls or groupies. Elvis always had "the pick of the litter," often choosing three to five women to take into his bedroom, where he would encourage them to make love to each other while he watched and sometimes masturbated; sometimes he simply passed out, seldom joined in the action. One night he stepped out of the French doors of his bedroom and exhibited himself totally naked—it was unheard of that anyone saw Elvis naked—to the gang around the pool. Not only naked, "he had hooked one end of Colonel Parker's walking cane over his erect

penis." Biographer Goldman writes: "What an image! But what does it mean? Does it shout, 'Fuck you, Colonel Lardass!' Or is it an unconscious confession that Elvis has lived his whole adult life with the Colonel's hook deep in Elvis's dick?" Now there's a thought for the day.

RUBIROSA, PORFIRIO
(1909–1965)

Dominican diplomat with a penchant for pretty, rich, or famous women, proud of his presumably inexhaustible skill as a Latin lover. Rubi was a jet-setter before there were jets, hanging around the polo grounds at Deauville or poolside almost anywhere that privileged people go. Dark, handsome, flamboyant, he would have been perfect casting as the smooth continental fortune hunter in a Lubitsch comedy, except that Rubi's real life was a shade too extravagant for mere fiction.

PRIMARY SOURCES: *Million Dollar Baby: An Intimate Portrait of Barbara Hutton*, by Philip Van Rensselaer (Putnam's, 1949); *Zsa Zsa Gabor: My Story*, "written for me by Gerold Frank" (World, 1960).

★*DARRIEUX, DANIELLE* French actress and one of the brighter feathers in Rubi's cap, she had been Rubi's wife just ahead of Doris—and at the peak of her fame was considered by many to be the most beautiful woman in the world.

★*DUKE, DORIS* The next richest girl in the world after Barbara Hutton. Anyway, it didn't matter, there was plenty of money to go around, but not many men like Rubi. Doris married Rubi before Babs did and "spoke glowingly of him." How come? Stewart Granger's memoirs recall the time he and Mike Wilding asked Rubi about the secret of his success in bed. "Simple," he said. "A lot of whiskey. It becomes numb. It functions. . . . I feel nothing, but the ladies do."

★*GABOR, ZSA ZSA* Their affair was so on

and off and on again for so long a time that the paparazzi could barely keep up. It began in New York in 1952, when Zsa Zsa, sans hubby George Sanders, was celebrating the premiere of her film *Moulin Rouge.* "I was drunk that moment, drunk with power, drunk with achievement . . . so overemotional, so overmiserable . . . and here was Rubirosa, the most pursued of men, the only man whose name could make George grow pale . . . I said yes." Zsa Zsa goes on at length trying to put a handle on Rubi's appeal: "He has the instinct of a wild animal to sense your every mood. . . . He is completely, blindly, recklessly possessive. . . . When he wants you, and he wants you all the time, it's with a singlemindedness that gives you no time to think." Zsa Zsa stood by while Rubi briefly married Barbara Hutton (and came away with a settlement perhaps in the millions), but returned to her for a few more years of the madcap life before both grew disenchanted. (See also GABOR listing.)

★*HUTTON, BARBARA* Rubi was her fifth husband; the wedding took place on December 30, 1953, with Babs wearing a black Balenciaga gown. Friends thought she looked as if she were going to a funeral. The wedding night was upsetting for the bride, who found the sight of her naked husband "appalling." She didn't have to put up with it for long; after a total of seventy-three days of marriage, the couple separated, and Rubi went back to Zsa Zsa. (See also HUTTON listing.)

★*MINOUCHE* Pet name for famous French actress known to be on close terms with Rubi, Errol, Aly Khan, and all the other lads on the circuit.

★*RODIN, ODILE* French actress and only 19 when she married Rubi in 1957. She was apparently a steadying influence on him, for they were still happily wed up until the night he ran his car into a tree—and died, in an accident strangely similar to the one that had killed his pal Aly Khan just five years earlier.

★*TRUJILLO, FLOR de ORO* Daughter of Rafael Trujillo, the Dominican dictator. She was 17 when they wed, his first wife. Through the Trujillo connection, Rubi was launched into his diplomatic career, presumably causing scores of diplomats, right and left, to lock up their daughters.

ST. JOHN, JILL
(b. 1940)

The former Jill Oppenheim demonstrated some charm and insouciance as the babe with Frank Sinatra (in *Come Blow Your Horn*), Dean Martin (*Who's Been Sleeping in My Bed?*, 1963), or Sean Connery (*Diamonds Are Forever*, 1971). Even the titles say a lot. She was thought to have a high IQ. It just seemed that Jill collected more press clippings for dating the right people than for emoting. One Kissinger biography, cited here, devotes an entire chapter to her. She's clearly smart, a liberal, but not the kind of girl to let politics interfere with her plans for Saturday night.

PRIMARY SOURCE: *Kissinger: The Adventures of Super-Kraut,* by Charles R. Ashman (Lyle Stuart, 1972). A chapter is devoted to Ms. St. John.

★*BARNES, BENJAMIN* Onetime lieutenant governor of Texas. His conservative supporters were against his being seen with the flaming redhead in his own state. "He didn't listen."

★*BULGARI, GIANNI* Internationally known Italian jeweler. One of the jet set.

★*CONNERY, SEAN* A chess partner. But evidently not as much fun with his kings, queens, and pawns as Henry Kissinger. (See KISSINGER listing.)

★*DUBIN, NEIL* Laundry heir, Jill's first husband. It lasted one month, but just didn't wash.

★*JONES, JACK* Singer, her third husband. The worst part of their marriage was that they were *Jack and Jill Jones.* And they came tumbling down. To a divorce, that is.

★*KISSINGER, HENRY* She was a leader of the anti-Nixon forces in California when she met Dr. Kissinger. Nixon's number-two man. In no time at all. she found him "brilliant. thoughtful. kind. generous and lovely." Jill kept a lid on her political views during the time she became one of Kissinger's most frequent and most visible dates. (See also KISSINGER listing.)

★*PHIPPS. OGDEN.* Millionaire socialite and horse owner. A sometime date.

★*REVENTLOW. LANCE* The late race driver and playboy son of Barbara Hutton. heir to the Woolworth fortune. Jill's second husband. When she received a $100.000 property settlement in dissolving the Reventlow marriage. Jill said. "I don't believe in alimony if you work. . . . But a property settlement is okay."

★*SINATRA. FRANK* Jill was frequently seen with Ole Blue Eyes in Las Vegas and some other of the best places. until the time she met Henry Kissinger. They were close. (See also SINATRA listing.)

★*WOLPER. DAVID* Studio production chief in Hollywood. and another one of Ms. St. John's impressive escorts.

MISCELLANY

Quite a few who'd qualify for getting around with energetic Jill. but left no trace. They'll have to wait for *her* book.

SEBERG, JEAN
(1938–1979)

An American tragedy of the sort they used to dream up in Hollywood. A stunning would-be actress from Marshalltown, Iowa, 17-year-old Jean was chosen by producer-director Otto Preminger from a field of 18,000 eager applicants to star in his 1957 epic *Saint Joan.* The picture turned out to be a fiasco, and Jean's fairy-tale adventure in filmdom turned out even worse. Living mostly abroad, she appeared in *Bonjour Tristesse* and had her greatest success in Jean-Luc Godard's *Breathless.* co-starring with Jean-Paul Belmondo in what became a landmark movie of the French New Wave. The rest of her life seemed to be a moral tug-of-war between continental sophistication and the ingrained ethics of smalltown U.S.A. Bad marriages. bad movies. and thwarted ambition led to her involvement with black-militant political causes. and ill-advised relationships which prompted the FBI to initiate an insidious campaign of slander against her. Hounded and finally unhinged at the end. Jean committed suicide at 41.

PRIMARY SOURCE: *Played Out: The Jean Seberg Story.* by David Richards (Random House. 1981).

★*BERRY. DENNIS* Seberg's third and last husband. an American raised in France. Young Berry (then 27 to Jean's 34) was a struggling director when they met. Three weeks later, in March 1972, they made a round-trip flight from Paris to Las Vegas to be married, because all his life, he said. "I've had this mad desire to marry a movie star in Las Vegas." The entire cost of this trip, including wedding rings, went on Jean's credit cards. Though he directed Jean in one disastrous film, *Le Grand Délire,* Berry's career never really got off the ground. She wanted her independence. They split in 1976. But he continued to come to her aid when needed. And in her last years, Jean often *needed.*

★*DESMOND. PAUL* Saxophonist with Dave Brubeck Quartet. They met while Seberg was on a whirlwind tour to promote her first film, Preminger's forgettable *Saint Joan.* "He's much too old, much too complex and much too wonderful for me," she gushed. Convinced it was true love, she sent Desmond flowers and notes, called him from around the world. A sax fiend, Paul seemed indifferent to everything but his music.

★*EASTWOOD. CLINT* It was, said director Josh Logan, one of those things that can only happen on a location. The film was *Paint Your Wagon.* and the co-stars. Logan says. "how shall I put it—*enjoyed* each other." The romance was hampered by Eastwood's marriage and hers (to Gary) and ended when the filming did. Jean had regrets; if there was ever a fella she'd have been proud to take back to Marshalltown, she said, it was Clint Eastwood. "He's the sort of man who does his own dishes."

★*FRANCO, RICARDO* Aspiring Spanish film director who became Jean's constant companion for about a year, in 1971, with the approval of hubby Romain Gary, who treated Franco "like a son." The Spaniard was ten years younger than Jean, "a cross between Che Guevara and Toulouse-Lautrec." Her friends called them "Beauty and the Beast." Franco came into Seberg's life again in 1976; when he was happily married, she was exhibiting terrifying self-destructive tendencies. In Madrid, unable to see him, she began breaking her hotel windows and screaming anti-fascist slogans; some reports had it that she ran nude through the lobby. Dennis Berry got her back to Paris, and a sanitarium.

★*GARY, ROMAIN* French novelist-screenwriter-diplomat who was France's consul general in Los Angeles when Seberg, then Mme. Moreuil, came into his life. He was drawn to her "radiant naïveté," she to his "Clark Gable mustache and thick black hair." Gary's British wife, writer Lesley Blanch, refused to give him a divorce until after he and Seberg were openly living together and Jean had given birth to their son, Diego. When they married in October 1963, Romain was 49, Jean 25, Diego 1. Jean told friends that sex went out of their relationship almost immediately; he became solely her teacher, mentor, father figure, and friend. Jean and Romain would divorce in the early '70s but he was still her husband a few years earlier when she got involved in the scandalous affairs with Jamal and Hewitt (below). She once said that Gary had "created this Frankenstein. He pushed me to develop my own tastes." After Seberg's suicide, he also pushed for the public disclosure of Jean's harassment by the FBI regarding Hewitt, et al., which, he said, "destroyed" his former wife. In his own suicide note in December 1980, Gary

wrote: "No connection with Jean Seberg."

★*HAMADI, KADER* Swarthy Algerian, owner of Moroccan restaurant in Paris. He had a sporadic affair with Jean in early 1979. The uncle of Ahmed Hasni (see below), about whom he angrily said, "In my family, the men do not sleep with the same woman."

★*HASNI, AHMED* Unemployed actor and soccer player who met Jean in 1979 and moved in with her. He claimed to be 29, but was possibly ten years younger; more than Jean's lover, he was her "round-the-clock keeper and disciplinarian." They went through a mock wedding (not valid because Jean was still married to Dennis Berry) and Jean started to talk about having another child, moving with Ahmed to Algeria. When Ahmed started physically abusing her, she tried to leave him several times. He was still in her bed on the August night in 1979 when Jean got up, wrapped herself in a blanket, took a handful of barbiturates, and drove herself around the corner to die.

★*HEWITT, RAYMOND "MASAI"* Head of the Black Panthers chapter in Los Angeles, when Jean met him through Hakim Jamal. Jean contributed a great deal of money, time, and moral support to the Panther cause in 1969, and admitted having sexual relations with Hewitt—but he was *not* the father of the child she lost in a premature birth in 1970 (see Navarra below) as was suggested in press reports at the time, subsequently proved to have been planted by the FBI.

★*JAMAL, HAKIM ABDULLAH* A Black Nationalist, born Allen Eugene Donaldson, founder of the Malcolm X Foundation, who promoted his causes through association with a number of celebrities, including Jean, with whom he became "entangled, psychologically and sexually." Faded from favor after Seberg met Hewitt.

★*MOHAMMED* A Moroccan medical student in Paris. A brief involvement.

★*MOREUIL, FRANÇOIS* Young lawyer "whose considerable charm, some felt, masked his considerable ambition." Jean's first husband, he met her on the Riviera while she was starring in Otto Preminger's *Bonjour Tristesse*. Part of the St. Tropez set, he represented both glamour and freedom to young Jean. François followed Jean back to the states and personally took charge of their elaborate wedding on September 5, 1958, in Marshalltown, "the most celebrated social event in the city's history." The union was shaky from the beginning, cracked under the strain of Jean's success in Godard's *Breathless*, and fell apart altogether when she met Romain Gary.

★*NAVARRA, CARLOS* A young Mexican "revolutionary" with whom Jean fell in love during the making of a "bad movie" called *Macho Callahan* in Mexico. She became pregnant by him, decided to have the child; gallant Gary said he would "assume fatherhood." She gave birth two months early, and the baby died, an event that seemed to precipitate her eventual break with reality.

★*TESTI, FRANCO* A macho Italian actor who became enamored of Jean and was prone to jealous fits.

MISCELLANY

★*BEATTY, WARREN* They were co-stars in *Lilith*, and, as expected, "he preyed on Jean with all his powers as a seducer," said an observer. Surprisingly, Seberg was immune. She grew to despise Beatty, and wrote to a friend: " . . . Warren Beatty's behavior is just unbelievable. He's out to destroy everyone—including himself."

★*GARREL, PHILIPPE* Unconventional young filmmaker. Jean was drawn to his "creative madness," and became the subject of his film *Les Haute Solitudes* ("The Outer Reaches of Solitude"), much of which was improvised on Paris streets and in the apartment Jean shared with Berry. The camera caught Jean's "uncanny" resemblance to Marilyn Monroe, and it also reveals that she was "flirting dangerously with insanity." The film played only briefly in Paris, to a small band of cultists.

★*HOPPER, DENNIS* They were "close" when both took acting lessons in Hollywood from Paton Price.

★*PREMINGER, OTTO* The dictatorial di-

rector discovered Jean in 1956, and plucked the 18-year-old from obscurity to star in his ill-fated film *Saint Joan*. He would lavish her with gifts one minute, browbeat her the next; "Jean would be *made* to play Joan of Arc." On their next film, *Bonjour Tristesse*, Jean recalled that he almost drove her to suicide, and it took her years to "overcome the DTs about him." He was a father figure, not a romantic one, despite suspicious speculation at the time. And, although she was said to have admired Otto, "at the same time she hated his guts."

SELLERS, PETER
(1925–1980)

English screen comedian who began his career with Spike Mulligan's popular *Goon Show*, reached his peak of popularity as Inspector Clouseau in the *Pink Panther* comedies, but made one of his finest films, *Being There*, the year before he died. The heart attack that killed him came after a lifetime of frayed nerves, insecurity, and amorous exploits ad infinitum. From a theatrical family (his mother was a singer), he craved love, approbation, a live audience, and applause. Said one friend, "For Peter, making a film is like making love and not reaching a climax." In his youth, as a lover, another chum recalls that Sellers had the first automatic record player: "The trick was to make your date before the last record ended. . . . if you hadn't got anywhere by then, you'd had it. The records would play a total of 24 minutes. . . ." Offscreen, Sellers appeared to devote a lot of time to breaking records.

PRIMARY SOURCES: *Peter Sellers: The Mask Behind the Mask* by Peter Evans (New English Library, 1980; Signet, 1980); *P.S. I Love You* by Michael Sellers (with Sarah and Victoria Sellers; Collins, London, 1981).

★*EKLAND, BRITT* Six months after clairvoyant Maurice Woodruff told Sellers he would meet and marry a woman with the initials B.E., he did. On their first date (in February 1962), he asked for details of her sex life, treated her to champagne and her first whiff of Acapulco Gold. Then they made love. Or so *he* said. They were married eleven days later, and four months after that Sellers had a series of massive heart attacks (Britt says they might have been triggered by his use of amyl nitrate "poppers" to heighten orgasm), and Peter's bride was plunged into responsibilities that, at 21, "she was hardly prepared for." She wasn't prepared for Sellers's jealous furies either. They had a daughter, Victoria; their fights became more frequent and more public. The marriage, his second, ended in 1968. (See also EKLAND listing.)

★*FARROW, MIA* After Britt he found consolation, but only briefly, with Mia, who had divorced Sinatra. (See also FARROW listing.)

★*FREDERICK, LYNN* She was 21, his fourth and last wife. They spoke their vows in Paris in February 1976. Lynn felt Peter needed a woman who would dedicate herself to him entirely: "I like mothering people a bit. I love cooking and spending evenings at home. I'm content to put Peter's career first." Yet Lynn advanced her own career by becoming Sellers's leading lady in *Prisoner of Zenda*. She found she enjoyed being in front of the cameras; meanwhile, Sellers was growing morose. "The marriage ticked away, like a time bomb." After another heart attack, before he took the role of Chance in *Being There*, Sellers announced that the union was over. Lynn denied it; they seemed to reconcile—but she was in California when Sellers died in July 1980. Lynn inherited Sellers's considerable fortune, as he left only token amounts to his three children—who are still involved in contesting their father's will. Michael Sellers doesn't have too many kind words for his former step-ma, but says he was against his Dad's last marriage from the beginning. Widow Lynn married TV mogul David Frost—an old beau.

★*HAYES, ANN* Australian actress who, at 19, met Peter in London at the Royal Academy and "it was love at first sight—for both of them." They married in September 1951, and

soon after Peter's "prime objective" was to persuade his bride to give up her acting career. "Once Dad arrived at the stage door to inform her that he had swallowed a hundred aspirins because she refused to give up work." (He hadn't.) Still, for eleven years, Ann was to exert "a calm yet formidable influence over her husband." Until he developed his grand passion for Sophia Loren (see below) and Ann began to fall in love with a South African architect named Elias Levy. She married Levy after Sellers sued *her* for divorce, charging adultery.

★*HILTON, FRANCESCA* Daughter of Zsa-Zsa Gabor and Conrad Hilton. She was only 21 at the time, and Michael Sellers feels that Peter was "cautious" about her, "fearing her loquacious mother might have something to say on the subject of their relationship." It didn't last.

★*JOYCE, ALICE* Pan American stewardess. She entertained Peter's guests with her "demonstration of the airline's safety procedures." She couldn't take Peter's proposal seriously.

★*LOREN, SOPHIA* She was already a big star, and he wasn't—so Sellers never thought "it" would happen. But, when they appeared together in *The Millionairess*, he went "absolutely round the bend about her." Michael Sellers recalls that Peter brought Sophia home to meet the wife and kids, and that, finally, in a "frenzy" of passion for the voluptuous donna, "he was suffocated by the urge to confess all to Mum." He told his wife, for example, about Sophia's "loving asides" on the set, how they kissed when no one watched. Most observers feel that La Loren's involvement with Peter was minimal—perhaps nothing more than a display of her "natural, warm Neapolitan generosity." She stayed with Carlo.

★*MINNELLI, LIZA* On the rebound from marriage to Miranda Quarry (below) Pete met Liza at a London dinner party, and they announced their engagement forty-eight hours later. He said he was "walking on air"; soon after Liza moved into Sellers's digs, "she realized she was walking on eggshells." She consulted a clairvoyant, who said that marriage to Sellers just wasn't in her future. "That's what I thought," said Liza. "Why didn't she go to *my* fucking clairvoyant?" said Peter.

★*QUARRY, MIRANDA* A 22-year-old "flower of the British aristocracy." They had a two-year "feuding and forgiving, clashing and kissing affair," finally wed in August 1970. Miranda, calling Sellers "a dear sweet man," brought along as "bridesmaids" her two Pekinese dogs, Tabitha and Thomasina. Their friends thought they went through with it out of boredom. He was presumably proud to lure a real blueblood into his bed; and she, probably, "wanted a bit of a rough, a stroll across the tracks." They were divorced in early 1974.

★*SCHOOL SWEETHEART* She gave birth to Peter's illegitimate daughter, who was given up for adoption. So says Sellers's legitimate son, Michael.

★*SCOTT, JANETTE* Former English child star, "a professional virgin figure." Their "strange love affair" came after Peter's divorce from first wife, Ann, and they talked of marriage. But "one morning she packed her bags and left for New York . . . later to meet and marry and divorce Mel Torme."

★*SWEDISH BEAUTY QUEEN* Peter found her in New York, installed her in his temporary digs in a Long Island mansion. The kids Michael and Sarah were there, too. They didn't like her. *They* went back to England.

★*WACHTMEISTER, CHRISTINA ("TITTI")* The "leggiest, dolliest bird" Sellers ever set eyes on. She was the daughter of Sweden's ambassador to the U.S., living in Cyprus— where he was making a film. Sellers couldn't stand her flirtatious response to other men. One night, in a fury, he went home, packed Titti's bags and flung them in front of her in a local nightclub. "I want you out of here on the next plane," he declared in his best Inspector Clouseau manner. Titti blinked. "But I live here," she told him.

★*WIFE'S BEST FRIEND* Sellers once told his wife Ann that if she really wanted a divorce, "she could cite *her* best friend as co-respondent, as he'd recently had an affair with her." The "friend" later admitted it was true.

MISCELLANY

★*DAHL, TESSA* Daughter of Patricia Neal. She was 18 when Peter began to take notice. Flattered, young Tessa set about organizing Peter's life, answering phones, etc. However, Michael writes that "this time, thankfully, Dad recognized the danger signs and asked Tessa to leave."

★*MARGARET, PRINCESS* Pete and Britt and P.M. (Princess Margaret) and Tony were all good friends during the mid-'60s in swinging London. And, "inevitably, perhaps, Sellers' relationship with Margaret became the subject of speculation." Sellers himself fanned the flames of gossip, hinting a liaison with "somebody *very* high up in the social tree." Once while smoking dope with Laurence Harvey, Sellers confided that the thing was, P.M. had the very same-sized breasts as Sophia Loren, "the same cup size exactly!" Harvey mused blandly that "large breasts and small husbands must be an irresistible melange for some chaps." Sellers said, "They're my undoing." The alleged affair between Pete and P.M. was even celebrated by Spike Mulligan in a ditty which the Princess herself is said to have chuckled over: "Wherever you are/Wherever you be/Please take your hand off the PRINCESS's knee." The Princess's later romance with Roddy Llewellyn gave some credence to Sellers's boasts, and jealous Peter was known to put Llewellyn at the very top of his "shit list."

SHAW, ARTIE
(b. 1910)

Clarinetist and big-band leader of the swing era, an inveterate swinger with or without his licorice stick. Way back, when name bands used to be featured in films, Shaw appeared in *Dancing Co-Ed* and *Second Chorus*, somehow developed a habit of dating—and frequently mating with—movie stars. He later dabbled with some success in film production, wrote a novel, *The Trouble with Cinderella*, and went into semi-retirement in Spain, more or less abdicating from both music and marriage.

PRIMARY SOURCES: *Ava: A Life Story*, by Charles Higham (Delacorte, 1974); *Judy Garland: A Biography*, by Anne Edwards (Simon and Schuster, 1974); *Betty Grable: The Reluctant Movie Queen*, by Doug Warren (St. Martin's, 1981); *Scarlett O'Hara's Younger Sister, or, My Lively Life in and out of Hollywood*, by Eleven Keyes (Lyle Stuart, 1977); *Lana: The Public and Private Lives of Miss Turner*, by Joe Morella and Edward Epstein (Citadel, 1971).

★*ALLEN, MARGARET* Wife no. 2, before the stars got into his eyes.

★*CARNS, JUNE* Wife no. 1, apparently just a warmup exercise.

★*DOWLING, DORIS* Movie character actress whose sister Constance was also in films. Shaw's seventh wife, mother of his son John, Doris got away from it all and resided in Italy.

★*GARDNER, AVA* He was her second husband, she was his fifth wife. They met at a time when Shaw was depressed about the breakup of his marriage to Turner, and the decline of his personal fortune through alimony and various other bad investments. He was won over by Ava's beauty, but turned off by her lack of education. So he started her on a Great Books regime. He once caught Ava with a copy of the current best-seller, *Forever Amber* by Kathleen Winsor, and publicly berated her for reading "shit like that." A few years later Ava was amused to learn that Artie's sixth wife was Kathleen Winsor. (See below . . . also see GARDNER listing.)

★*GARLAND, JUDY* Musical superstar, a teen prodigy when she used to step away for secret dates with Shaw, hoping her studio bosses wouldn't find out. (See also GARLAND listing.)

★ *GRABLE, BETTY* Blond song-and-dance gal in numerous Fox musicals. Her divorce

action against Jackie Coogan was still in progress when Betty went east to conquer Broadway in a new musical, *Du Barry Was a Lady*, with a Cole Porter score—and be near her new love, Shaw. Reporters followed the handsome couple everywhere, and Grable's bio quotes Artie's exuberant announcement that "he was thinking of writing a song or two for Betty to sing in the show." Cole Porter let it be known that he didn't really need Shaw's help. The show turned out just swell without him. So did Betty, when Artie abruptly left her for another lady. (See also GRABLE and TURNER listings.)

★*KERN, ELIZABETH* Wife no. 4, mother of son Steven. After Lana, before Ava.

★*KEYES, EVELYN* She met him in France after her breakup with Mike Todd, who had already discovered Liz. "His talk was dazzling . . . his subject matter making wide sweeps round the globe . . . his vocabulary soaring in infinite variety," chortles Keyes in her autobiography. After they were married (she was no. 8), Shaw's exacting demands and outbursts of temper unnerved her, but his vocabulary was still impressive: "A stream of words so vindictive, malevolent and vicious it boggles the imagination: Harridan, lunatic, cheat, selfish, unfeeling, blind, dense, unreachable, untrustworthy . . ." Worse yet, she notes: "To tell Artie to shut up was like lighting a firecracker under a herd of buffalo and standing in front of it." He ultimately stampeded her into divorce, and both stopped trying. (See also KEYES listing.)

★*MARCIA* New interest Artie discovered when his marriage to Keyes hit heavy weather. "She was beautiful—and young," Evelyn recalls. "That she was somebody's wife didn't seem to bother Artie." She also had a yen to dance professionally, but Shaw "talked Marcia out of dancing and into being his secretary—success and romance all wrapped up in a neat package." For once, however, they didn't marry.

★*TURNER, LANA* Artie, at the time, was wooing Betty Grable and Judy Garland as well as Lana. Artie called to wish Lana a happy

20th birthday and learned that her date for the evening, Greg Bautzer, had canceled out. So Artie and Lana spent the evening together. And the morning—for they eloped to Las Vegas, her first trek to the altar, Artie's third. That was on February 8, 1940. (Betty Grable remembers that the Shaw-Turner wedding occurred over the New Year's weekend, but who's counting?) Lana's version of their brief marriage (it lasted just short of four months) recounted Artie's constant commands to "get rid of those ridiculous high heels. Wear low heels. . . . Also that damn lipstick. Wipe it off your mouth." (See also TURNER listing.)

★*WINSOR, KATHLEEN* Novelist best known as author of 1944 best-seller *Forever Amber*, about a rambunctious Restoration lady. Made into mildly controversial movie starring Linda Darnell in 1947. Kathleen was the fifth Mrs. Shaw. They went back to their books.

SHORE, DINAH
(b. 1917)

The durable thrush from Tennessee has not aged a day that anyone can detect in decades. Though her movie career began with wartime musicals and never came to much, Dinah herself went on and on, mostly upward in TV where the *mmm-wah* kiss-off closing shot on her Chevrolet variety show became an All-American ta-ta as popular as *Ciao, baby*. A fitness freak, Dinah in recent years has stayed in the public eye by hosting daytime talk shows, and going out nights with the likes of Burt Reynolds—whose long relationship with her helped to burnish his image as a man of distinction, with a taste for vintage wine. (Burt's boyish foolery with all those other babes has not yet been collected in book form, though he has been offered handsome advances to get going.)

PRIMARY SOURCE: *Dinah! An Intimate Biography*, by Bruce Cassiday (Franklin Watts, 1979; Berkley, 1980).

★*"G.I."* Dinah was already a big radio and recording star when a "certain G.I." stole her heart in 1942. Ticker Freeman, her arranger and accompanist, thought the guy a phony and warned Dinah she'd be sorry. She wouldn't speak to Ticker for weeks. Then the soldier suddenly disappeared. Dinah had no idea where he'd gone until she received a Dear Dinah letter from his hometown saying he had married his old sweetheart. Dinah cried her eyes out.

★*MONTGOMERY, GEORGE* Later in '42, Dinah had an engagement in Atlantic City, and while there saw a movie starring George Montgomery. She promptly announced to all who would listen that she was going to marry George Montgomery. Bing Crosby sighed, "Poor George. . . . That Dinah Shore gal may look like cotton candy wouldn't melt in her mouth, but she knows what she wants, and she's harder than flint about getting it." George, at the time, was engaged to glamorous Hedy Lamarr; but that didn't last long after he met Dinah at the Stage Door Canteen. He joined the army and began to grow frantic about Dinah's being left on her own in big, bad Hollywood. On his first leave they eloped; it was December 5, 1943. Their daughter Melissa arrived in 1948, a few years later they adopted a son, Jody. Dinah was into tennis, George into building furniture; though her career kept building while his hit a plateau and definite downward slide. Dinah pinpointed the real problem in their marriage: "The whole world had an image of us and so did we, a beautiful Technicolor image. We never quarreled. But if you don't share your private distress and sadness there is something fundamentally wrong with the relationship. In the end, we just drifted apart." They divorced in 1962. Dinah went on to major TV stardom for the next twenty years. George directed a few offbeat movies and eventually became very successful at his furniture business.

★*REYNOLDS, BURT* Dinah invited Burt to be a guest on her television show. The year was 1971. Three significant things happened to Burt that year. The first was his appearance as a nude centerfold in *Cosmopolitan* magazine. The second was his appearance in the

critically acclaimed film *Deliverance*. The third was his affair with Dinah. On that first TV show where they began it all, Burt recalls blurting spontaneous, unexpected things. "I said, 'I want to talk to you about going to Palm Springs with me for the weekend.'" Burt immediately liked her mind: "I fell in *like*." It got to be more than that, and the affair was big news not just because of who they were but because of the disparity in their ages. Dinah was nearly 20 when Burt was born. When asked how he felt about marriage, Burt replied, "I believe in good marriages. I also believe in the Tooth Fairy." Dinah kept insisting she didn't want to marry Burt, and "I don't want to grow old in his arms." In time they broke up, reconciled, then started seeing other people, though Burt insisted that he considered Dinah his best female friend, "maybe *the* best friend." Burt *still* squires Dinah around town on occasion. When Barbara Walters cornered him for one of her intimate TV interviews, she asked who he'd like to be if he came back in another life as a member of the opposite sex. "I'll tell you who," Reynolds grinned, "Dinah Shore, that's who!"
★*SMITH, MAURICE F.* They met in Palm Springs, he was a building contractor, Dinah a tennis nut, and they loved to play tennis together. "On May 26, 1963, just a few days over a year after her divorce from George was final, Dinah married her tennis partner." It lasted less than a year. Love-0.

MISCELLANY

★*COLLEGE BEAUS* Three of them proposed to Dinah within two days after she graduated from Vanderbilt University.
★*SINATRA, FRANK* When they were young singers starting out in New York, this skinny kid from Hoboken made it known that he didn't think Dinah added much to the radio show on which they both appeared. "My accent was all wrong, even for South Jersey—*he* said." Later, much later, Dinah invited Frankie to her TV show and they got along like gangbusters.

Among those Dinah dated in recent years

were *RON ELY*, one time Tarzan on TV; *IGGY POP*, far-out rock star; and *JOE IACOVETTA*, former pro tennis star.

SINATRA, FRANK
(b. 1915)

Ole Blue Eyes, still the reigning King of Crooners. By any name, Hoboken's gift to pop music and headline writers began as a band singer with Tommy Dorsey and became a one-in-a-million entertainer, an Oscar-winning actor, and indefatigable ladies' man. He has had a love-hate relationship with the public since bobby-soxers started swooning in his honor back in the early '40s. The pendulum of popularity has swung both ways many times during a career spanning four decades. His altercations with the press are famous, as are his sometime palship with gangland toughs he seems to admire, and his weakness for beautiful women. Sinatra has attributed his romantic adventures, in or out of marriage, to his unquenchable Italian thirst for passion and sex. The Man should know.

PRIMARY SOURCE: *Sinatra: An Unauthorized Biography*, by Earl Wilson (Macmillan, 1976; New American Library/Signet, 1977).

★*BACALL, LAUREN* One of Sinatra's "most charming qualities is his comforting people in grief," writes Wilson, "and he especially has a way with widows." Frankie was Bogart's best friend, soon Bogie's widow would become his new love. Press reports had them ready to marry, "barring an act of providence or Ava Gardner." Sinatra didn't like to be publicly hemmed in, and cooled it; Bacall felt crudely rebuffed. (See BACALL listing.) Sinatra's reaction to her side of the story, as told in her book, *By Myself*, prompted Bacall to tell Barbara Walters on network TV, "the man has as much sense of humor as this floor."
★*BARBATO, NANCY* The first Mrs. Sinatra. A plasterer's daughter from Hoboken

who saved the pennies she earned as a secretary to buy young Frank sandwiches and coffee while he made the rounds of radio stations and nightclubs looking for a gig. They were wed in February 1939, divorced in 1950 after several separations and three children, Nancy, Frank Jr. and Tina. Nancy had loved Frank unreservedly, and had striven to keep up with him when his life moved into the fast lane. "What do other girls do for him in bed that I don't do?" she supposedly asked her girlfriends.

★*CONNOLLY, PEGGY* Beautiful brunette actress and singer, longtime girlfriend. Frank brought her to Spain when everyone *thought* he might reconcile with Ava.

★*COREY, JILL* Perky songstress who maintained a relationship with Frank for about six years in the late 1950s. "I think we thought about marriage," she remembers.

★*DICKINSON, ANGIE* Before Bacharach, there was Sinatra, whom she considered a "dear, dear friend," although not the kind of man she could ever live with.

★*EKBERG, ANITA* Their friendship established, he paid her air fare to come see him at the Copacabana in New York. Anita blew it by walking in with another date.

★*EXNER, JUDITH CAMPBELL* The notorious party girl. Sinatra introduced her to both John F. Kennedy and mob boss Sam Giancana, a link recently brought to light in the lady's own exposé. Judith says she gave up sex with Sinatra because he had "kinky" tastes. Frank snapped back: "Hell hath no fury like a hustler with a literary agent."

★*FARROW, MIA* As the 19-year-old star of the TV series *Peyton Place*, she was thought of as a "rebellious, unglamorous, unsexy-looking teenager." Sinatra, at 50, was one of the best catches around, and Mia caught him. Frank didn't like jokes about their age differences (e.g., "He's got *ties* older than she is"). After an on-again-off-again courtship, they managed to sneak away for a private wedding in Las Vegas on July 19, 1966. They seemed so much in love; Frank gave her "a car, a

horse, diamonds." But Mia wasn't into expensive baubles; she became captivated by Indian gurus, and hanging out at Arthur discotheque, where one could get "all the guru news." In early 1967, Mia went to India to meditate with "the Maharishi," which only widened the growing rift between them. "Mia went back to Arthur; Frank stayed on at Jilly's." In August 1968, after nearly a year's separation, the couple obtained a Mexican divorce. (See also FARROW listing.)

★*GARDNER, AVA* The cliffhanger courtship and marriage of Ava and Frankie gave the world a four-year soap opera in the early 1950s. "Indifference was Ava's charm," writes Wilson, and her coolness drove Frank crazy. While still tied to Nancy, and while his singing career suffered a slump, Sinatra began chasing Ava across the country and around the world. He saw red when he read she was dating a Spanish bullfighter. Sinatra's divorce came through in 1951. Twenty-four hours later, Ava and Frank flubbed one attempt to marry, called the whole thing off, then got it on again for real. About a year later came their big blowup in Palm Springs over the Lana Turner incident. (See GARDNER and TURNER listings.) Other crises intervened, including Frank's sudden acting success in *From Here to Eternity*, for which he won an Oscar as Best Supporting Actor, and after which, said Ava, Frank became his old arrogant self: "We were happier when we were on the skids." The divorce was announced in late 1953. Ava would claim that she and Frankie were always "great in bed . . . The quarreling started on the way to the bidet."

★*GARLAND, JUDY* She had "love tremors for the King," and was allegedly with Sinatra the night he dumped a press agent "on his fanny" for asking Frankie, "Who's the broad?" Judy was married to Sid Luft at the time. (See also GARLAND listing.)

★*MARX, BARBARA* Former Las Vegas show girl, former wife of Zeppo Marx. They began dating around 1973, broke up a lot and got together a lot. She is known to be extremely patient with Frank, popular with his cronies, able to cope. She married him July 11, 1976, and is still his missus. His fourth.

★*MAXWELL, MARILYN* Beautiful, busty, blond Marilyn was the first woman back in the 1940s coupled with Frank in the gossip columns, when he was supposedly happy with Nancy and the kids.

★*MONROE, MARILYN* When Marilyn split with Joe DiMaggio she became "one of Sinatra's many girlfriends," and, for a number of weeks, his houseguest. Frank said he was just trying to help her get out nights, joked about her infidelity: "She's staying at my house and going out with other guys." (See also MONROE listing.)

★*NOVAK, KIM* After Sammy Davis, Jr., and after Aly Khan, Kim was a frequent guest of Frank's in Las Vegas, "leaning over the baccarat or blackjack table, wide-eyed, whispering breathily to him as he flung in his chips."

★*PROVINE, DOROTHY* Bouncy, energetic singer and "a Sinatra enthusiast."

★*PROWSE, JULIET* Statuesque dancer from South Africa; Frank adored her and was a help in advancing her career. Juliet used to open his act, as they say. But he insisted she step *out* of the spotlight if she wanted to become Mrs. Sinatra. She didn't want to *that* much; their announced engagement was canceled.

★*ST. JOHN, JILL* Jill joined in Sinatra's high-living days at the Cal-Neva Lodge in Lake Tahoe. She rated high enough to be taken home to New Jersey for a home-cooked meal with Sinatra's mom. They both went on to other entanglements. (See also ST. JOHN listing.)

★*TAYLOR, ELIZABETH* Liz's biographer Kelly insists he lit her fire, though Wilson on Sinatra failed to detect even a trace of smoke. (See also TAYLOR listing.)

★*TURNER, LANA* The columns said they were a hot item in the late 1940s. Probably true. What else *could* they be? Does the Pope wear red shoes? (See also TURNER listing.)

MISCELLANY

★*BEATTY, LADY ADELE* Formerly Adele O'Connor, press agent from Texas who married into British nobility (then divorced out of it), was considered one of London's great beauties when Sinatra squired her around in the late 1950's. Later when Lady Adele married director Stanley Donen, she received a one-word cable: WHY? The Donens believed it was sent by Sinatra.

★*DE PORTAGO, MARQUESSA* Shapely, titled, bejeweled beauty who caught Frankie's eye in Rome. They weekended it in Monte Carlo.

★*DIETRICH, MARLENE* She said of Sinatra: "*Mais oui* . . . the Mercedes Benz of men!" She ought to know, being a hard driver.

★*GABOR, EVA* Mama Jolie Gabor once told Earl Wilson about Eva and Frankie: "They loff each other, dolling, but eet's just a leetle flirtation."

★*KAZAN, LAINIE* In her nightclub act, Lainie would refer to herself as "Lainie Levine, the walking sex machine." She met Sinatra in Miami, and later told Earl Wilson, "Listen, if anything happened, do you think I'd tell you?"

★*KENDALL, KAY* There was an incident at a party: Frank was talking to Kay, suddenly her husband Rex Harrison came up; something was said about something or someone "being yellow," and Harrison slapped Sinatra in the face. But Harrison recalls that it was a harmless fracas; he and Kay had dinner with Sinatra the next night.

★*LANGE, HOPE* Beverly Hills gossips, says Earl, were frequently heard to say: "Sinatra's seeing Hope Lange again." Ms. Lange, once the wife of Don Murray, hasn't said much.

★*MARGARET, PRINCESS* When the Princess and her consort Tony visited the U.S., Sinatra was "the one man" she wanted to see, 'tis said. But a requested "command performance" never came off.

★*MILES, SYLVIA* The "tempestuous" actress has been "a Sinatra friend." She told Earl with a provocative smile, "I found out he reads *Nugget."* Sylvia was in it.

★*ONASSIS, JACKIE* On their one public date, doubling with the Peter Duchins after one of Sinatra's New York concerts, the speculation was (1) that Jackie had arranged the evening (which she had) to try to obtain Sinatra's memoirs for publication; (2) it was all a plot by New York Governor Hugh Carey and Jackie to woo Sinatra back into the Democratic Party. Another source swore that Frankie and Jackie had met at least five times—secretly—before that.

★*REED, DONNA* She dated Frank right after they both won Oscars for supporting roles in *From Here to Eternity.*

★*VANDERBILT, GLORIA* He introduced his "sweep-them-off-their-feet technique" to high society when he romanced Vanderbilt shortly after the end of her marriage to conductor Leopold Stokowski. Miss Vanderbilt was supposed to appear in the next Sinatra movie. Those plans melted away, canceled, as was the romance.

★*WOOD, NATALIE* Sinatra took Natalie to Broadway shows and Jilly's, "when both were free."

STEINEM, GLORIA
(b. 1935)

Toledo-born journalist, now a leading spokesperson for the women's movement, beautiful Gloria went to Smith College, discovered the wonders of Washington, D.C., and began to command attention as a strikingly articulate representative of her sex when she wrote a magazine piece about the pill, titled "The Moral Disarmament of Betty Co-Ed." A founder of NOW (National Organization for Women). As activist lecturers go, Steinem is about as chic as they come, and has been known to say, "If you don't want to be a sex object, you have to make yourself unattractive, but I'm not going to walk around in army boots and cut off my hair.

There's no reason for us to make ourselves look like men." Little danger of that. Gloria's displeasure with men allows for all sorts of exceptions, though the Kissinger bio (below) goes a step beyond that, saying, "If you could poll the men who have known Gloria, few of them would think she's above or below bedding down with anybody or everybody to achieve the goals of her campaign."

PRIMARY SOURCE: *Kissinger: The Adventures of Super-Kraut,* by Charles R. Ashman (Lyle Stuart, 1972). A chapter is devoted to Ms. Steinem.

★*GALBRAITH, JOHN KENNETH* He was asked by publisher Guinzburg (see below) to write an introduction for Gloria's *The Beach Book* (1963). They met to discuss the project, "and Gloria put aside her liberationist tendencies *and* Guinzburg long enough to fall in love. . . . Galbraith is still a close, close friend and adviser." JKG also respects her gifts as a political infighter, and has said, "When she cuts up people, the blood shows."

★*GUINZBURG, TOM* Former president of Viking Press. He picked up rights to Gloria's book (see above) and "also picked up certain rights to Gloria." Guinzburg recalls: "I won't say we were exactly Scott and Zelda, but we were very cute together."

★*JOHNSON, RAFER* Black Olympic star and one regular date for Gloria.

★*KISSINGER, HENRY* It was front-page news when Gloria felt compelled to announce that she was not then and never had been a girlfriend of Henry Kissinger's. Author Ashman goes so far as to say that Gloria was "maybe the most important filly in Kissinger's life—perhaps because he has been totally unsuccessful in getting her into the hay." Make of it what you will. (See also KISSINGER listing.)

★*NICHOLS, MIKE* Actor-director. Seen about town with Gloria when not being seen about with Jackie O. and other ultra-chic luminaries.

★*SARGENT, HERB* Writer in TV and film, *Saturday Night Live,* etc. Occasional date.

★*SORENSEN, TED* Adviser to President

John F. Kennedy. Gloria moved in on *him,* it's said. But he lost his appeal when he began telling Gloria not to drink or smoke, to wear her hair in a bun, and to act more feminine.

MISCELLANY

★*HEFNER, HUGH* Gloria got his goat when she went undercover as a bunny in the New York Playboy Club, and blasted the club's policies in an article for *Show* magazine. She got to him again years later while on an interview for *McCall's* magazine. "Instead of an interview, she ended up telling him off, saying that his crusade for sexual liberation was 'beating a dead horse.' "

Gloria has had many buddies, and usually in high places; she has been close to *ALL THE KENNEDYS, GEORGE MCGOVERN, CESAR CHAVEZ,* many others in the world of politics, entertainment, and publishing.

STRASBERG, SUSAN
(b. 1938)

Actress-daughter of famous teacher-director-actor Lee Strasberg and his first wife, Paula Strasberg (best known as Marilyn Monroe's acting coach). Raised in a heady theatrical atmosphere, she made her stage debut at 15 and achieved an overnight success in *The Diary of Anne Frank.* Competent but never charismatic, she made a number of so-so films, suffered through an impossible marriage and years of psychoanalysis before she put it all down in book form—life upon the wicked stage, as seen from several rungs below the top.

PRIMARY SOURCE: *Bittersweet,* by Susan Strasberg (Putnam, 1980).

★*ADLER, RICHARD* Broadway lyricist. Susan was starring in her first Broadway play (*Diary of Anne Frank*), so "it was inevitable that I would have my first love affair." Richard was 36 and his maturity "relieved me of any re-

sponsibility," she writes. Susan's mother, Paula, thought otherwise. For her daughter's 18th brithday, Paula arranged for Susan to acquire a diaphragm. Friends had told her she'd never forget the moment she lost her virginity. "They lied. I have forgotten."

★*BEATTY, WARREN* In Rome, after he finished shooting *The Roman Spring of Mrs. Stone,* opposite Vivien Leigh, Warren moved in with Susan for what she calls his "vacation." She found he had a "tremendous need to please women as well as conquer them," and his needs could sometimes become urgent. They were at a party at Luchino Visconti's mansion (the Italian director found Beatty "enchanting") when Warren pulled Strasberg into the bathroom and locked the door. She laughed nervously—complaining, "Isn't it a little close for *that* in here?" But Warren managed very well. When he asked her to go to Paris with him, she begged off.

★*BURTON, RICHARD* Young Susan's second Broadway play was *Time Remembered,* co-starring Burton, who *literally* swept her off her feet, lifting her into the air and hailing her as his "beautiful Hebrew princess." Out of town with the show, she "longed to consummate" things with Richard, but darn, she'd forgotten to bring her diaphragm. Later she threw herself into the affair "with total abandonment and passion. . . . I did not care about the consequences." Richard sometimes slept over with Susan at her parents' place and she felt some guilt at making them co-conspirators. But mother Paula was actually delighted, having dreamed "that I would have affairs with the great writers and actors of our generation." Then came the misery of those nights when Burton didn't come. Or didn't even call. At play's end, Richard returned with his wife Sybil to Switzerland, leaving Susan to "a period of hysteria." Reunited back in New York six months later, they drank champagne, had sex. And, suddenly, Strasberg began to see that Burton was, well, "human."

★*GRANT, CARY* They met in Hollywood and dated briefly, restlessly. "He was at a restless period of his life, as was I."

★*ITALIAN ACTOR* An "overnight sensation" in the movies, and with Susan. But after a few weeks, she awakened in his apartment one night feeling "suffocated and isolated." She looked at his sleeping face, "and realized he drank too much, made love too quickly, and in typical Italian fashion deprecated any attempts at analysis or introspection." *Finita la commedia.*

★*"JERRY"* Successful older businessman whom Susan describes as ultra-conservative, even though "he wore silk undershorts with his initials hand-stitched on the fly." Pressing for marriage, he told her she'd never find anyone to take care of her as he would. She conceded that was true, but "he was also *buying my life.*" She said no.

★*JONES, CHRISTOPHER* After Burton, Susan vowed "no more actors." But Jones was persistent. While admiring his handsomeness, she continued to have doubts, and scolded herself, "Susan, you don't want to wake up in the morning with someone prettier than you." After they spent two weeks together in New York, "hardly leaving the apartment," the commitment was made. They moved to Hollywood, she suffered through his many jealous rages, and he introduced her to LSD, to help her "cut loose from all your tight-assed conventional crap." After two and a half years of a stormy, druggy, on-and-off affair in the U.S. and Europe, Susan became pregnant. They were wed in September 1965, in Las Vegas. In March she gave birth to daughter Jennifer Robin. Next step was divorce.

★*LOEW, ARTHUR JR.* Scion of the motion-picture family. He liked actresses, and was seeing Joan Collins at the same time he dated Susan. When Susan found out, "I halfheartedly threw an ashtray at him, but it was not an intense enough relationship for me to work up any real indignity." (See also LOEW listing.)

★*"WILLIAM"* A musician and gentleman farmer, recently separated. Susan was "wild about him." But he couldn't decide whether he loved her or his absent wife, "so we separated by mutual consent." The last romantic entry in Susan's rueful autobio.

MISCELLANY

★*DEAN, JAMES* He knew her folks; adolescent Susan was fascinated by him—but he was fascinated by Pier Angeli.

★*FONDA, PETER* The script of Jack Nicholson's film *The Trip* called for co-stars Fonda and Strasberg to do a love scene in the nude. Fonda said, "Susan, I just want you to know—if I get an erection, it's nothing personal."

★*KHAN, ALY* They were introduced by Elsa Maxwell; he sent her flowers and they began to date. At the end of the evening Aly and Susan would sit in the back of his limousine and kiss passionately, but he never went further. "I thought he had some kind of terminal disease. . . . after we disengaged ourselves from these passionate embraces, his legs would shake so uncontrollably they would rattle the seat." Susan figured he figured she was still a virgin, and she was too shy to indicate otherwise. Mama Paula sighed; "Wouldn't Susan make a perfect begum?"

★*OLIVIER, LAURENCE* A picture of Larry and Susan appeared in a New York newspaper captioned "Olivier to Divorce," implying that *she* was the femme fatale he was after. At the time, Olivier was actually involved with future wife Joan Plowright, Susan with Burton.

STREISAND, BARBRA
(b. 1942)

When she was a skinny, shy, slightly cross-eyed, unpopular Brooklyn schoolgirl, Barbra used to imagine being Vivien Leigh or Carole Lombard. She grew up to be just as big if not as beautiful, having discovered how to make an asset of her strikingly unconventional looks, better still having discovered she had a singing voice. Everyone else made the discovery when she was booked into a modish Manhattan *boite* called the Blue Angel, which led to Broadway, *Funny Girl*—an Oscar for the film version her first time at bat—and a phenomenal career thereafter. She's so assuredly box-office that even her worst movies make money. Streisand has a mind of her own, and has rarely been known to keep an opinion to herself. Romantically, after one unsuccessful marriage wrecked by bad timing—seldom a problem for her—she seems to have formed a powerful partnership with Jon Peters to do things her own way, which is apt to mean uninhibited, risky, brilliant, maybe off-the-wall, but virtually never dull.

PRIMARY SOURCES: *The Greatest Star: The Barbra Streisand Story,* by Rene Jordan (Putnam, 1975): *Streisand,* by Jonathan Black (Leisure Books, Norden); *Streisand: The Woman and the Legend,* by James Spada (Doubleday/Dolphin, 1981).

★*BEATTY, WARREN* He and Barbra were "seen together" on occasion in 1971. With Beatty, usually, any miss is good for some mileage. Barbra considered him one of her "flings" between important romances. (See also BEATTY listing.)

★*BUSINESSMAN* As she was basking in the critical raves of *The Way We Were,* Barbra fell into "the throes of a grand passion that proved to be fleeting." She did tell an interviewer that she "enjoyed being subjugated" by her new lover, and "I like to accompany him in his business travels."

★*DENNEN, BARRY* Her first real romance, and the first man to have an influence on her career. An actor himself (he played Pontius Pilate in both the stage and screen versions of *Jesus Christ Superstar*), he persuaded Barbra to move into his Greenwich Village pad, then to enter a talent contest in a club called the Lion. She won; the prize was $50 and a week's engagement. That was in 1960, a turning point. Barbra considered Barry more than a lover, he was "a teacher, a driving force." For a girl who "never even had dates for proms," the end of the affair left her embittered. Barbra was referring to Dennen when she said later, "When I used to sing *Cry Me a River,* I had a specific person in mind. I don't sing it quite the same way anymore because I don't feel the same way. . . ."

★*GOULD, ELLIOTT* They were both getting their first big break on Broadway in *I Can Get It for You Wholesale.* When he first encountered Barbra, Gould recalls, "I thought she was the weirdo of all times. But when I saw her next, I offered her a cigar." Barbra remembers: "I thought he was funny-looking. . . . I saw the back of his neck, and I just liked him." "Ellie" soon moved into her apartment above Oscar's seafood restaurant. "We worked together, we lived together, we thought of ourselves as Hansel and Gretel," said Barbra. *Wholesale* became a hit—but though Gould was the leading man, "Barbra got the Tony nomination, TV guest shots, recording offers, etc." That was the story of their marriage, which began in September 1963. By March 1964, Barbra became the toast of Broadway in *Funny Girl.* They divorced in 1971 after a two-year separation, about the time Gould's professional star began to rise. It was the first marriage for both; a son, Jason, was born in 1966.

★*GREYSON, RICHARD* British ex-husband of Natalie Wood, still brokenhearted over Natalie when he met Barbra and said: "I guess I'm a bit starry-eyed. . . . I can't find a single thing wrong with Barbra except the way she spells her name." Greyson stuck around just long enough to discover that Barbra yearned to be dominated, but on most of their dates, he recalls, "It was impossible to get a word in."

★*KRISTOFFERSON, KRIS* Another "fling" in the wake of her romance with O'Neal (see below), long before they co-starred in *A Star Is Born* several years later.

★*O'NEAL, RYAN* In a "paroxysm of rancor," writes biographer Jordan, some Hollywood wag dubbed O'Neal and Streisand "the Prince and the Frogess." The pair tried to keep their affair secret, lest the scandal (Ryan was still married to Leigh Taylor-Young) "would strip O'Neal of all chances of winning the Oscar for *Love Story*." But the glittering pair nevertheless made news—with their pictures in the papers under headlines like, "A New Love Story?" The romance "sputtered uphill like a wheezing cable car" and expired during the San Francisco shooting of Peter Bogdanovich's *What's Up, Doc?* (1972). Barbra found the whole film just silly, "a puff of smoke, a piece of fluff." Ryan thought it was hilarious. Personally, they were kaput, though the movie was a hit. Professionally, the duo came back for a rematch in 1979's *The Main Event*. Ryan today calls her "a delicately made creature, a great lady."

★*PETERS, JON* At last, a man who could take charge. Jon was a "star" in his own world—as owner of a chain of Beverly Hills beauty salons (and one of the prototypes for the sexy hairdresser Warren Beatty played in *Shampoo*). Barbra called him to her manse for a coif, kept him waiting for an hour and a half, then finally requested that he trim her *wig*. Insulted, Jon thought she was rude and told her so, then remarked, as she flounced across the room, "You've got a great ass." That did it. Streisand had met her match, and loved it. Jon and Barbra have been together since 1974, partners in a production company and apparently steady-as-they-go despite (or because of) their reluctance to marry. Jon has been quoted: "She is like ten different women, and I love them all." Adds Barbra: "I get all the ego nourishment I need from him."

★*SHARIF, OMAR* Moon-eyed Egyptian actor. Omar started the talk when they were teamed in *Funny Girl* by telling a *Life* reporter, "This woman is beautiful, and I am *lusting* after her." Still married, Barbra supposedly responded with "I am crazy in love with Omar and I have told my Elliott about it." Sharif later described their four-month affair as a domestic idyl, eating at home, watching TV: "When I'd used up all my Italian recipes—Barbra would heat TV dinners." When their first kissing scene in the film was publicized, during the Arab-Israeli Six-Day War, an Egyptian newspaper condemned Sharif in a front-page editorial. Quipped Barbra, "You think *Cairo* was upset? You should have seen the letter I got from my Aunt Rose."

★*TRUDEAU, PIERRE* Soon after her split with Gould, Barbra mused that she needed a "mature, non-narcissistic man who had nothing to do with the arts." Canada's handsome Prime Minister appeared to fill the bill. Tru-

deau responded by dating Barbra, even invited her to Ottawa, where she sat in the visitors' gallery and distracted him from government business. Had she ever *seriously* considered becoming Canada's First Lady? In her 1977 *Playboy* interview, Barbra said: "Oh yeah. I thought it would be fantastic. I'd have to learn how to speak French. . . . I would only do movies made in Canada. I had it all figured out." Rumors of marriage plans were finally shot down, however, with the gossip columns citing "career conflicts." That's known as putting it mildly.

MISCELLANY

★*MATTHAU, WALTER* No romance, more like mutual misanthropy with her testy co-star in *Hello, Dolly* (1969). Barbra was miscast, Matthau disgusted. Walter told one interviewer that he had asked Barbra to "stop directing the fucking picture, which she took exception to, and there was a blowup in which I also told her she was a pipsqueak who didn't have the talent of a butterfly's fart. To which she replied that I was jealous because I wasn't as good as she was." He wound up referring to her as "Miss Ptomaine." Barbra's pet name for Matthau was "Old Sewermouth."

SWANSON, GLORIA
(b. 1898)

The only comeback that counted was her tour-de-force as an aging, paranoid star of the silent screen in Billy Wilder's *Sunset Boulevard*, for which she won an Oscar nomination in 1950. It might have been Swanson's own story, but not quite. Monumentally self-sufficient, she entered movies at 17 and by 1919 she was ready to challenge all comers as Hollywood's most glamorous dramatic damsel in a series of glossy romances produced by Cecil B. DeMille. Though she has done very little acting in the past thirty years, Swanson remains luminous, amazingly youthful, a much-married superwoman known for her lifelong dedication to high style, pure foodstuffs, and good sex.

PRIMARY SOURCE: *Swanson on Swanson,* by Gloria Swanson (Random House, 1980).

★*BEERY, WALLACE*   Gruff, heavy-set character actor, Gloria's first husband. They eloped on her 17th birthday. She thought the marriage license would be "a ticket to heaven," but her wedding night turned out to be a form of hell, with Beery literally raping his virgin bride. "I had only managed to be brutalized in pitch blackness by a man who whispered filth in my ear while he ripped me almost in two." Within weeks, Gloria became pregnant. One night Beery brought her some "medicine" to ease her cramps. She awoke in a hospital, having miscarried, and learned later that her husband's medicine was a powerful poison to induce abortion. That ended the brief marriage.

★*DAVEY, WILLIAM*   Fifth husband. An affable, well-groomed, rich young man who in 1945 proposed to Gloria on very short acquaintance. She accepted and soon discovered he was an alcoholic. Annoyed with her attempts to steer him to Alcoholics Anonymous, he packed his bags and left. The marriage lasted just over a month.

★*DE LA FALAISE, HENRI, MARQUIS*   "A gallant French nobleman, the kind every American woman dreams about." She met him in France in 1924 and they agreed they belonged together in holy matrimony. A couple of problems, though—she was still married to Somborn (see below) but was pregnant by Henri. Knowing that having a child so soon after her marriage would ruin her career, Gloria decided to abort—the day *after* the wedding. One day "my gorgeous marquis lifted me to the very pinnacle of joy," and the next, she was plunged into an "abyss of despair." The surgery gave her blood poisoning and nearly cost her her life. The Marquise returned to Hollywood, where she went on to produce movies as well as star in them. He felt out of it. Especially when Gloria took up with Joseph P. Kennedy. They divorced in 1930 but remained friends.

★*DUFTY, WILLIAM*   Miss Swanson's sixth and current husband. They met at a conference on cancer research; she admonished him not to put sugar in his coffee. He smiled. Years later, in 1965, they became friends, sharing a keen interest in nutrition. Dufty wrote a book, *Sugar Blues,* citing the evils of sugar consumption, and Gloria accompanied him on a promotional tour. He finally popped the question. She demurred until he said he wanted to *take care of her.* "The words traveled through me like lightning, warming as they went." They were married quietly in 1976, just before he turned 60 and she turned 77.

★*FARMER, MICHAEL*   A moody Irish playboy. She met Farmer on his yacht off the coast of France. "Some Black Irish playboy tips his yachting cap to me once in the moonlight—and bingo! I'm pregnant!" She wasn't so sure about making it legal, but he convinced her. Their daughter Michelle was born in 1932. Tired of hat tricks, Gloria divorced Farmer in 1934. Her fourth husband.

★*KENNEDY, JOSEPH P.*   Banker, businessman, film distributor, etc., father of John F., Robert, and Edward Kennedy, etc. Business brought them together. Kennedy, Gloria, and her husband Henri went to Palm Beach, Fla., to talk over the financing of a film she wanted to produce. Quite unexpectedly one day Kennedy appeared at her door, "in his white flannels and argyle sweater," and after staring at her wordlessly for a full minute or more, he attacked her in the manner of "a roped horse, rough, arduous, racing to be free. After a hasty climax he lay beside me, stroking my hair." Somehow, Gloria knew that "this strange man *owned me.*" Throughout their long affair she lived in fear of becoming pregnant; Kennedy wanted to have a child by Gloria, and he pointed out to her that in an entire year his wife hadn't become pregnant either, which was proof that he had been "faithful" to her. Toward the end of 1929 Gloria was visited by Cardinal O'Connell, one of the highest officials of the Catholic Church. He told her there was no way that Kennedy, as a Catholic, could be at peace with his faith and continue the relationship with Gloria. She never found out who sent the Cardinal to her, but was told it *wasn't* Joe himself.

★*LE ROCQUE, ROD* Valentino-type leading man ("he was taller than Rudy") with whom Gloria starred in *Society Scandal*. In ten years of movie making, this was the first time her love scenes were *real.* "Within three days I was in love, within a week Rod proposed." Then he turned surly about Gloria's spending so much time with others; they decided to remain "just friends."

★*MARSHALL, HERBERT* British actor. Within a week of their meeting, Gloria and "Bart" Marshall were in love; "I could no more have prevented it happening than I could have blown out a klieg light in one small breath. . . . Beside him, all the other cultivated men I had ever known seemed just a bit coarse." Actually, Marshall was too cultivated, so "overly docile" he could not bring himself to divorce his wife back in London, and Gloria agreed they should end the relationship.

★*NEILAN, MARSHALL ("MICKEY")* Director who helmed most of Mary Pickford's movies. Young, handsome, and popular, he came along just as Gloria got engaged to Somborn. Mickey vowed he'd marry her himself one day, meanwhile they would each have other partners. After her divorce from Somborn, Gloria ran into Mickey in Paris, and "he waltzed me into my first real love affair." As it turned out, they were never free to marry at the same time, but, "I would go right on loving him; for that, there was no help."

★*SCHIRMER, GUSTAVE* Heir to the music-publishing firm. A "dear friend" of Gloria's, who asked her to marry him many times. Through him she learned that she couldn't be dishonest when it came to love.

★*SOMBORN, HERBERT* President of Equity Pictures Corp., Gloria's second husband. She was 20, he twice that; she was impressed by his serious manner, but "I felt no strong passion for him, he had given me no cause." They married, and Gloria gave birth to her daughter Gloria (1920). Herbert decided to take charge of their business affairs, but she

wound up paying all the bills. She hadn't loved Herbert, they didn't have any fun, she had married him for security, and he wound up being the least secure person in her life.

★*WALSH, RAOUL* Veteran Hollywood director of macho films, Gloria's director and co-star in '20s version of *Sadie Thompson* based on the Maugham classic *Rain*. When Walsh first told her the story, Gloria sniffed: "You mean they kicked this Sadie What's-her-name out of San Francisco for whoring? Why, that's ridiculous. Whoring is a national pastime." She was his kind of woman, albeit married at the time to the Marquis.

MISCELLANY

★*BUSHMAN, FRANCIS X.* Early screen star. Young Miss Swanson was sitting in the studio wardrobe department when Mr. Bushman came in and casually put his hand on her right knee. "She slapped him and they didn't exchange a word."

★*CONWAY, JACK* Director of Gloria's first major film, *Smoke*, in 1917. She developed a "serious crush." Gently, Conway told her that his wife was "a jealous, vindictive woman," and an affair with him could only damage Gloria's career.

★*GARTZ, CRANEY* Cynical young millionaire; 18-year-old Gloria was impressed with how much he knew, but they were always arguing and he was always pressing her to run away with him. She couldn't—too busy. "But nobody could dance like Craney Gartz."

★*MENOCAL, MARIO* Ex-President of Cuba. During a visit to Havana in 1924, Gloria received a rather pornographic note, along with two cut rubies, from a mysterious "Señor X." She learned it was from the same Señor Menocal who was her official host. "I guess in Havana, an actress—*any* actress—is simply considered a prostitute." Menocal had no hard feelings re her rejection.

★*PARMALEE, LIVINGSTON, JR.* The first boy who ever kissed Gloria Swanson. She was 15, they danced at a party, and then, "with his buttons scraping the front of my dress, he kissed me on the mouth." Later that evening

Gloria told a girlfriend that she thought she was going to have a baby: "All I know is, something powerful happened. I'm sure you don't have a baby *every* time you kiss someone . . . only when you kiss a certain person a certain way at a certain time of the month. . . . Anyway, I don't care. If it means marrying Livingston I will." Gloria didn't marry Livingston; she went to Hollywood and learned all the things Mother never told her.

TAYLOR, ELIZABETH
(b. 1932)

Former child star who grew up to be the most beautiful girl in the world and an indestructibly glamorous woman. From *Lassie Come Home* in 1943 to her smashing Broadway success in *The Little Foxes* in 1981, the life and work of Elizabeth Taylor have been a saga of sex, illness, broken marriages, scandal, and heartbreak that any tragedienne might envy. Liz, however, persists in playing the Taylor story as a romantic comedy—the famous violet eyes remain bright, her raucous guttersnipe humor irrepressible. Through seven marriages (two with Richard Burton, after a tumultuous courtship that rocked several continents) and childbirth and frequent surgery for a plague of ailments, Taylor always seems to come back swinging. The extent of that swinging was not generally known, for she used to insist she married every man she slept with. A recent biography suggests that the Senator's wife wasn't telling *quite* all, though it seems dubious that the flamboyant superstar's indiscretions, at home or abroad, past or future, would surprise a world grown accustomed to Taylorgate revelations.

PRIMARY SOURCE: *Elizabeth Taylor: The Last Star*, by Kitty Kelley (Simon and Schuster, 1981).

★*BURTON, RICHARD* Celebrated actor and veteran of many previous affairs, but none with anyone "so fucking famous . . . she knocks Khrushchev off the bloody front page." Le scandale between Burton (then 37 and married to Sybil) and Elizabeth (in her fourth marriage, at 30, to Eddie Fisher) began, in Rome, on the set of *Cleopatra* in 1962. After headline-producing breakups, suicide attempts, reconciliations, and, finally, divorces (she from Eddie, he from Sybil), Liz and Dick were wed on March 15, 1964. He had drunk himself silly by 10:00 A.M. that fateful day and when Elizabeth was late for the ceremony, Burton bellowed, *"Isn't that fat little tart here yet?"* In their nearly eleven years together the Burtons lived like rajahs, spending a fortune on jewels, villas, hotel suites, cars, yachts, private jets; they traveled constantly, accompanied by children and unhousebroken dogs. Of the several movies they made together, *Who's Afraid of Virginia Woolf?* may have been the most accurate mirror of their public private lives. They laughed, fought, made love, and drank together. In time he couldn't handle the booze, she couldn't handle his extramarital dalliance. Divorced in 1974, they continued to yearn for one another. Elizabeth proposed that they remarry in Africa, "in the bush," she said quixotically, "amongst our kind." Commenting on the occasion in October 1975, the *Boston Globe* reported, "Sturm has remarried Drang and all is right with the world." But it wasn't right with the Burtons. They were divorced again the next year—he married Suzy Hunt, she wed John Warner. *However*, both Liz and Dick split from their respective spouses in late 1981, and were reunited—with strobe lights flashing—in early 1982 at her 50th birthday party in London. Do stay tuned. (See also BURTON listing.)

★*CLIFT, MONTGOMERY* Elizabeth and Monty certainly looked like the perfect lovers in *A Place in the Sun*. Whether their intense, long-term real-life relationship actually included sex is debatable. As Elizabeth reportedly told Truman Capote, "Well, one doesn't always fry the fish one wants to fry. Some of the men I've really liked didn't like women."

However, Monty and Elizabeth did profess an undying love, each always there when the other was in need. (See also CLIFT listing.)

★DARMANIN, PETER   Advertising executive from Malta. Claims he gave comfort to Liz while Burton was getting to know Suzy. It happened in Gstaad, and lasted seven weeks, "But it was like seven months—no, seven years—because we were with each other every moment. She needs that kind of loving."

★DONEN, STANLEY   He was directing Elizabeth in *Love Is Better Than Ever* at the end of her marriage to Nicky Hilton, "and their affair was no secret to anyone on the set." Donen's wife filed for a divorce, making Liz, at 19, suddenly a "notorious woman."

★FISHER, EDDIE   She was Mike Todd's young widow; he was Todd's best friend. Taylor told one of her later loves that after a decent interval, she and Eddie had spent four days and nights in bed together, "and that's how Eddie got her over her grief." They were wed in May 1959, with the bride proclaiming the honeymoon should last "thirty or forty years." It was late 1961 when they got to Rome, and *Cleopatra*, and Burton. Fisher went back to the nightclub circuit. When asked why he opened his act with "A Rivederci Roma," he said, "What did you expect, 'Take Me Out to the Ball Game'?" (See also FISHER listing.)

★HILTON, "NICKY"   Son of Conrad Hilton, chairman of the Hilton Hotel Corp., 23-year-old Nicky lived on a huge Beverly Hills estate that absolutely awed Elizabeth and her ambitious mom. Liz said there was "no doubt in her mind" that Nicky was the man she wanted to be with the rest of her life. For the wedding, on May 6, 1950, MGM (which was then releasing *Father of the Bride* starring Elizabeth) commissioned Edith Head to design dresses for the bride and attendants. Over 3,000 hysterical fans waited outside the church to see the happy couple off on their European honeymoon—which turned into disaster, with Nicky spending most nights in gambling casinos. "The thing that hurt her most is when he began refusing to go to bed with her." The marriage, Elizabeth's first, lasted exactly seven months. MGM demanded the return of the $3,500 wedding dress but presumably let Liz keep the shoes. She still had *miles* to go.

★LERNER, MAX   The columnist. He was 57 in 1961 when he met Elizabeth, and when, it is written, they began their startling affair during her supposedly "happiest times" as Eddie Fisher's bride. Lerner and Taylor, "the perfect complement of The Brain and The Body," continued whatever they did together while Liz was in California convalescing from her tracheotomy. Lerner considered marrying her, but reflected, "In the end I realized . . . she would use me the way a beautiful woman uses an older man—as a front while she goes on fucking everything in sight."

★LOEW, ARTHUR JR.   Theater-chain heir. She dated him after Hilton, again after Todd; considered him a close enough friend to take charge of her kids while she went for R&R—secretly meeting Fisher in New York. (See also LOEW listing.)

★PAWLEY, WILLIAM D.   Multimillionaire, 28 when he met 17-year-old Elizabeth, offering her her first serious proposal and first diamond—a 3.5-carat solitaire. But he also demanded that she give up her career in movies to be his wife exclusively. She agreed, then George Stevens asked her to star with Clift in *A Place in the Sun*. Bill Pawley did not marry for nearly twenty-five years.

★SINATRA, FRANK   Biographer Kelley offers no direct evidence, but refers several times to the fact that she *had* had an affair with Sinatra. Presumably while married to Mike Wilding. (See also SINATRA listing.)

★TODD, MIKE   Hollywood romantics prefer to believe that if Todd had lived, Liz would still be married to him. For sure, they were temperamentally in tune, loving to fight as much as they loved to kiss and make up. Todd said, "She's been on a milk toast diet all her life with men. But me—I'm red meat." Liz thought so, anyway. In a reporter's presence she once yelled at Mike to come back to bed with her immediately: "I want to fuck you *this minute!*" For an engagement ring, Todd gave Taylor a 29.7-carat diamond that "looked like an ice cube," and that was just the beginning. He had tons of lobster, cracked crab, champagne, and white orchids and gladioli flown in for their Mexican wedding in February 1957. The bride was several months pregnant (with Liza) and *mucha boracha* at the ceremony. Just over a year later, one of the few times they were separated, Mike was aboard his private plane, *The Lucky Liz*, when it crashed in the New Mexico desert, killing everyone aboard. (See also TODD listing.)

★*WARNER, SENATOR JOHN* Elizabeth's sixth husband, her seventh marriage. It all began when he was her blind date at a Bicentennial bash in Washington, D.C. The next day he took her to his Virginia farm—acquired, along with a hefty lifetime income, when he divorced Catherine Mellon of *the* Philadelphia Mellons—where they spent the night. Elizabeth fell in love. She and John got engaged there, in a mad moment on a rain-swept hill, and chose that very spot for their wedding on December 4, 1976. As Liz walked toward him, clad in lavender and gray, he "startled everyone by loudly summoning his herds of cattle with shouts of 'Hoo-ee! Hoo-ee!'" As a wedding present, Farmer Warner gave his bride a corn silo, painted blue, on which was drawn a heart saying "John Loves Elizabeth." The farmer's wife gave her husband two cows and a bull. Taylor gamely campaigned alongside Republican Warner (though she still claimed to be a Democrat) and stood proudly by John's side in January 1979, when he was sworn in as a U.S. Senator. An event which prompted one wag to remark: "Looks like Virginia just elected the three biggest boobs in America." Warner's Senate career, however, seems to be standing the test of time. Not so the marriage. At the end of 1981, after five years as man and wife, Elizabeth and John announced their separation. Since then she has been seeing other men—including her ever-popular ex, Richard Burton. While insisting she won't

marry *anyone*, ever again, one never knows what Miss Taylor will do next. Do one?

★*WILDING, MICHAEL* British actor and Liz's second husband. Young Ms. Taylor admitted *she* proposed to Wilding, and even bought her own engagement ring—so sure was she that things would work out. At the time, reluctant Michael was also in love with Marlene Dietrich, who, at 47, was eight years older than he. But Elizabeth pointed out that at 19, she'd be able to give Michael the children he never had. Their wedding was held in 1952, in London; "She wore a dove-gray suit. He wore an air of surprise." Sons Michael Jr. and Christopher were born, and in 1956 (after Wilding's Hollywood career "had turned to ashes"), the couple divorced. From then on they became the best of friends, remaining so until Wilding's death in 1979.

★*WYNBERG, HENRY* Used car salesman who met Liz in the throes of her first divorce from Burton. When friends expressed their doubts about Wynberg, she said she knew he didn't have a "big mind," but that he took care of her, "and he fucks me beautifully."

★*ZAHEDI, ARDESHIR* Former Iranian ambassador to Washington. During her *second* split from Burton, Taylor became captivated with the dashing ambassador. They began inviting each other to gala events and "three weeks later, after he sent a chartered jet for her," the love affair began. Apparently Liz moved into the Iranian embassy in D.C. for a while, not wanting to leave until she was Mrs. Zahedi. The Shah wouldn't hear of it.

MISCELLANY

★*BRISKIN, TED* He was Betty Hutton's ex when he dated the former Mrs. Nicky Hilton.

★*BROOKS, RICHARD* Director of *The Last Time I Saw Paris*, a piece of romantic fluff with Liz and Van Johnson. Richard fell in love with her, "and killed himself to get a good performance out of her," later directed her more successfully in *Cat on a Hot Tin Roof*.

★*DAVIS, GLENN* Elizabeth's first big romance. He was an All-American football player, a soldier about to ship out to Korea. It was a summer romance, he says, "with family barbecues and touch football on the beach." Other than a little necking, Davis swears he never touched 16-year-old Elizabeth—though he did buy her an engagement ring she never got. When Davis returned from the wars, Liz was already dating Pawley.

★*HUGHES, HOWARD* An offer of $1 million wasn't nearly enough to get Elizabeth to marry Howard Hughes, she said. In their few dates together, "He was an out-and-out bore . . . and he needed a bath." It was shortly after her well-publicized "romance" with Howard, however, that ex-husband Nicky said, "Every man should have the opportunity of sleeping with Elizabeth Taylor—and at the rate she's going, every man will."

★*JOHANNSON, INGEMAR* Heavyweight boxer. Max Lerner took Elizabeth to the Johannson-Patterson fight and she expressed admiration for Johannson but said, "Don't get me wrong about Ingemar. I'm not fucking him." But Lerner thinks she was.

★*McCLORY, DEVIN* One of Mike Todd's assistants, who dated Elizabeth before Mike did.

★*MOFFAT, IVAN* Associate producer who took Liz out après Hilton.

★*ONASSIS, ARISTOTLE.* Seeking revenge for Burton's dalliance, Elizabeth flew to Rome to have dinner with Ari. The place was stormed by paparazzi wanting to get shots of "Jacqueline Kennedy's husband with Richard Burton's wife."

★*STEVENS, GEORGE JR.* Son of the director, another sometimes date.

TIERNEY, GENE
(b. 1920)

1940s dream girl and former New York socialite, with Otto Preminger's provocative *Laura* (1944) as the glittering jewel in her crown. That she had genuine talent was also clear in *Leave Her to Heaven* (1946) and *Whirlpool* (1949), though on many other oc-

casions her creamy complexion and unmistakable class were used to dress up some pretty empty film frippery. Tierney's 1979 autobiography spelled out the sad tale of marital woes, personal tragedy, and a nervous breakdown that kept her out of movies for years. When last seen, she was still a breathtaking beauty, and her memoirs inspire the piquant notion that she *might* have been JFK's First Lady.

PRIMARY SOURCE: *Gene Tierney: Self-Portrait*, by Gene Tierney (Wyden, 1979; Berkley, 1980).

★*CASSINI, OLEG* Russian-born fashion designer. Gene's first husband. He was a 28-year-old divorced man-about-town when 20-year-old Gene met him at a Hollywood party. "I thought he was the most dangerous-looking character I had ever seen—dangerous in a seductive way." He was also the exact opposite of everything Gene's parents told her a husband should be: "He wasn't a Yale man. He hadn't even gone to Harvard. On top of that, he was a foreigner." Gene and Oleg eloped in 1941; in 1943, they had a daughter, Daria, who was born deaf and retarded, adding a strain to their already shaky marriage. They split but reconciled and had another daughter, Christina, in 1948, before the final split and divorce.

★*HUGHES, HOWARD* He zeroed in on Gene when she first arrived in Hollywood in 1940. She fell hard for Hughes; "he was sweet and quiet and almost aesthetic-looking." However, Howard wasn't marriage-minded, and Gene was. The problem, reflected Gene, was "I don't think Howard could have loved anything that didn't have a motor in it." When she pulled out of the relationship he remained her friend, as was his style, casually performing many favors for Gene and her family over the years. But she did not date Hughes after the time the jealous Cassini, then her estranged husband, angrily confronted Hughes, demanding to know his intentions toward Gene. (See also HUGHES listing.)

★*KENNEDY, JOHN FITZGERALD* In 1946, still wearing his navy lieutenant's uniform, Kennedy visited Hollywood and the set of

Gene's movie *Dragonwyck*. While playing a scene she turned "and found myself staring into what I thought were the most perfect blue eyes I had ever seen on a man. . . . He smiled at me. My reaction was right out of a ladies' romance novel. Literally, my heart skipped." They began seeing each other; before long she was telling family and friends she had met a young man who would be President someday. "That was his goal. He talked about it in a way that was unself-conscious." Gene recalls that gifts and flowers were not Kennedy's style: "He gave you his time, his interest. He knew the strength of the phrase 'what do *you* think.'" One day at lunch, out of the blue, he said, "You know, Gene, I can't marry you." At the end of lunch, Gene said in small voice, "Bye bye, Jack." She, of course, was a divorced woman, and an Episcopalian, not a proper wife for a Catholic Kennedy. Their ill-fated romance was "sweet," says Gene, and she remembers Jack as "a serious young man with a dream." (See also KENNEDY listing.)

★*KHAN, PRINCE ALY* Gene was on the verge of her mental breakdown in 1953 when she became involved with Aly. In fact, her sister considers the romance was a symptom of the illness to come: "She meant that he was not the kind of man I would have picked out if I had been well and secure," says Gene. She found Aly "very kind . . . one of those rare men who do not force themselves on you," and they had a wonderful summer traveling around Europe. "We swam together, sailed together, danced and laughed together." She also acted as hostess at his many parties, noting it was "easy to be dazzled by that role . . . greeting his rich and important and sometimes royal friends." The Prince had just divorced Rita Hayworth, and his father, the Aga Khan, was not eager to have another movie star in the family, so the romance between the Prince and this show girl ended. Tierney recalls, "He was an intelligent man who dissipated his powers by being a playboy." (See also KHAN listing.)

★*LEE, HOWARD* Texas oil man. Gene's second husband (and former husband of Hedy Lamarr). They met in 1958 in Aspen on a blind date of sorts. At first Howard was reluctant, claiming he'd had "his fill of movie stars." But he turned out to be kind and gentle, "and not put off or overly curious" about the fact that she had been in a mental hospital. Any qualms Gene had about being a *burden* to someone began to fade. In fact, Howard insisted that if she married him, "it would free my mind forever." Not quite; Gene signed herself into another mental hospital for a while. But Howard waited and they became husband and wife in 1960. Still are, living in Houston.

MISCELLANY

★*ABBOTT, GEORGE* Producer of Gene's first New York play; she was 17, he 53, and by the time the play reached Broadway, "I knew I was developing a whale of a crush on him." On their first night out, both nervous, he didn't know quite what to do, so he bought her a bag of hard candy. At last he blurted, "Gene, I could never marry you. In years to come you'll want to dance. And I won't feel like dancing." He would remain one of Tierney's "true friends."

★*MORLEY, ROBERT* The British actor was a casual date when Gene was 18 and first on Broadway. She had a weakness for caviar, which he used to tease her about. But one day at lunch, he ordered a *salad bowl* filled with caviar. "Now, my dear girl, you may have all your heart desires."

★*POWER, TYRONE* Friends and co-stars in *The Razor's Edge* in 1946. Power tried hard to promote a romance, according to Gene, sending little notes of endearment and such gifts as a silk scarf with the word "love" embroidered on it. Gene was so wrapped up in Jack Kennedy at the time, she almost didn't notice Ty's attentions. "Ty was warm and considerate. He had a beautiful face. But I could not fall in love with Ty Power—having met Jack Kennedy."

TODD, MIKE
(1907–1958)

Flamboyant Broadway showman who did nothing in a small way, and was famous for saying, "You're not rich unless you owe at least a million." Todd owed plenty, made plenty, spent most of it, and tried everything. He won a 1956 Academy Award with the lavish spectacle *Around the World in 80 Days,* the only picture he ever personally produced, which was the opening gun in his plan to take Hollywood by storm. He took Elizabeth Taylor, made numerous friends and enemies, and gave the Todd-AO wide-screen system his name before his death in a plane crash.

PRIMARY SOURCES: *Linda: My Own Story,* by Linda Christian (Crown, 1962); *Marlene: The Life of Marlene Dietrich,* by Charles Higham (Norton, 1977); *Scarlett O'Hara's Younger Sister, or, My Lively Life in and out of Hollywood,* by Evelyn Keyes (Lyle Stuart, 1977); *Elizabeth Taylor: The Last Star,* by Kitty Kelley (Simon and Schuster, 1981).

★*CHRISTIAN, LINDA* Todd could not resist a beautiful dame, and she *was* that. They met on a transcontinental flight, with Todd coming on in his usual suave fashion: "Stick with me, babe, I'll make you the most loved and most wanted woman in the world." Linda said it was the most original monologue she'd ever encountered. Todd's pursuit continued on the ground; he offered to put her in movies, he wanted to give her jewels and paintings—all of which she refused. And "he began to get the point," says Linda. She generally preferred people as beautiful as she was. (See also CHRISTIAN listing.)

★*DIETRICH, MARLENE* A lavish spender herself, Marlene admired that trait in Todd. "Wouldn't it be wonderful if everyone spent money like Mike?" Todd was on the verge of falling deeply in love with Marlene, but she told him to cool it, and left behind, as a souvenir, a delicious cameo in *Around the World in 80 Days.* (See also DIETRICH listing.)

★*KEYES, EVELYN* In her account of their tempestuous romance, during the early '50s, Evelyn notes that she wasn't thrilled at first by Mike's looks, or that "monstrous cigar." She did laud his generous stream of little surprise gifts, "the see-through bag covered with enormous rhinestones, and with a card reading, *Happy Arbor Day to the love of my life—your Mike.*" Things got better with "a glorious choker, an inch and a half wide, of solid diamonds. Plus five thousand shares in some venture of Bing Crosby Enterprises. I took it as a sign of true love." Their love withered because of Todd's unreasonable jealousy, and constant quizzing about his predecessors in bed. Keyes recalls, "He found himself a running joke—'If I didn't make friends with your ex-husbands and lovers, who would I talk to?'" He ultimately struck up a conversation with Elizabeth Taylor and that was that. (See also KEYES listing.)

★*TAYLOR, ELIZABETH* According to Todd's onetime fiancée Evelyn Keyes, Elizabeth was "everything Mike professed not to care for . . . she was the epitome of movie star in dress, attitude and demands." Yet showman Todd and spoiled movie star Taylor hit it off like gangbusters—despite the twenty-seven-year difference in their ages. Liz claims he first fell in love with the way she could "coo, gurgle and chirp." He was not so delicate, calling her things like "my fat little Jewish broad, Lizzie Schwartzkopf." Mike and Liz got married in a lavish ceremony in Mexico in February 1957, with Eddie Fisher and Debbie Reynolds as best man and matron of honor. Their made-in-heaven relationship thrived on fighting and making up, and they did both in public as much as in private. Liz had their daughter Liza by Caesarian on August 6, 1957, and when the doctors told Mike she should not risk childbirth again, he okayed a tubal ligation to prevent pregnancy. When told of the operation as she awoke from the anesthesia, Liz said it was "the greatest shock of my life." But that was far overshadowed by her next shock—Todd's death in a plane crash in New Mexico in March 1958. (See also TAYLOR listing.)

TRUDEAU, MARGARET

(b. 1947)

How does a failed flower child become the First Lady of Canada? That is the fairly remarkable tale of Margaret Trudeau, daughter of a former Minister of Fisheries, who left the government to make his fortune in the cement business. Of Scottish descent, raised in Vancouver, young Margaret Sinclair attended university in her hometown, dated a football player, dabbled in student activism during the volatile '60s, later became what she calls "an established part of the North African hippy circus." And still later, Margaret became a controversial political Cinderella who made headlines while letting the world know, as she states in her autobiography, "that there was a real human being inside the Barbie doll."

PRIMARY SOURCES: *Beyond Reason*, by Margaret Trudeau (Paddington, 1979; Pocket Books, 1980); *Consequences*, by Margaret Trudeau, copyright Margaret Trudeau Enterprises, Ltd. (Seal Books [Canada], 1982).

★*AMERICAN FRIEND* During a restless period in her marriage to Pierre Trudeau, Margaret went to New York and fell in love. "It was sudden, it was fantastic. He was a high-powered American, a charming southerner whose name was of no importance." Well! His name *might* be important, especially if it's Yankee Senator Edward "Ted" Kennedy, as "rumor" would have it—a rumor repeated by Margaret herself in the second volume of her memoirs. Are the rumors correct? "That's a secret I intend to keep," she writes. In the first book Margaret recalled that hubby, Pierre, became suspicious about her N.Y. fling and asked if she'd been faithful. In reply she seized a kitchen knife and ran out into the snow, "tearing off my clothes to find a bare spot" for the lethal blade. "O.K.," she screamed at Pierre, "O.K., I've fallen in love." "You're sick," he answered. Maggie eventually realized that her American lover *(whoever* he may be) had

not been directly responsible for the breakup of her marriage, "I had simply used him to escape my own unhappiness."

★*BUSINESSMAN* Another American, "who groomed his crinkly hair with a blow dryer." He invited the Prime Minister's estranged wife for a weekend in Las Vegas; she pleaded nothing to wear. "Charmer that he was, he presented me with the best Valentine's present that ever came my way—*carte blanche* at my favorite store, Ungaro's." But the romance was shattered once they got to Vegas, in a "bloody and brutal" fight.

★*JOHNSON, JIMMY* A Canadian lawyer, businessman, "terrific skier," and Margaret's current no. 1 beau, at least at the time she wrote *Consequences*. Their relationship works, she feels, because Jimmy is about her age, also separated, also a parent to three children. They talk about getting married when they're, oh, about fifty, but meanwhile, Mrs. Trudeau has no plans to divorce her husband.

★*LEWIS, YVES* On holiday with her family in Tahiti, young Margaret met Yves, a handsome Frenchman whose father created the Club Méditerranée. But Yves was the apotheosis of that world—a rich hippy who introduced her to pot smoking, mysticism, and "the quest for freedom." She went the whole route, frizzing her hair, starving herself on a macrobiotic diet, etc. "I wanted to bake whole-wheat bread and talk love and peace, but Yves Lewis, my liberated lover, was unimpressed." When she presented herself to him in San Francisco, to be his live-in flower child, he turned her down. Yet, for years, everything she did was judged by whether Yves would approve. They eventually lost contact; Margaret learned in the late 1970s that he had committed suicide.

★*LOVERS IN MOROCCO* At 19, Margaret spent seven months "on a hippy trail" in Morocco. "I smoked dope with the best of them and came to love it; I shed all my bourgeois belongings and came home with nothing but a small knapsack." But, while there, she behaved in a way some people might call promiscuous, "though it was probably no wilder than the life of a girl my age in Pennsylvania . . . I finally learned to treat men as brothers, while enjoying making love to them in a way my puritan upbringing had not allowed me to consider possible." Her adventures in Morocco included getting so ill she almost died, taking her first LSD trip, and opening a hostel—somewhat like a boardinghouse—for international hippy drifters.

★*NEVINS, BRUCE* President of the Perrier Company; they met on a plane to Paris in 1977 and dated regularly in New York. "A strong, big-shouldered man, with the warmest brown eyes a woman could hope for. . . . We had Sunday brunches at the Tavern on the Green in Central Park, cozy dinners at Elaine's . . . It was months before I realized with sadness that Bruce is a confirmed lifelong bachelor."

★*NICHOLSON, JACK* It was the summer of '78 in London; she was writing *Beyond Reason*, he was starring in *The Shining*. They met at a party and Margaret knew in a trice that Nicholson was "the first real rival to Pierre. . . . It was an exciting moment . . . and I wanted Jack." She *got* him a few nights later, after another party, in the back seat of his chauffeur-driven car. "I discovered just how much room there is in the back of a Daimler," she recalls. Thereafter, they spent a lot of time together, even though she awoke each morning to hear Jack on the phone ordering flowers for his true love, Anjelica Huston, back in Los Angeles. Then Jack broke the dreaded news that Anjelica would arrive in London the very next day. "We made love all night . . . the episode had shaken me, but I was not broken. For one thing, I was making good progress on my book. . . . I wanted him badly, but I didn't *need* him." (See also NICHOLSON listing.)

★*O'NEAL, RYAN* They met briefly in New York, then on her arrival at the Beverly Hills Hotel a phone message awaited: "Mr. O'Neal will be picking you up for dinner at seven-thirty." Margaret calls her fling with Ryan "a one-week stand of Hollywood romance . . . a rather sordid affair." She actually thought him

a bit shallow, but they did have fun. However, at the end of the week, when she went banging on Ryan's door, she was told to go away— as Ryan's son was visiting. "Hitching up my short red leather skirt, I scaled the incredibly high wall around his house. . . . Ryan was far from pleased, though he soon started preening under my insistent attentions." Margaret admits that she went over the wall in more ways than one with O'Neal, "carried away by the Hollywood nights and my image of myself as a sort of female Errol Flynn, with Ryan as my leading man." She soon concluded she'd had enough of "Ryan's conceit, his self-obsession. He was too much for me." Perhaps the feeling was mutual. (See also O'NEAL listing.)

★*SULLIVAN, TOMMY* He represented something new for Margaret. As a rock musician "he was offering me a glimpse of another culture, one laced with drugs and sex, just at a time when I was looking for ways of escaping the increasingly painful reality of having left Pierre." She and Tommy tasted the high life in New York and London. She was dazzled by his attitude toward money, the way he kept his jeans pockets stuffed with hundred-dollar bills; "We had endless champagne, more caviar than I could eat." And, of course, all that cocaine: "coke to get me up, Valium to bring me down again." She was already disenchanted with Tommy when Jack Nicholson drove up in his Daimler.

★*TRUDEAU, PIERRE* Prime Minister of Canada. She was taking the sun on a raft in the waters off Tahiti, when this Pierre Someone-or-other swam up to rest and chat. She remembered him as a nice, middle-aged chap. He was among the first to ask her for a date on her return from Morocco. She never stopped to wonder what an unsuitable couple they were: "One cerebral, clearheaded, rational, devout and almost 50; the other confused, scatty, certain of wanting to avoid all social responsibility, and barely 20." Nevertheless, she knew from that first date "that I wanted this man for myself." So, the handsome statesman and the scatterbrained, pot-smoking hippy married on March 4, 1971.

Margaret's rebellion began in 1974, and continued for three more years before the couple formally announced their separation. In the interim, Pierre had gotten Maggie to stop smoking dope (for a while), taken her around the world, and introduced her to some of the most important political figures of the twentieth century. He had also fathered her three sons—Justin, Sacha and Micha. Margaret says her overriding problem was that "no amount of careful schooling, no amount of anxious warnings by Pierre, could ever really have prepared me for the role of a prime minister's wife."

MISCELLANY

★*AHMED* The drug king of Tangier, one of her pre-Trudeau adventures. She quickly caught on to his game—when he began to invite her to dinner, and offer her clothes and jewelry. He also wanted to give her a villa, set her up in business, providing all the drugs she needed, while she *entertained* potential buyers. "Ahmed had to be fought. I saw it as a mission to go around warning new arrivals about him."

★*CASTRO, FIDEL* Cuban Premier. On a state visit, Maggie quickly discovered that Castro loves women. He paid her the most outrageous compliment: "You know, my eyes are not very strong, so every day to make them stronger I force myself to look at the sun. I find it very hard. But do you know what I find even harder? That is, to look into the blue of your eyes." The Canadian Prime Minister's wife *loved* Cuba.

★*CHARLES, PRINCE* Margaret arranged the placecards so that Charles would be her dinner companion at a state function in honor of the Royal Family. As they stepped on to the dance floor she caught him peering down the décolletage of her Valentino dress, Charles blushed and laughingly admitted that his father always told him to look into his partner's eyes when she was wearing a low-cut dress. Replied Margaret: "Feast ye while ye may. If I wasn't three months pregnant, there would be nothing to see."

★*NIXON, RICHARD* He was then the U.S. President. Margaret was seated next to him at a banquet. She was in awe, didn't know what to say. Finally, Nixon turned to her and "embarked on a tedious story about how his pandas had never mated." Margaret found herself still in awe. "The only conversation I have now had with the President of the United States is on the sex life of pandas."

★*ROLLING STONES* The headlines read: PRIME MINISTER'S WIFE AND ROLLING STONES. . . . MARGARET IN HOTEL CORRIDOR IN WHITE PAJAMAS. . . . SEX ORGY IN CANADIAN PRIME MINISTER'S SUITE!!! It was definitely Margaret's most publicized post-Trudeau "affair." What really happened, she says, is this: She met the Rolling Stones one night in Toronto and went out to dinner with a couple of them. Then the guys dashed off for an all-night recording session. On their return to the hotel at 6:00 A.M., the entire group invited themselves to Maggie's room for a game of dice. "Does it matter what currency?" she asked Mick, "since, rather surprisingly, I had a pile of yen with me." They settled down to drink, play dice, smoke a little hash. "It was fun." At 9:00 A.M., everyone departed to his or her own room to sleep. *C'est tout, c'est tout, vraiment c'est tout*, says Margaret.

TURNER, LANA
(b. 1920)

The fabled "sweater girl" was discovered by Hollywood at 17, allegedly while sipping a soda at Schwab's drugstore. According to a co-worker, Hollywood's definitive blond sexpot "had the morals and the attitudes of a man. If she saw something she wanted, she took it. . . . If she saw a muscular stagehand with tight pants and she liked him, she'd invite him to her dressing room." Lana went to the altar (or equivalent) seven times, making her Hollywood's most-married glamour girl. She once explained: "If they're clever and if they give me the right story, I'll take the bait. Then I get kicked in the teeth again." Her most publicized and tragic affair was with Johnny Stompanato, who was stabbed to death by Lana's teenaged daughter Cheryl.

PRIMARY SOURCE: *Lana, The Public and Private Lives of Miss Turner*, by Joe Morella and Edward Z. Epstein (Citadel, 1971).

★*BARKER, LEX* Socialite, screen *Tarzan*, husband no. 4. They wed in Italy in 1953, a month before Barker's divorce from Arlene Dahl was final. So, Lex and Lana later remarried, legally, in Hollywood. Lana's friends reportedly had a betting pool on how long the marriage would last. Divorce ended it in 1958. At the trial she spoke of Lex's "uncontrollable" temper, and "implied that he belonged back in the trees like the character he portrayed on the screen."

★*BAUTZER, GREG* Super-handsome Hollywood attorney, frequent escort of many famous ladies; Lana's first serious affair. He was *everybody's* first serious affair. (See also BAUTZER listing.)

★*BEY, TURHAN* Exotic star of *Sabu* and such. Lana announced, in September 1945, her plans to marry Bey. A month later, the romance was fini. (See also BEY listing.)

★*CRANE, STEPHEN* Businessman and husband no. 2. After knowing each other less than a month, in July 1942, Steve and Lana eloped to Las Vegas, hitched by the same justice of the peace who had tied the knot for Lana and Artie Shaw. In January 1943, Lana sued Crane for annulment because his divorce from his first wife had not been final. Annulment granted. Later, Lana (already With Child) refused to remarry him and Crane tried suicide. "It's all so terrible and everybody's so unhappy," said Lana. One day before he joined the army, when she was six months pregnant, Steve and Lana exchanged vows once again, "in as drab and shabby a ceremony as was ever performed, in the heat and squalor of Tiajuana." Daughter Cheryl born in July, 1943; her parents divorced in 1944.

★*DANTE, RONALD* A nightclub hypnotist who became Lana's seventh husband after a three-week courtship. Eight months later, in 1969, Lana filed for divorce, claiming Dante had defrauded her of $34,000. The charges were dropped, but she got the divorce.

★*EATON, ROBERT* "A startlingly handsome" thirty-four-year-old, and husband no. 6. It lasted from 1965 to 1969. He later wrote a book, "a work of fiction," called *The Body Brokers*, with a fictional character named Marla, "a 45-year-old movie queen . . . an alcoholic in constant competition with her daughter for the favors of young lovers." Eaton's fictional heroine is a woman "who not only delights in fellatio, but switch-hits, and was once found in bed with another Hollywood glamour queen."

★*GARDNER, AVA* Sultry, raven-haired star of the late '40s and '50s. There are several versions of what *really* happened the night Ava and then-hubby Frank Sinatra had a terrible fight in their Palm Springs home; some say Frankie came home to find Ava and Lana "lying around drinking with not many clothes on." Later, Lana and Ava were set to co-star in a film called *Intimate Friends*. It was canceled. (See also GARDNER listing.)

★*HARTFORD, HUNTINGTON* Much-married millionaire, Lana's occasional date on trips east.

★*HUGHES, HOWARD* Howard and Lana grandly announced they would announce their engagement after a madcap flight from New York to Los Angeles in Hughes's private plane. But on arrival, the brief betrothal was inexplicably over. They made up later, but that old feeling was never the same. (See also HUGHES listing.)

★*HUTTON, ROBERT* Handsome young actor. Walter Winchell once called him "Lana's biggest thrill yet," which became a curious joke to certain Hollywood insiders.

★*LAMAS, FERNANDO* Latin leading man who met Lana as co-star in *Latin Lovers*. Their relationship was described as "spontaneous combustion." Both were still married —Lana to Bob Topping—but after respective divorces, the affair came to an abrupt end at a party at which Lamas flew into a rage over the way Lana danced with Lex Barker. "If you must be intimate with this man," Lamas lambasted Lana, "don't do it in public." Note: Barker was then in the process of divorcing Arlene Dahl who would later marry Lamas, after Lana married Barker. Ah, la ronde, la ronde.

★*MARTIN, TONY* Hollywood's "society" singer. Lana dated him after splitting from Artie Shaw. (Lana told Shaw she was "doing it" with a well-known crooner, who said, she reported, "Boy, can you imagine how many guys out there would like to be in my place right now?")

★*MAY, FRED* Sportsman, horse breeder, rancher, millionaire, and Lana's fifth husband—acquired after the Stompanato affair. They had been quietly dating for months before marrying in November 1961. Lana said to the groom, "I know it's going to be a very happy marriage." And her friends agreed that she'd *finally* made the right choice; "May was handsome, cultured and seemed truly in love with Lana." But he and his star came unhitched in less than a year. Said May to a reporter: "I can't even tell you what caused the rift. It's too bad . . . Real life can't be lived as if it were a movie script."

★*PERO, TAYLOR* A "secretary-companion" and Lana's sometime escort during the breakup of her marriage to Ronald Dante. Pero was her date, for example, at Harold Robbins's Christmas party one year. Also, on occasion, he accompanied her on excursions to a night spot in the San Fernando Valley "frequented by homosexuals."

★*POWER, TYRONE* Swashbuckling matinee idol, said to be *the* love of Lana's life. "The most beautiful couple you'd ever hope to see" made news from the fall of 1946 through the end of 1947, while Power was still married to Annabella. They were expected to announce their engagement when Ty took off on a round-the-world goodwill trip, met Linda Christian in Rome, and later married her. "This is where Lana's self-destructive impulses

took over," whined Louella Parsons. (See also POWER listing.)

★*RICH, BUDDY* Jazz drummer and bandleader. Lana called a surprised friend to say, "Buddy wants to drive to Mexico tonight and get married. What should I do?" She sat this one out.

★*SHAW, ARTIE* "King of Swing" bandleader and Lana's first husband. On her 20th birthday, after being stood up by Greg Bautzer, Lana went out with Artie. On a whim, they flew to Las Vegas and were wed by a justice of the peace. "It was then that I kissed Mr. Shaw for the first time." She called the marriage "my college education," with Artie constantly telling her how ignorant she was. It was all over in just over four months; both went on to take their places among Hollywood's most-married citizens. (See also SHAW listing.)

★*SINATRA, FRANK* Legendary crooner/actor. Frank was "dazzled" by Lana. The two were seen smooching in his car on the MGM lot, for starters. Some observers held Lana responsible for the breakup of Frank's first marriage to Nancy. (See also SINATRA listing.)

★*STOMPANATO, JOHNNY* Smalltime racketeer. Lana met him in 1957 when she was 37, he 29. A flashy dresser with a good physique, Stompanato appeared to be "wildly in love" with Lanita, as he called her, but he became jealous and possessive and began to badger her for money. Lana confided to a chum: "I wonder if the screwing I'm getting is worth the screwing I'm getting." In April 1958, after hearing Stompanato repeatedly threaten her mother ("I'll cut your face up. . . .") during a violent quarrel, Lana's daughter Cheryl entered their bedroom, said, "You don't have to take that, Mother," and plunged a butcher knife into Stompanato's abdomen. A coroner's jury ruled it "justifiable homicide," and adolescent Cheryl was not brought to trial.

★*TALBOT, JOHN ALDEN JR.* New York socialite whose wife named Lana in a divorce suit.

★*TOPPING, HENRY J. ("BOB")* Connecticut millionaire and Lana's third husband. He looked hurt when Lana rejected the large diamond earrings he offered on their very first date. "Well, I *could* just try them on," Lana finally conceded. Lana wore a "gown of cocoa lace over nude satin" at their lavish wedding ceremony in 1948, then she temporarily settled down as a homebody. After two miscarriages, "the Topping-Turner marriage disintegrated fast." They were divorced in 1952, shortly after she was hospitalized with cut wrists in a rumored suicide attempt. She claimed she had injured herself by losing her balance and falling through the shower door.

MISCELLANY

★*CALHOUN, RORY* They dated while she recovered from Turhan Bey.

★*COOPER, JACKIE* One of Lana's earliest Hollywood "dates."

★*DANIELS, BILLY* Singer and celebrated swinger. During her early fame, Lana reportedly made visits to New York, donned "slacks and dark glasses," and made nightly visits to Daniels's Harlem nightclub, the Red Rooster.

★*GARFIELD, JOHN* Lana's hot-blooded co-star in the steamy *The Postman Always Rings Twice.* They experienced "an unmistakable chemistry."

★*JAEGER, CHARLES* ABC network executive who once proposed to Lana. She headed for New York saying, "He is just what I want." Changed her mind.

★*ROONEY, MICKEY* Hollywood's perennial juvenile. Dated Lana when she was a sweet 17 and both were contract players at MGM. "I spent all my time fending off learning and fending off Mickey Rooney."

★*SACHS, MANNY* Record company executive; a fling, after Crane.

★*STACK, ROBERT* Good-looking actor, a frequent escort in the early 1940s.

★*STEWART, JAMES* Easygoing leading man. "They were fun-loving and got along famously." Kind of fun unspecified.

★*OTHER HOLLYWOOD ESCORTS: GENE KRUPA, PETER LAWFORD, JOHN HODIAK, JOHN DALL, PETER SHAW,* etc.

VADIM, ROGER
(b. 1928)

French film maker celebrated for the women he has met, mated with, occasionally even married while masterminding their movie careers. His films are generally perceived as being the glossy French postcards of international cinema, erotic souvenirs of his own amours with protegées, models, starlets, nearly always stunning beauties. It follows, then, that he seems to be most famous as the man who launched the career of Brigitte Bardot, and—very briefly—made Jane Fonda, All-American, look as if *she* might be the new international sexpot. Surprisingly, Vadim's volume of memoirs (see below) gives a remarkably pastel picture of a life generally thought to be lurid, and decadent if not downright depraved.

PRIMARY SOURCES: *Memoirs of the Devil,* by Roger Vadim (Harcourt Brace Jovanovich, 1975); *Bébé: The Films of Brigitte Bardot,* by Tony Crawley (Citadel, 1977); *Bardot: Eternal Sex Goddess,* by Peter Evans (Leslie Frewin Ltd., London, 1972).

★*BARDOT, BRIGITTE* First wife, and Vadim's first major filmic creation—probably his masterpiece—was BB herself. He was a restless young bohemian with his eye on the main chance, Brigitte a teenaged dance student whose extraordinary possibilities were still unplumbed. She preferred ballet to cinema, but found Vadim "handsome as a god." Their clandestine love affair started under her bourgeois family's watchful eye, but to Vadim, "One night with her was worth a lifetime." They married in 1952. In 1956, he wrapped her in a sheet and made *And God Created Woman.* The moment she dropped the sheet, Bardot was big time. Which boosted Vadim's reputation, too, though he paid a heavy price—losing his delectable wife to her leading man in the picture, Jean-Louis Trintignant. BB thought he looked like James Dean (he didn't). Seeing his marriage and his film finished at the same time, Vadim waxed philosophical, sort of: "I can't have an erection on the set when the woman I love is naked and masturbating or making passionate love to another man." Bardot's "obsession with happiness" became so intense she just took off with Jean-Lou (his *wife* didn't like it much). Bébé and Roger have remained good, good friends to this day, *bien sur.* (See also BARDOT listing.)

★*DENEUVE, CATHERINE* Famed blond French beauty whose face has become synonymous with Chanel in American TV commercials. In 1962 she had dark-chestnut hair and "was dancing the Charleston" the night Vadim found her. Mother of Vadim's only son, she took a giant step toward superstardom in his *Vice and Virtue* (1962). Vadim first saw her as "a flayed cat in an ermine coat." Their marriage plans were sidetracked, however, and Vadim's veiled irony hints that blond ambition may have hastened the inevitable split: "She took the rough with the smooth with apparent serenity. I never noticed that she was quietly sharpening her claws."

★*FONDA, JANE* Third wife and mother of second daughter, Vanessa, born 1968. Love at first sight. Vadim starred her in *La Ronde* and *Barbarella,* but found Jane insecure about herself as well as uncertain how to balance career, marriage, and motherhood. Among other things, militant politics finally came between them, leaving Vadim to ponder: "In all frankness, I cannot decide whether it is more distressing to lose one's wife to a guitar player or to a noble idea." (See also FONDA listing.)

★*FRANÇOISE* Fellow theatrical student, who claimed Vadim's virginity in a hayloft in Normandy on D-Day, June 6, 1944. At the climactic moment, "The walls began to move, the ground trembled." His loss of innocence thus accompanied by heavy artillery, Vadim concludes: "I have always had a sense of history."

★*LANE, SIRPA* Finnish model discovered to star in Vadim's *La Jeune Fille Assassinée* (1974-75), titled *Charlotte* in the U.S. No newsworthy follow-up.

★*P., NICOLE* Green-eyed blonde with a golden body and "a Botticelli face painted by some satanic forger." Vadim's first headlong experience with love at first sight. He stole her from a friend, "he lectured on sensuality while she silently promised me her thighs," then lost her to another old love, a brute who beat her.

★*SCHNEIDER, CATHERINE* Fourth wife, socialite heiress to an armament fortune. A non-pro. And it didn't last.

★*STROYBERG, ANNETTE* Danish-born model, mother of Vadim's firstborn Nathalie, and subsequently became his second wife. Lazy but wishing to work, "she took the easy way and decided to go into films." Starred in Vadim's successful erotic epic *Les Liaisons Dangereuses* (1959), Annette finally left him because of her own incurable attachment to a pop singer who played the guitar. Nathalie stayed with her father.

★*WELLES, GWEN* American discovery, starred in Vadim's autobiographical *Helle* (1971), then resumed career at home, most notably as the poignant, untalented stripper in Robert Altman's *Nashville.*

MISCELLANY

Many *autres femmes* were phoned and amorously fooled with, but precious few mentioned in print except for Vadim's acknowledgment of "a girlfriend who was Ernest Hemingway's mistress. She used to insult him in restaurants in my presence, and Hemingway seemed to find this vastly amusing." Takes all kinds.

WAYNE, JOHN
(1907–1979)

His hawkish right-wing politics during and after Vietnam did not endear him to young moviegoers, but John Wayne on the screen—in *Stagecoach* or *Red River* or *The Quiet Man*—was larger than life, overwhelming anything about him as a private citizen, pro or con. The Oscar he won for *True Grit* in 1969 was merely—as is so often the case—the Oscar he had earned in much earlier, much better movies. The prototypical western hero was born Marion Morrison in Iowa, unlikely as that sounds, and went to USC on a football scholarship before Hollywood discovered him. In his lifetime he became a towering national monument, more familiar to more Americans than the great stone faces of Mount Rushmore. He seemed to favor small dark Spanishy women, black-and-white issues, and three cheers for the red, white, and blue. He was not overfond of horses, but loved his wives, his sons, his booze, his career, and his country.

PRIMARY SOURCES: *Duke: The Real Story of John Wayne,* by Jean Ramer (Universal Award House, 1973); *Shooting Star: A Biography of John Wayne,* by Maurice Zolotow (Simon and Schuster, 1974).

★*BAUER, ESPERANZA* "Chata," so called, was a beautiful Mexican "spitfire," who liked to talk and drink and go on fishing trips with Duke and his friends. Wayne met Chata in Mexico, soon after his first divorce, married her in 1946. Chata hissed and spat and threw things, had wild jealous rages, but not just over Wayne's leading ladies; she accused him of going to bed with the movie business: "You make love with John Ford and heem, the other one, the ugly one, Bond, heem, not me you make love. You not love me." Chata was actually taking others into her bed—notably Nicky Hilton, whose name came up in the divorce trial in 1953. Soon after, Chata went back to Mexico, ended up living in one small room, eating rarely, never going out, subsisting mainly on brandy. She died of a heart attack the next year, at age 36.

★*DIETRICH, MARLENE* They made three movies together, and "in Wayne she found an actor who was an animal, an animal of honor and dignity, the sort she always played most excitingly against." And Wayne was just as exciting offscreen. Duke found in Marlene a sensual and intelligent woman who was also a man's woman, "and could even have been called a man's man." They went fishing and hunting, ate simple hearty food like steaks—

and Marlene was always a good drinker. Their intimacy lasted about three years and was public enough to alarm the first Mrs. Wayne. (See also DIETRICH listing.)

★*GODDARD, PAULETTE* When they became friends during the filming of *Reap the Wild Wind,* "he learned another chapter in his book on the varieties and diversities of *Woman.*"

★*GURIE, SIGRID* Co-star with Wayne in *Three Faces West.* She, like most women he met, was charmed by John Wayne's politeness and shyness. "It was Duke's first intimate knowledge of the European female, specifically the erotically liberated Scandinavian woman." She made most of the moves, which Duke found helpful, still being "awkward" about romance. The depth and length of the liaison remains unknown.

★*MASSEN, OSA* Wayne's next Scandinavian experience. She was *not* one of his leading ladies, but an actress recommended to help him acquire a Swedish accent for *The Long Voyage Home,* in which Wayne played a Swedish sailor. Their lessons usually took place over dinner and drinks, followed by what is often suggested as the best way to learn a language—with love.

★*PILAR, PALETTE* Peruvian actress and wife of Wayne's friend Dick Weldy when they met. That first encounter was nothing out of the ordinary, except that petite Pilar was bowled over by Duke's size: "I felt as if I had been hit with a telephone pole." He had no intention of marrying again, but Wayne was hooked. "I can tell you why I love her. I have a lust for her dignity. I look at her wonderfully classic face and I see hidden in it a sense of humor that I love." He said that marrying her (which happened November 1, 1954) was "the greatest thing that ever happened to me. . . . this is the best." Pilar was Wayne's third and last wife, and gave him a "second family," children Aissa, John Ethan, and Marisa. They were still very much a happily married couple when he died.

★*SAENZ, JOSEPHINE* Duke's first wife, and his steady girl when he was a student—

and football star—at the University of Southern California in 1926. The daughter of a Panamanian envoy, Josie was a highborn socialite, beautiful and dignified. She defied her family to become engaged to Marion "Duke" Morrison. The engagement lasted seven years, during which time Josie remained a virgin, in accordance with her Catholic beliefs. Duke finally began earning enough money to support a wife, so they tied the knot in June 1933. Josie kept a beautiful home, entertained lavishly, did good works for her church, and gave Wayne four children— Michael, Antonia, Melinda, and Patrick. But she was not cut out to be a movie star's wife. After a long period of anguish, she agreed to a divorce, which became final in December 1945. Josephine never married again, always called herself Mrs. Morrison.

★*TREVOR, CLAIRE* Wisecracking blond character actress (and Oscar winner for *Key Largo*). It was more than a rumor that the romance between Wayne and Trevor was not just on the screen. They were teamed the first time in *Stagecoach*, the 1939 film that made both their careers, and again in *Allegheny Uprising* and *The High and the Mighty*.

MISCELLANY

★*HOLMES, HELEN*   She was the ravishing star of a Saturday-afternoon two-reeler serial titled *The Hazards of Helen*. Wayne was about 10 when he fell totally in love with her, even took to skulking about in the vicinity of her house in the early morning. Every day she'd come out, mount her palomino, and gallop away, "like a princess, her auburn hair flying in the wind." Young Marion not only fell in love with movie star Helen, but through her he fell in love with the movies.

★*RUSSELL, GAIL*   It was during the stormiest period of Wayne's marriage to Chata that he became friendly with co-star Gail Russell, whom he saw as a troubled girl in need of a friend. Chata dragged her name into the divorce proceedings, charging that Wayne had given Gail a car (he said it was to make up for her low salary on loan-out from Paramount)

and spent the night at Gail's house (he said he drove her home from a party and went in for a drink). Wayne testified to his version of the association and added, "I deeply regret that Miss Russell has been subjected to this kind of mud-slinging." The two remained friends, and Duke urged her to call him whenever she was unhappy. She did, when her marriage to Guy Madison broke up, and her drinking became a problem. Russell died in 1961, at 36.

WEST, MAE
(1892–1980)

Mae went to jail back in the 1920s for writing and appearing in a play called *Sex*. What could be simpler? What she did then would still look daring today because she was decades ahead of her time in realizing that sex was one of the few sure things we've got, and we'd just have to make ends meet until they found something better. Suggestiveness became harmless in her care, defused by mockery. When she said, "Beulah, peel me a grape," West somehow relayed the message that a real Babylonian orgy would probably be as innocuous as bobbing for apples. Mae's concern, she drawled, was "not the men in my life, but the life in my men," and no sex symbol before or since ever put it more succinctly. Considering the reputation she enjoyed, a woman pushing 40 when she made her first movie, Mae had a fool-proof formula. Hardly anyone knew or wondered what she did between films, though she often arranged to be seen in public with scantily-clad musclemen (the male equivalent of big-bosomed starlets), a clear statement that brawn not brains would light her fire. She was the late great-grandmother of the sexual revolution, a bona-fide pioneer whose tongue-in-cheek wiles still outdo *Deep Throat*.

PRIMARY SOURCES: *Goodness Had Nothing to Do with It*, by Mae West (McFadden, 1970); *Come Up and See Me Sometime: A Confidential Biography of Mae*

West, by David Hanna (Tower, 1976); *Mae West: A Biography*, by George Eells and Stanley Musgrove (William Morrow & Co., Inc., 1982).

★*BAER, MAX* The heavyweight champ. Their attraction was "immediate and mutual." One day soon after they met he dropped in, out of the blue, and one thing led to the next. Their lovemaking over, Baer, still naked, went to the window, pulled up the shade and waved to somebody down the street. When Mae asked what that was about, "he replied he had won a $500 bet with his agent, who had opera glasses trained on her bedroom window." Mae was so amused, she told the story on herself.

★*COCHRAN, STEVE* Actor who appeared in 1949 stage revival of *Diamond Lil*, and during rehearsals, he frequently "rehearsed" in Mae's dressing room—although he was "too seriously involved with French actress Denise Darcel to offer anything more than physical gratification—which was all Mae demanded."

★*COOPER, GARY* He'd kept a couple of dates with Mae in her dressing room—until West watchdog Timony (see below) had the studio order him to stay away. (See also COOPER listing.)

★*DEMPSEY, JACK* Another heavyweight champ. In his screen test with Mae, she whispered, "Listen, champ, hold me tighter. I can take anything you can throw." Their next few scenes together were in private.

★*DIERO, GUIDO* Disguised in Mae's autobiog as "Mr. D," an accordionist and vaudeville headliner who became so smitten with Mae he temporarily abandoned his own career to follow her on the circuit. He turned out to be overly jealous, however, and *married*. Mae claimed she never "fooled around" with husbands, but "she was more emotionally stirred by Diero than any other man she had ever been involved with." But because Mae's basic orientation was to "sexual variety," she moved on.

★*DU BOIS, RICHARD* He was Mr. America of 1954, and what he wanted more than anything was to meet Mae West. She invited Du Bois and some of the other contestants to drop by. "In this magnificent herd of males, the 30-year-old Mr. America was outstanding." She found he was more than a mere body; "he had depth and sensitivity and an inquiring mind." Du Bois became her lover and one of the musclemen in her act.

★*HAMMERSTEIN, OSCAR II* He wrote his first song, "Make Yourself at Home," for a 1917 production featuring Mae. In her later years she couldn't remember the number, but she did remember Hammerstein: "I think I had a little thing with him. In fact, I know I did."

★*HARGITAY, MICKEY* Hungarian-born Mr. Universe. He was reportedly the only muscleman in Mae's troop who failed to show her "respect." His ambition made Mae uneasy, and also, she resented his very public affair with blond bombshell Jayne Mansfield. After a fight with Mae's new man Chuck Klauser (soon to become Paul Novak), Mickey and Mae parted company.

★*INDRISANO, JOHNNY* Trainer and Mae's live-in lover for a time in the late 1930s. He introduced her to jogging, and, says one observer, "he exercised her like a promising young pug."

★*JONES, WILLIAM ("GORILLA")* Black boxer. Mae became his manager, and was credited with helping him attain the middleweight title. She also advised him on his investments. Which may be one reason why he turned down $250,000 to film his life story—as Mae's lover. Besides, said Jones, "That would have been a lie, because she was just my manager and friend." Others are sure there was more to the relationship than that.

★*LAPIN, DAVID* Another member of the 1949 *Diamond Lil* company. Mae "went crazy" over Lapin, even though he was married. She gave him a Rolls Royce and let him run her life for a few years.

★*LA RUE, JACK* He had been in the *first* version (1928) of *Diamond Lil*. "I was in love with her and didn't particularly care who knew about it."

★*LAWLER, TEDDY* He was on tour with Mae in *Pleasure Man*, "and before you knew it, Miss West had him in the kip . . . alternating with Jack La Rue, George Raft and a few others—when she wasn't busy with Timony."

★*LOPEZ, VINCENT* World heavyweight wrestling champ, Mae's bodyguard in the 1950s. They were on-again, off-again for several years. The big problem was his fierce jealousy. He returned to his native South America, but stayed friends with Mae until the end.

★*LUCAS, JERRY* Cast as a guard in Mae's ill-fated production of *Catherine the Great*, the tall, powerfully built Lucas was soon elevated to the role of a Captain. For a while he had a great deal of influence over Mae, but as always, the star could not tolerate a man with ambitions of his own. As authors Eells and Musgrove note: "Once again she chose public success over private ecstasy—and was seemingly able to do so without regret."

★*MAZURKI, MIKE* Wrestler turned actor—thanks to Mae West. Hired as a bodyguard, to keep him near her Mae put him in costume as an extra in her film, *Belle of the Nineties*. Their alliance continued for more than a year. He remembered how, in private, he could call her "dear, darling or honey"; but in public she said, "call me Miss West."

★*MR. A.B.C., ETC.* Mae had many men in her life, but in her own book discreetly referred to them by an anonymous letter of the alphabet. David Hanna wrote: "Her suitors included lawyers, brokers, film magnates, judges, operatic tenors, French importers, chorus boys, casual diners in a restaurant. . . . there were big boys with the sleek cars and the three-hundred dollar suits, the Filipinos, weight lifters, muscle boys, athletes—and a lot of gay men." Mae enjoyed gays—and even wrote a play about them, called *Drag*. And a lot of men in all of Mae's categories were black. Along with their names, Mae's book—and Hanna's—kept secret most of what went on in her boudoir with these men.

★*NOVAK, PAUL* Also known as Chester Ribonsky (his real name) and Chuck Krauser. He was the love of Mae's life during her last 27 years. He was 33 when they met, about half Mae's age. Handsome and rugged, he was also a gentle man who obviously "adored" Miss West and cared for all of her needs. Once complimented on his deep concern for the woman who was his life, if not his wife, he replied, "I believe I was put on this earth to take care of Miss West."

★*PERRONI, PATSY* Ex-fighter identified by Eells and Musgrove as the anonymous "sexual athlete" Mae referred to in her autobiography. He was the one who reportedly climaxed 26 times in 24 hours.

★*RAFT, GEORGE* Raft was still working for a big-time New York bootlegger when Mae saw him, "and liked what she saw." They both had strong sex drives, it's said, which led them to *do it* wherever they could—in cars, elevators, etc. "It was love on the run with half the buttons undone," remarked Mae; "the results were like a high speed film—blurred but excitin'." Looking back, Mae admitted she would have married George, "if I coulda."

★*RICHMAN, HARRY* Comic who became "a vaudeville sensation" while sharing the bill with Mae. He had been warned that once he'd entered into an affair with her, "he'd be fired, just like that." But he decided to risk it. "The next day the performance was fantastic. It had never gone so well. But right after that he was given his notice." As time went on, Mae changed her views about keeping lovers in her employ.

★*SCHENCK, JOE* Studio executive. In her early days in Hollywood, Mae paraded Joe as one of her escorts—and found it helped open a few doors. Schenck later married actress Norma Talmadge and, much later, in his dotage, he "entertained" Marilyn Monroe.

★*SKINNER, JOE* A member of the *Diamond Lil* cast; his jealousy of Teddy Lawler got him fired.

★*SRI DEVA RAM SUKUL* A holy man from India, who in the 1950s helped Mae "open her consciousness to the Forces." During rehearsals he'd give Mae daily Yoga lessons consisting of "exercises which ended with the Sri, fully clothed, lying on top of Mae while she experienced an orgasm."

★*TIMONY, JAMES* One of the few men close to Mae throughout most of her life. He was her lawyer, business adviser and lover. He became part of Mae's scene in 1918, when she was on Broadway doin' a show called *Sometime*, in which she introduced the shimmy. Although Mae seldom spoke about Timony, he was always around, and most people assumed he was her secret husband. (Most people *didn't* know about Frank Wallace, below.) In time, Timony—with his girth and his bald pate—proved an embarrassment to Mae, and she also felt constricted by his jealousy. "He was a friend," says an observer, "but the friendship was based on a con woman's respect for a super con man." They remained friendly until his death in 1954.

★*WALLACE, FRANK* A song-and-dance man who shared billing with Mae, then but 17. He proposed. Mae wanted to do the respectable thing, so on April 11, 1911, she married Frank, who was 21. She was not in love with him, and told him while still a bride: "You don't move my finer instincts." When he asked what her finer instincts were, she said, "I don't know yet. But I must have them." Mae made some excuse that her parents, vaudevillians themselves, wanted her to do a single act from now on, so she thought she should live at home. That ended her professional partnership with Wallace, and presumably the marriage. Nothing was heard from him until the mid-1930s, when he showed up in California suing to have Mae declared his legal wife so he could claim community property. Her community property then added up to six figures. With all the notoriety, down-on-his-luck Wallace started getting nightclub dates as "Mr. Mae West." For publication, Mae denied all. "I've never heard of the fellow . . . Eight guys have called me up since January . . . They tell me they're married to me . . . must be those other girls." Mae finally went to court, "laid a bit of the green on the line" for Wallace and got her divorce in 1942.

★*WRIGHT, CHALKY* Fighter who became Mae's chauffeur. Authors Eells and Musgrove claim that "Even though Mae and Wright won

a 1950's retraction from *Confidential* magazine for alleging they once had been lovers, intimates insisted there could be no question that their relationship was a passionate one."

MISCELLANY

★*GRANT, CARY* He was her handpicked leading man for *She Done Him Wrong* and *I'm No Angel* (both 1933). When asked to name her favorite co-star she said, "Cary Grant. I like him so well I had him twice—in pictures, you understand. He seems to get better every year. . . . When better men are made, I'll make 'em." Grant himself is quoted in the new biography of West as saying that Mae "taught me all I know about timing." In pictures, that is. There's no evidence that theirs was any more than a professional relationship, extremely profitable to both. (See also GRANT listing.)

WINTERS, SHELLEY
(b. 1922)

A brash "blond bombshell" type in her early Hollywood career, but evolved into a serious actress in such prestigious films as *A Place in the Sun* (1951), won two Oscars for Best Supporting Actress in *The Diary of Ann Frank* (1959) and *A Patch of Blue* (1965). Garrulous and voluptuous, the kind of performer who knows how to milk laughs on a TV talk show, Winters sometimes seems to be a dedicated artist masquerading as a clown. The first volume of her bestselling autobiography (a second volume is imminent) takes her colorful life only up to the mid-1950s, and irrepressible Shelley uses romantic cliché movie imagery to describe her many-splendored past as a woman in love.

PRIMARY SOURCE: *Shelley . . . Also Known as Shirley*, by Shelley Winters. (Morrow, 1980).

★*BRANDO, MARLON* After a spartan dinner party in Brando's really cold cold-water flat in New York in the late '40s, Brando told her: "My body generates a great deal of heat." Shelley's cryptic footnote: "He was right." They later smoozed around in Hollywood. Like the night she was on a downer over her affair with the very married Burt Lancaster. Brando bought her drinks and dinner, told funny stories to lighten the mood. Then he quoted Shakespeare: "Men have died from time to time and worms have eaten them, but not for love." Shelley slapped him for that. "After all, it was *my* heartbreak." He returned the slap with a kiss—a "passionate kiss," so they decided to skip the entree and go straight for dessert—at Shelley's place. Brando was still there at 5 A.M. when Lancaster started pounding on the door. At her insistence, Marlon escaped via the roof—leaving behind his sneakers. Moments later, as Shelley welcomed Burt into her bedroom, "I started to draw the drapes to shut out the sunrise, and looking down, I saw Marlon limping down Santa Monica Boulevard." (See also BRANDO listing.)

★*COLMAN, RONALD* Shelley mentions an "intimate lunch" with Ronnie after he kissed her bare breast during a rehearsal on the set of *A Double Life.*

★*FLYNN, ERROL* Their first encounter was dinner and a movie at his place—double-dating with Clark Gable and Yvonne de Carlo. About an hour into the film, Flynn pressed a button, a twelve-foot sliding panel slid open, "and there on a raised platform was a huge bed covered with cream-colored satin sheets and pillows." When Flynn whispered some sweet nothing in her ear, "all I could think of to answer was: 'I wonder what the poor people are doing.'" Nevertheless, when the film ended, Errol told Yvonne that he'd see Shelley home; Yvonne told Flynn to remember that Shelley had to be at work at 6:30 Monday morning. "What the hell was she talking about?" Shelley wondered. "This was only 11 P.M. Friday night." She didn't make it to work until nearly noon on Monday. As to the interim, "Cut to . . . A fire roaring in a fireplace, waves pounding a beach . . . Fireworks exploding . . . Tchaikovsky's 1812 Overture, complete

with cannons." Flynn and Winters became close pals. (See also FLYNN listing.)

★*GASSMAN, VITTORIO* Italian stage and screen star, Shelley's second husband. They met in Rome and that night he awakened her to "the passionate beauty of Italy . . . and you can't cut to anything because it hasn't been invented in pictures or words." Their international affair was idyllic, tempestuous; after Gassman's divorce in 1952 they had a quickie wedding in Nevada, then, for legal reasons, another in Mexico. Vittorio was again in Mexico, working on a film, when Shelley flew to him—"with just a nightgown and toothbrush"—in a desperate effort to take advantage of her ovulation cycle and conceive a child. Vittorio had yellow roses in their room, mariachis playing outside, "So after two margaritas we put our hearts and souls into fulfilling Dr. Krahulick's instructions." It worked; daughter Vittoria was born on Valentine's Day 1953. After two troublesome years working in Hollywood, Gassman returned to Italy. They had never discussed whether he wanted to remain in the U.S., or if she would move to Italy. "It seemed too stupid a thing to admit to myself that we had not settled this enormous life question before." The breakup was public and a bit nasty, but today they are close again.

★*GRANGER, FARLEY* They met on a blind date, became "inseparable friends, sometimes lovers, certainly as close as brother and sister." At one point, partially as a studio publicity stunt, Farley and Shelley announced their engagement and took off on a round-the-world trip—funded by Howard Hughes. In Italy, Shelley met Gassman; Farley went on without her. Today, Granger and Winters are New York neighbors. When they're both in town.

★*HOLDEN, WILLIAM* During a Christmas party at Paramount, Shelley was waylaid in his dressing room. She can't remember exactly how it happened, but . . . "Cut to: Waves pounding on a beach . . . Trees swaying in a storm." As he drove away at dawn he asked her name. "Sonia Epstein," she told him. Then, "before I—knew it, it was Christmas Eve again." And, again, Shelley went to a party on the Paramount lot. Holden was waiting for her in his dressing room, with champagne, flowers, a lavish dinner. "He kissed me and said, 'I've been waiting for you all year . . . I wanted to surprise you, Sonia.' " He also surprised her with a diamond wristwatch, plus waves pounding, fireworks exploding, etc., etc. "This strange relationship with Bill Holden went on in this manner for seven years . . . I only missed two Christmases when I was married." Shelley claims those holiday encounters were more fun than most relationships in her life.

★*HUGHES, HOWARD* At a New Year's party, Shelley started talking to a tall, skinny fellow in a shiny tux and tennis shoes, "some poor guy named Hugh something." Later, in the powder room, Ava Gardner thanked her "for taking Howard Hughes off my hands." They made a date for the next day, and he called for her. Her father immediately got into an argument with Hughes, and after eyeing the billionaire's scruffy attire, suggested that Hughes come down to the Peerless Pants Company where he could get him a new jacket wholesale. Later Hughes took up the offer. Meanwhile Shelley's big date consisted of dinner in an abandoned restaurant followed by a screening of *Hell's Angels* (directed by Hughes, starring Harlow) in an abandoned theater. "At the door he shook my hand . . . I felt a little strange, as if something had happened and I hadn't noticed." Hughes never again went to a big Hollywood party, notes Shelley, but he did do many favors for her in years to come. As always. (See also HUGHES listing.)

★*IRELAND, JOHN* Second rank leading man, and Shelley's first serious affair after divorcing her first husband. Ireland introduced her to marijuana (which she didn't like) and gambling (ditto). It was a comfortable, long affair and Ireland believed that Shelley brought him luck. He later married a co-star, Joanne Dru.

★*LANCASTER, BURT* On a first date in New York, they saw *South Pacific*, enjoyed a romantic dinner at Le Pavillon, then to Burt's room. Again, she can't recall how it happened, but there they were on a thick white rug "and Burt didn't have any clothes on and he was gorgeous and I didn't have any clothes on and I felt gorgeous and now Gigli was singing 'O Paradiso' on the phonograph . . . Cut to: A galloping army with banners, meteors flashing in a spangled sky . . . and the Top of the World." The affair was one of the deepest and most chaotic of Shelley's life, colored by guilt because Lancaster was married, with children. It was an announcement in the trades that Burt's wife was expecting another child that finally prompted Shelley to make the break. She told Brando: "I know in my heart it's true. That bastard's fucking his wife." When she wound up in a hospital with a mild nervous breakdown, Burt sent her some flowers and $3,000. "I told him to keep the roses, but I kept the $3,000. My severance pay, I guess."

★*MILLER, PAUL* A phony name for the "handsome, Jewish, intelligent" Chicago salesman Shelley married at 17, just after he signed up for the Army Air Corps following Pearl Harbor. On returning to Hollywood, he decided he could not be *"Mr. Winters."* The marriage ended in divorce in 1944.

★*PELLIGRIN, RAYMOND* French actor working in Italy during Shelley's breakup with Gassman. He knew how to pamper a girl: He ran a bubble bath for her, threw in rose petals and handed her a goblet of champagne with strawberries, then sat on the edge of the tub to sing a chanson d'amour. "Cut to: The fountains at the Place de la Concorde . . . the Seine flowing tenderly through the city of Paris . . . etc."

★*SPELVIN, GEORGE* Anonymous name (used by long tradition in the theater) for "a handsomely homely and brilliant young actor" with whom Shelley arranged to destroy her virginity, at age 15, by plying him with Southern Comfort and potato chips. The maneuver resulted in pregnancy and a particularly nasty abortion.

★*TIERNEY, LAWRENCE* Moody actor. A

one-night stand the night of VE day (the end of World War II) after Tierney had gotten into a fight with Nazi sympathizers at a bar.

MISCELLANY

★*EDDY, NELSON* Singing star. He lurched into her dressing room one day, lunged for Shelley—but missed. She begged him to consider his image: "What would Jeanette MacDonald say?" asked Shelley. "Who cares?" Nelson answered. "She slides off her C's."

★*OLIVIER, LAURENCE* In their one Hollywood evening together, no action. Although, as Shelley's roommate Marilyn Monroe pointed out, Olivier was on Shelley's list of the famous men in the world she wanted to sleep with. (Marilyn's list included Albert Einstein; after MM's death, Shelley found among her belongings a framed photo of Einstein signed "To Marilyn, with great respect and love and thanks —Albert Einstein.")

★*STEVENSON, ADLAI* While he was Ambassador to the United Nations, Shelley was hostess at an official dinner at Waldorf Towers.

★*WALKER, ROBERT* They were just "good friends."

ZANUCK, DARRYL F.
(1902–1979)

Superproducer and a founding father of 20th Century–Fox, where he guided some of that studio's greatest hits. A pint-sized dynamo with an ever-present cigar stuck in his mouth, Zanuck began to rise in the Hollywood hierarchy by writing scripts for Rin Tin Tin movies. He traditionally had better luck judging stories than judging stars, and he sponsored the careers of several European actresses whose slim chances for success rested largely on Zanuck's blind faith in them. Throughout his long career, Zanuck had an eye for the ladies, though he hotly denied gossip linking him with virtually every major female star on the Fox lot. Undocumented stories abound of his chasing star-

lets around his executive suite, yet Zanuck swore to his biographer, "I never touched a soul." A former director at Fox once put it this way: "The single most important thing in Darryl Zanuck's life—bigger than movies or success—is sex." He was also famously fond of croquet and polo.

PRIMARY SOURCE: *Don't Say Yes Until I Finish Talking: A Biography of Darryl F. Zanuck*, by Mel Gussow (Doubleday, 1971).

★*CALL GIRL* Part-time or semi-pro prostitute whom Zanuck saw often in San Francisco when he was 20 and a hack short-story writer. He enjoyed telling the tale of a friend who met the same call girl years later in New York—she had a photo of DFZ, autographed *With love—from Darryl*. By then a powerful studio chief, Zanuck snapped: "Jesus Christ! How can we get it back?"

★*DARVI, BELLA* Polish-born divorcée, survivor of wartime concentration camps, introduced to the Zanucks at a sidewalk café in Paris in 1951. She moved into the Zanucks' California home for a time, until Mrs. Zanuck booted her out. Zanuck's efforts to make Bella an actress ("She's got zip, zoom, and zowie," burbled the press ballyhoo) fizzled in such forgotten flicks as *Hell and High Water*, then she played a courtesan in *The Egyptian* (Brando turned the movie down, his agent said, because "he doesn't like the role . . . and he can't stand Bella Darvi"). Bella went back to Europe, and Zanuck followed. "Still infatuated or sex crazy or whatever you call it," he said. Over the years, Bella became a compulsive gambler, and took an overdose of barbiturates in 1968, but rallied to say, "I regret I regret I regret."

★*DEMICK, IRINA* French-Russian model in Paris, chosen as Zanuck's third protégée-mistress, following Darvi and Greco. He gave her a role in *The Longest Day*, and Demick was never defensive about her satellite role as the girl who became famous chiefly for being photographed with Zanuck. Said she: "If the sun is not there, we die. I cannot be Irina Demick without Darryl Zanuck . . . I am a cabbage." The critics generally concurred, and Irina drifted out of his life, married, but remained Zanuck's loyal friend.

★*FOX, VIRGINIA* Pretty West Virginia girl, unrelated to the 20th Century–Foxes. She came to Hollywood on vacation from boarding school, worked as a bathing beauty in Buster Keaton movies, and met Zanuck. He bombarded her with flowers and phone calls, married her six months later, in January 1924. The Zanucks' Palm Springs home, Ric-Su-Dar, was named for their three children—(Darrylin, born 1931; Susan, 1933; and an only son Richard Darryl, 1934—today a top producer himself). Weekends at Ric-Su-Dar, which became a social hub for the movie colony, involved fun and frolic and killer croquet. The marriage ended, bitterly, but without a divorce, in 1956. Mrs. Zanuck moved to their beach house in Santa Monica, but kept the home fires burning for DFZ, with a humidor full of his favorite cigars locked in a safe. Retired at 70, Zanuck reconciled with Virginia, and they returned to Ric-Su-Dar, together until his death.

★*GILLES, GENEVIEVE* The last of the important Other Women in Zanuck's life. When they met at Maxim's in Paris, she was a 19-year-old model, he was 63. Genevieve airily dismissed her predecessors: "The first thing he recognized was that I was elegant. All the girls about him—no class." The Gilles movie career was launched with a spectacular $48,000 short titled *The World of Fashion,* then a so-so romantic comedy, *Hello-Good-bye.* Back in New York, it was beautiful while it lasted, and Genevieve said that Zanuck, always preoccupied with sex, kept a book of girls' names rated by the number of stars he wrote next to them. Her own rating? "The moon!"

★*GRECO, JULIETTE* Onetime street urchin who became a great French singing star on a par with Piaf, discovered for films by Zanuck, though she initially detested even the sound of his name ("Zanuck sounded to me like Coca-Cola"). She made movies *(Roots of Heaven, The Sun Also Rises)* but had small impact on the screen. "Greco couldn't be photographed," Zanuck said later. She felt herself "an object without a soul operated by remote control"; movieland for her was a "golden, asphyxiating, absurd merry-go-round." Greco's Parisian chums thought Zanuck a joke, and she finally left him—with a dog she had given him, a schnauzer named Iago, and a drinking habit. Zanuck was livid later, when Greco's mocking memoirs were serialized in London and Paris weeklies and held him up to ridicule. He sued her in an Italian court, and managed to suppress publication of the book. Greco now claims not to have written all those bitchy revelations herself.

★*STARLET* The one nameless contract player he admitted fooling around with during his early years at Warner Brothers. It was she who put fear into him one day in his office. Zanuck claimed: "She turned out to be impossible as an actress. When I came to the conclusion she didn't have it, she suddenly started to undress, getting out of her dress and panties. . . . She scared hell out of me, but I was saved by the bell." Zanuck's secretary buzzed on his private wire to say: "Urgent—the White House calling."

MISCELLANY

★*COLLINS, JOAN* Her experience was believed typical of the Zanuck approach. Though Joan ultimately eluded him, Mr. Z was said to have given chase in his office, and thus summed up his sexual credentials: "You've had nothing until you've had me, I am the biggest and the best. I can go all night and all day."

INDEX

The names and page numbers in bold type refer to the celebrities who have main listings of their own.